The Human
Tradition in Modern Africa

The Human Tradition around the World
Series Editors: William H. Beezley and Colin M. MacLachlan

The Human
Tradition in Modern Africa

Edited by
Dennis D. Cordell

ROWMAN & LITTLEFIELD PUBLISHERS, INC.
Lanham • Boulder • New York • Toronto • Plymouth, UK

Published by Rowman & Littlefield Publishers, Inc.
A wholly owned subsidiary of The Rowman & Littlefield Publishing Group, Inc.
4501 Forbes Boulevard, Suite 200, Lanham, Maryland 20706
http://www.rowmanlittlefield.com

Estover Road, Plymouth PL6 7PY, United Kingdom

British Library Cataloguing in Publication Information Available

Library of Congress Cataloging-in-Publication Data
The human tradition in modern Africa / edited by Dennis D. Cordell.
  p.   cm. — (The human tradition around the world)
  Includes bibliographical references and index.
  ISBN 978-0-7425-3732-3 (cloth : alk. paper) — ISBN 978-0-7425-3733-0 (pbk. : alk. paper) — ISBN 978-1-4422-1383-8 (electronic)
  1. Africa—Biography. 2. Africa—History—19th century. 3. Africa—History—20th century. 4. Africa—Social conditions. I. Cordell, Dennis D., 1947– II. Series: Human tradition around the world.
  DT18.H86 2012
  960.0922—dc23
                                                                        2011036159

∞™ The paper used in this publication meets the minimum requirements of American National Standard for Information Sciences—Permanence of Paper for Printed Library Materials, ANSI/NISO Z39.48-1992.

Printed in the United States of America

For Michael and Selena and Our Little Family

Contents

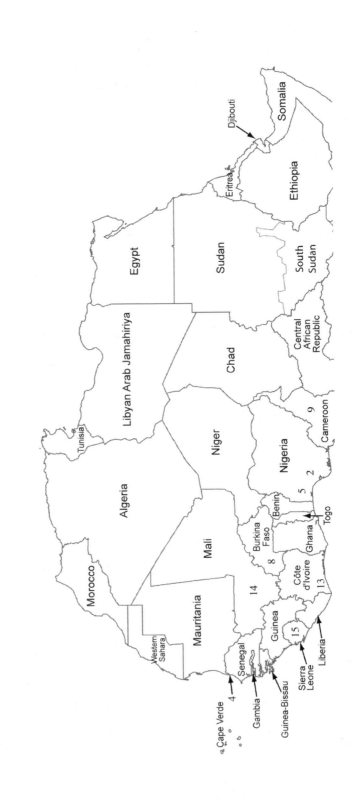

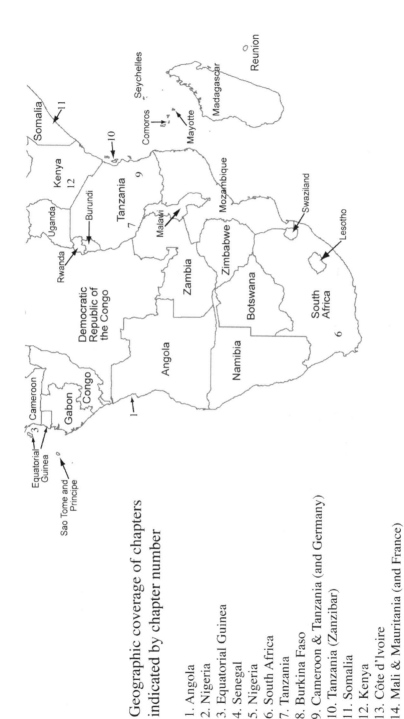

Geographic coverage of chapters
indicated by chapter number

1. Angola
2. Nigeria
3. Equatorial Guinea
4. Senegal
5. Nigeria
6. South Africa
7. Tanzania
8. Burkina Faso
9. Cameroon & Tanzania (and Germany)
10. Tanzania (Zanzibar)
11. Somalia
12. Kenya
13. Côte d'Ivoire
14. Mali & Mauritania (and France)
15. Sierra Leone

Contemporary Countries of Africa

INTRODUCTION

~

People and History in Modern Africa

Dennis D. Cordell

This collection enlivens the history of Africa with people—not with su-
perheroes like Sunjata of ancient Mali or Shaka the Zulu or the Queen of
Sheba, whose everyday lives are clouded by the mists of myth and fantastic
feats—but with individuals whose day-to-day lives are at once real and a
part of larger themes in the continent's history since the early nineteenth
century. The volumes in the Rowman & Littlefield series The Human
Tradition around the World add crucial human dimensions to the study of
the past of many societies. In the case of modern Africa, this contribution
is particularly valuable because the sources usually used to write about the
history of Africa in this era—travel narratives by outsiders, oral traditions,
and anthropological accounts—do not easily lend themselves to biography.
As a result, African history courses have frequently and profitably turned
to novels written in the last half-century to explore the ways that historical events and trends have shaped individual lives. In contrast, the fifteen
chapters that follow recount the life or lives of real, identifiable people from
societies across Africa south of the Sahara or from African communities in
Europe over the last two hundred years.

To underscore the obvious, many major changes have occurred in Africa
since 1800. This book divides these two centuries into four periods, each

covering a half-century or so. The even decade dates attached to each of them signal that these divisions are rough approximations, since human societies evolve over time and clearly delineated boundaries between eras are rare.

The first period, which we call "Encounters: Two Worlds and New Worlds," covers the first half of the nineteenth century. Overall, this era is characterized by a greater European presence in the interior of Africa—beyond the slave-trading outposts on the coast that in some cases dated from centuries earlier. The increased European presence was very uneven. For example, in parts of West Africa and Southeast Africa, respectively today's Angola and Mozambique, Portugal already had a long history of colonial rule and administration on the ground. Other international powers established new outposts on the coast, sometimes for people liberated from slaving ships—such as the British in Freetown in today's Sierra Leone, the French in Libreville in today's Gabon, or even the Americans in today's Liberia—but their effective control did not extend very far inland. South Africa was an exception. The Dutch had established a resupply station at Cape Town in 1652, and Dutch settlers slowly expanded their area of settlement over the next century and a half. The British took definitive control of Cape Colony in 1806, so that British settlers joined descendants of Dutch settlers now called Afrikaaners in enlarging their hegemony over local African societies. A few European missionaries had made their way to Africa as early as the fifteenth century, but in the first half of the nineteenth century their numbers also grew significantly. As a result, local people in many scattered places on and near the coast became more intimately acquainted with Europeans and imported European institutions between 1800 and 1850. Some of them challenged European power.

After 1850, Africans found themselves dealing with a much more intrusive European presence. European powers competed for formal control of African territories, fueled by new knowledge of tropical diseases and how to combat them; more sophisticated military, maritime, and communications technology; and competition for new resources and markets in an era of rapid industrialization. Each country feared that it would be deprived of the chance to profit from Africa's imagined riches, and the "scramble for Africa" took off after 1885. Africans and their societies were not at all passive in the face of this onslaught. Out of choice and necessity, they acted on the possibilities presented by this topsy-turvy world. Hence our title for the second part of the volume: "Fashioning African Identities in the Era of European Conquest."

The decades between 1910 and 1960 were an era of contradiction and rapid change. The European conquest of Africa had concluded by 1910, although areas in the far interior, such as Ubangi-Shari in Equatorial Africa or southern Sudan, had only recently fallen to European control. Often referred to as the high tide of colonial rule, the interwar years were marked by intensified efforts to extract labor and resources from African societies everywhere—particularly during World War I and the Great Depression of the 1930s. In order to rule their vast domains, though, European administrations had to turn to Africans for help. By this time, expanded numbers of missions had brought schools and rudimentary medical infrastructure to much of the continent, and as we see from the biographies of some of the people in this book, many individual Africans sought Western education in an effort to improve their fortunes and those of their children. In so doing, they also learned how to leverage their labor power, how to manipulate Western institutions, and very often, how to use the colonial presence to enlarge their own arenas of action. Moreover, they began to do so on the scale of the colonial political borders that had been drawn around them and in new colonial cities. With time they perceived quite clearly the contradictions between how European powers recognized democratic principles and individual rights at home—with notable exceptions such as Germany—and how they administered their colonial possessions. Across the continent at different times and in different places over these five decades, people claimed and campaigned for greater rights. The infrastructure of colonial rule made it possible for them to learn what was happening in other European colonies in Africa and in the wider world. In the last decade of this era, their struggles led to the political independence of most former colonies, even though Portugal did not relinquish its colonies until the 1970s and the white minorities that ruled South Africa and Southwest Africa recognized majority rule only two decades later. What is clear, in general and from the stories of men and women included in this volume, is that Africans possessed a sophisticated understanding of the instrumentation and culture of European colonial rule.

In the last few chapters of this volume, covering the decades since 1960, we read about people attempting to deal with political, economic, gender, and cultural issues that have brought together the local and the global in new ways. Unfortunately, independence did not bring true democracy to the countries of Africa—not surprising given that as colonies they had been subjected to many decades of authoritarian rule. In the 1980s and 1990s people in many countries again set out to limit or overthrow dictatorial rule. "Presidents for life" looted national resources for their personal advantage and politicized differences between ethnic communities in order to remain in power. In some places, conflict led to failed states where violence undermined the national community. In other countries and regions, local people turned to local institutions in order to maintain social and economic life. There are some countries—for example, Mali, Senegal, Cape Verde, Ghana, Benin, Sao Tome and Principe, Botswana, South Africa, Namibia, Mauritius and several others—that have weathered these storms reasonably well.[1] And in many places, forms of African cultural expression have remained vibrant, as known and anonymous artists attempted to interpret and understand their worlds.

So, how do reading and thinking about the lives of the people in this book deepen our understanding and enhance our engagement with these many dimensions of the history of modern Africa? Before beginning to answer this question, stop to think about how knowing about your own life might help us understand the broader forces and trends in the larger society around you. How have major economic developments in recent years impacted you and your family? What, if any, social or political movements have prompted you or your friends to take action? Most important, how do you think knowing about your life and the lives of members of your family and friends deepens our understanding of these larger happenings?

The biographies in this book help us understand the human tradition in modern Africa in four ways. First, learning about the actions of real people underscores the importance and the power of individual action or agency. Moka was a chief on the island of Bioko in the second half of the nineteenth century (chapter 3). Bioko, now part of Equatorial Guinea, had been divided up into smaller chiefdoms for a long time. Yet Moka came to see the possibility of uniting the island—which he did. The life of Tina (chapter 13), a woman in southwest Côte d'Ivoire, also illustrates how individual action may influence historical events. Despite the predominance of men in commercial agriculture in Côte d'Ivoire, for example, the woman Tina became a major producer of palm oil. In the 1960s, Samba Sylla (chapter 14) arrived in Paris with minimal knowledge of French, but through language classes offered by French unions, he learned labor-organizing skills that he later applied to mobilize migrant resistance to discriminatory housing practices. His fellow migrant Doulo Fofanna (also chapter 14) helped in these campaigns. Their experiences and those of their fellow migrants paved the way for Djénébou Traore, a young girl who followed her parents to France (chapter 14). Although her experiences built on those of her parents, her life was different because they had preceded her. All of this is to say that individual agents and their actions do have an impact on how human societies change through time. Not all change is the result of large, impersonal forces.

Second, the biographies of individual people also often serve to show that reality is more complex than the generalizations produced by too exclusive a focus on broad historical trends. Painting the past with very broad strokes also may produce stereotypes. Knowledge of what is local informs and enriches our understanding of what is global. Life histories complicate the big picture by adding other perspectives; in so doing, they may even alter our view of the big picture. A prime example of this phenomenon is the struggle of Nbena and her daughter to regain their freedom in the hinterland of Angola in the late 1810s (chapter 1). While Nbena's fight seems quite natural to us today, you will perhaps be surprised by what she did after she regained her liberty. Clearly her own victory did not lead her to conclude that everyone should be free. The life story of Adolphe Taillebourg (chapter 8), a French colonial administrator in what is today Burkina Faso, also defies the comfortable presumption that European officials were uniformly evil, which tends to be embedded in survey texts on the history of Africa under European rule.

Even the sketches of the lives of Louis Brody and Mohammed Bayume Hussein (chapter 9), men from the former German colonies of Kamerun (today's Cameroon) and German East Africa (today's Tanzania) who found their way to Germany after World War I, challenge our much too simplistic imaginings of what life would be like for African immigrants living in the open society of Germany in the 1920s or in the horrific Nazi years between the early 1930s and the end of World War II. Moreover, their experiences were different. On the other hand, the story of Foday (chapter 15), a boy soldier in Sierra Leone in the 1990s, confirms in a concrete way what we might imagine to be the horrors of such a life, based on global accounts of the treatment and suffering of children forced to become killers. But even in his confined environment, he found room for action.

Third, individual life stories help us see more clearly how people and their societies deal with times of transition. The nineteenth century in Africa was such an era. Looking back at the period of outright European conquest and colonial rule in the late nineteenth and first half of the twentieth centuries, along with the movements toward independence after World War II, we have been encouraged to divide people into two groups—those who collaborated with European domination and those who fought against it. But these opposed categories do not exhaust the range of reactions to the extraordinary changes that were taking place. Many people forged a middle way through these transitions. For example, Hamet Gora Diop (chapter 4), a prominent figure in the local Muslim religious and merchant class in the Senegal River valley in the second half of the nineteenth century, joined with others of his social group to shape an accommodation with the French officials of the colony of Senegal. The arrangement served the economic position of these "notables," enabling them to preserve their own African-Islamic society while fashioning a new place for themselves. Several hundred miles to the south in today's Sierra Leone, Samuel Johnson (chapter 5) was born in 1846 into a recently freed and newly converted Christian Yoruba family—the same year that Diop was born. Freed from a slave ship and settled in Sierra Leone, John-son's father returned with four of his children to their homeland in today's Nigeria. Johnson promoted Christianity and championed Western education as a way of using the European presence for personal development. Although enamored of things Western, he nonetheless wrote a book on the history of the Yoruba that attracted wide readership and undoubtedly ensured the recognition of their importance by the new British colonial administration.

A little later and much farther away, in today's Tanzania in East Africa, Mama Adolphina Unda (chapter 7) was also a transitional figure. Born into the aristocracy of the Fipa people, Mama Adolphina engaged with Catholicism but then returned Christian ritual objects to the missionaries who preceded the German colonial administration. Later she returned to the Church. Her actions were not simply aimed at manipulating the Europeans. She found herself situated between the power and religion of her royal fore-bears and the new faith. She was truly attracted to Christianity, indeed going so far as to convince the missionaries to found an order of African sisters, which she led as mother superior. Still later, the complexity of royal politics, the coming of World War I, the ensuing paralysis of Church institutions, and the illness of her brother the king dampened Adolphina's ardor, and she sought the shelter of family. Although remembered among the Fipa, she was unknown to the British officials who arrived later to replace the Germans. Mama Adolphina Unda personified the ambivalence of transition.

Fourth and finally, this collection of biographies offers concrete examples of the important and diverse roles that women have played in the history of modern Africa. Earlier paragraphs have introduced us to Nbena, Tina, Djénébou Traore, and Mama Adolphina Unda. Other chapters add more women, such as Efusetan Aniwura (chapter 2), who like many other Yoruba women was a successful trader. What set her apart was the great scale of her commercial success and how she parlayed that achievement into a position of military and political power. In addition, the stories of family in the Cape region of today's South Africa (chapter 6) in the era of slavery and eman-cipation include portraits of women of several generations who displayed courage and strategic thinking in their efforts to remake their lives. Steyntje went to court in 1815 to demand her liberation in accordance with a resolu-tion issued by the Court of India in 1772 that a slave women who had had children with her owner would be freed upon his death—a decision that had never been recognized in Cape law even though the Cape fell under the jurisdiction of the India Office. In the end, Steyntje and her children were freed following a decision in London by the king in council about 1819! For-mer slave Katie Jacobs recalled that their owner gave her mother to his son, who went to live elsewhere. She never saw her mother again. Later, after being formally freed in 1838, Katie and her husband had to stay on three years with their former master because they had no alternative. They eventually managed to make their way to Cape Town. The chapter includes vignettes of many other women (and men) who struggled for freedom and survival.

Following emancipation in 1897, the slave woman Siti binti Saad courageously left the countryside of Zanzibar Island for the city in 1911 (chapter 10). She sold pottery in the streets of Zanzibar Town, composing and singing songs in Kiswahili as she made her rounds. She often sang of the tribulations of her fellow former slaves of black African heritage. Despite her low social status, her popularity led her into the houses of the Arab elite on the island, where she contested their prominence in song. Having taken on one elite, she turned to another, learning the ways of the British colonial administration sufficiently well to travel with her band to India to record her music. Siti's records were hits in Tanganyika (today's Tanzania), Kenya, the Belgian Congo (today's Democratic Republic of the Congo), and throughout the Indian Ocean region.

Two other East African women, Maryan Muuse Boqor of Somalia (chapter 11) and Wambui Waiyaki Otieno Mbugua of Kenya (chapter 12) also figure prominently in these years. Maryan's story is a tale of solidarity among women of several generations, showing how women supported each other. Building on the recognized family roles of women, Maryan had an expansive view of the world—gleaned from visits by male relatives whose commercial activities took them up and down the East African coast and later from overhearing the extended debate among the Allied powers after World War II about what to do with Somalia, a colony of Italy that they had defeated. The men listened to these discussions on the radio in a courtyard below, while the women listened by clustering around the windows above. Maryan learned what women could do in politics by observing how her stepmother, through poetry and persistence, supported the Somali Youth League. When she went off to school in Egypt in the later 1950s, Maryan took this heritage of women's solidarity and political awareness with her, eventually ending up in Boston.

Over the course of her life, Wambui Waiyaki Otieno Mbugua of Kenya has always been politically engaged, beginning with her commitment to the nationalist movement in Kenya in the 1950s. She went from supporter to engaged revolutionary in the Mau Mau movement. Following independence, she served in the national assembly. But her greatest struggle has been around women's family rights in contemporary Kenya. When her husband died in the 1980s, she challenged traditional practices that gave rights over her husband's body and burial to his extended family—setting her against his male relatives. The court case was long and she lost, but her challenge to patriarchy mesmerized Kenya. In recent years she has pushed her challenge to accepted gender roles even further by marrying a much younger man. Advocates for women's rights rallied to Wambui, while her own children boycotted the ceremony. Once again, Wambui's life story crystalized controversy across the nation and opens a window into the social history of Kenya.

In conclusion, a few paragraphs and questions are in order about biography and history. To be sure, biography, literally "the drawing or writing of life," focuses on the life course of an individual, while we tend to think of history as embracing larger numbers of people in societies and how societies change through time. So the scale is different—which leads us to ask to what degree a biography, or small-scale history of the individual, is representative of the large-scale history of a region, a country, a continent, or the globe. In the chapters of this book, the authors and the editor explicitly link the lives of the people who figure in them to larger events and patterns of change that have usually emerged from their other research. Most of the time the relationship is very direct; sometimes it is less so.

Another question concerns just how historically accurate a biography may be—even how accurate it is possible for it to be. First, since biographers can never learn all there is to know about their subjects, they inevitably fill in gaps in their evidence with their interpretation. They speculate about why the person they are writing about may have done one thing or another; they even try to imagine what she or he might have been thinking at the time. Second, and not surprisingly, the subject or subjects of the biography themselves also regularly offer their own interpretations of why they did what they did—whether in the written documents they leave behind or in oral accounts to others. We have examples of both in this collection. Third, life histories, unlike daily diaries, are written or told backwards—after the events in a person's life have taken place. Hence, later happenings may influence what is remembered, written, or said about earlier ones. Fortunately, documents contemporary with the events may serve as a corrective for these kinds of problems. And fourth, how accurate or complete a life history may be is also tied to the question of why the biography or life story is recalled at all. In African societies as in Western ones, life stories sometimes aim more at teaching lessons, documenting status, or claiming rights than at transmitting truthful information.

But despite all of these questions, the stories of people who lived in the past are compelling because they describe real experiences. In the chapters that follow, we encounter men and women from across Africa. We may or may not identify personally with each of them, but taken together these life stories add a human dimension to the history of modern Africa. We are drawn to them because, we too are individuals, living our own life stories.

Note

1. See the "Map of Freedom, 2010," produced by Freedom House at www.freedomhouse.org.

PART I

ENCOUNTERS: TWO WORLDS AND NEW WORLDS, 1800–1850

CHAPTER ONE

~

José Manuel and Nbena in Benguela in the Late 1810s

Encounters with Enslavement

José C. Curto

By the time of the dramatic events that José C. Curto describes in this chapter, the Portuguese had been in Angola for more than three hundred years. The tumult of conquest had long since given way to colonial rule and with it the routinization of authority. The Portuguese colonial authorities, people of mixed African and Portuguese heritage in the port of Benguela, individual Africans from the town, and African societies in the near hinterland had developed mutually accepted and expected ways of dealing with each other. New identities also developed with the emergence of a new African/Portuguese society and an indigenous Christian tradition.

Given the length of the Portuguese presence, this evolution is perhaps not very surprising. It is quite ironic that this new colonial order took form in a broader context of extreme violence and disorder occasioned by the continued capture, sale, and export of slaves. The tale that follows shows that the order and civility underpinning colonial society were the products of a delicate balance. First, local African individuals and groups such as the Ndombe, whose cooperation and participation were necessary for the operation of the slave trade, enjoyed rights and privileges not extended to the people of the interior, who were the target of raids and enslavement. Nonetheless, the struggles of José Manuel and Nbena and her daughter show that even these safeguards were fragile and subject to violation at any time, not only by the colonial authorities but as much as, if not more so, by others of African descent seeking gain. Indeed, their experiences suggest that Portuguese authorities were more concerned to protect the integrity of local arrangements than were some of the locals themselves. Second, the concern and admiration inspired by the valiant struggles of José Manuel, Nbena and her daughter, and their families for their liberty are undoubtedly tempered by the fact that they were slave traders themselves, both before and after their ordeals. This is not a lofty tale of the struggle for human rights.

Finally, this story illustrates the immensity of the African continent and the disjointed character of the movement to abolish first the slave trade and then slavery itself. By the later 1810s, Britain, the United States, and several continental European powers had abolished the slave trade north of the equator. Indeed, in 1833, a decade and a half after the events recounted in this chapter, Britain officially abolished slavery in the entire British empire. Yet in Benguela at the time of José Manuel and Nbena at least, no one seems to have raised questions about the legality or morality of the slave trade. It would be another decade or so before the legal commerce to Brazil ended (1830), and even longer before the ensuing clandestine trade dissipated in the 1860s.

Enslavement in Africa took place under a myriad of contexts: warfare between states, chiefdoms, and villages; raids, or *razzia*; kidnapping by bands of thugs or unscrupulous individuals; the contortion of court proceedings to enslave both insiders and outsiders for the violation of trivial and other rules of society; witchcraft accusations designed to turn people accused of such activity into slaves; tribute exactions, with subordinates forced to provide captives to higher authorities; and the sale of kin or even self-enslavement, particularly during times of famines and epidemics. These methods turned the slave trade in sub-Saharan Africa into a truly monumental enterprise.

Indeed, from the early sixteenth through the nineteenth century, tens of millions of Africans were taken into slavery. Over these four centuries, the slave trade forcibly took more than eleven million people to the Western Atlantic world and another five million to the Muslim world. Beginning in the late seventeenth century, both of these currents experienced spectacular growth. In addition, other people taken as captives supplied various internal slave trades within Africa. The historical writing about the slave trade has tended to focus on the aggregate dimension of this experience. As Patrick Manning has pointed out, however, slavery was not a mass phenomenon, but rather the sum total of all of the individual lives spent partly or wholly in slavery.[1] Every person taken into slavery had a face, a name, and a story to tell.

Forty years ago, Philip Curtin published a collection of personal narratives of several West Africans who were taken into slavery and reconstructed the contexts of their enslavement.[2] Despite his example, historians of slavery and the slave trades in Africa have been slow to turn their attention to individual victims and their stories. According to a recent appraisal,

> The historiography of Africa has yet to capture the horror and terror that accompanied the African dimension of the slave trade. Within world history it is the narrative of those who became African American slaves that has taken pride of place and come to exemplify a universal chronicle of suffering, pain, and eventual triumph. However, the contemporary political agenda of African descendents within the Americas has led historians to shy away from tackling the complex and contradictory narrative of the circumstances under which these people were enslaved, as well as the story of those enslaved Africans who did not end up in the Americas, across the Sahara, or in the Indian Ocean but remained within the continent. In other words, this haunting silence creates a void where the voice and experiences of Africans on the continent should be articulated.[3]

But this situation is changing. Concerned with the de-individualization of the people who were enslaved that is characteristic of quantitative approaches to slavery and the slave trades in Africa, historians have recently begun to reconstruct and analyze the lives of real people under all kinds of contexts within this nexus.[4]

This chapter articulates two individuals' experiences with enslavement. The stories of José Manuel and Nbena unfolded in the central Angolan port town of Benguela and its immediate interior during the second half of the 1810s. Their experiences are important on several levels. First, each incident is relatively well documented, which allows a detailed reconstruction of their encounters with enslavement.[5] When José Manuel and Nbena were threatened with enslavement, they did not experience the ordeal alone: Their kin quickly mobilized to rescue them. With such support, each of them took the unusual, though not uncommon, approach of a legal challenge against enslavement in this central Angolan town before they were to be deported to the Americas. José Manuel and Nbena argued before Benguela's highest colonial administrator that as freeborn persons they could not be enslaved. Nbena's case rested on the claim that, as a freeborn resident of a Ndombe village located about twenty kilometers from Benguela, she was assured safe passage to and from her village and this central Angolan port. In Benguela she was involved in selling produce—some that she produced and some produced by her slaves—both to feed the port population and to supply the slave ships destined for the Americas. Vassals of the Portuguese crown since the late 1620s, Ndombe villagers were long-standing commercial and political allies of the Portuguese colonial administration in Benguela, which entitled them to certain privileges, including protection against enslavement.[6]

Identity, place of residence, and occupation were also part of the argument put forth by José Manuel. Either born as a free person in Benguela or having lived there as a free man for quite a long time, José Manuel was a part-time soldier in the local Henriques regiment, an unpaid militia of free blacks.[7] He also periodically traveled into the interior with trade goods, which he exchanged for captives. Manuel was part of a relatively large contingent of free creole blacks who, by virtue of their identity, place of residence, and occupations, were also protected from enslavement by the Portuguese colonial administration. Indeed, they were instrumental in underpinning Benguela's slave export trade. Yet, in spite of such protection, the cases of José Manuel and Nbena also demonstrate the insecurity generated by the enslavement process. The very individuals who sustained the slave trade could easily become caught up in its web and be enslaved themselves. Moreover, both cases show how the process of enslavement sometimes unfolded over days, weeks, months, and even years. Some victims lived for long periods with anguish stemming from their disputed status and dreaded deportation from their homeland. In short, the experiences of José Manuel and Nbena capture very well the horror and terror that accompanied the African dimension of the slave trade.

Before turning to their stories, however, let us contextualize the landscape where their experiences unfolded by looking at the town of Benguela. In the 1810s, Benguela was the second most important port in colonial Angola after Luanda, through which West Central African slaves were exported to the Americas and notably Brazil.[8] Over the course of the decade, about 45,178 slaves were legally shipped out of Benguela, 85.5 percent of whom were destined for Rio de Janeiro.[9] Although a large number, this figure represented a drop when compared to the height of the trade in the 1790s. In that decade, 83,355 slaves left Benguela as legal exports.[10] In September 1816, when Manuel de Abreu de Mello e Alvim assumed the governorship of Benguela and its hinterland, one of his major concerns was to expand the commerce in captives. The permanent population of Benguela was then overwhelmingly African: Between 1813 and 1819, it averaged 2,290 individuals; half were African slaves and 44 percent were free Africans.[11] Many of them were creoles, locally born individuals who were artisans or worked in commercial or other occupations linked to the slave trade.[12] The large supply of food needed by the permanent population of the city and the hundreds upon hundreds of slaves awaiting shipment on any given day led to frequent food shortages.[13] Benguela depended largely upon African farmers in the immediate hinterland for its food. As for defense, the white population was quite small, so the responsibility for defending the port town fell partially upon the Henriques regiment, whose ranks included José Manuel.

José Manuel

Some time following the rainy season of 1816, José Manuel set out alone from Benguela into the hinterland. He was laden with trade goods to exchange for slaves.[14] There was nothing unusual about this journey. José Manuel was part and parcel of an army of black, mulatto, and white petty traders based at Benguela who, with the coming of the *caçimbo*, the dry season, annually left central Angola's slave-exporting town to trade for captives throughout the interior. Unlike many other petty traders, he apparently did not obtain his trade goods on credit. More likely, he amassed them through his own work and/or by drawing upon the economic resources of kin, who also lived in Benguela. Consequently, he was not burdened with debt as were so many of his counterparts. But he was not rich, either.

This particular journey did not go well. Somewhere in the interior, local people stole his trade goods. To add insult to injury, he was also arrested and, for reasons that remain completely obscure, condemned to pay a fine of forty-six *panos*, or small pieces of cloth. This number of panos would have been worth between 18$000 and 20$000 *réis* at Benguela, or about one-fourth of the average cost of an exportable slave. Inland, the same forty-six panos would have probably represented half the average cost of a slave.[15] Alone and imprisoned in the interior, José Manuel had few ways to pay this fine. Fortunately, he was soon delivered from this predicament. Upon learning of the incident, the *sova*, or chief of the area, offered to pay the penalty if José Manuel agreed to repay him. José immediately agreed to these generous terms, regained his freedom, and headed straight for Benguela.

This episode clearly indicates that in Angola, as well as elsewhere in Africa, the risky business of slaving required trust between traders on the coast and African suppliers inland.[16] José Manuel could have, once back in his hometown, reneged on his word to settle the debt. But to do that would have made it nearly impossible for him to return to the interior to trade, thus undermining his livelihood. The debt of forty-six panos, even if incurred inland and with an African chief, was thus a powerful liability. Consequently, once he reached his hometown, José Manuel wasted little time in attempting to settle his obligation.

For this purpose, José Manuel could think of no one in a better position to help than António Leal do Sacramento. Although he appeared to be an old man in his seventies, the nominal census of 1797 in Benguela reported him to be thirty-five years old.[17] In 1816, then, he would have been around fifty. Sacramento had deep roots in Benguela. The 1797 census also registered him as *homen preto*, or a black man, owner of a number of *cazas terrias de telha* (single-storied, red-clayed shingle houses) in Benguela, as well as owner of eight male and seven female slaves who worked for him in town. In mid-1798, another document records Sacramento as also owning in "Quissequelle, where the mouth of the Katumbela River begins, a hamlet comprising of eight *cubattas*, where seven of his female slaves live, an agricultural estate [annually] producing 35 *canzungueis* of corn and 30 of beans, and a spread of orange, palm and banana trees." The *cazonguel* was a unit of dry measure equal to about 14 liters, while *cubattas* were the single-room homes of the local African population. This economic success was probably responsible for the fact that Sacramento had already risen to the rank of captain in the Henriques regiment. When José Manuel thought about turning to Sacramento for assistance, the older man still owned the agricultural estate in the immediate interior of Benguela, as well as a retinue of slaves both in town and near the mouth of the Katumbela River. Some time before, this wealth had already allowed Sacramento, who was black, successfully to seek appointment as the lieutenant colonel of the Henriques, the highest military position open to a local black male in Benguela. Sacramento was hence José Manuel's senior officer.

Because Lieutenant Colonel Sacramento was black like himself, the senior military officer in his regiment, and a person of considerable means, José Manuel probably came to the conclusion that the older man would rescue him from his dire predicament. And so the soldier-trader anxiously approached Sacramento for an advance, which he would use to repay the debt that had secured his release in the interior. The lieutenant colonel, however, flatly refused. José Manuel may well have sought other options. If so, these did not produce anything concrete. Pressed for financial assistance, he addressed a second plea to Sacramento, with the same result. Discouraged, José Manuel approached him a third time, though now with a proposition that could hardly be refused. To cover the pledge incurred with the African chief, José Manuel offered Lieutenant Colonel Sacramento his personal services until the debt was liquidated. This time around, Sacramento found the offer far more alluring, most likely because the value of the debt was not specified. He agreed to help his subordinate. José Manuel soon received forty-six panos, as well as a coat of arms and a bottle of *aguardente*,[18] which he promptly forwarded to the African chief who had come to his aid in the interior. At last the debt was repaid, but as a result José Manuel became Sacramento's personal servant.

To settle his new debt, José Manuel performed all kinds of chores for his senior military officer. He even carried Sacramento on a *tipoia* or palanquin, a task usually reserved for slaves. José Manuel endured these hapless circumstances, "like a slave," for about two years. But even after this term of service, Sacramento judged that his subordinate's services fell far short of the original value of the goods. To get what he thought he was still owed, Sacramento began to consider selling José Manuel into slavery.

In the middle of 1818, José Manuel somehow learned of the lieutenant colonel's intentions, and the news aroused great concern. Because he worked in Sacramento's household, he must have known that his patron and senior officer had recently kidnapped, branded, and sold Nbena and her daughter, also free blacks, as slaves to a ship captain heading for Brazil by way of Luanda. Now José Manuel was also at risk of losing his freedom and being deported across the Atlantic into, as a Brazilian proverb put it, the "hell for blacks"—the epithet used for Brazil. Once aware of the plan brewing in the mind of the lieutenant colonel, José Manuel lost no time in alerting his kin of the plot.

Upon learning of Sacramento's intentions, the family quickly sought a meeting with Governor Mello e Alvim. During their audience, they argued that although José Manuel had turned himself into a servant, he remained nevertheless a free person and consequently could not be sold into slavery. They hence claimed the privilege of "original freedom," a right granted to Africans by the Portuguese crown almost from the beginning of the Angolan slave trade, so that those "unlawfully" enslaved would not be unjustly compelled to serve a life of bondage. In addition, ecclesiastic and civic dispositions required that slaves exported from Angola be "instructed in the religious truths and baptized before embarkment." Beyond overseeing such nominal conversion to Christianity, priests in Benguela also functioned as *carimbador e inquiridor das liberdades*, which is to say that they were responsible for overseeing the branding of export slaves and fulfilling the obligations of the "inquisitor of freedoms," who questioned slaves before they sailed about whether they had already been slaves before the Luso-Brazilians traders and their local agents bought them. Predictably, as Manuel Nunes Gabriel points out, "there was a great deal of carelessness both in catechizing . . . and in verifying the previous condition of those brought before them."[19] Slave traders tried to get around or otherwise minimize contact with priests, who, despite their responsibilities, generally were not particularly interested in protecting the enslaved. Even when some captives were able to prove that they had been enslaved illegally, few actually succeeded in regaining their freedom. Most were hastily declared to have been slaves before purchase by Luso-Brazilians or their agents, branded, and shipped to the Americas.

José Manuel and his kin were clearly aware of the formal privileges reserved for Africans who, like themselves, were integrated into the Portuguese colonial world—especially in Benguela. As permanent residents of a major Angolan port, they had benefited a long time from such protection. It was specifically on these grounds that José Manuel's family asked the governor of Benguela to "oppose the sale" and "give them enough time to gather the merchandise" that their kinsman owed Lieutenant Colonel Sacramento.[20] The governor agreed.

The family of José Manuel immediately turned their efforts to getting the goods to repay Sacramento. They then set out to compensate Sacramento and obtain José Manuel's release from debt bondage. The lieutenant colonel, however, refused the reimbursement. Instead, he demanded a *peça d'India*, a prime male, adult slave, valued at the considerable sum of 90$000 réis in 1819. Otherwise, he insisted, he would sell José Manuel into slavery.

With the repayment of the original debt rejected, the kin of José Manuel desperately searched for someone who could help them meet Sacramento's new demand. They eventually turned to José Nunes Romão, a lieutenant in Benguela's militia regiment, the outfit headed by Sacramento in which José Manuel also served. They humbly asked Romão if he could "lend them a good black female or male slave with which to satisfy" the lieutenant colonel. Romão promptly lent them a "good black *molecana*" or young female slave, valued at 64$000 réis. The family immediately took the young slave woman to military headquarters in Benguela, so that Mello e Alvim could witness the payment. The governor called Sacramento into his office, where he instructed him to accept the young female slave as reimbursement of José Manuel's debt. The lieutenant colonel acquiesced, but with the proviso that he be paid, in addition, the difference between the value of the slave and that of a *peça d'India*—a packet of cloth, a matter of some 26$000 réis. This proviso was totally unacceptable for the governor, who told Lieutenant Colonel Sacramento that he should acknowledge that he had been repaid appropriately and free José Manuel.

Sacramento walked home with the molecana, which suggested that he had accepted the governor's final ruling. But he did not release José Manuel, holding him for sale. The failure of the lieutenant colonel to set José Manuel free, in spite of having been duly reimbursed, led the family to return to see the governor. They bitterly complained, requesting now that the molecana given to secure José Manuel's freedom be returned to them. Mello e Alvim again agreed. He soon ordered the lieutenant colonel not only to return the female slave to José Manuel's relatives, but also not to sell him into slavery. By this time, however, Sacramento had already sold the molecana. Learning of this turn of events, the governor immediately ordered the woman's new owner to return her to the family of José Manuel. But the new owner, without Mello e Alvim knowing, had already paid Sacramento 70$004 réis for her.[21] Nonetheless, in November 1818, the female slave was again brought to Sacramento. He accepted her for the second time and finally released José Manuel from his personal service.

The upshot of these machinations was that Sacramento parleyed an initial debt of slightly more than 20$000 réis into a net profit of around 300 percent above the value of the goods originally extended to José Manuel in Benguela. In addition, he had profited from the services of José Manuel for a period that, in itself, more than compensated for the value of the original loan. José Manuel's kin, on the other hand, spent the average price of a slave to rescue their relative from slavery but still remained indebted to Lieutenant Romão, who had lent them the molecana in the first place. As for José Manuel, over and beyond suffering the humiliation of two years' service under Sacramento—"like a slave"—he lived for several months in fear that he would be sold into slavery and deported.

Nbena and Her Daughter

If José Manuel's struggle to avoid enslavement was over in a matter of months, in the case of Nbena and her daughter, horror and terror went on for years. Early one morning in late May or early June 1817, Nbena and her young daughter set out from an Ndombe village in the Katumbela area for Benguela to the southwest. Ndombe women regularly made this trek to sell agricultural produce in Benguela, and Nbena subsequently made the same trip for this reason. She was probably part of a small army of enterprising Ndombe women who sold foodstuffs in the Angolan port. The road to and from Benguela, however, was not safe, even for regular travelers like Nbena whose services helped sustain the town. Ndombe women were often robbed and sometimes suffered worse along the way.

Not long after Nbena left her village that morning, she encountered an old and frail slave woman who worked on the nearby agricultural estate of Lieutenant Colonel Sacramento, the same man who played a major role in José Manuel's life. The woman convinced Nbena to follow her to the estate house, where she introduced Nbena to Sacramento's wife. Advanced in years and tired of laboring as a field hand, the female slave told her mistress that because she was now too old to be useful, she had brought the much younger Nbena to replace her. She had conned Nbena and her daughter into slavery. The following day, Nbena was given an ax and forced to work on Sacramento's estate. Born a free woman, Nbena would have none of it. As fortune would have it, an opportunity to escape arose the same day, and Nbena fled with her daughter. In countryside that she knew well, Nbena headed straight for the secure world of her village. Once there, she returned to life as a free person, living amidst her relatives and possessions—ironically made up, in part, of her own slaves. Nonetheless, Nbena's brief experience as a slave had scared her, and she did not venture out of her village for some months. About six months later, in late November or early December 1817, either because she was no longer afraid or for other reasons, Nbena once again set out for Benguela early in the morning to sell produce.

The trip was uneventful, and Nbena, her daughter tagging along, arrived safely in Benguela. Unfortunately, someone recognized her as a fugitive from the Sacramento estate. Word was sent to Sacramento, who happened to be in town. Suddenly, a few of his trusted slaves encircled Nbena and her daughter and kidnapped them. Sacramento lost little time in dealing with his recaptured runaway. Nbena was branded on the spot and then sold with her daughter for 70$000 réis to João de Oliveira Dias, captain of the *Astréa*, a Lisbon vessel about to set sail for Luanda. The *Astréa* was almost certainly ultimately headed for Brazil, the destination of almost all ships that left the capital of Angola.[22] Nbena and her daughter were on the point of suffering the difficult Atlantic crossing.

News of Nbena's abduction, sale, and imminent departure quickly reached her village. Alarmed, relatives quickly mobilized and headed for Benguela. A few hours later, they descended in large numbers on military headquarters. Among them were five or six Ndombe *sovas*, one of whom was Nbena's uncle. They did not come to ransom her. Rather, they created a great uproar, clamoring in favor of Nbena, complaining about her unlawful enslavement, and demanding justice from the governor. For Mello e Alvim, such a large number of rowdy people was frightening. But their cause was also very disturbing. He soon decided to look into the matter and scheduled a hearing.

An even larger crowd assembled in front of Benguela's military headquarters for the hearing. Mello e Alvim first called for his *tandalla*, or translator, and others in Benguela who acted as translators. He summoned the plaintiffs, including Nbena's relations, the Ndombe chiefs, and other witnesses. Their depositions were in complete agreement: Nbena had been born free and lived as such until her abduction. She was not a slave and had been wrongfully enslaved. The governor asked Lieutenant Colonel Sacramento to respond to these allegations. Sacramento said that Nbena had been brought seven months before to his household by an old female slave of his as her replacement and that she had subsequently fled. He had ordered his slaves to recapture her and then sold her to Captain Dias. Without further proof, Mello e Alvim judged this to be an "extremely scandalous" matter and ruled in favor of Nbena. He ordered Sacramento to have Nbena and her daughter returned from Luanda without delay, at his own expense. When they learned of the decision, Nbena's relatives and the crowd dispersed peacefully, hoping for the best.

But where were the unfortunate Nbena and her daughter? Were they still in Luanda, or were they already on the *Astréa* headed for Brazil? Equally important was the issue of whether Sacramento would keep his word. To make sure that both Nbena and her daughter were returned to Benguela, Mello e Alvim wrote Luiz da Motta Feo e Torres, the governor of Angola in Luanda who was his immediate superior, describing the details of the case. He asked that Motta Feo take "the necessary measures, so that the said Negro female returns [to Benguela] from the authority of the Captain who bought her, or from wherever she may be."[23] When Mello e Alvim's letter arrived in Luanda, Nbena and her daughter were still in the possession of Captain Dias, and the *Astréa* had not yet sailed. Motta Feo ordered Captain Dias to comply with the Benguela governor's request. He complied and in late 1817, the governor of Angola in Luanda let Mello e Alvim know that Nbena and her daughter had been freed and were on their way back to Benguela. They arrived early the following year. Nbena and her daughter had barely escaped being dispatched to the "hell for blacks."

Back in Benguela, Nbena and her daughter were convened before Mello e Alvim. Nbena claimed her liberty on the basis of "original freedom"—which is to say that having been born and lived her life as a free person, she could not be enslaved in the circumstances of her original capture at Sacramento's estate.[24] Where or how Nbena learned of this privilege of "original freedom" is not known. Of course, she lived near Benguela and went to the city regularly. In addition, her people, the Ndombe, had lived with such protection for a long time. Hence it may be assumed that the principle of original freedom was general knowledge among them, sustained through direct contact with Portuguese colonial society. Whatever the case, Sacramento questioned the applicability of the principle in Nbena's case. Contradicting her claim to original freedom, he petitioned the governor to hold her and her daughter in custody while he initiated judicial proceedings to prove his claim that he was their owner. Mello e Alvim had no choice but to grant the petition. The mother and daughter were thus placed in the custody of a local merchant, Manuel Pereira Gonçalves, who also happened to be a second lieutenant in Benguela's militia, the unit that Sacramento commanded. Nbena and her daughter had escaped deportation to Brazil as slaves, but they were still not free.

The living conditions that characterized this fettered freedom are unknown. It is known that Nbena and her daughter languished in the custody of Gonçalves for quite a while before Sacramento initiated judiciary proceedings. The governor's patience grew thin, and he issued a decree requiring that Sacramento explain the delay in presenting proof that he was the owner of the two women. Sacramento did not respond to the decree. Instead, he sent a letter to Mello e Alvim that failed to acknowledge his position as governor; this lack of deference earned Sacramento a trip to the dungeon in the fort. There, the governor ordered Sacramento to explain what rights he held over Nbena and her daughter and how long he had owned them. Sacramento replied that he had nothing to say to Mello e Alvim and had already brought the matter directly before the governor of Angola.

Mello e Alvim did not take long to react to this affront. In mid-July 1818, he bluntly informed his superior in Luanda:

> The said Lieutenant Colonel committed the absurdity of stealing, violently branding the mentioned free, black female Micia [Nbena], and deceptively selling her, never giving proof or showing whatever title through which he may have had rights favoring him in this matter. Consequently, he did not justify anything. . . . On the contrary, the said black female, today still in custody, gave the most convincing proof that is possible to give me, three *Tandallas* or Interpreters, and four *Sovas*, one of whom an uncle of [hers], and a considerable number of witnesses who were not all required to be questioned. All of this I have already informed Your Excellency. This matter is extremely scandalous and prejudicial; it thus requires austere measures, especially since Her Royal Highness recommends in Her Royal Instructions to the Governors of this Captaincy that they show great consideration respecting [the question of original] freedoms. Given the aforesaid, Your Excellency will take the measures that seem most appropriate.[25]

For Mello e Alvim, the situation was crystal clear. Sacramento had, through deceitful means, enslaved Nbena and her young daughter. The lieutenant colonel had, moreover, failed to provide proof of proprietary right. As a result, Nbena and her daughter should be given their unfettered freedom.

But this is not what happened. Nbena and her daughter remained in Benguela in the custody of Lieutenant Gonçalves, anxiously awaiting the decision of the governor of Angola, who in turn referred the matter to José

Verneque, the *ouvidor* or chief justice of the Portuguese crown in Luanda. After reviewing the case, Judge Verneque decided in favor of Sacramento. Given the overwhelming evidence in favor of Nbena and her daughter, it is unclear how he came to this decision. A few days later, Motta Feo confirmed the verdict. The case, he wrote Mello e Alvim, was not one of original freedom because the court had accepted Sacramento's claim of having had owned Nbena for years. Consequently, there was no doubt whatsoever that the matter should be litigated by the two parties in Benguela's court of first instance and adjudicated by its *juiz ordinário*, or justice of the peace. It could not, the governor of Angola continued, be adjudicated by the colonial administration, which could only hear and settle cases relating to original freedom, "as was consistently the practice [in Luanda]."[26] The fettered freedom under which Nbena, along with her daughter, had lived upon returning to Benguela from Luanda was thus further compromised. Her only recourse now seemed to be the municipal court in Benguela.

Yet, this was not to be. Mello e Alvim objected strenuously to the interpretation of the governor of Angola, considering the intervention a violation of the powers and responsibilities of his own governorship in Benguela. He appealed Motta Feo's decision. In his opinion, the governor of Angola was "erroneously persuaded" that the case should go to the judiciary when, in fact, it was a case of original freedom to be decided by the colonial government. He wrote that the governor's ruling was unbelievable because he (Mello e Alvim) had duly demonstrated that Sacramento's actions had been "scandalous" and "unjust," entailing as they did two episodes of holding Nbena and her daughter captive. Mello e Alvim further told his superior that a second investigation of the case had recently been completed. The governor of Benguela appended depositions from all the parties and their respective witnesses to the appeal, noting that the proceeding had confirmed his previous findings. Only one new element was discovered. The local *carimbador* found that Sacramento had branded Nbena's right breast with a false mark hoping it would pass as the royal stamp, thereby sullying his case even more. As a result, Mello e Alvim declared,

> the malicious intent of the Lieutenant Colonel to steal the liberty of the said black female and her daughter, who are both freeborn, being well known, Your Excellency will fully recognize that he carried out the same practices as the barbarous natives in the execution of their laws; and I, not having accepted them, for he would have abusively offended the laws of our August Sovereign, the King, especially in such decisive case, given the substance of the charge, will thus not execute the order of Your Excellency.[27]

The governor of Benguela thus "freed the unfortunate black female, and her daughter, who protested the extremely grave affronts and the scandalous injuries committed by the Lieutenant Colonel."[28] Having been deceived into slavery by an old female slave, kidnapped, branded, sold by a wealthy and influential black man for shipment to Brazil, rescued before deportation, and then forced to witness, from a distance, a protracted battle over her status, Nbena, with her daughter always in tow, was finally allowed, almost two years after her ordeal had begun, to return to her home, family, friends, and slaves as a free woman.

Conclusion

José Manuel and Nbena were lucky. Identity, place of residence, and occupation protected both José Manuel and Nbena against enslavement—which was not lost upon Governor Mello e Alvim, who understood well that keeping them in bondage could threaten the future of Benguela as a major slave-exporting town. Although both were traumatized by the possibility of spending the rest of their lives as slaves, neither in fact experienced that fate. Yet their experiences reveal some of the horror and terror that millions of other individuals faced on the African end of the slave trade. The fact that individuals such as José Manuel and Nbena could be threatened with enslavement makes it clear that few Africans were immune from bondage. The shadow of slavery darkened the daily lives of nearly everyone. Most enslaved people could neither call on the protections claimed by José Manuel and Nbena nor make their pleas to high-ranking colonial administrators. Most people were captured in much more horrific and terrorizing ways. Without protection, they were simply uprooted to confront the traumatic experiences that came along with being turned into a commodity. In addition to examining the lives of slaves on the middle passage across the Atlantic and their situations in the Americas, these African dimensions of enslavement must also be explored. Only then will we begin to understand the total experience of the slave trade and slavery—for Africa, for Africans, and for us all.

Further Reading

On the Atlantic and Muslim slave trades, see, along with titles included in the notes, Philip D. Curtin's now classic study, *The Atlantic Slave Trade: A Census* (Madison: University of Wisconsin Press, 1969); Ralph A. Austen, "The Trans-Saharan Slave Trade: A Tentative Census," in *The Uncommon Market: Essays in the Economic History of the Atlantic Slave Trade*, ed. Henry

A. Gemery and Jan S. Hogendorn (New York: Academic Press, 1979), 22–76; Ralph A. Austen, "The Mediterranean Islamic Slave Trade out of Africa: A Tentative Census," in *The Human Commodity: Perspectives on the Trans-Saharan Slave Trade*, ed. Elizabeth Savage (London: Frank Cass, 1992), 214–48. The victims of the internal slave trade numbered in the millions by the time it reached its climax in the 1800s. See Patrick Manning, *Slavery and African Life* (Cambridge, UK: Cambridge University Press, 1991), 60–148; and Paul E. Lovejoy, *Transformations in Slavery: A History of Slavery in Africa*, 2nd ed. (New York: Cambridge University Press, 2000), 140–245.

In addition to studies that offer an overview of the slave trade, there is a substantial literature on individual African encounters with enslavement. Among those on people taken from West and West Central Africa, see Cugoano Ottobah, *Thoughts and Sentiments on the Evil and Wicked Traffic of the Slavery and Commerce of the Human Species* (Legon: Institute of African Studies, University of Ghana, [1787] 1965); Olaudah Equiano, *The Life of Olaudah Equiano: or, Gustavus Vassa the African, 1789*, 2 vols. (London: Dawsons, [1789] 1969); Mary F. Smith, *Baba of Karo: A Woman of the Moslem Hausa* (New York: Praeger, 1954); A. C. de C. M. Saunders, "The Life and Humour of João de Sá Panasco o Negro, Former Slave, Court Jester, and Gentleman of the Portuguese Royal Household (fl. 1524–1567)," in *Mediaeval and Renaissance Studies of Spain and Portugal in Honour of P. E. Russell*, ed. F. W. Hodcroft et al. (Oxford, UK: Society for the Study of Mediaeval Languages and Literature, 1981), 181–91; Sylviane Diouf, *Servants of Allah: African Muslims Enslaved in the Americas* (New York: New York University Press, 1998); Terry Alford, *Prince among Slaves: The True Story of an African Prince Sold into Slavery in the American South* (New York: Oxford University Press, 1986); Robin Law and Paul E. Lovejoy, eds., *The Biography of Mahommah Gardo Baquaqua: His Passage from Slavery to Freedom in Africa and America* (Princeton, N.J.: Markus Wiener, 2001); and Claire C. Robertson, "Post-Proclamation Slavery in Accra: A Female Affair?" in *Women and Slavery in Africa*, ed. Claire C. Robertson and Martin A. Klein (Portsmouth, N.H.: Heinemann, 1997), 220–45.

For encounters with enslavement in East Africa, see A. C. Madan, ed., *Kiungani, or Story and History from Central Africa* (London: G. Bell & Sons, 1886); W. F. Baldock, "The Story of Rashid bin Hassani of the Bisa Tribe, Northern Rhodesia," in *Ten Africans*, ed. Margery Perham (London: Faber and Faber, 1936), 81–119; James J. Mbotela, *The Freeing of Slaves in East Africa* (London: Evans Brothers, 1956); Marcia Wright, *Strategies of Slaves and Women: Life-Stories from East/Central Africa* (London: J. Currey, 1993); Richard Pankhurst, "The History of Bareya, Šanqella, and Other Ethiopian

Slaves from the Borderlands of the Sudan," *Sudan Notes and Records* 58 (1977): 1–43; Margaret Strobel, *Muslim Women in Mombasa 1890–1975* (New Haven, Conn.: Yale University Press, 1979), 43–100; and Edward A. Alpers, "The Story of Swema: Female Vulnerability in Nineteenth-Century East Africa," in *Women and Slavery in Africa*, ed. Claire C. Robertson and Martin A. Klein (Portsmouth, N.H.: Heinemann, 1997), 185–219.

Notes

1. Patrick Manning, *Slavery and African Life* (Cambridge, UK: Cambridge University Press, 1990), 110.

2. Philip D. Curtin, ed., *Africa Remembered: Narratives by West Africans from the Era of the Slave Trade* (Madison: University of Wisconsin Press, 1968).

3. Carolyn A. Brown, "Epilogue: Memory as Resistance: Identity and the Contested History of Slavery in Southeastern Nigeria, an Oral History Project," in *Fighting the Slave Trade: West African Strategies*, ed. Sylviane A. Diouf (Athens: Ohio University Press, 2003), 219.

4. Paul E. Lovejoy, "Biography as Source Material: Towards a Biographical Archive of Enslaved Africans," in *Source Material for Studying the Slave Trade and the African Diaspora*, ed. Robin Law (Stirling, UK: University of Stirling, 1997), 119–40; Paul E. Lovejoy, "Identifying Enslaved Africans in the African Diaspora," in *Identity in the Shadow of Slavery*, ed. Paul E. Lovejoy (London: Continuum, 2000), 1–29; Jerome S. Handler, "Survivors of the Middle Passage: Life Stories of Enslaved Africans in British America," *Slavery and Abolition* 23, 1 (2002): 25–56.

5. Full reconstructions are found in José C. Curto, "The Story of Nbena, 1817–1820: Unlawful Enslavement and the Concept of 'Original Freedom' in Angola," in *Trans-Atlantic Dimensions of Ethnicity in the African Diaspora*, ed. Paul E. Lovejoy and David V. Trotman (London: Continuum, 2003), 43–64; and Curto, "Struggling against Enslavement: The Case of José Manuel in Benguela, 1816–1820," *Canadian Journal of African Studies* 39, 1 (2005): 96–122.

6. The thrust of the privileges emanating from vassalage is found in Beatrix Heintze, "The Angolan Vassal Tributes of the Seventeenth Century," *Revista de História Económica e Social* 6 (1980): 57–78; and Heintze, "Luso-African Feudalism in Angola? The Vassal Treaties of the Sixteenth to the Eighteenth Century," *Revista Portuguesa de História* 18 (1980): 111–31.

7. Founded in 1760, the Henriques regiment was manned exclusively by free black soldiers. See Ralph Delgado, *O Reino de Benguela (Do descobrimento à criação do govêrno subalterno)* (Lisbon: Imprensa Beleza, 1945), 247–48.

8. José C. Curto, "The Legal Portuguese Slave Trade from Benguela, Angola, 1730–1828: A Quantitative Re-Appraisal," *África* (Centro de Estudos Africanos, Universidade de São Paulo) 16–17 (1993–1994): 101–16; Curto, "Luso-Brazilian Alcohol and the Legal Slave Trade at Benguela and Its Hinterland, c. 1617–1830,"

in *Le grand commerce en Afrique noire, du 18e siècle à nos jours*, ed. H. Bonin and M. Cahen (Paris: Éditions de la Société française d'histoire d'outre-mer, 2001), 351–69.

9. Joseph C. Miller, "The Number, Origins, and Destinations of Slaves, in the Eighteenth Century Angolan Slave Trade," in *The Atlantic Slave Trade: Effects on Economies, Societies, and Peoples in Africa, the Americas, and Europe*, ed. Joseph E. Inikori and Stanley L. Engerman (Durham, N.C.: Duke University Press, 1992), 77–115; David Eltis, Stephen D. Behrendt, David Richardson, and Herbert S. Klein, eds., *The Trans-Atlantic Slave Trade: A Database on CD-ROM* (Cambridge, UK: Cambridge University Press, 1999).

10. José C. Curto, "Experiences of Enslavement in West Central Africa," *Histoire sociale—Social History* 41, 82 (2008): 386.

11. See census documents for these years found in the collection titled "Mappa da Cidade de Benguela . . ." in the Arquivo Histórico Ultramarino, Angola.

12. Tito Omboni, *Viaggi nell'Africa Occidentale: Già Medico di Consiglio Nel Regno d'Angola e Sue Dipendenze Membro Della R. Accademia Peloritana di Messina* (Milan: Civelli, 1845), 60–81; Gustav Tams, *Visit to the Portuguese Possessions in South-Western Africa* (New York: Negro University Press, [1845] 1969), vol. 1, 75–182.

13. Joseph C. Miller, *Way of Death: Merchant Capitalism and the Angolan Slave Trade* (Madison: University of Wisconsin Press, 1988), 417.

14. Manuel de A. de Mello e Alvim [Governor of Benguela] to Luiz da Motta Feo [Governor of Angola], 21 November 1818, Arquivo Histórico Nacional de Angola [the National Historical Archives of Angola, hereafter abbreviated as AHNA], Códice 447, folios 32–32v. This account of José's capture and struggle to regain his freedom is based on documents from this archive and the Archivo do Instituto Histórico e Geográfico Brasileiro (the Archives of the Brazilian Historical and Geographical Institute, hereafter abbreviated as AIHGB). For the most part, individual documents will not be cited in this chapter, but may be found in the articles listed in note 5.

15. Curto, "Struggling against Enslavement," 101–2.

16. Paul E. Lovejoy and David Richardson, "Trust, Pawnship, and Atlantic History: The Institutional Foundations of the Old Calabar Slave Trade," *American Historical Review* 104, 2 (1999): 332–55.

17. "Relação de José Caetano Carneiro, primeiro tenente, da metade dos moradores da parte do norte da cidade de São Felipe de Benguela, de ambos os sexos, cor, escravos sem nomes, empregos e estados. Relação de senzalas às quais pertencem," 29 November 1797, (AIHGB), DL32,02.03, fl. 23.

18. A brandy, made from the must of grapes, which was rarely found in Benguela at the time. Here, as a result, the term *aguardente* was commonly applied to Brazilian sugarcane brandy, the most voluminous alcoholic drink available until the 1850s. See Curto, "Luso-Brazilian Alcohol and the Legal Slave Trade." The coat of arms and the bottle of "aguardente" were probably sent to cover the interest on his debt.

19. Manuel Nunes Gabriel, *Angola: Cinco Séculos de Cristianismo* (Queluz, Portugal: Literal, n.d.), 234–35.

20. Mello e Alvim to Motta Feo, 21 November 1818, AHNA, Códice 447, fl. 33.

21. Curto, "Struggling against Enslavement," 107.

22. Miller, "Number, Origins, and Destinations of Slaves."

23. Mello e Alvim to Motta Feo, 11 December 1817, AHNA, Códice 446, fls. 154v–155v.

24. Curto, "The Story of Nbena," 51.

25. Mello e Alvim to Motta Feo, 17 July 1818, AHNA, Códice 447, fls. 9v–10v.

26. Motta Feo to Mello e Alvim, 21 July 1818, AHNA, Códice 155, fls. 36–36v.

27. Mello e Alvim to Motta Feo, 26 September 1818, AHNA, Códice 447, fls. 16–17.

28. Mello e Alvim to Motta Feo, 26 September 1818, AHNA, Códice 447, fls. 16–17.

CHAPTER TWO

~

Efusetan Aniwura
of Ibadan (1820s–1874)

A Woman Who Rose to the Rank of a Chief
but Whom Male Rivals Destroyed

Toyin Falola

*The nineteenth century was a time of great change in West Africa and the rest of
the continent. The professional and political career of Efusetan Aniwura, a prominent Yoruba woman and chief in the new city of Ibadan whose life spanned the
middle decades of the century, illustrates how these turbulent times affected her both
as a trader and as a leader who was a woman. Some of the tumult was internal to
the Yoruba. Aniwura grew up during the Yoruba civil wars that marked the eclipse
of older Yoruba city-states and the rise of new regional Yoruba powers. Other influences came from without, such as the increased circulation of imports from Europe
and the Americas, more intense interaction with European traders to the southwest
on the coast of today's Nigeria, and the arrival of white Christian missionaries
and former Yoruba slaves intercepted on the high seas and initially resettled farther
west on the African coast at the British outpost of Freetown in Sierra Leone or in
the African American settlements in Liberia. Aniwura's career demonstrates that
classifying influences as internal or external sometimes suggests a false dichotomy.
For example, the arms that Aniwura imported from the outside played a strategic
role in internal Yoruba wars. Like Hamet Diop, the Muslim trader and religious
leader featured in chapter 4, Aniwura maintained ties with Europeans, but she also
operated beyond the sphere of their direct control, using her in-between position to
her advantage.*

Aniwura's life also offers proof that women in Africa—in this case Yoruba women—were not rigidly confined to the roles of wife and mother. Most women in Africa worked outside the house, even in Muslim societies—the notable exception being the relatively few women confined to the home in conservative Muslim urban settings. Among the Yoruba and other peoples along the West African coast, women played very visible roles in commerce. Aniwura was not exceptional in being a Yoruba woman trader; rather, she was extraordinary because of her enormous success. In addition, women in many West African coastal societies, including the Yoruba, held leadership roles—most often among other women or among officials responsible for running the markets. A few women also made their way into the circles of male political leaders. What made Aniwura special is that she not only became a leader with men but also challenged their dominance.

Aniwura's fall from power and wealth—and her eventual execution—illustrate that even in a time of tumult and change, when prevailing political arrangements among the Yoruba were being recast, an influential woman leader still could not completely ignore, much less erase, boundaries imposed by gender. She challenged men on their own terms—as political and military leaders. Ironically but not surprisingly, male rivals condemned her for witchcraft, a charge often levied against women in Africa and elsewhere. As evidence, they cited her failure to conform to the proper roles of women as wife and mother. They did not raise the other, probably more important, reasons for their resentment, such as her success in competing with them in their own arena.

The activities and relevance of women and female leaders in Africa are underreported in historical sources. The evidence needed to explore Aniwura's life and career is sufficient, but it is not plentiful. We possess rich oral traditions and evidence collected at the turn of the twentieth century. We are also fortunate that Samuel Johnson, author of *The History of the Yorubas*, published in 1921, included her in his observations about the nineteenth century (see chapter 5). Among the Yoruba, the sparseness of information on women and their contributions to state development undoubtedly stems from the patrilineal nature of the Yoruba family, which relegates women to a low position in the policy- and decision-making machinery.

Aniwura's Background

The city-state of Ibadan, which was the capital of a sprawling empire, provides the context for understanding Aniwura's rise and fall. In the 1830s, when the Yoruba empire of Oyo lurched into the political decline that ultimately led to its disintegration, a host of other city-states emerged to take its place. Indeed, refugees fleeing Oyo in the 1820s founded Ibadan, whose warriors laid the foundations for its fame. Aniwura contributed to the city's rise.

Efusetan Aniwura was born in the 1820s, although we do not know the exact year of her birth. She rose to prominence around 1850 and was assassinated in 1874. Her life and death are illustrative of the lives and careers of a surprising number of extraordinary women in nineteenth-century Nigeria. Her first name, Efusetan, indicated that her parents believed in the Yoruba god of creation, Obatala. Aniwura, a second name that she probably acquired later, means "owner of gold"—a reference to her wealth and prestige. Like many powerful chiefs of her generation, Aniwura came to Ibadan as a migrant from Abeokuta. Her father was from Orile Ikija, an Egba community to the south. Abeokuta was the capital of the Egba, and Aniwura maintained her ties with the city after she emigrated. Earlier in the nineteenth century, Aniwura's family had produced a distinguished general named Ogundipe. Her mother came from the Yoruba sacred city of Ile-Ife. Her brother, Aniwura's uncle, was Oluyole, the first ruler of Ibadan.

What we know about Aniwura's childhood shows that she was a normal girl socialized into the roles of the Yoruba household. She must have observed that many Yoruba women engaged in trade. She also grew up in a time of rapid political and economic change. The Yoruba were undergoing a major political and cultural revolution. Clusters of refugees fleeing war had founded Abeokuta, her birthplace. Abeokuta itself was attacked in 1832 and 1835 by its Ijebu neighbors, and in turn, Abeokuta attacked its Awori and Egbado neighbors in the 1830s and 1840s to gain access to trade routes to the Atlantic coast. Aniwura's life experiences, then, would have taught her that warfare was critical to the survival of a state. These many conflicts also underscored the importance of regional trade in guns and gunpowder. Aniwura probably could not have avoided overhearing conversations about the provenance of guns and gunpowder, and about the traders who profited from their sale.

As she grew up, she also witnessed the arrival of a wave of newcomers to Abeokuta—notably liberated Yoruba slaves from Sierra Leone and Liberia and white Christian missionaries. In the 1830s and 1840s, about three thousand people migrated to Abeokuta from Sierra Leone. These events would have taught Aniwura that trade provided an avenue to profit from both the wars and the returned Yoruba immigrants.

Aniwura the Trader

Before she moved to Ibadan, Aniwura traded in Abeokuta, although she maintained long-distance ties with Lagos, Porto Novo, and Badagry, cities on the Atlantic coast to the southwest. But her greatest success came in Ibadan, where she moved in the 1850s or 1860s. Ibadan was a larger and more prosperous city with a bigger army, which was almost always at war. The city attracted thousands of immigrants, including young people who came to make their fortunes. As the center of an emerging empire, Ibadan offered many commercial advantages: The large number of inhabitants created a demand for many different products. Perched on the edge of the savanna, it was also well placed for the distribution of imports from Lagos as well as crops from the Yoruba hinterland. Items from Lagos included salt, liquor, and foodstuffs. Ibadan's warriors and armies also needed guns and gunpowder and a substantial stockpile of both, should their Ijebu and Egba neighbors to the south block the trade routes to the coast.

In Ibadan, Aniwura settled near Oja'ba, the city's major market. Oral traditions are unanimous in recounting that when she emigrated from Abeokuta she left behind a failed marriage. Nor did she have children. She never remarried and died without children, a status that her enemies later used against her—a potent weapon in a society where it was thought that a woman's natural role was to bear children. In Aniwura's case, this misfortune also afforded opportunity. Freed from the demands of children and family, she found herself with the time and social space to build her trading network.

Aniwura traded in three complementary sets of items: (1) essentials such as salt and foodstuffs; (2) luxury items such as beads, rum, and cloth; and (3) products such as guns and gunpowder that the state required to extend its power. This balanced mix of strategic and essential goods brought substantial wealth. In return for imported salt, guns, gunpowder, liquor, and other items from the coast, for example, Aniwura exported palm oil, textiles, palm kernels, and foodstuffs. She also dispatched slaves to Lagos. Such exchange involved complex negotiations with traders who were themselves enmeshed in several regional and international markets. Her trading partners at Lagos, for example, included European merchants and firms from Germany, Great Britain, Austria, and France. She also traded with other African merchants. Apart from slaves and the goods mentioned above, Aniwura's profits derived from a diverse array of other products: expensive locally woven textiles; imported cloth such as velvet, wax prints, and shirting; tobacco, which mainly came from Brazil and which people smoked, inhaled as snuff, and used as an ingredient for medicine; coral and *segi* ornamental beads; imported sea salt, which was superior to the local variety; liquor, notably rum and schnapps; casks from Portugal for bottling local palm wine; metal boxes used as containers for a variety of products; cutlery; and guns and gunpowder, as mentioned earlier. Aniwura grew rich from buying and selling, all the while taking care to operate within established structures and commercial institutions.

She used well-established routes and markets. Ibadan lay at the center of a regional network that apart from the areas already described also included regions farther away in the northern part of today's Nigeria. Aniwura stayed in Ibadan to coordinate her affairs, but her operations mobilized an army of carriers and agents who bought in bulk and sold as retailers. Usually her agents had to walk several days to places where they bought and sold their wares. Commercial success relied on trust as well as Aniwura's ability to provide necessities, make arrangements for lodging, and above all, assure security.

Aniwura, then, was a broker. She received goods wholesale and sold retail to small-scale traders. Not only was she able to determine prices, oftentimes as a member of a guild of brokers, but she created a trading empire to collect the goods she needed. For example, her agents traveled to Bida in northern Nigeria to buy a sodium carbonate compound called natron, to Abeokuta for livestock, and as already noted, to Lagos for salt and guns. She acquired canoes for navigating the Ogun River. Aniwura invested in the tobacco trade, buying in large quantities in order to control the market. She was also astute in advancing credit. She exchanged guns and gunpowder with warlords for booty, notably slaves. She was also a producer, creating a textile manufacturing industry to make handwoven products, notably the durable *kijipa* cloth. She established three large farms, where several hundred farmworkers worked to grow vegetables, corn, yams, and other products, which she both sold and distributed to many of her followers.

Aniwura's trading career not only tells us about her but also reveals a lot about the broader role of women in trade. In order to achieve their ambitions and fulfill their other obligations, women appear to have worked more than men. Their activities were various, ranging from domestic labor to high-profile duties in public administration and service in the priesthoods of important cults.[1] Like most other societies, the Yoruba believed that everyone must work, irrespective of gender, both to survive and to earn respect, fame, and prowess. To be sure, some activities associated with women were designed to support husbands and raise children, but Yoruba society did not frown on women creating opportunities to make money on their own. They spent their profits to maintain their households, fulfill social obligations, and purchase chieftaincy titles.

In precolonial Yoruba societies, men were almost always farmers and craftsmen, while women engaged in food processing and trade.[2] In general, women's entry into many occupations was unrestricted, although they avoided the military and some crafts. Farming was the main occupation, although Yoruba women were less involved in farming than was the case among the Ijo and Igbo of Eastern Nigeria, the Akan of Ghana, or the Tio of the Middle Congo. Yoruba women helped bring in the harvest, processed food for final consumption or storage, kept livestock, and sold farm products. Women of means sometimes reinvested their profits in large-scale farming—as in the case of Aniwura.[3] Women also manufactured goods such as oil, dye, ceramics, and textiles.

However, the most important activity of women was trade, and being a trader was a professional occupation. The emphasis was on selling what they or their husbands produced from their farms, what they manufactured on their own, and the goods they bought from others for resale. B. W. Hodder, author of one of the earliest studies of the Yoruba market, was fascinated by the central role played by women in commerce, which he dated to the nineteenth century. He suggested that such prominence was due "to the conditions of internal insecurity in which it was unsafe for men to move away from their farms, while women enjoyed relative immunity from attacks."[4] Although the nineteenth century was a very turbulent era and women did receive better protection than men, there is no strong evidence that incessant warfare was solely responsible for women's domination of trade. Sources from earlier periods also note the degree to which women dominated trade.

Studies by Niara Sudarkasa [née Gloria A. Marshall] have established a close correlation between the roles of women as wives, mothers, and traders.[5] It was expected that a man would assist his wife by providing some capital to begin trading on a small scale. A woman assisted her husband with money, but more importantly she took care of her children, who competed with the children of rival wives for their father's favor. Among the Yoruba, a wife often stayed closer to home in her younger years to bear children and help her husband on the farm. As the children got older, she had more time for herself, while the husband often took another, younger wife. Thus, Yoruba marriages matured in such a way that women acquired greater independence over time.

The process of capital accumulation in the precolonial setting is best described by N. A. Fadipe, the first Yoruba sociologist. Fadipe concluded that having a husband and network of relatives allowed women to amass the wealth necessary to begin trading:

A percentage of the payment made as brideprice by her husband was passed on to her before her marriage. A few days before marriage her own relatives made her, in addition to clothing and other articles of personal wear, presents of cash—especially among the Oyo-Yoruba and the Egba—where a young woman has to go round the houses of her relatives on both sides in order to say farewell. A few days after her marriage—between seven and nine days—she has an opportunity of receiving presents of money not only from the various households in her husband's compound, but also from some members of the neighborhood, and from principal members of her husband's kindred group. The money collected in these various ways would total considerably in excess of what the husband alone could give her for starting a trade. Out of it she buys an animal (goat or sheep) or two and some fowls for rearing. If a wife was not brought up in any trade, these animals and fowls would remain her principal investment. If she was skilled in some trade, part of it would be used for starting it.[6]

Fadipe presents one of the best descriptions of the ways that "sentiments of kinship and social solidarity" created mobility for a woman who had to start from scratch—sentiments devoid of "mercenary motives" or expectations of interest. A new wife benefited from more "sentiments," in the form of gifts and other support up until the birth of her first child. Starting out with minimal wealth, an enterprising woman expanded her operations by plowing capital back into commerce. In so doing, she raised more capital, obtained more credit, and was in an increasingly advantageous position to manipulate new market opportunities.

In precolonial society, women traders everywhere hawked cooked food. Others conducted house trade in foodstuffs, cosmetics, and tobacco. These traders were patronized by those who could not go out to market. This practice of house-trading was common among older women and among new brides, for whom full-time commerce was not acceptable until they had spent a few years at home. Women and commissioned agents also obtained crafts products to sell from the craftsmen who made them. Aniwura undoubtedly launched her career from similarly modest beginnings.

Beyond the notable example of Aniwura in Ibadan, it must be underscored that Yoruba political systems created titles that were specific to women, thus recognizing the need to incorporate successful women into the system. Such opportunities were not many, compared with those available to men, and the distribution of principal functions and roles was no doubt dominated by men. A survey of prominent women shows that many of them exploited and benefited from these avenues to success. Women's political influence varied from one polity to another. Although such claims remain to be verified, it is said that a few women even reached the apex of authority, reigning as *oba*, something akin to a king. For instance, a tradition from Ile-Ife, the ritual heart of the Yoruba world, recalls the reign of the tyrannical woman *ooni* Luwo.[7] There were similar cases in Akure[8] and Ilesa.[9] In any case, there was no town without a woman chief of some kind, although the power attached to such offices varied. In Ondo, for example, the *lobun* was a powerful woman chief, excluded from farming and secluded to her palace like the male oba. She took part in the selection of a new king, settled quarrels among the male chiefs, and officiated at the opening of new markets. In addition, she was regarded as the priestess of Aje, the god of money.[10] Towns and villages other than Ibadan also had their own *iyalode*, who were the heads of women chiefs.[11] A few women chiefs were also members of the secret societies responsible for executive and judicial functions in some Yoruba societies.[12]

Aniwura the Chief

Participation in trade gave women the chance to become wealthy and enjoy high status. They did what wealthy men did: collecting titles, building a following, and acquiring status symbols such as fine clothes and fine horses. The relationship between the market and power was more than a simple one-to-one correspondence. Aniwura's life demonstrates the kinds of opportunities open to women and how a savvy woman profited from them. To start with, there was control and management of the marketplace, where the bulk of community wealth circulated. The marketplace was also an important locus of local politics, not only because of its economic influence but also because of the opportunities it offered for communication and its function as a site for social functions. For the members of the political class, the market was a venue to collect revenue through taxes, tolls, fees, dues, levies, and gifts; to benefit from largess in the form of stall allocation; and to exercise power by making the laws that regulated the use of physical coercion and violence. Market women took advantage of these possibilities.

Invisible to buyers and other visitors to the market were powerful associations and guilds, which sought to dominate the space in order to maximize economic gains, create order, and mix in the muddy terrain of politics. Traders who dealt in similar commodities came together in guilds. Each guild had an executive group that admitted new members, set prices, and oversaw market administration. Market women also joined together in associations or unions, which set up micro-administrations that the city respected and recognized. Such organizations governed expulsions from the market, enforced discipline, checked the activities of illegal traders, and sought to improve market facilities.

The iyalode, a woman of means and influence, presided over the association of market women. Aniwura became an iyalode. The iyalode's power derived from her individual abilities and charms, her personal resources, and the role of the associations that she represented. She was both the formal and informal link between the market, market women, and the political authorities. She allocated market stalls in accordance with the wishes of the association, and she presided over the admission of new members. She made it her business to know all the traders who had stalls, while keeping an eye on the floating population of street traders and hawkers. Finally, she supervised the internal administration of the market, settled disputes, and interacted with external suppliers to assure fairness.

The political institution of the market extended well beyond the office of iyalode. The iyalode had lieutenants, in some cases elected by the women's association, and in others appointed by the town's traditional political authority. In Ibadan, for example, there were subordinate titles such as *otun*, *osi*, and *balogun*, and other honorary titles were bestowed on successful and prominent women. Each guild set up a parallel order, headed by an official called the *iya egbe* and chairwomen known as the *alaga*, who presided over subcommittees. These practices resulted in a forest of titles. For those who could mobilize enough capital to expand operations, such organizations and offices made it possible to turn business acumen into social and political benefit.

Given their overall dominance in Yoruba society, the men who controlled the political order assumed that they could easily manipulate both the marketplace and women traders through these women's associations and their leaders. They were often wrong. Women also manipulated prominent men and political institutions. A detailed analysis of how prominent women used their positions to influence the male-dominated political order is beyond the scope of this chapter. We may underscore several examples of the ways that women manipulated the politics. A crucial dimension of women's strategy was to incorporate politically prominent men into market organizations by conferring on them offices and honorary titles. The men did not become part of these women's associations because women were not capable of managing their affairs. Rather, the women included them as a way of forging useful alliances with men, who in turn established critical links with other men who exercised political power, controlled resources, and manipulated social groups beyond the market in ways that supported the interests of women traders.

In Aniwura's case, success in the marketplace and market politics catapulted her to visibility in the city at large and positioned her to climb the ladder of city titles. Like the successful men of her time, she invested her wealth in the display of honor, affluence, and generosity. She acquired followers and obtained titles for herself and her supporters. Aniwura's clientele was numerous. Apart from the hundreds of slaves who worked on her three huge farms, she possessed two large grazing farms for cattle taken care of by specialized Hausa workers from the north. Two hundred domestic assistants also lived in her sprawling compound. Contemporary traditions describe Aniwura's luxurious lifestyle, recalling her baskets of expensive beads (the *okun, lagi-digba, segi, iyun,* and *opoto*); silver trinkets commissioned from Lagos; custom-made brass and copper bracelets from Ibadan; and elaborate wardrobes of local and imported textiles that included brocade and velvet of bright colors.

Aniwura's political career beyond the marketplace began when she be-came a *mogaji,* or chief, of a compound and ward in Ibadan. This position was normally conferred on a senior male, so the title elevated Aniwura to the male-dominated council of ward chiefs. Her service to her lineage and com-pound were remarkable. She attracted more people to the lineage, expanded and added to the buildings in the compound, and administered justice. These achievements led to her elevation to iyalode, the highest rank, and to still more ostentatious displays of affluence. Aniwura had to wear fine clothes all the time. A convoy of followers accompanied her when she moved about. She also kept horses and maintained a retinue of poets and drummers whose tasks included singing her praises.

The rank of iyalode also brought new responsibilities. As iyalode, Aniwura was expected to contribute to Ibadan's ambitious efforts to build an empire. In one victory after another, Ibadan's military machine added numerous new territories to its political network and colonies. Aniwura did not go to war herself, but she contributed to the military campaigns from her base in the city. For example, Aniwura and other major traders were expected to ensure an adequate supply of ammunition. Indeed, she extended credit to the war-riors to buy guns and gunpowder. She also sent many of her male followers to serve in the army. Moreover, she also fielded her own military unit, made up mainly of slaves who served under their own commander.

Beyond these contributions, Aniwura took on the role of a queen, repre-senting the interests of women. She joined the council of chiefs to mediate conflicts, engage in diplomacy, and deliberate on city regulations and other matters. She held court in her compound to listen to complaints. She par-ticipated in city festivals. Finally, she played an active role in the annual celebration commemorating the worship of Ori, the god of fate and des-tiny—offering a feast to several thousand people.

Aniwura's Assassination

In 1872, Are Latosa became the leader of Ibadan and launched ambitious military policies that led to the longest war and, ultimately, to the collapse of the empire. The new ruler attempted to concentrate power in his own hands through appointments that favored his kin and loyalists. These measures increasingly alienated older chiefs such as Aniwura. In turn, Are Latosa and his supporters condemned Aniwura for being too independent and decided that her power had to be curbed. Other male chiefs who were also jealous of her success joined what became, quite literally, a witch hunt.

The ruler's attack came in several stages. He began by finding fault with Aniwura's personality. She was accused of being high-handed in the way she treated her slaves, cruel in preventing many of them from marrying and having children, and unsympathetic when they fell ill. Second, warriors to whom she had extended credit conspired not to repay their debts. As wars multiplied and lasted longer, Aniwura refused to advance additional credit, which increased the ranks of her enemies and led Are Latosa to accuse her of political insubordination and arrogance.[13]

These attacks culminated in 1874 when the warrior chiefs deposed her and appointed another woman in her place. Aniwura's fall brought humiliation and loss of prestige. Her former peers shunned her, and the public was ordered not to visit her. Indeed, she was not allowed to receive any visitors at all. Her drummers and singers were forced to leave. Not surprisingly, her business began to collapse.

In the nineteenth century, a disgraced chief generally committed suicide or went into exile. In contrast, Aniwura opted to fight. She lobbied a number of chiefs who were loyal to her and spent a substantial sum to appear before the council of chiefs to proclaim her innocence. Latosa was not persuaded, and fearing that Aniwura's refusal to either commit suicide or leave would undermine his power, he plotted to assassinate her. Fellow conspirators included her kin and her slaves, who set up an "accident." Aniwura was crushed when a stack of heavy imported casks from Portugal fell on her on May 1, 1874.

Aniwura's death upset many people, who expressed their sympathy. The Christian missionaries in Ibadan arranged for her burial in her own compound. Abeokuta sent an official delegation to protest her death. Angry chiefs at Ibadan accused Latosa of ordering the assassination. The upheavals almost led to civil war. Several people were arrested in connection with her death, another was banished from the compound, and two others were executed in public.

Aniwura's life ended in tragedy, but her life offers insights and evidence about the relationship between gender and power among the Yoruba.

Gender and Political Power

Studies of women in the history of Nigeria have often targeted high-profile political women—the "queens" of African history—in order to glorify and enhance the political value of women and their contributions.[14] Such research is an entirely justifiable reaction to the many historical accounts about men. Unfortunately, such a focus on queens limits the range and possibility of social and political history. The stories of market women demonstrate that the less structured informal sector produces its own queens, mythology, and conception of order and value. On the face of it, such biographies appear to be less dramatic, although Aniwura's life and career were certainly not lacking in drama. Her story makes it clear that despite marginal roles in formal political institutions, women could wield political clout. Success in the market offered Aniwura a route to power. Her marketplace relationships led to the exchange of information, gave rise to networks of influence, and even provided opportunities to relate and negotiate with the political authorities. Aniwura was so successful in these kinds of negotiations that a number of male chiefs became her clients.

Insofar as the marketplace was linked to productivity and prosperity, it was also tied to religious and political power. Women's control of the marketplace brought religious influence in a society that sought spiritual balance through all of its institutions. Religious influence translated into political power because the market rituals were necessary for maintaining prosperity and power as well as spiritual equilibrium. Some of Aniwura's male rivals attributed her commercial success to her enormous spiritual power—to the point of charging her with witchcraft.

But Aniwura's spectacular achievements should not obscure the problems that most women faced during her era. Amassing capital always presented a challenge, and men tended to have more chances at success in such endeavors. For most women, trade did not translate into wealth or power. Trade was competitive, many people lost money, and some of the highest profit-yielding commodities like palm oil and guns remained in the hands of male dealers. Women also contended with other constraints. Domestic responsibilities usually curtailed economic activities in the early years of marriage. Women needed to devote considerable time to social and religious events, and they were the first in line to care for those who were ill.[15] Aniwura was a great woman who acquired wealth, titles, and honor, like any of the leading men of her time. Her demise reveals how difficult it was to achieve and maintain prominence and legitimacy in a patriarchal society.

In the wake of her death, Aniwura received *oriki*, classical Yoruba eulogies which recounted her life with pomp and exquisite language. Set within its Yoruba setting and idioms, the following excerpt from an oriki for her is brilliant. When delivered, its impact would have been enhanced by drumming and dancing. This oriki includes metaphors of greatness: abundant slaves, horses, "graceful fashion," and guns and gunpowder. Power is reflected, too, in references to slaves, the poor, and access to weapons of violence and warfare. Nor does this eulogy shy away from mention of her rivals. Aniwura was "the Iyalode who instills fear into her equals." To top it off, the oriki boldly compares her to the Are, the male political leader of Ibadan, perhaps the very one who plotted her assassination. In proclaiming that Iyalode Aniwura's possessions surpassed those of the are himself, the oriki—and by extension, Aniwura herself—has the final word:

> Efusetan, Iyalode
> One who has horses and rides them not
> The child who walks in a graceful fashion
> Adekemi Ogunrin!
> The great hefty woman who adorns her legs with beads
> Whose possessions surpass those of the Are
> Owner of several puny slaves in the farm
> Owner of many giant slaves in the market
> One who has bullets and gunpowder
> Who has the gunpowder as well as guns
> And spends money like a conjurer
> The Iyalode who instills fear into her equals
> The rich never give their money to the poor
> The Iyalode never gives her wrappers to the lazy

The oriki resonates beautifully with grace, evoking the horses in the compound, the "great hefty woman," "the child who walks in a graceful fashion." Aniwura was a woman so rich that she spent money like someone who was conjuring or minting it. Aniwura's aspirations centered on the "good things of life": money, long life, power, children, and good health. Her compound is now known as Iyalode's Compound, and a village now bears her name. Like the oriki, they are monuments to her greatness.

Further Reading

A contemporary view of Aniwura may be found in Samuel Johnson, *The History of the Yorubas* (Lagos: Church Missionary Society, 1921). On women in Nigerian history in general, including mention of Aniwura, see Bolanle Awe, ed., *Nigerian Women in Historical Perspective* (Lagos: Sankore and Bookcraft, 1992), and Nina E. Mba, *Nigerian Women Mobilized: Women's Political Activity in Southern Nigeria, 1900–1965* (Berkeley: Institute of International Studies, University of California, 1982). About the institution of iyalode, see Bolanle Awe, "The Iyalode in the Traditional Political Yoruba System," in *Sexual Stratification*, ed. Alice Schiegal (New York: Columbia University Press, 1977).

Broader surveys of women in African history have grown in number over the years. For one of the first and now classic essay collections, see Denise Paulme, ed., *Women of Tropical Africa* (Berkeley: University of California Press, 1971). Margaret Jean Hay and Sharon Stichter coedited a second survey two decades later titled *African Women South of the Sahara* (New York: Longman, 1995). In 1997, Catherine Coquery-Vidrovitch published the first single-author survey in English. See her volume *African Women: A Modern History*, trans. Beth Gillian Raps (Boulder, Colo.: Westview Press, 1997).

For more focused topical studies on women and gender in African history and societies, see Nancy Hafkin and Edna Bay, eds., *Women in Africa: Studies in Social and Economic Change* (Stanford, Calif.: Stanford University Press, 1976); Edna Bay, ed., *Women and Work in Africa* (Boulder, Colo.: Westview Press, 1982); Claire C. Robertson and Martin A. Klein, eds., *Women and Slavery in Africa* (Madison: University of Wisconsin Press, 1983); Margaret Jean Hay and Marcia Wright, eds., *African Women and the Law: Historical Perspectives* (Boston: Boston University Press, 1982); and Patricia Romero, *Life Histories of African Women* (London: Ashfield Press, 1987).

Monographs focused on particular regions or individual societies include Christine Oppong, ed., *Female and Male in West Africa* (London: Allen & Unwin, 1983); Claire Robertson, *Sharing the Same Bowl: A Socio-Economic History of Women and Class in Accra* (Bloomington: Indiana University Press, 1984); Mary Smith, ed., *Baba of Karo: A Woman of the Muslim Hausa* (London: Faber and Faber, 1954); Gracia Clark, *African Market Women: Seven Life Stories of African Market Women* (Bloomington: Indiana University Press, 2010); Margaret Strobel, ed. and trans., *Three Swahili Women: Life Histories from Mombasa, Kenya* (Bloomington: Indiana University Press, 1989); Margaret Strobel, ed. and trans., *Three Swahili Women: Life Histories from Mombasa, Kenya* (Bloomington: Indiana University Press, 1989); and Belinda Bozzoli with Mmantho Nkotsoe, *Women of Phokeng: Consciousness, Life Strategy, and Migrancy in South Africa, 1900–1983* (Portsmouth, N.H.: Heinemann, 1991).

The history of Ibadan is narrated in Toyin Falola, *The Political Economy of a Pre-Colonial African State: Ibadan, 1830–1900* (Ile-Ife, Nigeria: University of Ife Press, 1985). On Ibadan, also see Peter Lloyd, A. L. Mabogunje, and Bolanle Awe, eds., *The City of Ibadan* (Ibadan and Cambridge: Institute of African Studies and Cambridge University Press, 1967). Kristin Mann analyzes aspects of gender in Lagos in *Marriage, Status, and Social Change among the Educated Elite in Colonial Lagos* (Cambridge, UK: Cambridge University Press, 1985). Finally, for a survey history of Nigeria, see Toyin Falola and

Matthew M. Heaton, *A History of Nigeria* (Cambridge, UK: Cambridge University Press, 2008).

Notes

1. See, for instance, Samuel Johnson, *The History of the Yorubas* (Lagos: Church Missionary Society, 1921), 64–65, and E. Bolaji Idowu, *Olódùmarè: God in Yoruba Belief* (London: Longman, 1962), chapter 8.

2. Several works describe the sexual division of labor among the Yoruba. For instance, see N. U. Beier, "The Position of Yoruba Women," *Presence Africaine*, nos. 1/2 (1955): 39–46; A. Izzett, "Family Life among the Yoruba in Lagos, Nigeria," in *Social Change in Modern Africa*, ed. Aidan Southall (Oxford, UK: Oxford University Press, for the International African Institute, 1961); and Niara Sudarkasa, *Where Women Work: A Study of Yoruba Women in the Marketplace and in the Home* (Ann Arbor: University of Michigan, 1973), chapter 2.

3. Johnson, *History of the Yorubas*, 393.

4. B. W. Hodder, "The Yoruba Market," in *Markets in Africa*, ed. Paul Bohannan and George Dalton (Evanston, Ill.: Northwestern University Press, 1962), 110.

5. Gloria A. Marshall [Niara Sudarkasa], "Women, Trade, and the Yoruba Family," PhD diss., Columbia University, 1964; Sudarkasa, *Where Women Work*.

6. Nathaniel A. Fadipe, *The Sociology of the Yoruba*, ed. Francis Olu Okediji and Oladejo O. Okediji (Ibadan, Nigeria: Ibadan University Press, 1970), 156. Fadipe presented this study as his PhD thesis to the University of London in 1939.

7. Michael Ajayi Fabunmi, *Ife Shrines* (Ile-Ife, Nigeria: University of Ife Press, 1969), 23–24.

8. The thirteenth *deji* of Akure is said to have been a woman who did not wear a crown. See National Archives, Ibadan (hereafter NAI), *Intelligence Report on Akure*, compiled by N. A. C. Weir, 1935, 10.

9. Toyin Falola, "A Descriptive Analysis of Ilesa Palace Organisation," *African Historian* 8 (1976): 78–79.

10. NAI, A. F. Bridges, *Intelligence Report on Ondo*, 1934–1935, 10.

11. NAI, John Blair, *Intelligence Report on Abeokuta*, 1937, 48; NAI, E. A. Hawkersworth, *Intelligence Report on Ijebu Ife*, 1935, 9. For an overview of this institution, see Bolanle Awe, "The Iyalode in the Traditional Political System," in *Sexual Stratification*, ed. Alice Schlegel (New York: Columbia University Press, 1977).

12. For instance, in Ago, an Ijebu village, "female members, known as *Erelu*, were allowed to join the Osugbo society. The *Erelu* were consulted in all matters that concerned the female community, though they did not sit with the other members in judicial matters." See NAI, A. F. Abell, *Intelligence Report on Ago*, 1934, iii.

13. Johnson, *History of the Yorubas*, 391.

14. See, for instance, D. Sweetman, *Women Leaders in African History* (London: Heinemann, 1984); Nina E. Mba, *Nigerian Women Mobilized: Women's Political*

Activity in Southern Nigeria, 1900–1965 (Berkeley: Institute of International Studies, University of California, 1982); Cheryl Johnson, "Grassroots Organizing: Women in Anti-Colonial Activity in Southwestern Nigeria," *African Studies Review* 25, 2 and 3 (1982); Folarin Coker, *A Lady: A Biography of Lady Oyinkan Abayomi* (Ibadan, Nigeria: Evans Brothers, 1987); and Bolanle Awe, ed., *Women in Historical Perspective* (Lagos: Sankore and Bookcraft, 1992).

   15. Fadipe, *Sociology of the Yoruba*, 166.

~

CHAPTER THREE

Moka of Bioko (Late 1820s–1899)

The Chief Who United a Central African Island

Ibrahim Sundiata

The story of Moka, who rose to become the paramount chief among the Bubi people on the island of Bioko in the nineteenth century, is a powerful testimony to the complexity of African political, social, and economic development in the modern era. Bioko, which lies in the Bight of Biafra off the coast of today's Cameroon, was arguably at the epicenter of the slave trade that forcibly shipped millions of men and women from West Central Africa to the Americas for four hundred years. European and African slave traders regularly sailed the sea-lanes around the is-land. Despite this location, however, the Bubi maintained their autonomy, in large part by retreating toward the interior of the island. Yet they did not seek to isolate themselves completely from the outside; rather they sought to situate themselves strategically to be able to control contact with outsiders.

Moka's career concretely illustrates debates around two important issues in African history. The first is state formation. Historical accounts make it very clear that the numerous Bubi chiefdoms were at odds with each other in the first half of the nineteenth century. Moka successfully united them in the decades after 1850 and reigned supreme in the 1870s and 1880s. How did he make this happen? Trade with the outside world through the English and Kru settlement at Clarence played a role in this achievement. The Bubi supplied palm oil and foodstuffs to their foreign neighbors. But trade by no means explains everything. An emerging broader sense of religious authority across the island may also have been an impetus toward unity. In addition, Moka's large household points to the important role that kinship and marriage alliances played in his success. Finally, there is the greatest challenge—assessing how Moka's personal attributes and leadership skills contributed to the rise of centralized authority.

The second issue turns around how Moka managed relations with outsiders— whether they were the English naval personnel and their Kru workmen from Liberia who lived in Clarence; the Kru and English renegades who from time to time raided Bubi villages; the Sierra Leoneans in the coastal areas; or later, the Spanish missionaries and colonial authorities. In the mid-nineteenth century, Moka limited contact in order to maximize his autonomy, but he needed to trade with outsiders to get firearms and other imports to defend himself. Toward the end of the century, he developed apparently positive relationships with several Spanish missionaries, but he very consciously continued to limit their influence. Neither a collaborator nor a rebel, the king of the mountain displayed great sophistication and nuance in dealing with foreigners, whose provenance and intentions must have been, at least in large part, unknown to him. Following Moka's death, Spanish colonial authorities imposed greater demands on the Bubi of Bioko, and more foreigners arrived from Spain and Rio Muni, a Spanish colonial territory on the African mainland. Despite resistance, later Bubi leaders were not able to regain control over their island. Today it might be said that Bioko is itself a dependency of the mainland territory of Equatorial Guinea.

As recently as the middle of the nineteenth century the Bubi people, Bantu-speaking inhabitants of the island of Bioko, remained a mystery to outsiders. Their island, formerly called Fernando Po, is forty-four miles in length from northeast to southwest and twenty-two miles across. With an area of roughly eight hundred square miles, it is larger than either Zanzibar or any of the Mascarene Islands in the Indian Ocean. At its nearest point, the distance between this mountainous volcanic island in the Bight of Biafra and the African mainland in Cameroon is about twenty miles. The island is roughly rectangular with several mountainous peaks. Basile Peak is a volcanic cone that covers most of the northern part of the island, and the contemporary city of Malabo lies at its base. Moka Peak (formerly called Riabba) in the south rises to 2,009 meters.

Despite their nearness to the coast, the Bubi islanders deliberately avoided the gaze of foreigners. Indeed, during the first three centuries of the Atlantic slave trade, they successfully resisted settlement by outsiders. Europeans first encountered the island in the 1470s, and one of them, Fernando Po, gave it his name. Over the century after 1640, the Dutch raided the island for slaves, but the Bubi repelled all attempts at alien settlement. Although the last quarter of the eighteenth century saw a upsurge in slave trading in the Bight of Biafra, Spanish efforts to claim the island and set up a slave-trading post in 1778–1780 failed.

Fast-forwarding to a century later, a king named Moka ruled the entire island. The story of how this happened offers glimpses of a state in formation. Through persuasion and diplomacy, Moka forged a confederacy to mediate intra-ethnic strife. Only in the 1890s did a Spanish missionary succeed in reaching the reclusive ruler, and he was impressed by what he encountered. He marveled at the ruler's abode, a "palace of grandeur and splendor."[1] He negotiated his way beyond a barrier that sheltered the king's servants and their families, where he was able to observe Moka's seventy-odd wives and concubines:

> There followed a second barrier that separated the family of the *mochuku* [king], his wives and children. A double stairway constructed with rough trunks, supported and attached to posts, . . . gave entrance to the dwellings of the latter. From here continued a narrow alley which led to a small square in the middle of which was found a somewhat spacious dwelling which served as a dining room and reception room . . . in which only persons of the nobility and [those] very intimate with the king had admittance; the royal bedroom adjoined. From there led off some alleys . . . in which were put, in order of their dignity, the bedrooms and kitchens of the wives and concubines, and their respective children of less than seven years of age—because those over this age slept in separate apartments, one for the youth and another for the girls.[2]

The Spanish missionary, Antonio Aymemí, came to know Moka, writing that "he was a person of majestic presence, just and noble in his conduct."[3] Despite such access, we still have no word portrait of Moka. He studiously avoided the gaze of outsiders. Was he tall? Was he short? Was he corpulent? For most of his life, he kept his distance from non-islanders. In the 1840s, John Clarke, a Baptist missionary, traveled around the island extensively, but he heard no mention of a paramount chief. Thirty years later, in the early 1870s, Primitive Methodists heard about Moka's rule and made an unsuccessful attempt to visit him in 1874. From the fragmentary tales of these travelers and missionaries, an image of the king emerged from the shadows. Having read these accounts, Sir James Frazier cited Moka in his now classic compendium on myth, *The Golden Bough*, as an example of "savage" religiosity: "As might have been expected, the superstitions of the savage cluster thick about the subject of food. . . . In Fernando Po [today's Bioko] the king after installation is forbidden to eat *cocco* (*arum acaule*), deer, and porcupine, which are the ordinary foods of the people."[4] Spanish missionaries came to serve as intermediaries with the Spanish colonial administration. Yet Moka still maintained distance from interlopers. When he died in February of 1899, the local missionary was not allowed to see Moka's body, nor was he told where it was buried.

In the early nineteenth century, well before Moka's rise, the Bubi were divided into twenty-eight districts embracing two hundred villages, all of them located inland. The ruler and his people lived behind a veil. So how and why did Moka succeed in uniting the Bubi, and just who were the people he brought together? Travelers were divided about the physical appearance and origins of the Bubi. The name "Boobe" was given to them by a British naval officer in 1821. In the same year, another British naval officer thought their appearance peculiar:

> The hair of these islanders were [sic] matted into several locks; a mixture of palm oil and red ochre affords a protection against the rain as well as against vermin, the whole body was smeared over with this composition, even to their hands, and gives them the appearance of North American Indians rather than African Negroes.[5]

Two years later, in 1823, an English geographer opined that Bioko

> has been peopled from the neighboring continent by malefactors and runaway slaves, who are determined to sell their liberty dearly, and any persons attempting to deprive them of it will have cause to regret their temerity.[6]

Thirty years after that, in the 1850s, the British consul concluded that "the Fernandians [Bubis], who are the aborigines of the island, do not seem to have an affinity with any of the races of the continent." On the basis of Bubi facial scars he came to the sure conclusion that the Bubi were "of a mixed race between the Okoos [Yoruba of Nigeria] and the Portuguese, who visited Lagos some hundreds of years ago."[7] Around the same time, a German philologist determined that Bubi was a Bantu language.[8]

Descriptions of the character of the islanders seemed often to be no more than projections of cultural bias or products of chance encounters. Indeed, one visitor correctly observed that "of the natives of Fernando Po every person will be disposed to speak as he may by actual experience find them."[9] The naval officer who encountered them in 1821 found them to be unaggressive, but he had heard from a previous visitor that they were "extremely savage and untractable [sic], never to be trusted."[10] In the late 1840s, according to another observer, it was said to be "impossible to speak too highly of the disposition and character of this singular race."[11]

Geography, History, and Socioeconomic Contexts

Rugged and relatively isolated Bioko has had a rich and varied history. Linguistic research suggests that the "language cluster of Bioko" was one of the first to break away from the parent Western Bantu more than two thousand years ago.[12] The Bubi are associated with a sequence of stone-using cultures, the last of which endured into the nineteenth century.[13] The fundamental linguistic division is between the dialects in the north and those in the south. There are four principal dialects and various secondary ones, which in some cases are not mutually intelligible. Analyses of origin stories have concluded that the migrations came in four waves. The last migrants described in oral tradition used iron and arrived by the fourteenth century.[14] In addition to more complex military organization, the new Bantu invaders would have had the advantage of iron weapons during the initial period of conquest. The newcomers imposed themselves on the existing population but at some point adopted their language.

Bioko's inhabitants depended largely on the land. Interestingly, fishing was not the mainstay. Perhaps because they feared invaders from the sea, the Bubi fished from dispersed encampments on the coast. Agriculture was the major economic activity; people lived in villages for only part of the year, dispersing to work in their fields the rest of the time. The village (*bese* or *ería*) was made up of a group of houses, often widely separated. Yams were the staple crop and only men were allowed to eat them. Each male head of household participated in yam planting rituals, along with his dependents and relatives. In addition to yams, the Bubi also raised cocoyams. Unlike yams, cocoyams were women's crops, and men only ate them in case of necessity. The Bubi rounded out their diet by keeping chickens and collecting honey and palm oil. They also hunted antelope, deer, monkeys, squirrels, and other forest animals.

Nineteenth-century Bubi material culture was sparse. The most prevalent artifacts were conical hats, digging sticks, canoes, and short sections of log that served as pillows. In contrast to this fairly simple material culture, most nineteenth-century observers reported that the Bubi had an elaborate system of socioeconomic levels. The population was divided into nobles (or *baita*), who were the descendants of late-arriving conquerors, and commoners (or *babala*). Nobles and commoners were divided by rules of social segregation.

District chiefs, drawn from the baita, collected fines and tribute. By the nineteenth century, a new title for "lord," *botuku* in the north or *monchuku* in the south, had come into use. Succession was passed on among brothers of noble status born of the same mother. Following the death of the last of a group of brothers, a council composed of all the local nobles and perhaps neighboring chiefs elected a new leader. The new chief was usually unrelated but of noble class.

Within chiefdoms there were age sets based on generation. From birth, each man belonged to such a set, called a *buala*; membership was not contingent upon an initiation or other ceremony. In some villages there were three or four buala.[15] Sometimes these generation sets corresponded to the four living generations: great-grandfathers, grandfathers, fathers, and sons. The buala had military and ideological functions. Songs and dances associated with them emphasized loyalty across kin groups. The power of a buala manifested itself in a cult object, or *lobedde*, that often was a miniature clay canoe or other object that symbolized migrant origins. One buala directed affairs, and when most of its members had become aged and infirm, power passed on to its "son" in a series of ceremonies that took place over a year.[16]

The Bubi believed that each newborn had an individual male guardian spirit (*mmo* or *morimo*) for life, who initially bought the infant's soul from the spirit who created embryos. In addition, each person belonged to the spiritual lineage (*loka*) of his father. Membership in the lineage stemmed from a spiritual connection between the spirit of the place (or the *boteribo* of the land) and the people who lived on it. The Bubi believed that this spiritual connection was passed on from father to son beginning with the first inhabitant. This connection between descent and land also expressed a wider sacred force called *mohula*.

Challenge and Response in the Nineteenth Century

Interlopers breached Bioko's relative isolation in the early nineteenth century. While the slave trade continued in the Bight of Biafra, trade in palm oil began to burgeon. Newcomers on the northern coast traded for palm oil even as they facilitated the spread of firearms and disease. Between 1827 and 1834, the British government maintained an anti-slaving base called Clarence at what is now Malabo. When this official British presence was withdrawn, a community made up of about a thousand Sierra Leoneans and Kru laborers (from present-day Liberia) remained behind. Increased trade and warfare led to the creation of a loose Bubi state structure. At the same time, the little colonial nucleus implanted in 1827 did not have the power to conquer the island. In the wake of the British withdrawal, Baptist missionaries arrived in the early 1840s. Leadership of the settler community was in the hands of a small group of black and white palm oil traders. In 1843 and again in 1858, Spanish efforts to claim control of the island failed.

As for the Bubi, by the 1840s they were fighting among themselves and also faced serious incursions by alien palm oil traders and runaway migrant laborers with firearms.[17] Raiding parties descended on the northern districts, demanding oil, food, and women. By 1841, Kru laborers who had escaped to the western side of the island had set up their own independent encampment. The recalcitrant laborers were said to be forcing the local fishing Bubi to supply their settlement with fish and women. In response, the leaders of Clarence (Malabo) took action against the Kru, captured their leader, and deported him. But then, at the end of 1841, the Kru and the Bubi on the western side of the island clashed violently. Upheavals persisted for several years, and Kru wreaked havoc in the settlement's hinterland. Only at the end of the 1840s did a semblance of stability emerge.

Over this period, the Bubi extracted palm oil at a fairly steady pace, but they largely left the business of trading to outsiders. At first, trade was conducted only by barter, but later Bubi currency (*chibo*), consisting of strings of shells, figured in exchange. Bubi living near the Anglo-African trading settlement traded goods on to Bubi in the southern part of the island at a good profit. As a result, people living in more remote areas took an interest in direct trade. In the 1820s, a Briton had already observed that "the natives are not only divided into distinct tribes, but that each tribe possesses a distinct portion of territory, and is extremely jealous of admitting others within its boundaries."[18] More than sixty years later, in 1888, a Spaniard still described the reluctance of the Bubi to permit travel inland as a "ruse employed by the tribes of the littoral, interested in preventing us from communicating with those of the interior, in order to be the intermediaries between these [interior people] and the whites."[19] Violence broke out frequently. By the 1840s, war among the Bubi was increasingly destructive. Visitors in 1843, for example, reported that a terrific war was going on between the Bubi of the north and the Bubi of the south. Five years later, an English missionary noted that among the Bubi in general "often, wild and savage war prevails . . . and after the battle, a fierce spirit of revenge . . . takes possession of the breast of the contending parties."[20] In the early 1870s, warfare was so intense that "neither age nor sex" was spared.[21]

Moka Becomes King of the Mountain

Moka emerged out of this environment of intense competition and war by about 1875. As economic and demographic patterns shifted after the 1820s,

Moka's dynasty, the Bahftaari dynasty, managed to sustain and spread its preeminence. To be sure, Moka is the most memorable of the Bahftaari rulers, but the dynasty also included the shadowy Buadjamita (Moadyabita) (c. 1860–c. 1875).[22] Two other dynasties, the Babuuma and the Bapolo, preceded the Bahftaari. According to tradition, the noble branch of Babuuma had become extinct, as women married outside the noble group and their descendants lost status. In the period of transition, the Bapolo dynasty acquired greater importance, leading the last Babuuma king to turn over power and spiritual authority to it. Later traditions stress that the Bapolo were, in turn, related to the Bahftaari.[23] All three families that gave rise to these dynasties—the Babuuma, Bapolo, and Bahftaari—had their origins in Ureka on the far southern coast.

Moka's home, Riabba, stood at more than eighteen hundred meters above sea level on the island's second-highest peak. Although Moka's rise to paramount chief is said to have begun in the 1850s, the custom of brother-to-brother succession makes it unlikely that a single brother would have reigned through the largest part of the nineteenth century. But Moka did live a long life; when he died his followers claimed that he was 105 years old. In any case, Moka was a major political figure by the 1870s, suggesting that he was born in the late 1820s, about the time of the founding of the Anglo-African settlement on the northern coast. It is tempting to conclude that Moka's state was the inevitable result of the concentration of military power by groups of traders. But the story is more complex. Indeed, some earlier attempts to unify the island relied on claims of superior spiritual powers.[24]

From his seat at Riabba in the southern highlands, Moka was better placed than his northern counterparts to resist the military and epidemiological threats presented by interlopers. He tried to limit the disruption caused by foreign contact by restricting his use of European wares to guns and machetes. He scorned European cloth, rum, salt, and tobacco. As we have already read, Moka also steadfastly refused to see Europeans, while at the same time increasing his control over the Bubi. Footpaths led to his residence from all directions.

A notable innovation of Moka's rule dealt with the dispensation of justice. In the 1880s, a visitor said that "the most beautiful achievement of Moka's is: unity of the Bubi, abolition of war [and] introduction of the people's court."[25] This court adjudicated all murder cases; as "soon as murder had taken place, delegates from all communities immediately unite on the dance square of the village of the presumed murderer." Often the assembled numbered more than two thousand people. Moka had a judicial militia of 150 men called the *lojua* or *lohua*, which had the right to the property of people found guilty of crimes. When the militia was created, its members were armed with hardwood lances, javelins, and large shields made of animal hide, but the use of guns gradually increased.

Moka was known as *etako ote*, or "great chief." He was also called *mocuku m' oricho*, "the lord of the world." All other chiefs claimed kinship with him. His court became the model for chiefs beneath him. It had a variety of titleholders, including, among others, the *abba mote* (chief priest) as well as the chief military leader, called the *takabaala* or *takamaala*. Another official was the *botuku oboho*, the leader of the baita. Another title was that of *koracho*, or head judge, and yet another, *buac* or *sam*, keeper of the treasury. The *tchoko o botuku*, keeper of the palace, and the *looba lo botuku*, chief executioner, also served on the council. Moka's subchiefs or *botukus* bore the titles of the districts over which they ruled, such as *botuku bo Isupu*, *mochuku mo Elacha*, or *mochuku mo Motehe*—respectively, chief of Basupu, of Balacha, of Batete, and so on. These chiefs also had subordinates whose titles resembled those of the royal court.

The size of Moka's household, with seventy wives and concubines, symbolized male wealth and status. With the rise of chieftainship on the island, harems proliferated and the accumulation of women became a conspicuous sign of wealth and power. By 1850, some harems included two hundred wives. Adultery was harshly punished, sometimes by crucifixion. So fierce was the competition for women that even a widow could become a concubine, with the understanding that the offspring belonged to the dead husband. Some women also possessed their own goats and cattle and commanded considerable respect in political deliberations. For example, the daughter of the eldest sister of the king, or the *obele*, was among the most distinguished persons at the royal court. Considered the first lady of the realm, she lived in the palace, ate with her uncle the king, and received half of all gifts and debts paid to him. In addition, elderly and venerated widows of the nobility were of great social importance. All the inhabitants of a district gave them an annual gift of yams.

Unity and Centralized Power

How were the Bubi able to create at least a semblance of unity by the 1870s? Trade was important, but trade does not automatically give rise to states. Spiritual in-gathering may have played a role, along with more obvious events. Moka's political preeminence was supported by well-established religious prestige across the island. His court housed the abba mote, a chief priest who maintained a sacred fire and played a significant role in rituals guaranteeing the well-being of the whole island. It may well be that the abba motes were descended from the earliest group to rule at Riabba, as symbolized by the fact that they were not subject to the authority of the paramount chief, even though their presence upheld it. Bubi religious practice had many dimensions, but by the late nineteenth century it emphasized loyalty.

Only in the 1880s did the Spanish colonizers of Bioko attempt to enter into direct communication with Moka, the man who had emerged as the paramount leader among the Bubi. After Jesuits and other missionaries failed to gain followers and influence, the order Hijos del Immaculado Corazón de Maria, or the Claretians, entered the mission field. The Claretians consistently labored to win over Bubi political authority. They worked in Basile and Banapa, and in 1886 founded a mission at the village of Bolobe in the Concepción area, led by a missionary fluent in Bubi. The following year they established a mission at San Carlos, through the goodwill of the botuku of the Batete group of Bubi. In 1889, the fathers set up a health station and mission at Musola. Nevertheless, missionary success was far from rapid. Fewer than fifty Bubi were baptized. The traveler Mary Kingsley observed in the 1890s that "a priest had enterprisingly settled himself one night in the middle of a Bubi village with [the] intent to devote the remainder of his life to quietly but thoroughly converting it. Next morning, when he rose up, he found himself alone, the people having taken all their portable possessions and vanished to build another village elsewhere." She wryly noted that "the worthy Father spent some time chivying his flock about the forest, but in vain."[26]

Some in the Spanish colonial administration looked eagerly at the Bubi as potential labor—not as souls to be saved. Although some islanders voluntarily worked for non-Bubi as early as the 1880s, most Bubi followed the example of their king and did what they could to avoid prolonged contact with outsiders. Planters complained that Bubi workers were prone to abruptly abandon their jobs and return to their villages. Again, Mary Kingsley offered her observations: "Now and again a man or woman will come voluntarily and take service in Clarence [Malabo], submit to clothes, and rapidly pick up the ways of a house or store." However, she went on to note that "just when their owner [sic] thinks he owns a treasure, and begins to boast that he has got an exception to all Bubidom . . . a hole in that man's domestic arrangements suddenly appears." The woman or man would leave "without giving a moment's warning and without stealing his master's property."[27] Islanders resisted the poor working conditions on cocoa plantations with reason. Most Bubi preferred to meet their need for cash by selling crops, small animals, or the products of hunting and gathering. Non-missionized Bubi were ostracized by their families if they worked for outsiders, so workers on the cocoa estates tended to be Catholic converts. Some Bubi surreptitiously collected palm oil on outsiders' plantations. Planters sometimes retaliated by destroying palm trees, which drove some Bubi poachers to suicide.

In 1887, a Spanish colonial official and two clerics went to Riabba to induce Moka to acknowledge Spanish sovereignty and to entice the Bubi to become laborers. The embassy had little effect. Moka continued to act independently of any other authority. Bubi-Spanish relations oscillated between tepid friendship and flashes of hostility, but most of the time they were simply indifferent to each other. A visitor observed: "I once received the answer: The whites are fish, not humans; they may well lose their way onto land; . . . in the end they again enter their ships and disappear with them at the point of the horizon in the ocean. How can a fish own land?" He went on to say, "Even the Bube near Sta. Isabel [formerly called Clarence and now Malabo] respect the Spanish Governor not perhaps as their superior, but as chief of the town of Sta. Isabel. . . . The other Bube [sic] worry themselves about him about as much as he worries himself about the Bube."[28]

A year later, in 1888, missionaries in Concepción seemed to succeed in gaining Moka's friendship. In June the king dispatched an embassy to them that included one of his sons and various relatives, escorted by a hundred men of the lohua armed with rifles and lances. Moka offered his protection, but he also warned the missionaries not to molest their Bubi neighbors, reminding all that he had the power of life and death: "I have the right to end the life of those who violate my decrees."[29] Moka's embassy was repaid with a visit by the head of the Concepción mission to Riabba in September of 1888. In March 1889, two missionaries went to Moka to ask him to make education mandatory, to which he replied, "We are not European and we don't need it."[30] The two Spaniards deliberately challenged Bubi religious beliefs by drinking from the sacred lake in the environs of the Bubi capital. Children watching the Europeans eventually followed their example and were not punished by the spirits for their temerity.

A little over a year later, another Spanish missionary went up to Riabba to discuss with the king rumors that the Bubi were about to attack a mission. Moka denied any such intention. He went on to urge the missionary to accompany him to the village of Bantabare, where a villager had been fined for murder but had refused to pay the penalty. Indicative of the shifting power dynamic between the colonizer and the colonized, the missionary reinforced the king's judgment by pronouncing it correct. In the end, the accused Bubi paid the fine, but Moka was, no doubt, disconcerted by the implication of such compliance. A few days later the commander of the Spanish gunship visited the paramount chief. The Spanish flag was raised and given a rifle salute. Six years later, in 1895, when the Spanish governor-general visited Moka personally, the king received him with pomp and circumstance. By that time, Moka flew the Spanish flag.

When the Spanish Claretian missionary order had come to the island in the 1880s, efforts had increased to pull the decreasing population of Bubi into the cultural orbit of European imperialism. Moka sought to manipulate European influence without letting it overwhelm him. This strategy was obviously fraught with dangers, both known and unknown. By this time, contact with outsiders had brought disease and precipitated population decline. Whereas the population of Bioko may have been as high as thirty thousand people in the 1820s, John Clarke put the number of inhabitants at twenty thousand in 1848.[31] At the time of Moka's death in 1899, the population was thought to have dropped to no more than 14,818 people. A series of epidemics that hit the island in the late nineteenth century were the probable causes of this decline: yellow fever in 1868, smallpox in 1889, whooping cough in 1893, and dysentery in 1896. To make matters worse, Fang laborers from Rio Muni on the African mainland introduced trypanosomiasis, or sleeping sickness, on the eastern side of the island. By the last decade of the century, the decline in population was sufficiently dire that authorities and observers thought that the Bubi would become extinct.

As for the missionaries, the Claretians were a potential source of both help and political meddling. In December 1888, the superior of the mission at Batete stopped the decapitation of a botuku who had disobeyed Moka. Eight years later, missionaries again came to the aid of one of Moka's subordinates. The chief of Mueri was accused of failing to accord proper respect to the administrator of San Carlos and imprisoned. The Bubi chief escaped, convinced the Claretians to present his case to the Spanish governor-general, and was restored to office. In 1897, Moka accepted one missionary innovation—potato cultivation. A Catholic missionary asked for a field to grow the crop and, when the endeavor produced a fruitful harvest, Moka followed suit. At the same time, the king demurred on requests to allow more missionaries into his area.

By the end of the 1890s, then, the king of the Bubi was maintaining peace with the Spanish, even though there was ominous discontent within his own camp. In late 1897, the year he accepted potato cultivation, three missionaries went to Riabba and were well received. During the visit, however, Moka's lieutenant, Sas Ebuera, objected and returned cloth given to village children. Angry, Moka took away Sas Ebuera's house, and differences between the two men came out into the open. Moka favored a policy of conciliation designed to retain as much freedom of action as possible. His chief subaltern stood for a firmer policy. The tension between them burst into violence in September 1898, when Sas Ebuera openly defied Spanish rule. As in the past, the confrontation was resolved through the intercession of the Claretians.

Moka died in February 1899 following two years of bad health. During his illness, Padre Antonio Aymemí was accustomed to taking him coffee liqueur, or *chuaho choe*, "of which he was most fond."[32] The rebellious Sas Ebuera elbowed aside Moka's presumed successor, Malabo, and was crowned in October 1899. A few days later, the new king forbade all contact with Europeans. In 1904, he revolted against European authority again, in response to Spanish attempts to step up labor recruitment. After a time, Sas Ebuera gave himself up and died a short time later. With his death, a pivotal era of Bubi culture came to a close.

The Spanish Colonial Era on Bioko

Events in the decade following Moka's death sounded the death knell of traditional culture on Bioko. The colonial regime asked for new authority over native justice and labor, and the Bubi of San Carlos revolted in 1906 over rumors that forced labor would be imposed. The crisis was successfully mediated by Catholic missionaries, but rumblings of discontent continued among both the Bubi and the colonial administration. In April 1907, Spanish officials ordered the Bubi to present themselves to work on roads. In May, a decree proclaimed that disputes would be settled by colonial authorities if the Bubi could not settle them themselves. At the same time, the government strenuously pushed the planting of cotton, cocoa, tobacco, oil palms, and rubber trees. In 1910 the colonial governor followed up with demands for labor. This time around, chiefs who resisted were threatened with the confiscation of their guns and hunting licenses. Resentment was especially strong in the south. A rumor circulated that Bubi were being beaten to death on European farms and that the Bubi king, Malabo, had been kidnapped and was being held prisoner. These fears gave rise to a guerrilla movement, but Luba, the local leader of the resistance, was eventually killed. As in the past, the two sides negotiated. While Malabo, the Bubi leader, had not joined the revolt, he had not actively opposed it, either. He remained in place as the Bubi paramount chief.

Despite Malabo's continued rule, these events marked the final eclipse of Bubi leadership. Moka's successors were alcoholic relics of a bygone age:

Malabo (1904–1937), Alobari (1937–1943), and Oriche (1943–1952). The increasing impact of the outside world and especially demands associated with colonial rule proved to be disastrous. The Spanish government finally resolved to develop the island it had claimed since the eighteenth century. Clerics and *finqueros*, or planters, arrived in greater numbers, as Bubi numbers declined. In 1911, a year after the last Bubi armed resistance, they numbered about 10,000.[33] A year later, according to another authority, the total had fallen to only about 6,800—54 percent of a total African population of 12,545.[34] By this time, the Bubi were nearly outnumbered by immigrants from other parts of Africa. By 1917, the disarmament of the Bubi was finished. They turned over a thousand rifles and more than a million cartridges to the Spanish. Bubi culture had also reached a turning point. The sacred fire of the last abba mote was extinguished in 1909, and the Claretian missionaries launched an extensive program of Hispanicization. Once pacification was complete, the missionaries embarked on a campaign to gather the islanders into concentrated villages, a movement that was almost complete by the 1940s.

Moka's achievement in creating a kingdom and defending the Bubi from outside interference in the nineteenth century was followed by demographic decline that lasted until after the Second World War. Twenty-odd years later, with the coming of independence, the name of the island changed from the Fernando Po to Bioko. Despite this facade of freedom, the Bubi remained a closed-off minority on their own island. By 1970 their European colonial masters had departed, only to be replaced by a postcolonial dictatorship run from the African mainland. Symbols of the past were dusted off in a wave of neo-traditionalism—for example, Santa Isabel was renamed Malabo, for Moka's successor. Another gesture was at least appropriate: Riabba was renamed Moka.

Further Reading

Equatorial Guinea is one of the least known of Africa's republics, and the Bubi are among its least-known peoples. As a Spanish colony under the rule of the Spanish dictator Francisco Franco's regime until 1975 and for a time thereafter, the country was off limits to scholars. Books in English that deal with the history of Equatorial Guinea and the island of Bioko include Max Linger-Goumaz, *Small Is Not Always Beautiful* (London: Rowman & Littlefield, 1988); Randall Fegley, *Equatorial Guinea: An African Tragedy* (New York: Peter Lang, 1989); and my two volumes, *From Slaving to Neoslavery: The Bight of Biafra and Fernando Po in the Era of Abolition, 1827–1930* (Madison: University of Wisconsin Press, 1996) and *Equatorial Guinea: State Terror and the Search for Stability* (Boulder, Colo.: Westview Press, 1990).

A reliable exploration of prehistory may be found in P. De Maret's "Fernando Po," in *The Archaeology of Central Africa*, ed. F. Van Noten (Graz, Austria: Akademische Druck-u Verlaganstalt, 1982). Jan Vansina's encyclopedic *Paths in the Rainforests: Toward a History of Political Tradition in Equatorial Africa* (Madison: University of Wisconsin Press, 1990) ties the Bubi to the larger saga of the Bantu migrations. The island of Bioko also figures in a more recent story of DNA and the black diaspora. Beaula McCalla, a black Briton, claims that DNA testing proves she is of Bubi descent. A British TV program chronicled her visit to Bioko and her reunion with her ancestral folk. See Beaula McCalla, "Family History," Portcities Bristol, http://www.discoveringbristol.org.uk/showNarrative.php?sit_id=0&na.

Travelers' accounts from Moka's time are few but varied. A firsthand description of Bioko is given in Oskar Baumann, *Eine afrikanische Tropeninsel, Fernando Poo und die Bube* (Vienna, 1888). After the First World War, Gunter Tessmann, a German with earlier experience in Cameroon, published *Die Bubi auf Fernando Poo* (Darmstadt, Germany: Filkwan, 1923). Because the island eventually fell under Spanish rule, most of the other relevant sources are in Spanish. Spanish scholars, many of them missionaries, produced several studies with a historical dimension. Armengol Coll, *Segunda memoria de las misiones de Fernando Póo y sus dependencias* (Madrid: Imprenta Iberia, 1911) describes missionary activity during Moka's lifetime. A much later work, Cristóbal Fernandez's *Missiones y missioneros en la Guinea española* (Madrid: Editorial Co. Cul. S. A., 1962) also describes missionary labors. But the best missionary accounts are by Antonio Aymemí, who worked among the Bubi from 1894 until his death in 1941. Some of his articles were collected and published as *Los Bubis en Fernando Póo, Colección de artículos publicados en la revista colonial "La Guinea española"* (Madrid: Galo Saez, 1942). An excellent English translation of his writings can be found online at www.Bubi.com. Amador Martin del Molino, a Spanish Claretian missionary, produced masterful work over a fifty-year period. See his article on the workings of Bubi kingship titled "La familia real," in *La Guinea Española* 59, 1553 (1962), 37–40. His major work, *Los Bubis, ritos y creencias* (Malabo: Centro Cultural Hispano-Guineano, 1989), includes substantial ethnographic data. Although not a history, it thoroughly probes theories of origin and/or migration.

Luis Ramos-Izquierdo, a colonial governor, published an early description of the administration, *Descripción geográfica y gobierno, adminstración y colonización de las colonias españolas del Golfo de Guinea* (Madrid: F. Pena Cruz,

1912). After the Second World War, the Spanish Instituto de Estudios Africanos in Madrid published three books that treat, among other topics, the historical evolution of Bioko: Abelardo de Unzueta, *Historia Geográfica de la isla de Fernando Póo* (1947); José Antonio Moreno-Moreno, *Reseña historica de la presencia de España en el Golfo de Guinea* (1952); and Manuel de Teran, *Sínteis geográfica de Fernando Póo* (1962).

Notes

1. www.thebubis.com/Chapters%20through%2025.htm, quoting Antonio Aymemí.

2. From the collection of his articles mentioned above, see Antonio Aymemí, "Los Bubi en Fernando Póo," 66.

3. www.thebubis.com/Chapters%2060%20and%2061.htm.

4. J. G. Frazer. *The Golden Bough: A Study in Magic and Religion* (New York: Macmillan, 1922), 277.

5. *Parliamentary Papers*, Slave Trade 64, Sessions 1821–1822, Navy, Communications to the Admiralty 1822 (233) XXIII, 17, "Extract of a Report from Commodore Sir George R. Collier on the Coast of Africa," 27 December 1821.

6. John Adams, *Remarks on the Country Extending from Cape Palmas to the River Congo*, 2nd ed. (London: Frank Cass, [1832] 1966), 148.

7. Thomas Hutchinson, *Impressions of Western Africa* (London: Longmans Brown, 1858), 187.

8. Wilhelm Bleek, "On the Languages of Western and Southern Africa," *Transactions of the Philological Society of London* (1855): 40–50.

9. *Parliamentary Papers*, "Extract of a Report from Commodore Sir George R. Collier," 27 December 1821.

10. *Parliamentary Papers*, "Extract of a Report from Commodore Sir George R. Collier," 27 December 1821.

11. William Allen and Thomas Thompson, *Narrative of the Expedition Sent by Her Majesty's Government to the River Niger in 1841*, 2nd ed. (New York: Johnson Reprint, [1848] 1967), 196.

12. Jan Vansina, "Western Bantu Expansion," *Journal of African History* 25 (1984): 132.

13. Vansina, "Western Bantu Expansion," 132.

14. Jan Vansina, *Paths in the Rainforests: Toward a History of Political Tradition in Equatorial Africa* (Madison: University of Wisconsin Press, 1990), 117.

15. A. Martin del Molino, *Los Bubis, ritos y creencias* (Malabo: Centro Cultural Hispano-Guineano, 1989), 485.

16. Martin del Molino, *Los Bubis*, 485. We have a list of the buala at Riabba, the seat of the Bubi paramount kings in the nineteenth century. Attributing to each buala a lifespan of forty years, Martin del Molino has set the dates of the first ruler

in the 1600s: Babiaoma (pre-1600), Bao (1600–1640), Balobedde (1640–1680), Beole (1689–1720), Bamaotedde (1720–1760), Balobicho (1760–1800), Badya (1800–1840), Barilaroote (1840–1924), Bidya (1924 to the 1960s).

17. The Baptist missionary John Clarke left two journals, which provide a detailed view of the turbulent 1840s. See Baptist Missionary Society (London), John Clarke Journals, first and second series.

18. J. Holman, *Travels in Madeira, Sierra Leone, Tenerife, St. Jago, Cape Coast, Fernando Po, Princes Island* . . . (London: George Routledge, 1840; Reprint edition: Freeport, New York: Books for Libraries Press, 1972), 1: 307–8.

19. Luis Sorela and L. Guxardo Faxardo, *Colonización en el Africa occidental* (Madrid, 1888), 24.

20. John Clarke, *Specimens of Dialects: Short Vocabulary of Languages and Notes: Countries and Customs of Africa* (Berwick-on-Tweed, UK: B. L. Green, 1848), 75.

21. Henry Roe, *West African Scenes* (London: Eliot Stock, 1874), 57.

22. There is a list of several kings who preceded Moka. Dating them is difficult, given the paucity of collected historical traditions on the island. It includes Molambo (prior to 1760), Loriite (1760–1810), Lopoa (1810–1842), Moadyabita (1842–1860), and Sepaoko (1860–1874). The last Bubi king was Fráncisco Malabo Beosa (1952–2001). See www.worldstatesman.org/Equatorial_Guinea_native.html.

23. A. Martin del Molino, "La familia real," *La Guinea Espanola* 59, 1553 (1962): 37–40.

24. Vansina, *Paths in the Rainforests*, 120.

25. Oskar Baumann, *Eine afrikanische Tropen-insel, Fernando Poo und die Bube* (Vienna: Hölzel, 1888), 106.

26. Mary Kingsley, *Travels in West Africa* (London: Macmillan, 1897), 57–58.

27. Kingsley, *Travels in West Africa*, 62.

28. Baumann, *Eine afrikanische Tropen-insel*, 123.

29. www.thebubis.com/Chapters 2060%and 2061.htm.

30. www.thebubis.com/Chapters 2060%and 2061.htm.

31. John Clarke, *Introduction to the Fernandian Tongue* (Berwick-on-Tweed, UK: Daniel Cameron, 1848), v.

32. Clarke, *Introduction to the Fernandian Tongue*, v.

33. See Manuel de Teran, *Síntesis geográfica de Fernando Póo* (Madrid: Instituto de Estudios Africanos, 1962), 87; Spanish Information Service, *Spain in Equatorial Guinea* (Madrid: Spanish Information Service, 1964), 23; Luis Ramos-Izquierdo, *Descripción geográfica y gobierno, administración y colonización de las colonias españolas del Golfo de Guinea* (Madrid: F. Peña Cruz, 1912), 345.

34. See Gunter Tessmann, *Die Bubi auf Fernando Poo: Volerkundlishe Einzelbescrhreibun eines westafrikanische Negerstammes. Kulturen der Erde. Materialien sur Kultur und Kunstegeshcite alle Volker* . . . (Darmstadt, Germany: Filkwan, 1923), 24.

PART II

FASHIONING AFRICAN IDENTITIES IN THE ERA OF EUROPEAN CONQUEST, 1850–1910

CHAPTER FOUR

~

Hamet Gora Diop (1846–1910)

Merchant and Notable
from Saint-Louis in Senegal

Mamadou Diouf

*Founded in 1650 at the site of a small fishing village inhabited by the Wolof people,
the French colonial town of Saint-Louis in today's Senegal was one of the first permanent European settlements in West Africa. French inhabitants were few, and
fewer still lived in Saint-Louis for their entire lives. With time, two local groups
eclipsed the European population in numbers. The first group, the métis or people
of mixed European and African heritage, were the children, grandchildren, and
later descendants of unions between European men and local women. Among
them, the* signares *became influential intermediaries between European and local
traders, as well as political leaders. Their ties and familiarity with both European
and African people, languages, and cultures allowed them to profit handsomely by
brokering exchange. Many métis and* signares *were Christians. Because of their
links with the French community, the colonial government recognized many of
them as French citizens and gave them the right to vote.*

*Another community made up the second most prominent local group. The
French called them* originaires[1] *or habitants, which is to say the first notable
inhabitants of Saint-Louis. In the Wolof language, they were referred to as the*
doomu ndaar. *As with the métis, the colonial regime recognized the doomu ndaar
as French citizens with voting rights. Mamadou Diouf's chapter explores the world
of the doomu ndaar from the founding of Saint-Louis du Senegal in 1659 to the*

firm establishment of colonial rule and the creation of French West Africa in 1895. Initially attracted to the town by the prospect of commerce, most doomu ndaar were of Wolof or Halpulaar ethnic heritage. Their numbers grew as their economic fortunes became increasingly intertwined with expanding French commerce—first on the coast and then in the Senegal River valley, which served as a commercial highway reaching eastward into the interior. In the late nineteenth century, they struck commercial alliances with French trading interests—indeed, they often worked as agents for the major commercial houses in the region—while at the same time cultivating exchange with Muslim political powers in the interior that actively resisted the Europeans.

Despite close ties with and intimate knowledge of French colonial society, the colonial legal system, and commercial practices, the doomu ndaar neither resisted nor collaborated with the French presence. They sought instead to see how they could benefit from it, while at the same time maximizing their autonomy and promoting their own African-Islamic culture. For example, they refused to submit to the French civil code. Many were patrons of Islamic learning; some were learned themselves. In the end, they drew on their multiple African and Islamic heritages along with their understanding of French society to build a vibrant civic culture.

This chapter presents a portrait of the *doomu ndaar* by building on a biography of Hamet Gora Diop, also known as Hamet Gueye. The economic and philanthropic activities of the doomu ndaar, along with what we know about how they ran their households, allow us to see how they combined and recombined a variety of resources to ultimately create their own culture out of the various social, economic, and political milieus around them. Their highly developed, urbane civic culture borrowed from the traditions of the Wolof and Halpulaar in Senegambia as well as the "religious library" of the Muslim world, all situated in political practice and structures that derived from the administrative, political, and institutional sources and resources of the French colony of Senegal.

Although members of the doomu ndaar became highly regarded merchants and represented their community to the colonial authorities, they were neither soldiers nor aristocrats nor Muslim religious figures, or marabouts. Despite collaborating with the colonial administration, they maintained an autonomous civic space. Educated in the Islamic sciences, arts, and jurisprudence, they also possessed a fine knowledge of the ins and outs of the colonial administrative system. They also mastered the professional rules of commerce.[2] Their sophisticated education led them to participate actively in the moral, theological, and political debates that gave rise to the civic[3] and political culture of the larger colony, as well as civil society in Saint-Louis.

Hence evolved a scriptural and literary Islamic modernity with an Arabic and Muslim textuality at its core, which offset the pretentions of the colonial *mission civilisatrice*, or "civilizing mission." Examples of this Islamic modernity would be the transcription of the Wolof language using Arabic letters, and genealogical constructions attaching the great Muslim families of the region to the tribes of Mecca. Through prowess, then, the doomu ndaar conjugated an indigenous Wolof version of colonial assimilation through the hybridization and vernacularization of Islamic, colonial, Moorish, and Senegambian resources.

This portrait of Hamet Gora Diop draws on several sets of archives, which are compared with each other and with other sources.[4] Some of the archives are oral traditions; others consist of account books preserved by the family that record the commercial activities of this famous Saint-Louis trader between 1882 and 1908.[5] They testify to Diop's success. The oral traditions about Diop come from three sources: family stories passed down from generation to generation; the accounts of *griots*, praise singers and serious oral historians often attached to prominent families; and the oral history of the Sufi brotherhoods. Together they recall a man of piety and situate Diop in his social world.

In 1950, Al-Hajj Sulayman Diop, a son of Hamet Gora Diop, wrote a short biography of his father.[6] Sulayman Diop was an inspector for Établissements Peyrissac, a French trading company. He also started to write a study of his father's business, which he never finished.[7] In these writings, Sulayman called into question the prevailing stereotype that Senegalese had no aptitude for commercial endeavors. He also raised questions about whether or not Senegalese merchants were subordinated to foreign economic interests. In effect, Sulayman mobilized a "usable past" based on his father's activities in order to imagine a more viable future for Senegalese merchants, whose survival at independence was threatened by the policies and practices of the postcolonial Senegalese political elite. The biography of Hamet Gora Diop documented the past achievements of Senegalese businessmen, thereby making the case for renewed success. This literary tradition continues. In 2004, Hamet Gora Diop's grandson, Moussa Iba Amett Diop, published a book on Saint-Louis that served as a backdrop for another biography of his grandfather.[8]

Hamet Gora Diop's private papers for the years 1882–1908, when he lived in Médine, Senegal, fill ten account books. *La Biographie* by Sulayman Diop includes information about his father's four years' residence in Rosso. Finally, oral traditions associated with the Muridiyya and Tijaniyya Muslim brotherhoods recounted in "La Biographie," and the memoirs of figures associated with them, link Diop to their founders.[9] He contributed both materially and financially to their endeavors. His activities are likewise recalled in the broader institutional memories of the brotherhoods. Taken together, these sources also illustrate how the higher literary and cultural traditions of Islam in Senegal came to take a backseat to efforts to spread the faith.

Commercial Spaces and Religious Frontiers

Two places demarcated Hamet Gora Diop's commercial operations: Saint-Louis, located in the west at the mouth of the Senegal River on the Atlantic Ocean, and Médine in the east, in the Khasso at the confluence of the Senegal and Kolombiné Rivers. In Diop's time, the commercial economy of the Senegal River valley focused on Saint-Louis, the first site of his activities. The city had been a colonial trading post since its founding in 1650.[10] The economic history of Saint-Louis and the colony of Senegal may be divided into two phases. The first dates from 1650 to the end of the eighteenth century, when French commercial houses enjoyed a monopoly. In this era, Africans and *métis*, people of mixed African and European heritage, were usually employed by the French companies. The second period began after 1780, with the rise of economic liberalism, when trade in Saint-Louis was divided among three professional groups: dealers or wholesalers, *habitants*, and administrators. This tripartite division led to tension over each group's place in the larger network of regional commerce. These tensions were often expressed in racial terms that set dealers and traders, and Europeans, Africans, and métis against each other.

In 1854, when Faidherbe became governor of Senegal, these questions shook the colony. The Faidherbe administration imposed a new logic on economic, political, and social life. Some aspects of this new logic grew out of the defeat of Al-Hajj Umar, a Muslim leader of the Fulani people who led holy wars or jihads against non-Muslim kingdoms on the upper Senegal River and middle Niger River between 1852 and 1864.[11] Following his defeat and death, the French took steps to establish their military and commercial presence in the area. These actions coalesced into what came to be called "French Muslim policy." This policy emerged from the reshaping of the École des Otages (School of Hostages), a school for the children of local notables, to an institution that more closely resembled its counterpart in Algeria (1856); the creation of Muslim courts (1857); and the granting of subsidies to prominent Muslims of Saint-Louis who wanted to make the pilgrimage to Mecca (1860–1861). David Robinson writes that "[the policy] in some ways offered legitimacy to Muslims who gravitated toward the French sphere."[12]

It also accorded Muslim traders an intermediary position that allowed them to shape the colony's commercial strategies and determine the nature of diplomatic and political relations between Saint-Louis and the hinterland.

The other anchor of Hamet Gora Diop's commercial operations lay in Upper Senegal, with its center at Médine. From there, his commercial reach extended north to Nioro in the Sahel on the edge of the Sahara, south as far as Bafoulabé, and east to Koniakary. Raw materials flowed from the surrounding hinterlands to each of these towns. In turn, imported manufactured goods made their way from Saint-Louis through these trading posts (escales) and out to these rural areas.

Two distinct periods mark the economic history of the Upper Senegal River in the later nineteenth century. The first, from 1850 to 1860, was marked by the jihads of Al-Hajj Umar with widespread consequences. Fighting between Umar's troops and local allies of the French opposed to the jihad led to economic collapse, neglect of agriculture, and generalized famine in the Futa Toro highlands, the Upper Senegal, and much of Kaarta. Merchants from Saint-Louis were the only people who profited from this dire situation.[13] They invested some of their earnings in buildings. Hamet Diop's father in Saint-Louis apparently benefited indirectly from the traders' success, because he specialized in the provision of building materials and other supplies.

After the jihads around 1860, Paris and Saint-Louis together took measures to resuscitate business in Upper Senegal. They focused on revitalizing trade in gum arabic and agricultural products and on raising animals—the reference item for commerce in the region. Two crops, peanuts and millet, became the symbols of a new dynamic economy in Upper Senegal. Encouraged by a colonial administration eager to find a replacement for gum arabic, commercial peanut production grew rapidly between 1861 and 1884. Due to a huge expansion in peanut production in western Senegambia, growers in Upper Senegal could not command what they considered to be a fair price in peanut production. In contrast, millet prices took off because political instability in the region stimulated demand.[14]

This rapid growth in commerce after 1850 is reflected in reports by the French commandants of Bakel and Médine and in the new infrastructure put in place for the colonial armed forces and financial system. In 1879, the administration launched new public works to support French expansion eastward to lands that would become French Soudan. Telegraph offices opened in Bakel and Médine in May 1880. With this solid institutional base, the colony's commercial reach extended to the east into a hinterland still controlled by the Tukulor empire of Ahmadu Seku, a son of Al-Hajj Umar. Indeed, Seku depended on the importation of between fifteen hundred and eighteen hundred weapons from the west each year to reinforce his domination, which also reinforced commerce on the Senegal River. Well implanted in the Kaarta-Malinké regions farther east, the Umarians maintained cordial relations with merchants whose attention was focused north toward the Sahara desert. These ties supported trade in salt and also allowed the Umarians to maintain forts in Murgala. In the other direction, links to the south assured access to gold, kola nuts, and slaves.[15]

This rapid sketch of the zone of Hamet Gora Diop's commercial operations identifies Upper Senegal as an important commercial crossroads. Despite this favorable environment, Saint-Louis traders were less successful after 1850 than they had been earlier. Perhaps to encourage trade, then, the colonial government granted Saint-Louis traders exclusive rights to do business on the Senegal River in 1863. These privileges, along with a monopoly on the purchase of sheep already accorded to Moors from the north, underscored the colonial regime's efforts to keep other Muslim traders from the interior—and notably the Jula—out of the river region.[16]

Despite the challenging economic environment faced by Saint-Louis traders, official correspondence described an expansive economic environment after 1850. In a letter to the governor, for example, the president of the chamber of commerce, A. Béziat, wrote that there was "no doubt that business on the Upper Senegal had brought profit to the colony overall. Existing trade in goods was increasingly supplemented by the exchange of products against imported currency, whose value came to be considerable." He noted that local people along the Upper Senegal, and even some from Segou Sikoro on the Niger River farther in the interior "now came to trading posts on the Upper Senegal, and even down to Saint-Louis to make their purchases." They then returned upriver with the goods, where they could undersell "similar merchandise already there that traders had acquired on credit."[17]

Economic data for the period suggest two conclusions. First, the volume of currency circulating in the Upper Senegal and Middle Niger regions increased significantly after the French conquered Ahmadu's empire. Second, Jula traders not only resisted colonial efforts to eliminate them, but successfully reorganized their networks by articulating them with the two poles of the river's economic geography—at Saint-Louis and along the Upper Senegal. In "La Biographie," Al-Hajj Sulayman Diop mentions that much later (in 1950) he met in Kankan (Guinea) "an old Jula who told us that he had been part of a group of Jula" who worked with his father.[18]

Despite testimonies to prosperity, the president of the chamber of commerce of Saint-Louis paradoxically emphasized that many traders found themselves in difficulty. Some of them filed petitions describing the deterioration in their economic fortunes. In September 1885, for example, "the traders of Médine and Bakel" complained:

> Foreign peddlers—Moroccans, Italians, Tukulors—who were not subject to obligations imposed by the administrative ruling of 28 December 1876 about keeping transparent books, compete with us in the trading posts along the river in a way that will force us to give up trading completely if the dealers in Saint-Louis, for whom we are the agents in Galam, do not take steps to bring this situation to an end.[19]

In another petition dated December 26, 1892, their recriminations are directed at the dealers themselves: "Allowing dealers to trade up and down the river in the name of free trade, while confining traders to designated trading posts where they compete with those who furnish them their goods, is to shift privilege from those who come from the poor masses to a handful of the wealthy." Between these two petitions, a request dated August 10, 1886, raised issues about both the "peddlers" denounced in 1885 and the dealers described in 1892 as a "handful of the wealthy."

During these hard times for many Saint-Louis traders on the Upper Senegal, Hamet Gora Diop actually achieved commercial success—at the same time that colonial commerce began to redirect attention westward toward the developing peanut basin. Given the slow pace of economic growth in Kaarta, Tukulor control of trade routes to the north and south, the integration of Jula traders into the colonial commercial network, and the westward orientation of Ahmadu's state, most Saint-Louis traders did not see river commerce as a viable alternative network. Hamet Diop took advantage of their failure to diversify his activities, thereby maximizing his profits and avoiding the fate of his colleagues who remained tied to older commercial networks.

This economic geography overlays a spiritual geography bordered on the north by the Berber and Moor marabouts of the Qadiriyya Sufi order or mystical brotherhood, on the east by the Halpulaar of the Tijaniyya Sufi order, and still farther east by Egypt, the land of Islamic letters. Superimposing these economic and spiritual geographies sheds light on the religious and commercial path that Hamet Diop chose to follow. Diop's grandson wrote with pride,

> Helped by ties of trust and friendship with the leaders, he [Diop] started by granting extensive credit to traders in the district without demanding guarantees for, or interest on, their loans which had been standard practice. . . . In so doing, and despite evident risk, he simply wanted to acknowledge the words of our Prophet Muhammad (Peace Be Upon Him), who, following a noble tradition, said, "trading is a privileged way of earning a living."[20]

The Life of Hamet Gora Diop

"La Biographie" gives 1846 as the year of Hamet Gora Diop's birth in Saint-Louis. Although many details of Diop's family history remain unknown, it is easy to get a sense of the social and familial context that nurtured him. His grandson Moussa Diop identifies the founding ancestor as Hamet Gora Diop's grandfather, Demba Diop. Demba Diop's son was Gora Diop Fabineta (1807–1877), who was Hamet Gora Diop's father.[21] His mother was Tabara Ameth Seck.[22] In calling his grandfather's grandfather the "founding ancestor," Moussa Diop perhaps suggests that he was the first in the family to gain public notoriety, maybe by becoming a member of the doomu ndaar, and probably the first in the family to settle in Saint-Louis in the late 1700s. The Diop family came from Kokki province in the kingdom of Kajoor. Kokki was said to be a stronghold of the Senegambian Muslim community because of its high level of Islamic learning and because some of its marabouts had become part of the aristocracy, playing important political and even military roles. Two remarks included in the family histories are of particular significance: that Gora Fabineta belonged to the "most respected of the great Muslim families," and that his family was among those "most listened to by the colonizers."[23]

Over time, the doomu ndaar welded a community from the diverse origins of its members, playing on knowledge and material resources that were both Senegambian and colonial, all the while endowing both with a palpable Muslim spirituality. They fashioned a distinctive culture and identity through constant negotiation and renegotiation among the diverse sources and resources that came from these origins. To be sure, this process evolved in the broader historical contexts that preceded and surrounded them. Islam and the Wolof language were the wellsprings of doomu ndaar culture and identity, while Sindoné precinct in the southern part of the Île de Saint-Louis offered the field for both to flourish.

Gora Diop Fabineta's notoriety and his prominent position are underscored by the central role he played in his son's religious and professional education, and his extensive marriage alliances and friendship and business networks. The community was made up of two circles, each allied with the other and both located in Sindoné precinct. The first and most prominent was comprised of métis Christians, while the Muslim doomu ndaar were the other. They shared Sindoné with commercial dealers or wholesalers from France, who constituted the third influential group in Saint-Louis. But the doomu ndaar and the métis stood at the head of the Saint-Louis and Senegal River valley commercial and economic networks.

Gora Fabineta, a learned Muslim, was of the generation that had profited from the policies of former governor Faidherbe, who had been inspired by the model of collaboration with Muslim elites elaborated in the French colony of Algeria. Allied with the colonial bureaucracy, Gora Fabineta engaged in trade and accumulated capital. He also joined in the networks of several marabouts—Sheikh Saad Buh (1850/1851–1917) of the Qadiriyya Sufi brotherhood,[24] who built a *zawiya*, or religious center, at Nimzat in the 1880s; Sheikh Siddiyya al Kébir (1780–1868); and his grandson Sheikh Siddiyya Baba, a prominent political figure from the 1880s to his death in 1924. Under Siddiyya Baba, the Qadiri *zawiya* at Boutlimit in today's Mauritania became the locus of a powerful coalition, bringing together disciples from Mauritania and Saint-Louis, on the one hand, and the French colonial administration on the other.[25] Sheikh Saad Buh, a recognized authority in *fiqh*, or Islamic jurisprudence, and Sufi initiation, consistently rejected holy war and violence.

The métis were heavily represented in the southern precinct of the island of Saint-Louis, where some doomu ndaar families also lived. Together, the two made up the community of habitants. In 1840, Charmasson Puy Laval, governor of Senegal from 1838 to 1841, described them as "an aristocracy that placed itself on the same level as the Europeans."[26] Indeed, according to M. Marcson, the habitants, both métis and black, controlled trade in the trading posts along the river.[27] The doomu ndaar, then, were closely tied to the métis, with whom they shared interests and economic activities, hostility toward merchants from France, and claims of French identity as originaires. The most influential of the doomu ndaar lived in Sindoné, which was otherwise mainly occupied by Catholic originaires and agents of the administration. They lived up against a Christian space whose landmark was the Catholic Church. The doomu ndaar built a mosque in the northern part of the island where most of them lived, but they also created a Muslim space that was both public and private in this southern precinct. They bought buildings to house their families and dependents, and labored to establish mosques and undertake philanthropic work—like Hamet Gora Diop's building of the Minbaar mosque. Located in the heart of colonial space, these activities underscored both doomu ndaar spirituality and civic culture.[28]

The doomu ndaar did not work solely through colonial institutions. In the midst of this colonial "architecture," they inscribed their own Islamic modernity in a religious infrastructure of mosques, tribunals, and philanthropic and social projects, as well as in the universal language of Arabic and the two regional vernaculars, Wolof and Hassaniyya (Mauritanian colloquial Arabic). They labored toward the recomposition, hybridization, and shifting of resources from their own civic spaces—the mosque and the houses of their leaders—to elaborate a broader civic culture that then very quickly became part of the French imperial identity of the colony of Senegal. In particular, they spoke out against partisans of holy war, a critical issue in light of the conflicts with Al-Hajj Umar Tall.[29]

Hamet Gora Diop grew up in this community. Born in Sindoné, he learned the Qur'an first from his father, who was a learned Muslim and notable fully engaged in affairs vital to the doomu ndaar. Gora Fabineta's learning and rich library fostered relations of mutual esteem and friendship with the Moorish marabouts who had thrown in their lot with the Senegalese colony.[30] Hamet Gora Diop furthered his education by going on to the school of a disciple of Mor Massamba Jeery Dieng, where he mastered the Qur'an and became literate in Arabic. He then studied "theology taught by eminent religious scholars of religion from Saint-Louis and Mauritania, with particular attention to . . . mathematics and astronomy."[31]

After his studies, Hamet Diop launched his commercial career under the watchful eye of his father, "a trader who excelled in deals involving lumber for construction and the cottage industry of brick-making [and whose . . .] sales of wood and bricks, particularly to the administration, made a comfortable fortune, allowing him to front sufficient money to his son Ahmed [Hamet]."[32] Hamet Diop's father's death marked a turning point in his life. His father had been part of the generation of Saint-Louis doomu ndaar who had negotiated the contours of the Senegal colony with governor Faidherbe. The next generation tested this identity, which had been forged in an unstable compromise of religion, local cultural traditions, and the political economy of an expanding European colony.

Hamet Diop first set up business in about 1877 in Rosso on the Senegal River, where he stayed until 1881.[33] In Rosso, he launched a "network for the purchase and distribution of diverse merchandise," which reinforced his presence among Moorish, Wolof, and Halpulaar marabouts. Les Lumières d'une cité points out that "during the Rosso years, he . . . welcomed [marabouts] at his house for months at a time, profiting from their presence to deepen his knowledge of theology and esoteric [topics]. In return, the marabouts profited from his extremely rich library." A few years later, "these Islamic learned men, who perceived [Hamet Gora Diop] as a man of great Islamic culture, profound altruism, and humility," named him a sheikh.

Oral traditions among both the family and Muslim brotherhoods underscore Hamet Diop's good works when he lived in Rosso, notably his service to the poor and marabouts. Such dedication shows that he belonged to a religious as well as an economic network and also testify to his success.

Such character traits also fostered his commercial success. For example, the commercial house of Devès & Chaumet had confidence in him due to his seriousness and his piety.

The wealth he amassed in Rosso led him in 1881 to move to Médine, a trading post in the Upper Senegal–Niger region on the frontier between the French colony and the Tukulor empire of Ahmadu Seku, son and successor of Al-Hajj Umar Tall. Médine was a long way from Hamet Diop's nearest trading posts and required a much larger investment. In moving to Médine, Hamet Diop apparently followed the pattern of other traders.[34]

The years in Médine from 1882 to 1908 were of great significance for Hamet Diop, and thanks to the surviving account books, are the easiest to reconstruct. His Islamic education and pedigree as a notable from Saint-Louis favored his rapid integration into the local and regional trading communities. Both attributes also made it easier to build bridges to the Tukulor empire of Segou and Nioro farther east. In the Médine region as in Rosso, Islamic models continued to be de rigueur due to the reticence of the Tukulor establishment to enter into direct contact with the French. Such a situation benefited traders from Saint-Louis, who acted as intermediaries.

From Médine, Diop's commercial network took shape in a larger geography dominated by Saint-Louis. "La Biographie" reports that he commissioned "a veritable flotilla to transport his goods down river to Saint-Louis." Indeed, when he set up residence in Médine, Diop had purchased a lot of matériel for shipbuilding—wood, beams, nails, sail canvas, and so on. His barges, which took to the Senegal River in both directions, were complemented by a fleet of canoes that plied the waterways of the Middle Niger. Hamet Diop's network hence crisscrossed the region. It was also closely connected to local Jula routes. Although he continued to be part of the Devès family commercial network, Diop diversified his sources of supply after 1895 by making direct contact with commercial houses in Bordeaux and Rufisque. He frequently went or sent close associates to Bordeaux. At the other end of the network, he also took on numerous subcontractors in Upper Senegal.

The account books give an idea of the products exchanged, the nature of commercial transactions, and the financial status of Diop's agents. He furnished them with trade goods and they reimbursed him in other goods or cash. Of Saint-Louis provenance, according to Bathily, were cloth, firearms, sea salt, and fish. Hamet Diop also distributed copper plates, silver rods, fishhooks, matches, rice, construction materials (tile, beams, whitewash, paint), blankets, sugar, knives, mirrors, candles, balls of yarn, pliers, prayer beads, rigging, glass beads, sacks for gum arabic and peanuts, bedclothes, white cotton caps, mosquito nets, and a whole range of trade goods of modest quality.

The diversity of goods dispatched to Médine suggests that Diop's clientele was heterogeneous. Some items were clearly destined for marabouts and other people literate in Arabic, while others were meant for ordinary people. Tobacco and snuffboxes were traded in all of Diop's markets, which underscores their profitability and testifies to a demand so high that it could not be met through local production. Indeed, many people in the regions ceased growing tobacco in the aftermath of the Umarian jihad and the spread of the Tijaniyya brotherhood, which forbade its consumption.

The catalog of imports also identifies Hamet Diop as a supplier to French businesses, Saint-Louis traders, and the colonial administration—signaled by bedclothes, crockery dishes, construction materials, and even telegraph equipment. He attracted the business of the colonial administration between 1884 and 1900, just as it was gearing up for conquests farther east in the region that later became French Soudan. Whenever he left Saint-Louis, Diop usually took a lot of cash. He also sent cash back to Saint-Louis, because he received payments for his imports in cash as well as local products. Export products to Saint-Louis included large quantities of gum arabic and peanuts amassed by his agents, as well as gold and ivory that he acquired himself. Between 1882 and 1908, Hamet Diop's trading activities made him a rich man.

Charitable Works:
The Contours of Civic Culture and Community

Hamet Gora Diop's real estate investments, trips, and good works give us an idea of the size of his fortune. He was clearly wealthy. The account books record the accumulation of his real estate holdings. For example, "Carnet No. 2" (Notebook 2) records for January 1884 the purchase of building materials, salaries paid to masons and laborers, and registration of a mortgage for a building on rue Neuville in a southern quarter of Saint-Louis. "Carnet No. 3" lists property taxes paid in July 1884 on a house on rue Ribet. The accounts dated July 1890 include a detailed list of properties and the taxes Diop paid on them. They note eight buildings in the southern sector and three others in the north. The houses were several stories high, and Diop rented them to commercial agents, the administration, or the colonial army. Not surprisingly, they brought in substantial revenue. Judging from the orders for tile, bathtubs, and water tanks in the account books, the houses offered the modern comforts of the era. "La Biographie" also noted that "he built a large mosque in the southern quarter. . . . He [also] donated another house of several stories with a cistern [to the mosque] whose rent financed mosque repairs."[35]

Diop's charitable works, along with his commercial activities, reflected the Islamic model of the successful notable. He made the pilgrimage to Mecca several times, and he visited Alexandria and Jerusalem to fulfill other religious obligations and buy books for his library. He also often sent for books and prayer beads from these cities. As mentioned above, his large library earned him the friendship of the marabouts of the major religious brotherhoods—in particular Sheikh Saad Buh and Sheikh Siddiyya Baba of the Qadiriyya, Al-Hajj Malick Sy of the Tijaniyya, and Amadou Bamba Mbacké of the Muridiyya.

The social works of Hamet Diop overlay and were integral to his commercial activities. In the Khasso region they supported the expansion of Islam, while in Rosso and Saint-Louis they helped anchor the faith.[36] Diop's brief residence in Rosso did not allow him to plant the first of his usual two pillars of intervention—an institution for social work such as a mosque or Qur'anic school. On the other hand, his charity and almsgiving in kind and in cash were more significant in Rosso. His departure for the Khasso region did not bring an end to his charitable activities in the middle Senegal River valley. In Rosso, he was well known for distributing subsidies to the sick and handicapped and to people who suffered from the famine that hit areas north of the Senegal River valley in 1890. In the 1903 famine, he gave major gifts in millet and cash. Every year during the months leading up to Ramadan, he also gave money to Moorish marabouts.

In Khasso, on the other hand, Diop's social works paired charity with the building of Islamic infrastructure. At the center of his large estate in Médine stood the Petite Mosquée (Small Mosque), whose prayer hall and surrounding wall were dusted with fine white sand imported from Saint-Louis each rainy season. *Les Lumières d'une cité* suggests that the contrast between the "red-ocre of the laterite soil" of the region and the white of the Saint-Louis sand gave rise to the mosque's name, Threshold of Paradise, which recalled "another in Medina in the Mosque of the Prophet."[37] Diop promoted the founding of Qur'anic schools associated with the mosque. Beyond that he financially supported teachers who often were imams of mosques representing the major ethnic groups of the region—Halpulaar, Fulani, Moors, and Manding. He commissioned a well dug in the center of the complex, which also supplied water to neighboring houses.

The Petite Mosquée and Diop's house came to be gathering places for political discussion, religious instruction, and conversation about philosophy and theology. Numerous disagreements were mediated within their walls. All of these activities promoted cooperation in the Muslim community.

The square in front of the mosque was also the site of business meetings and ceremonies. Many programs were devoted to the recitation of the Qur'an or introductions to Islamic law and theology—particularly during the fasting month of Ramadan. Hamet Diop's economic, social, religious, and political activities stand witness to the creation of a civic space and community nurtured by a universalist and assimilating Islam that bridged ethnic boundaries. This faith was bountiful, open, compassionate, and thankful—and inspired by the tradition of Saint-Louis civic culture. It was positioned to fill the void in local societies created by the French colonial conquest.

Diop's sojourns in Saint-Louis following long periods in the Upper Senegal–Niger region followed the same rhythm. They were in keeping with his status as a rich merchant and Muslim notable, but were grander in style than when he was in Médine. He helped the handicapped, the elderly, and the poor. He made gifts to marabouts and learned Muslims, and he convened religious gatherings in the Minbaar religious complex, built a long time before he returned definitively to Saint-Louis after 1900. The mission of the Minbaar religious center grew out of competition with the assimilationist policies of a Catholic colonial administration. It was "a fortified structure that had once belonged to the *signares*."[38] To be sure, the transformation of a signare edifice into a Muslim religious center was a powerful symbol in the competition to define Saint-Louis civic culture. Persuaded that the mosque was the most significant historical monument in the evolution of Islam, Diop built the Minbaar mosque in the huge courtyard of this fortified compound. Located a long way from Christian neighborhoods, the complex consisted of a "prayer hall crowned by a library reknowned for the variety and splendor of its collections" and "a room adorned with Persian carpets and perfumed by incense from distant Asian lands. Here [learned men passing through Saint-Louis and others of Saint-Louis origin] debated theological questions until the wee hours."[39] In Saint-Louis, then, Diop's charitable works supported by religious institutions built an Islamic civic community that openly displayed its identity and ideology in a colonial space.

In Saint-Louis, Hamet Diop's associations with prestigious Wolof, Moor, and Halpulaar marabouts along with his "great learning, . . . extensive knowledge of the *Qur'an*, the *sunna*, or islamic tradition, and his nuanced knowledge of the religious sciences elevated him to the level of the 'Great religious dignitaries.'"[40] His support of the marabouts took the form of monetary gifts, loans of books, and access to the Minbaar center. Diop also provided financial and administrative help in arranging the pilgrimage and acquiring real estate. Although he did not join the Tijaniyya and Muridiyya brotherhoods, which spread rapidly in the late nineteenth century, Diop supported their implantation. He also provided significant and continuous support for the building of the great mosques at Tivaouane and Touba.

Hamet Gora Diop died in 1910, having made the pilgrimage to Mecca four times. He provided for the financial security of the Minbaar religious center in Saint-Louis, which he judged to be his most important legacy. He thought it was perhaps the most significant institutional expression of the doomu ndaar—a civic culture that flowered in the heart of French colonial space, both cooperating and competing with European political, economic, cultural, and religious ambitions. The record of his life reproduces quite accurately the contours of the doomu ndaar community, whose religious practices, lifestyle, and consumption patterns translated quite effectively, and clearly a desire to introduce a local rhythm and sense of civic culture into a colonial modernity. They took as much care formulating ways to become part of colonial society as they did in determining how and to what degree they wished to remain apart from it.

Conclusion

The doomu ndaar shaped for themselves a thoughtful culture and a collective representation to present to the colonial authorities. This approach created a culture of petition that routinely turned to the law, lawyers, and the courts. The quest for representation and acceptance of the concept of representativity led to the configuration of a public space produced by both the colonial administration and the doomu ndaar. The integration of some of them into the colonial administration, the distance maintained by others such as Hamet Gora Diop, the recognition of formal (the Tamsir and Qadi) and informal representative institutions in the doomu ndaar community, and the development of a culture of public assistance and support for the disadvantaged eventually led the colonial administration to delegate much of the day-to-day governing of the population to the doomu ndaar. In getting out from under the authoritarianism of the administration, then, the doomu ndaar subverted colonial formulas promoting assimilation and the mission civilisatrice.

Hence emerged a particularly Saint-Louis brand of humanism that in the colonial context maintained civic community through its recognized practices, ceremonies and commemorations, commemorative plaques adorned with texts in Arabic letters in gold, and deliberations that drew on ties with the colonial administration and links with Senegambian religious circles. By competing with the good works of the Christians, the doomu ndaar notables imposed their civic tradition as the defining feature of Saint-Louis colonial society. Their influence is intimated by the recriminations and violent indictments that Abbé Boilat hurled at the Catholics of Saint-Louis, who had taken to wearing Muslim amulets and even adopting aspects of Muslim baptism and marriage ceremonies.[41]

The biography of Hamet Gora Diop is a privileged site for tracing the development and shape of this civic community and culture. "La Biographie" and *Les Lumières d'une cité* shed light on the paradoxes in the life of Diop and his community by presenting the varied inflections of their narrative strategy. A first strategy was designed to restore doomu ndaar identity by comparing their economic success in the past with their marginalization in the present—emphasizing their literary creativity and mastery of idioms and techniques related to commerce and exchange. The second strategy aimed at "correcting" the historiography and memory of Islam in this part of West Africa, which limited its recollections to holy war and the rise of Islamic brotherhoods and neglected the illustrious history of a faith associated with commerce and higher culture. The life of Hamet Diop perfectly illustrates these broader facets of Islamic history in Senegal.

The reconstitution of the history of the doomu ndaar community also offers an opportunity to rethink the long-standing conventional wisdom about the adoption and so-called Africanization of Islam in West Africa.[42] The Islamic political economy of the doomu ndaar, with its storehouse of universal spiritual and doctrinal formulations of Arab origin, suggests a trajectory for Islam in Africa that does not superimpose Islamization and Africanization. The community and culture of the doomu ndaar consequently calls into question a long-standing belief in a "black Islam" that, due to the supposed linguistic and ideological ignorance of local Muslims, edited out Arab racial and cultural elements, altering its spiritual message and producing a hybrid faith that inadvertently brought success in black Africa.[43] The doomu ndaar did not at all seek to produce an alternative Islamic public space. In a very nuanced and judicious manner, they created a civic community that grew out of a combination of Senegambian, Islamic, and French colonial sources and resources. The result was a culture that competed with the French colonial administration through confrontation, negotiation, and guile. The grandson of Hamet Diop described him in a way that also applies to the larger community of the doomu ndaar:

> The concept of "marabout" is too restricted a meaning because it refers to a
> single kind of religious figure who worked in the context of a brotherhood

which he was called to lead. Despite his great knowledge of the *Qur'an* and the religious sciences, his perfect mastery of the Arabic language, [my grandfather] was preoccupied by a quest to be elevated to the ranks of the 'best Muslims,' incorruptable guardians of Islamic morals, and not by the ambition to be the guide for some religious community or another. His concern as a good Muslim was always to warn the Believers of Saint-Louis about Muslim leaders who labored for an Islam of brotherhoods or marabouts whose followers would obey them. [In contrast, he] thought that, at a time when the colonialists never ceased in their oppression of Islam and its institutions, it was very important for Muslims to join in a common front to protect the sacred principles of the faith and create the conditions for perfect Islamic unity.[44]

Further Reading

On the growth and economic development of Senegal, there is a large literature in French. See the following key titles in French: Mbaye Gueye, "La fin de l'esclavage à Saint-Louis et Gorée en 1848," *Bulletin de l'IFAN*, series B, 28, 3–4 (1966); Abdoulaye Ly, "Sur le site et les origines de Saint-Louis," *Notes Africaines* 58 (1953); and Mamadou Diouf, *Le Kajoor au 19ème siècle. Pouvoir ceddo et conquête coloniale* (Paris: Karthala, 1990). In English, see David Robinson, *Paths of Accomodation: Muslim Societies and French Colonial Authorities in Senegal and Mauritania, 1880–1920* (Athens: Ohio University Press, 2000); James Searing, *"God Alone Is King": Islam and Emancipation in Senegal; The Wolof Kingdom of Kajoor and Bawol, 1859–1914* (Portsmouth, N.H.: Heinemann, and Oxford, UK: James Currey, 2002); Philip D. Curtin, *Economic Change in Precolonial Africa: Senegambia in the Era of the Slave Trade*, 2 vols. (Madison: University of Wisconsin Press, 1975).

The literature on Islam in West Africa is likewise abundant, but the following titles are particularly valuable for understanding the creation of public space in colonial Saint-Louis: A. Bathily, "Aux origines de l'Africanisme. L'œuvre ethno-historique de Faidherbe dans la conquête française du Sénégal," *Cahiers de Jussieu* 32 (1976); R. Pasquier, "L'influence de l'expérience algérienne sur la politique de la France au Sénégal," *Mélanges offerts à H. Deschamps* (Paris: Publications de la Sorbonne, 1974); C. Harrison, *France and Islam in West Africa: 1860–1960* (Cambridge, UK: Cambridge University Press, 1988); David Robinson, *Muslim Societies in African History* (Cambridge, UK: Cambridge University Press, 2004); Cheikh Anta Babou, *Fighting the Greater Jihad: Amadu Bamba and the Founding of the Muridiyya of Senegal, 1853–1913* (Athens: Ohio University Press, 2007).

Accounts of politics under French colonial rule during the nineteenth and early twentieth centuries include G. W. Johnson, *The Emergence of Black Politics in Senegal: The Struggle for Power in the Four Communes, 1900–1920* (Stanford, Calif.: Stanford University Press, 1971), and Alice Conklin, *A Mission to Civilize: The Republican Idea of Empire in France and West Africa, 1895–1930* (Stanford, Calif.: Stanford University Press, 1997).

Notes

1. See Mamadou Diouf, "The French Colonial Policy of Assimilation and the Civility of the Originaires of the Four Communes (Senegal): A Nineteenth-Century Globalization Project," *Development and Change* 29, 4 (1998): 671–96.

2. On the history of commerce and trading diasporas, see Abner Cohen, "Cultural Strategies in the Organization of Trading Diasporas," in *The Development of African Trade and Markets in West Africa*, ed. Claude Meillassoux (London: International Africa Institute and Oxford University Press, 1972).

3. On civic culture, which they define as "a set of orientations towards a specific set of social objects and processes," see G. Almond and S. Verba, *The Civic Culture: Political Attitudes and Democracy in Five Nations* (London: Sage, 1989), 12. See David Robinson, *Paths of Accommodation: Muslim Societies and French Colonial Authorities in Senegal and Mauritania, 1880–1920* (Athens: Ohio University Press; Oxford, UK: James Currey, 2000), chapters 5 and 6.

4. See Abdoulaye Bathily, "Guerriers, Tributaires, et Marchands," PhD diss., Université de Dakar, 1985, vol. 2; also David Robinson, *La Guerre sainte d'Al Hajj Umar: Le Soudan Occidental au milieu du XIXe siècle* (Paris: Karthala, 1988), which deals with the region where Hamet Gora Diop traded.

5. I wish to thank profoundly my friend Makane Fall for his remarkable work in classifying these registers and compiling an alphabetical index of names, places, and topics.

6. Or, as transliterated in French, El Hadji Souleymane Diop, "La Biographie de El Hadj Ameth Gora DIOP, dit Ameth GUEYE Cheikh, 1846–1910." The text is dated "Saint-Louis 1950," but the body includes a reference to Jacques Diouf, "Secrétaire Exécutif de l'ADRAO et Secrétaire d'État à la Recherche Scientifique et Technique," 6, which signals that this eight-page biography was either written or rewritten in the 1970s. The work is divided into the following sections: (I) Introduction, 1–3; (II) Oeuvres charitables (Charitable Works), 3–4; (III) Relations, 4–5; (IV) Logements (Houses), 5–6; and (V) Ses épouses (His Wives), 6–8.

7. El Hadji Souleyman Diop, "Le difficile problème du commerce au Sénégal" (Saint-Louis, n.d.). We have only recovered the following outline and the first ten pages of the first chapter of this work:

> Introduction
>
> (I) "Grandeur et décadence" du commerce au Sénégal. De l'inaptitude du Sénégalais aux affaires mercantiles: mythe ou réalité? (The Rise and Fall of Trade in Senegal. On the Inability of Senegalese to Become Successful Businessmen: Myth or Reality?)

(A) Aperçu historique: Le commerce au Sénégal avant l'indépendance (A Brief History of Trade in Colonial Senegal)

(B) Velléités de renaissance du commerce sénégalais depuis l'indépendance (The Rebirth of Senegalese Business since Independence)

(II) L'Avenir du commerçant sénégalais (The Future of the Senegalese Trader)

(A) Perspectives (Prospects)

(B) Quelques suggestions (Some Suggestions; with a reference to the economic policy of Nkrumah's Ghana)

(III) Conclusion. Nécessité d'une option nationaliste véritable et d'un protectionnisme éducateur (Fréderic List) (The Need for a True Nationalist Option and a Formative Protectionism)

8. Moussa Iba Amett Diop, *Les Lumières d'une cité: Ndar* (Dakar, Senegal: Presses Universitaires de Dakar, 2004). The first chapter of the second part is entirely devoted to "El Hadji Ahmed Gaura Diop" (87–170).

9. Souleymane Diop, "La Biographie," 2. The author furnishes a list of the informants whose testimonies he collected.

10. L. L. Faidherbe, "Notice sur la colonie du Sénégal," *Annuaire du Sénégal et Dépendances* (Saint-Louis, 1885); L. Jean-Baptiste Durand, *Voyage au Sénégal, 1785 et 1786*, 2 vols. (Paris: H. Agasse, 1803); Archives Nationales du Sénégal (ANS), 1B6, Correspondance de Huzzard à Portal, 13 April 1822; R. Rousseau, "Le site et les origines de Saint-Louis," *La Géographie* 49, 2 (July–August), 116–28; 49, 3: 282–301; 49, 4: 424–38.

11. David Robinson, "'Umar ibn Sa'id Tal," in *New Encyclopedia of Africa*, ed. John Middleton and Joseph C. Miller (New York: Scribner: 2008), 5: 127–28.

12. Robinson, *La Guerre sainte*, 203.

13. Robinson, *La Guerre sainte*, 226.

14. Bathily, "Guerriers, Tributaires, et Marchands," 2: 628.

15. Bathily, "Guerriers, Tributaires, et Marchands," 2: 628; Y. Saint Martin, *L'Empire toucouleur* (Paris: Karthala, 1975), 61; Robinson, *La Guerre sainte*, 341.

16. Bathily, "Guerriers, Tributaires et Marchands," 2: 635–36.

17. ANS, 15G 6bis, Président de la Chambre du Commerce au Directeur de l'Intérieur, Saint-Louis, 11 December 1885.

18. Souleymane Diop, "La Biographie," 3.

19. The three petitions discussed in this paragraph are also found in the ANS, 15G 6bis: "Pétition à M. Léon d'Erneville des traitants de Médine et Bakel," 27 September 1885; ANS, "Pétition des traitants du Haut Fleuve adressée au Gouverneur du Sénégal et Dépendances, Saint-Louis," 26 December 1892; ANS, "Réclamation des traitants de Médine," 10 August 1886.

20. Moussa I. A. Diop, *Les Lumières d'une cité*, 104.

21. See Moussa I. A. Diop. *Les Lumières d'une cité*, 91, 259, for a genealogical diagram. In the text, a genealogical reference cites the mother's given name (Fabineta), Gaura Fabineta, illustrating the matrilineal character of Wolof. The genealogical diagram makes reference to the father's name (Demba), Gaura Demba, illustrating the patrilineal character of name-giving among Muslims. This oscillation, perceptible throughout the text, reflects the diversity of oral sources and periods. In

Saint-Louis, it would seem that the practice of choosing a first name along with the mother's name gave way to a formulation that added the father's first name, probably at the end of the nineteenth century.

22. Souleymane Diop, "La Biographie," 1. S. Diop is precise about the year of birth. In contrast, Moussa I. A. Diop is content to suggest "about 1840" (*Les Lumières d'une cité*, 89).

23. Moussa I. A. Diop, *Les Lumières d'une cité*, 90.

24. On Saad Buh, see Robinson, *Paths of Accommodation*, 178–93.

25. On Siddiyya Baba, see Robinson, *Paths of Accommodation*, chapter 9.

26. ANS, 2B 1820, September 1840.

27. Marc D. Marcson, "European-African Interactions in the Precolonial Period Saint-Louis du Sénégal," PhD diss., Princeton University, 1976, 30 and throughout.

28. According to Moussa I. A. Diop, in *Les Lumières d'une cité*, 90–91:

The first Catholic missionaries chose, as soon as they arrived in Senegal, to locate their first parish in the southern part of the island. Métis such as Devès, Carpot, Crespin, D'Erneville and the signares, although Christianized and living in a community between the square where the church was located and rue Repentigny (a zone called "keur-thiane," or, "thiane's neighborhood," a deformation of the French word "chrétien"), retained close ties with the dignitaries and Muslims of the southern quarter.

29. David Robinson, *The Holy War of Umar Tall: The Western Sudan in the Mid-Nineteenth Century* (Oxford, UK: Clarendon Press, 1985).

30. Souleymane Diop, "La Biographie," 1–2. For example, the marabouts Sheikh Saad Buh, Sheikh Siddiyya al-Kébir, and his grandson, Sheikh Siddiyya Baba.

31. Moussa I. A. Diop, *Les Lumières d'une cité*, 94.

32. Moussa I. A. Diop, *Les Lumières d'une cité*, 94.

33. A careful reading of the sources leads us to conclude that Hamet Diop must have come to Rosso in 1877 or 1878; he definitely left in 1882. For all three quotations in this paragraph, see Moussa I. A. Diop, *Les Lumières d'une cité*, 98.

34. David Robinson, "Brokerage and Hegemony in Senegal," unpublished paper, 1995, 13–16.

35. Souleymane Diop, "La Biographie," 3.

36. This orientation explains the interest of the doomu ndaar in the leaders of holy war and others who resisted the colonial advance in this part of West Africa, such as Ahmadu Seku, Samory Touré, and Mamadou Lamin Dramé, whom Hamet Diop assisted directly and indirectly.

37. Moussa I. A. Diop, *Les Lumières d'une cité*, 128–29. The information in the remainder of this paragraph also comes from Diop (125, 128, 137).

38. The signares were African or métis women who lived as concubines of and did business with European settlers, or whose forebears had engaged in commerce along the Atlantic coast since the Portuguese era. Their business, personal, and sexual relations gave rise to the métis community. They adopted the customs and lifestyles of their European partners, including Christianity. See George Brooks, "The Signares of Saint-Louis and Gorée: Women Entrepreneurs in Eighteenth-Century Senegal,"

in *Women in Africa: Studies in Social and Economic Change*, ed. Nancy J. Hafkin and Edna G. Bay (Stanford, Calif.: Stanford University Press, 1976), 14–44; George E. Brooks, *Eurafricans in Western Africa: Commerce, Social Status, Gender, and Religious Observance from the Sixteenth to the Eighteenth Century* (Athens: Ohio University Press; Oxford, UK: James Currey, 2003).

39. Moussa I. A. Diop, *Les Lumières d'une cité*, 137, 138.

40. Moussa I. A. Diop, *Les Lumières d'une cité*, 140.

41. Diouf, "The French Colonial Policy of Assimilation and the Civility of the Originaires."

42. For a broader reexamination of the multiple paths of Islam in Senegal, see M. Diouf and M. A. Leichtman, eds., *New Perspectives on Islam in Senegal: Conversion, Migration, Wealth, Power, and Femininity* (New York: Palgrave Macmillan, 2009).

43. On this question, see David Robinson, *Muslim Societies in African History* (Cambridge, UK: Cambridge University Press, 2004), 27; Paul Marty, *Etudes sur l'Islam au Sénégal*, 2 vols. (Paris: Leroux, 1917), 2; Vincent Monteil, *Islam Noir* (Paris: Seuil, 1964).

44. Moussa I. A. Diop, *Les Lumières d'une cité*.

~

CHAPTER FIVE

Samuel Johnson (1846–1901) and The History of the Yorubas

Christianity and a New Intelligentsia in West Africa

Toyin Falola

For a quarter century, Reverend Samuel Johnson was a missionary pastor, a native agent of the Church Missionary Society (CMS) in what is now known as Western Nigeria. Not only was he one of the first Yoruba—a major ethnic group in today's Nigeria—to publish a book, but his The History of the Yorubas from the Earliest Times to the Beginning of the British Protectorate *remains the most successful amateur history in West Africa. Johnson completed the manuscript in the 1880s, but he did not live to see it in print or to know that it would become one of the most-cited works on African history. Johnson's book is the foundational reading for most scholarly historical and anthropological work on the Yoruba.*

Johnson's life illustrates three major themes. First, his life parallels the establishment of Christianity in West Africa and shows how Africans became agents of their own conversion. Samuel Johnson's parents were liberated Yoruba slaves who lived in Sierra Leone and later returned to their Yoruba homeland in Western Nigeria, where they contributed to the spread of Christianity. Second, Reverend Johnson's life experience sheds light on the rise of a new Western-educated elite in Africa in the late nineteenth century. His book explores the consequences of the spread of Western education: the spread of literacy; the ability to use education to earn wages, and beyond that, to make a good living and attain social mobility; and the generation of a nationalist consciousness from a body of new ideas and experience.

Having benefited from the introduction of Western education, Samuel Johnson advocated for and devoted his energies to the expansion of educational opportunities for others throughout his life.

The third theme relates to new ideas of progress that grew out of the coming of Christianity and Western education. A new generation of Africans began to think about the future of the continent by drawing on ideas from beyond its shores. What was the meaning of civilization? Would Africa adopt Western ways of life or promote African traditions? Was culture important to development? Should Africans adopt Christianity or Islam? None of these new questions were easy to answer. Johnson provided us with one set of answers: that his people could unite, accept the new religion of Christianity, and receive and adapt new ideas from abroad to transform themselves.

To be sure, European traders, missionaries, military figures, administrators, and others challenged African societies in the early modern period. However, the life and work of Samuel Johnson and other Africans like him raise important questions about precisely how change occurred and how those within African societies interpreted and channeled new influences from outside. The story of how Johnson conceived and wrote The History of the Yorubas *shows that soon after Europeans established a foothold in the interior of Africa, Africans set out to seize the initiative and reinterpret European influences in ways that responded to both time-honored features of African societies and emerging new African identities.*

A Missionary Life

Samuel Johnson was a descendant of the powerful Yoruba king Alaafin Abiodun, who was very famous in the latter part of the eighteenth century. King Abiodun presided over the Oyo empire, creating a unity and prosperity that impressed Johnson when he later documented this era. Samuel's father, Henry Johnson, was Abiodun's grandson. "Henry" and "Johnson" were new English names acquired through the experience of slavery. In the last phase of the trans-Atlantic slave trade, dating from the last quarter of the eighteenth century, the Yoruba were increasingly drawn into the notorious commerce. Henry Johnson was captured in Yorubaland and sold into slavery around 1820, sometime after the slave trade had been outlawed in the Atlantic Ocean north of the equator. Luckily for him, he was later liberated and resettled in a farming village in Sierra Leone—probably the town of Regent. The Reverend William Augustine Bernard Johnson, who gave his own last name to many ex-slaves, presided over the town. At this time, many liberated slaves were settled in Sierra Leone and Liberia.

Henry Johnson lived as a farmer and devoted Christian, becoming a leading member of the Church Missionary Society (CMS) in the town of Hastings, a village in the hinterland of Freetown, the largest settlement in Sierra Leone. His education was limited to the ability to read and write, which supported his religious devotion. The CMS placed great hope in Henry; he was expected to help in converting other Africans to Christianity and in bringing "civilization," or Western culture. In European eyes, Christianity and Western civilization were allies in a project to launch a generation of new Christians who could also become entrepreneurs—combining the Bible with the plow to earn their living as members of a new middle class. Henry was sent to Kew Gardens near London to learn new farming techniques and crops, with the aim of changing agriculture in West Africa. In fact, he did not succeed as a revolutionary farmer, leading the CMS to focus instead on his ability to advance the gospel. But the idea of combining Christianity with commerce spread in West Africa and was inculcated in men such as Henry's son Samuel Johnson, who worked with this paradigm in mind.

Henry returned to his native Yorubaland in June 1846 with four of his children, including Samuel, the third son, born in Sierra Leone. At that time, no one could have predicted that Samuel would later be active as a peacemaker and diplomat. Henry's arrival coincided with a long period of wars among the Yoruba that did not end until 1893. In December 1857, he was named a Christian visitor—a position described by historian Ade Ajayi as "something between a lay reader and a catechist."[1] Posted to Ibadan, a Yoruba city in today's Nigeria, Henry assisted the Reverend David Hinderer, the pioneer missionary in the settlement. His children benefited from his association with the church, in terms of both religion and the Western education that came with it. Hinderer was proud of Henry, describing him in 1858 as "a sterling man, so straightforward . . . , a man well acquainted with his Bible, loving and referencing it: and he quotes it so readily and appropriately."[2] Henry worked actively in the CMS mission at Ibadan, dying eight years later, in February 1865. His obituary described him as a "sincere Christian," who lived a faithful life and had a "happy death."[3]

Hinderer and the CMS also took an interest in the career of Henry's children. The eldest, named after his father, Henry, was sponsored to the CMS Training School in Islington, London, and then sent to the University of Beirut to learn Arabic. He became an archdeacon of the Niger mission. Nathaniel, the second son, became a teacher and a pastor in Lagos. The fourth and youngest son Obadiah became a medical doctor and a prominent member of the elite in Lagos.

Samuel, the third son, was the most influenced by Hinderer and the CMS. He was born at Hastings, Sierra Leone, on June 24, 1846, about when his father became a committed Christian. He moved to Ibadan with his father at the age of eleven and was designated for missionary life from the beginning. Samuel was sent to Anna Hinderer's school, the first missionary school in the town, where he became close to Anna and her husband. The Hinderers were great believers in liberal education and the art of writing. Having advanced from craftsman to missionary himself, Hinderer viewed his own transformation through education and Christianity as an avenue for Africans to pursue as well. He deeply believed that the success and personality of people like Samuel depended fundamentally on the quality of their education. Samuel became a part of the small band of pioneer Christians in Ibadan, where he, like his mentor Hinderer, took an interest in Yoruba history and culture. Johnson indeed later dedicated his book to "the revered memory of the Reverend David Hinderer, . . . who has left an imperishable name, and record of labor hitherto unsurpassed in this country."[4]

When his father died, Samuel Johnson was at the CMS Training Institution in Abeokuta, which he attended from 1863 to 1865. The principal of the school was Reverend Gotlieb F. Bühler, another German missionary, whose educational philosophy resembled that of the Hinderers. Between 1857 and 1864, Bühler used his position to privilege the teaching of English, religious knowledge, Latin, Greek, general education, and mathematics, subjects in which Samuel excelled. Some of Bühler's colleagues accused him of not paying sufficient attention to missionary instruction, thereby encouraging a so-called superior education that made the students less oriented toward full-scale religious activities. But Bühler's orientation encouraged Samuel to broaden his mind and develop interests in writing and history.

When he graduated in 1865 at the age of twenty, Samuel qualified as a schoolteacher and was posted to a school at Aremo in Ibadan, where Hinderer served as his supervisor. Many jobs were available for the few Africans who had a Western education, and they exercised increasing responsibilities. For example, Hinderer retired in 1869, leaving his two critical missions of education and evangelization to his former students. One of them was Daniel Olubi, the first Yoruba to be trained locally after converting to Christianity. When Olubi became a deacon in 1867, Samuel became one of his assistants. Samuel went on church business to a number of towns to preach, encourage the small bands of Christians, and contribute to the building of chapels. He became catechist of the Aremo church in 1875. Affiliation with the schools and the church allowed Samuel to interact with young and old, Christians and non-Christians. Not only did he teach; he also preached and performed catechetical duties, which led him to confront "paganism" and Islam.

Working in the community and no longer under the watchful eyes of the Hinderers and other European missionaries, Johnson and his African colleagues became interested in local politics. Not only had his teacher left, but the movements of Europeans were curtailed in many parts of Yorubaland during the 1870s. The critical mass of the new elite lived in Lagos. This new autonomy allowed members of the local clergy like Samuel the space to develop more self-confidence. Moreover, they were also free to interact with non-Christians. Hence Johnson came to know the chiefs, including the Are Latosa, the leader of Ibadan in the 1870s and 1880s. The churches now prayed for the Yoruba chiefs and kings, worked toward ending the wars, and even attended public functions sponsored by the chiefs. In his journal, Samuel began to record the activities of kings and chiefs, their politics, and the movements of troops in the wars.

In particular, Johnson witnessed the unfolding of the Sixteen Years' War, which began in 1877 with a disagreement between Ibadan, where he lived, and the Egba at Abeokuta. Johnson became our most reliable eyewitness of a war that consumed the Yoruba. The conflict revived old political rivalries and alliances, and Ibadan lay at its heart. The Egba and Ijebu to the south wanted to maintain control of trade and keep Ibadan weak, whereas groups to the east like the Ijesa and Ekiti wanted to free themselves of Ibadan's imperial domination. Johnson collected rich accounts of the causes of this long war and recorded its complicated battles and peace negotiations. Johnson began to act like a trained scholar, visiting knowledgeable people to obtain valuable information. His Western education was now very useful to his people, as he had the skills to record in writing instead of relying on memory to preserve what he was told and what he observed.

By the 1880s he had become an influential Christian leader and was deeply involved in the search for peace, for he felt it destructive for one Yoruba group to attack another. As Johnson made clear in his book, he served as the liaison between the British and the chiefs of Ibadan and Oyo. In this role, he advised the chiefs of Ibadan, even helping them compose letters explaining their side of the story. The leaders of Ibadan and Oyo also eagerly fashioned a role for the missionaries in the war—assigning to them the duty of obtaining the scarce items of ammunition and salt from Lagos. Pointing out to the missionaries that the educated Ekiti and Ijesa men in Lagos bought supplies for their people in the hinterland, the leaders of Ibadan and Oyo prevailed upon Johnson and others to do the same for Ibadan. In addition, the chiefs sought the advice of the Yoruba missionaries in 1881 on how to seek the intervention of the British in Lagos to end the war. Johnson became a political intermediary. Missionaries like Johnson almost succeeded in brokering peace in 1886, when the major actors all declared a truce. The deal collapsed over difficulties in determining how to break up the war camps and return home. Each side feared that it could be attacked when it was not battle ready. In the end, then, the missionaries lacked the force to guarantee peace.

Samuel Johnson's career reached another high point in 1875 when he became a deacon. First posted to Ondo, he was then transferred to Oyo, where he became a pastor in 1887 and a full priest a year later. His influence in Oyo and his knowledge of Yoruba history grew during his residence at Oyo, which was the seat of the *alaafin* or ruler. Johnson's contacts with the *arokin* or court historians, his relations, chiefs, and other knowledgeable people deepened to the point that he was able to collect oral traditions. His intellectual abilities and his interest in Yoruba history peaked in Oyo. The alaafin and many senior chiefs trusted him, and he enjoyed respect in the community. He used his contacts to advantage, learning and recording a great deal about the military organization and politics of the Oyo empire. Oyo came to influence him so much that he put its history at the center of all Yoruba history, and its alaafin as the political head of all the Yoruba. Reflecting on the damage caused by the Yoruba wars, Johnson hoped that they would unite once again under the alaafin. So fond was he of Oyo that he fought not to be transferred out of the town in 1893, when he was deeply engaged in writing his book.

Johnson also continued to serve as a diplomat, and in that capacity he also put his knowledge of local politics to good use. Between 1893 and 1895, he mediated conflicts between the British and Oyo. He played a major role in finally bringing the Yoruba wars of the nineteenth century to an end. In negotiations, he did not adopt an aggressive posture, preferring instead to plead and to convey messages of peace sent by others. He was not part of the influential Lagos elite who occupied the limelight reported in the pioneer newspapers. After a prolonged illness he died on April 29, 1901, leaving behind a wife, five daughters, and his enduring book. An obituary in the *Lagos Weekly Record* summarized his life in a few words: "He was distinguished for his devotion to duty, well-known for his liberality and open heartedness and for urbanity, self-abnegation and patriotism."[5]

Johnson himself did not tell us much about his life, family, and career in his book and missionary reports. He chose to tell us about his people's history. It is for this great intellectual achievement, rather than for his career and life, that Johnson will be forever remembered.

Johnson's Book, *The History of the Yorubas*

Completed in 1897 but not published until 1921, Samuel Johnson's *The History of the Yorubas* remains the most frequently cited and the most influential volume about the Yoruba-speaking people. His seven-hundred-page *magnum opus* is the starting point in discussion of the precolonial history of the Yoruba of West Africa and the diaspora. More than a dozen local chronicles have been written to refute aspects of the book, while primary school primers of the 1930s and 1940s and a host of other small books simply paraphrase it. In many respects, most academic works published on the Yoruba since the 1950s have merely elaborated on Johnson's themes. Now a standard text, it is regarded as a bible by many knowledgeable people and traditional historians, who sometimes even disparage wisdom from other sources. Even when scholars have turned to other sources to question Johnson or correct such things as his chronology, local audiences usually ignore the revisions and reasoned suggestions. The book is held as an article of faith by many of its readers. The venerable Samuel Johnson is always right!

That the book even exists in print today was a stroke of luck. After laboring twenty years to compose a manuscript about one thousand foolscap pages long, Johnson mailed it to the CMS publishers in London. The response was unfavorable. They asked him to prune it and write it in Yoruba to meet the needs of the missionaries interested in education and general history. We do not know how Johnson responded to their suggestions. After his death, however, his younger brother, Obadiah, the medical doctor, had to "rewrite the whole history anew from the copious notes and rough copies left behind by the author."[6]

In terms of depth, breadth, and significance, *The History of the Yorubas* is beyond compare with any other book on the Yoruba. Divided into two parts, it successfully brings together a set of diverse issues and topics. The first part offers ethnographies on language, social organization, customs, and early history. Johnson links early Yoruba history with that of the Coptic Christians, a narrative that reveals his agenda as a missionary who believed in a past that linked the Yoruba to Christianity and a future when this lost history would be recovered. The second part, on Yoruba history, is far more extensive and is further subdivided into four parts. In the first, a "prehistory," Johnson offers a list of what he calls "mythological kings and deified heroes" of the Yoruba, which conjoins the two powerful kingdoms of Ile-Ife and Oyo. Although Johnson shows us how other Yoruba cities and kingdoms were connected with Ile-Ife, at the same time he places the history of Oyo at the center of his grand narrative. Hence, we read about Oyo's glorious rise to fame, reaching its apogee in the reign of Abiodun, who died in about 1789.

The tale of the collapse of the Oyo empire follows, with attention to how new states emerged and how Ibadan became successful. Johnson then turns to the years from the 1840s to the end of the century. In a section titled "Arrest of Disintegration. Intertribal Wars. British Protectorate," he offers more than three hundred pages of detailed narrative on the many wars of the period. Johnson did not regard these years as unmitigated disaster for two reasons. First, he regarded the rise of Ibadan as a positive development. He believed that the Ibadan were "destined by God to play a most important part in the history of the Yorubas, to break the Fulani yoke and save the rest of the country from foreign domination, in short to be a protector as well as a scourge in the land."[7] Second, the period laid the groundwork for the penetration and spread of Christianity, followed by the imposition of British rule.

Samuel Johnson's interest in Yoruba history developed early in his career, when he was a schoolteacher—perhaps even before he started work on his manuscript. In the 1870s, his journals and diaries show his concern for Yoruba history and culture. He noted such things as the worship and historicity of the thunder god Sango, the fall of Oyo, and the founding of Modakeke at Ile-Ife. Some of these themes are developed later in his history. He wrote very well—in excellent prose, with dramatic imagery and passion. He powerfully presented heroic characters such as warriors and kings and re-created dramatic episodes such as great battles and the fall of towns.

The Hinderers made a strong impression on Johnson. They probably interested him in the study of language and culture. Later association with Bühler exposed him to the history of Greek and Roman civilization. He was familiar with the Greek civil wars and includes allusions to them in his book. He also read the works of Caesar and Eutropius. Johnson attempted to link the great civilizations of Egypt and Greece with the history of the Yoruba.

The fact that Johnson lived in Ibadan and not Lagos was probably another important factor in his work. Because Europeans were prohibited from moving freely in the interior of Yorubaland, Samuel and other indigenous missionaries were free of excessive interference by the senior officers of the CMS and government officials in Lagos. Although he was a Christian and a missionary, Johnson's motives were patriotic: to understand the history of his country and its people. Together with many of his educated contemporaries, he shared a deep sense of history. Part of the cultural nationalism of the second half of the nineteenth century was the attempt to understand African history and the extent to which aspects of it were useful to contemporary society. Although Johnson did not carry his own nationalism too far, he nevertheless developed an awareness of integrating values and concepts from the indigenous past with Christianity and British rule. Among other factors, his family background, his association with the Hinderers, and his involvement in local politics served to deepen this historical consciousness. His patriotic concern to "rescue" Yoruba history probably led to some discrepancies in the book.

History as Traditions

Samuel Johnson was a jack-of-all-trades and master of many; his book is rich in all aspects of culture as well as history. To appreciate Johnson's book, we have to see it as a body of traditions told as history. To be able to assess his contribution to history, we should acknowledge his skill and endurance as a researcher, his ideological perspective, and his conception of history. The most impressive of these qualities were his skill and patience as a researcher. He was extremely dedicated in his search for evidence. His appetite for data was insatiable; he attempted to commit to writing all the major traditions that he gathered, despite his many other commitments. In addition, his literary gifts were unusual. He put to good use his liberal education and his active involvement in politics.

Not dissimilar from contemporary historians, Johnson acknowledged his sources. These included "bards" for the "ancient and mythological period," and eyewitnesses and participants for the most recent events. He even provided the names of some of his informants, such as David Kukomi, "the patriarch of the Ibadan Church"; Josiah Oni, "an intrepid trader of those days"; and the Timi of Ede, "so well known all over the country as a gifted and trusted historian of the Yoruba country."[8] He evaluated data and rejected those that he thought were offensive. He also rejected certain versions of some events. He read published works as well as the Lagos newspapers. This is not to imply that Johnson necessarily subjected all information to critical analysis. He knew the limitations of his sources, but he was not always able to resolve the contradictions in oral traditions. Conceptualizations of time and chronology that Johnson reports may also differ from those today, which are associated with Christian and Islamic reckoning. The Yoruba, like most other African groups, dated events in association with the reign of a king or other notable events such as a famine. Indeed, Johnson found it necessary to create a king list in order to give us a chronology; it is not always too clear, although very useful.

Johnson does offer us the opportunity to critique traditions. It is not always clear whether the traditions collected by Johnson were those in line with his motives, those doctored by informants, or those already reshaped by contacts with external influences such as Islam and Christianity. In interpreting some traditions, he imposed his own perspectives. As for chronology, he avoided assigning dates before the 1830s. Moreover, his king list of the Oyo empire is incomplete. Robin Law has suggested that the king list itself was Johnson's creation, although he cannot be accused of inventing any of the kings.[9]

Johnson also attempts to see Yoruba history from the point of view of the Oyo empire. His reconstruction of major events revolved around Oyo's origin, its rise, and its collapse. In some places his accounts telescope time; in others they stretch it out. For instance, his king list omits some names. His love for Abiodun, his own ancestor, whose career he praised in contrast to that of the "devil" Basorun Gaha, is one example of how he created an archetypal hero.

Many other scholars have addressed the impact of literacy on oral traditions, with the aim of showing that what is collected and recorded changes in character with the introduction of literacy.[10] Even the idea of writing about Yoruba history is an elite project, for which Johnson mobilized the power of education and literacy. The task fell on Johnson, who, because he reduced oral traditions to writing, was impelled to expose and test the contradictions in them. He also then had to live with the tendency to succumb to pressure to eliminate contradictions, and he also felt the need to relate "the history of the Yoruba communities to the history of the wider world."[11] These two concerns did not bother traditional oral historians, but they did preoccupy literate ones. All in all, then, the process of seeking out traditions, subjecting them to analysis, writing them down, and asking "unfamiliar sorts of questions" of them tends to change their character.

The Politics and Ideology of Scholarship

Johnson's book reflects several influences. In the first place, his Christian orientation runs through the book. For him, the coming of Christianity to the Yoruba was one of the great developments in the nineteenth century. Commenting on the beginning of the missionary enterprise in Abeokuta, he expressed jubilation: "Light began to dawn on the Yoruba country from the south, when there was nothing but darkness, idolatry, superstition, blood shedding and slave hunting all over the rest of the country."[12] His greatest wish was to see Christianity triumph over all other religions. On occasion, this desire influenced his interpretations of events. For instance, he regarded the adoption of Christianity as the only cure for the descent of the Yoruba into war. The advent of the new faith would fulfill an age-old prophecy that "as ruin and desolation spread from the interior to the coast, so light and restoration will be from the coast interior-wards."[13] He linked this prophecy to his belief that the Yoruba were formerly "either Coptic Christians, or at any rate that they had some knowledge of Christianity."[14] The legends of origin that he recounts, perhaps narrated in an attempt to create an identity and political distinctiveness for the Yoruba, were also linked with Christianity. He rejected versions of the legend that linked the Yoruba with Mecca, which would imply connection with Islam. Rather he opted for a Christian telling of the myth that, while still postulating links with Arabia, claimed that "proto-Yoruba were expelled on account of their practicing their own form of worship, which was either paganism or more likely a corrupt form of Eastern Christianity (which allowed of image worship so distasteful to Moslems)."[15] For Johnson, the nineteenth century heralded the beginning of a glorious return to Christianity.

In the second place, he believed in the idea of progress. To him, the Yoruba stood on the verge of modernization with their new links with the British. Integral to modernization was imperialism. Johnson rejoiced that the British were able to attack the Ijebu in 1892, a move which he thought opened a "prison door." He justified the high-handedness of the British administrators as "not unexpected," in order to establish a new regime and deal with Ilorin, "the real disturbers of the peace in the country." He called for changes in culture—improved habits of dress, enhanced sanitation, reform of the marriage system, and the instigation of town planning. Disturbed by the terrible consequences of the wars on intergroup relations and respect for elders, Johnson also called for "modern" changes in these areas.

Despite his commitment to modernity, it should be emphasized that Johnson did not recommend a full-scale incorporation of Western values. Such advocacy would have been grossly incompatible with his cultural nationalism. He was proud of the Yoruba and their achievements. Indeed, one of his aims in writing his history was to record enduring Yoruba values. Underlying his thinking was the high status that he accorded to Yoruba culture, comparing it to the achievements of the English people:

> The Yoruba it has been noted—are not unlike the English in many of their traits and characteristics. It would appear that what the one is among the whites the other is among the blacks. Love of independence, a feeling of superiority over all others, a keen commercial spirit, and of indefatigable enterprise, that quality of being never able to admit or consent to a defeat as finally settling a question upon which their mind is bent, are some of those qualities peculiar to them, and no matter under what circumstances they are placed, Yorubas will display them.[16]

He counseled the Yoruba to retain their names, dress, and language. They should also reject influences that could promote social vices.

A third source of influence was cultural nationalism, illustrated by Johnson's call to Yorubas to keep their names, language, and dress. This characteristic of his work may best be understood in the context of changing attitudes to Europeans. Samuel Johnson was trained by Europeans, and he had a genuine love for the Hinderers. Many like him had adopted English names and sought to imitate European culture. Some among them even despised African traditions and cultures, believing that change would only come to their people through the assimilation of European ways of life.[17] However, in the 1890s, educated Africans began to rethink their relationships with Europeans. This new perspective grew out of the belief of many Africans that Europeans disliked them intensely. To restore their dignity and self-respect, many Yorubas began to promote their own culture and history.

Johnson was not influenced by this cultural renaissance to an extreme degree. He already believed that the Yoruba must promote their culture. He saw the coming of the British as divine intervention, in large part because he was fed up with the wars. He did not live long enough to see the consequences of British rule and died believing that Yoruba kings would maintain their power. Hence Johnson responded to the European images of Africa, not in the same vein as contemporaries such as Wilmot Blyden, but with greater subtlety. His background in British and Greek history inspired Victorian or biblical phrases such as "When Greek meets Greek" and "Famine and the sword."

A fourth guiding influence grew out of Johnson's belief that the best way to present his epic account was to accept the arokins' framework for portraying the history of Oyo empire. These emphases led Johnson to equate Oyo history with Yoruba history. The alaafin played the leading role in this interpretation. Johnson tells more stories of successful kings and fewer stories about the early historical period. He pays more attention to recent events. While he admitted ignorance of the history of the other groups, he was, nonetheless, unapologetic about his approach: "The early history of the Yoruba country is almost exclusively that of the Yoruba Oyo division, the others being then too small and too insignificant to be of any import."[18]

When his history reached the fall of Oyo, Johnson shifted his focus to Ibadan, its most influential successor state. His admiration for Ibadan was boundless: "The history of the Yorubas centered largely at Ibadan. . . . While the rest of the country was quiet Ibadan was making history." Though he did not like wars, Johnson saw the hand of divine providence in the crisis: God wanted to use the military state of Ibadan to "play a most important part in the history of the Yorubas, to break the Fulani yoke and save the rest of the country from foreign domination."[19] Despite this support for Ibadan, Johnson voiced occasional disapproval of the excesses of Ibadan warriors.

Finally, Johnson believed in the unity of all the Yoruba groups, led by Oyo. In some cases, the evidence is clear that the traditions he recorded and the interpretations he imposed on them were meant to achieve this agenda. His anti-Fulani accounts of Egba and Ijebu probably derived from his desire to enhance the status of Oyo. He was obviously disappointed by the collapse of the Oyo empire, brought about in part by an intense internal power struggle and by an attack by the Ilorin army. He also thought that policies adopted by the Egba and Ijebu were partly responsible for the delay in ending the wars.

Johnson's concern for Yoruba unity has to be interpreted in the context of nineteenth-century nationalism and attempts by the elite to create or identify with a pan-Yoruba identity. Johnson was well qualified to promote such national sentiment. He was born in Sierra Leone, where a vigorous sense of Yoruba identity had developed. The migration to Nigeria thrust him into the geography that had given rise to this broader identity. Members of the new Yoruba elite of the nineteenth century were educated and westernized. For the "scholars" among them, it was appropriate to use traditions and history as tools to construct a Yoruba cultural identity and, if possible, a political one as well. To some extent these initiatives grew out of the legacies of the past, such as the concern by some traditional elites, like the Ibikunle of Ibadan, for a united Yorubaland. But efforts to build a broader identity also stemmed from attempts to deal with problems of the day such as warfare, British incursion, and racism. Like some of his contemporaries, Johnson defined the Yoruba country as a collection of tribes that traced their origin to one source and ancestor. Along with this common descent came a common culture. To be sure, Johnson pointed out differences among the tribes and the divisive impact of the wars of the nineteenth century, but he also beckoned to the eighteenth century when the whole country was politically united. He urged all the tribes to come together once again: "[That] the disjointed units should all be once more welded into one under one head from the Niger to the coast as in the happy days of Abiodun, so dear to our fathers, that clannish spirit should disappear . . . should be the wish and prayer of every true son of Yoruba."[20]

Conclusion: Intellectual Accomplishments

Johnson's *The History of the Yorubas* remains as useful today as it was a century ago. It should be seen as the clearest and most elaborate elucidation of the idea of a Yoruba nation. He captured the essence of his age and used his data to reveal the contradictions of peace and war, "darkness" and "civilization," "paganism" and Christianity. In telling us about these contradictions, he wanted us to understand the Yoruba as an important people who would create a powerful nation in a future full of new possibilities.

Johnson's book has also made it possible for scholars to write about the Yoruba and address research methodologies. Both his life and book have been subjected to a series of critical analyses. A host of scholars has pursued many themes that Johnson suggested, such as the warfare of the nineteenth century.[21] Scholars have also benefited from hindsight and academic training, and they have drawn on wisdom from other sources and disciplines to evaluate his many assertions and clarify some of his confusing points, thereby providing an appropriate framework for understanding both the author and his scholarship.

Johnson's life and book, then, tell us about the nature of early Yoruba intellectual life. Western education and Christianity contributed to the spread of literacy in the Roman script. Samuel Johnson, like others in this new generation of educated people, acquired an English education. Beginning in Sierra Leone where they lived, members of this new generation began to reduce the Yoruba language to writing and to write in English. When people like Henry Johnson returned home to Nigeria, they worked for the Christian missions to establish schools, which in turn led to the spread of literacy among the Yoruba. Literacy turned out to be the tool the Yoruba had been waiting for. Pioneer writers emerged, men such as Samuel Crowther (c. 1806–1891), who wrote the first book on the Yoruba language. Interest in Yoruba history and culture began to develop, giving rise to a variety of historical accounts about Lagos, Abeokuta, and other parts of Yoruba country. The oral traditions collected by Samuel Johnson during the nineteenth century have been put to extensive and careful use by scholars who write about West African history. Johnson's accounts enjoyed wide readership, and they have become a foundation for scholars undertaking new research.

Second, authors such as Samuel Johnson were strongly motivated by cultural nationalism. They clearly wanted to use, and wanted others to use, their writings to empower themselves. Johnson's motivation on this matter was unequivocal: "Educated natives of Yoruba are well acquainted with the history of England and with that of Rome and Greece, but of the history of their own country they know nothing! This reproach it is one of the author's objects to remove."[22] Others emulated his passion. Yoruba history and culture became part of the school curriculum. Johnson worried that if he did not write, the history of his people would be lost forever.

Finally, Johnson believed that his book had practical applications. We have already noted its impact on cultural preservation. We have underscored his interest in promoting thinking about progress. In that sense, Johnson and his contemporaries contributed to the invention of nations and ethnicities. Johnson wanted his historical research to assist in healing the "tribal feeling and petty jealousies now rife among us."[23] To this extent, he constructed the history of a common origin for the Yoruba and imposed a unified political model on its many groups. Johnson and his peers reflected on the Yoruba past to create a new nation. The idea of progress—modernization through education, formal economy, formal politics, and Christianity—came to be summed up in a single word, *olaju*, which the members of the political class turned into an ideology for mobilizing millions of people to follow them. So it was that by the time the Yoruba entered the twentieth century, a successful campaign had been launched that transformed them into the megapolitical unit that has played a dominant economic and political role in modern Nigeria.

Further Reading

For the place of Johnson's book in West African studies, see Toyin Falola, ed., *Yoruba Historiography* (Madison: University of Wisconsin, African Studies Program, 1991). See also the following book, dedicated to Johnson: Toyin Falola, ed., *Pioneer, Patriot, and Patriarch: Samuel Johnson and the Yoruba People* (Madison: University of Wisconsin, African Studies Program, 1993). For accounts of his life, see Michel R. Doortmont, "Recapturing the Past: Samuel Johnson and the Construction of the History of the Yoruba," PhD diss., Erasmus Universiteit, Rotterdam, 1994. On the beginning of missionary work among the Yoruba, see J. F. Ade Ajayi, *The Christian Missions in Nigeria, 1841–91: The Making of an Educated Elite* (London: Longman, 1965), and E. A. Ayandele, *The Missionary Impact on Modern Nigeria, 1842–1914* (London: Longman, 1966). Michael J. C. Echeruo's *Victorian Lagos: Aspects of Nineteenth-Century Lagos Life* (London: Macmillan, 1977) traces the creation of the pioneer elite and their lifestyles. Their movements from Sierra Leone to Nigeria are captured in J. H. Kopytoff, *Preface to Modern Nigeria: The "Sierra Leonians" in Yoruba, 1830–1890* (Madison: University of Wisconsin Press, 1965). Achievements of the Yoruba educated elite included the creation of a standard Yoruba orthography and the translation of the English Bible into Yoruba, as well as literary and historical studies. On their achievements, see J. F. Ade Ajayi, "How Yoruba Was Reduced to Writing," *Odu: A Journal of Yoruba Studies* 8 (1960): 49–58. For the reflections of Samuel Johnson and his generation on the future of Africa, see Toyin Falola, ed., *Nationalism and African Intellectuals* (Rochester, N.Y.: University of Rochester Press, 2001).

Notes

1. J. F. Ade Ajayi, "Samuel Johnson: Historian of the Yoruba," in *Pioneer, Patriot, and Patriarch: Samuel Johnson and the Yoruba People*, ed. Toyin Falola (Madison: University of Wisconsin, African Studies Program, 1993), 28.

2. R. B. Hone, *Seventeen Years in the Yoruba Country: Memorials of Anna Hinderer . . . Gathered from Her Letters and Journals* (London, 1872), 172.

3. Church Missionary Society Archives, CA2/049, Hinderer to Venn, 30 March 1865.

4. Samuel Johnson, *The History of the Yorubas from the Earliest Times to the Beginning of the British Protectorate* (Lagos: Church Missionary Society, 1921).

5. 4 May 1901.

6. Johnson, *The History*, ix.

7. Johnson, *The History*, 246.

8. Johnson, *The History*, vii.

9. Robin Law, "How Truly Traditional Is Our Traditional History? The Case of Samuel Johnson and the Recording of Yoruba Oral Tradition," *History in Africa* 11 (1984): 195–211.

10. See, for instance, Jack Goody, ed., *Literacy in Traditional Societies* (Cambridge, UK: Cambridge University Press, 1968).

11. Law, "How Truly Traditional Is Our Traditional History?"

12. Johnson, *The History*, 45.

13. Johnson, *The History*, 296.

14. Johnson, *The History*, 7.

15. Johnson, *The History*, 6–7.

16. Johnson, *The History*, xxi–xxii.

17. Michael J. C. Echeruo, *Victorian Lagos: Aspects of Nineteenth-Century Lagos Life* (London: Macmillan, 1977).

18. Johnson, *The History*, xxii.

19. Johnson, *The History*, 247.

20. Johnson, *The History*, 642.

21. See, for instance, S. A. Akintoye, *Revolution and Power Politics in Yorubaland, 1849–1893* (London: Longman, 1971).

22. Johnson, *The History*, Author's Preface.

23. Johnson, *The History*, Author's Preface.

CHAPTER SIX

~

Stories of Cape Slavery
and Emancipation in the
Nineteenth Century

Pamela Scully

*The Cape Colony, South Africa, was the earliest colony of European settlement
south of the Sahara. In 1652, the Dutch East India Company (abbreviated as
VOC in Dutch) founded a settlement on the site of today's Cape Town, whose
purpose was to resupply Dutch ships making their way between Europe and the
Dutch East Indies with water, meat, and other foodstuffs. Pastoralist and hunter-
gatherer communities lived in the region. In general, the Khoekhoe made their
living by herding and the San were hunters and gatherers, although individuals and
groups probably moved back and forth across this divide—thus the term Khoesan.
Once settled, the Dutch traded with the Khoesan for cattle, for themselves and for
the passing VOC ships. As the settlement grew, they also devised various coercive
strategies to make the Khoesan work for them on their farms.*

*The Dutch never succeeded in making sufficient numbers of local people work
for them. From the earliest years, they had to contend with a shortage of labor.
The number of settlers was limited by the VOC, which did not want to establish a
permanent colony, and the Khoesan increasingly resisted working for Europeans.
The VOC had a policy of not enslaving people indigenous to an area, so as a result
the company and the settlers very early turned to importing slaves from the Dutch
East Indies and, in later years, from elsewhere on the African continent. They also
devised ways of indenturing the Khoekhoe and the San to their service. Hence, the*

theme of unfree labor is central to the history of South Africa, including the Cape Colony: how to find people to provide it; how to control them; how, in the nineteenth century, to transform former slaves and indentured servants into docile wage workers—and finally, how Africans dealt with all of these schemes.

Pamela Scully introduces us to a handful of people who lived through the last years of slavery in Cape Colony in the 1820s and 1830s, through a transitional "apprenticeship" in the middle 1830s, and into the promised era of freedom. Her stories of these women, men, and children are vivid, describing how they set out first to find family members, and then how they worked to fashion what they hoped would be new lives in freedom. These tales display courage and tenacity. Slaves went so far as to lodge formal protests with government officials to free family members from indentured labor contracts that had been foisted upon them. Mothers, daughters, sisters, and grandmothers were as adamant in their pursuit of their rights as their male relatives. Some stories ended happily. More often they were poignant, because slaves usually did not succeed in overturning the hegemony of landowners and colonial officials. Other times, we do not know how their tales turned out because they disappear from the historical record. The stories come to us incomplete—from the records of various courts and government offices as well as from newspaper accounts and the very occasional book. As a result, we catch glimpses and even sometimes get a longer look as women, children, and men navigated through what truly were the rapids separating slavery from freedom and tried to bring their loved ones along with them. Taken together, their experiences offer a larger understanding of what it meant to live through a time fraught with both promise and resignation.

Slave emancipation in the British Cape Colony finally came to pass in 1838. The Dutch East India Company, which ruled the Cape from 1652 through 1806, bar a few years at the end of the eighteenth century, instituted slavery in the late 1650s. The VOC had a policy of not formally enslaving indigenous people, owing to the probability that they would more easily run away because they were familiar with the terrain and the local societies. Over some 180 years of the institution, slaves at the Cape were thus drawn from the Dutch East Indies, the east and west coasts of Africa, and the islands off the coast in the Indian Ocean. By the early 1800s, the slave population of the Cape was reproducing itself. Research on the Muslim community of the Cape has grown in recent years, and it highlights the emergence of new, hybrid communities and identities. Ebrahim Rhoda, for example, has established that a free black Javanese Muslim community existed in Mosterts Bay (now the Strand) by 1822. They brought their own imam from Java.[1]

In 1834, slaves across the former slave colonies of the British West Indies and the Cape were emancipated under similar legislation that also put in place a new form of dependence on their masters: a transitional status known as apprenticeship, which led up to final abolition four years later. Both abolitionists and the British government envisioned that former slaveholders and former slaves required a period of transition that would give them time to learn to be good employers and employees, respectively, in a wage-based economy. The upshot of this policy was that the period of apprenticeship and the decade that followed brought great contestation over the meanings of freedom.

As I have argued elsewhere, ideas of freedom were deeply entangled with individuals' conceptions of gender identity and the relations between men and women.[2] Various actors in the struggle for emancipation in the Cape, as indeed in many other emancipation movements, construed the idea of freedom through understanding that it would bring different experiences for men and women.[3] As a result, the family became an important site where freed people created and tested the many meanings of emancipation and sought both to create new relationships between gender and labor and to draw on older notions of femininity and masculinity. The kinds of questions that participants struggled over in defining the meanings of emancipation included the following: Would former slaves, in fact, be entitled to refuse to engage in wage labor if they so chose? Might freed people have control over the labor and lives of their children, or would the post-emancipation world re-inscribe the power of former masters over their former adult and child slaves in new forms that nonetheless echoed the dynamics of inequality constructed under slavery?[4]

In the tumult of swirling conversations and contestations over the meanings of freedom, we come to learn something of the lives and worlds of freed people and their families at the Cape in the era of emancipation. Much of our historical knowledge of these topics derives from complaints by slaves to the "protector of slaves" (see below) in the 1820s and early 1830s. In response to growing abolitionist pressure in London, the government of the Cape Colony made its first moves toward the amelioration of conditions of slavery in 1823 by passing legislation that allowed Christian slaves to marry. However, these provisions rang particularly hollow since Cape slaveholders had historically denied slaves access to Christian teachings and baptism. Indeed, from 1825 to 1829 only six legal slave marriages occurred at the Cape. Thus, the legislation had little impact.

In the decade of the 1830s, however, the colonial government passed other Orders in Council which recognized common-law marriages, forbade the whipping of slave women, and generally tried to bring the Cape in line with values of the metropolitan British middle class that emphasized domestic order and morality. Faced with such resistance in the Cape and elsewhere, the Parliament passed the ordinance of February 2, 1830, formally establishing the office of the protector of slaves, who was supposed to look after slaves' rights. Ironically, the credibility of the office was severely compromised because the protector at the Cape himself owned slaves at that time. In addition, few slaves at the Cape who wanted to register their relationships as marriages formally in church were, in fact, able to do so. Their aversion derived partly from expenses associated with the custom that such *banns*, or registration decrees, be published in church, and partly because of masters' unease with the recognition that the new law accorded personal lives to slaves.

Beginning with the era of amelioration in the 1820s, slaves complained when they saw slaveholders violating rights newly conferred on slaves by law. Apart from slaves, indigenous people of the Cape (variously called Bastard Hottentots or Bastards or Hottentots, depending on their kinship with local Khoesan, slave, and settler groups) were also held in states of bondage. They too protested to magistrates and other local officials called field cornets about ill treatment in the years before and after the ending of slavery. During the period of apprenticeship, we also learn about the lives of apprentices from the records of the special magistrates, whose duties included adjudicating disputes between masters and apprentices. In addition, justices of the peace and local magistrates in the decade after 1838 handled many cases regarding the illegal indenture of apprentices' children. Freed people also wrote memorials to the governor petitioning for land and education for their families.

This chapter provides vignettes of some individuals who appear in the Cape archives or were the subjects of rare newspaper interviews. These truncated autobiographies are far from coherent, but they do offer glimpses into the personal lives of former slaves and bonded laborers. Many slaves' complaints against masters revolved around not only patterns of abuse but also broken promises of manumission. The law permitted slave women to appear in court to complain of abuse, and many took advantage of this opportunity to complain to the protector of slaves. But taking such initiatives was not without risk. Slaves could be fined at least £10 if the protector found them guilty of bogus complaints. For slaves in rural areas, lodging a complaint often entailed long walks—it could take days to reach the nearest magistrate's office or office of the justice of the peace.

Nonetheless, two thousand of the approximately thirty-five thousand men and women who were slaves at the Cape in this era lodged complaints with the protector of slaves.[5] As mentioned earlier, the Cape protector of slaves himself owned slaves and socialized with slaveholders, which made for a rather biased judicial context. So it is not surprising that only half of these two thousand complaints went to trial and that only one-sixth resulted in the conviction of masters. Nonetheless, these numbers demonstrate that slaves persisted in their assault on Cape slavery. Slave women availed themselves of the opportunity to describe their lives in detail. Both slave men and women especially used the legal avenues available to try to secure their right to see partners and children. Prior to the ending of slavery, slave women also went to court to claim their right to manumission. The records of these cases sometimes allow us to learn of slave women's experience of sexual abuse by masters.

Slave Women and Slaveholding Men

As in other slave societies, slave women were those most likely to be manumitted.[6] It was precisely through enduring or perhaps even fostering relationships with their masters and having children with them that many women were able to secure their freedom. This strategy of showing abuse and sexual relations with slave masters in order to gain manumission predated the era of amelioration and emancipation. One earlier case comes to us because of its long journey through the local and British courts. We also learn about it because George Greig, a leading Cape Town publisher, featured it in an 1827 pamphlet, *Papers Relating to the Manumission of Steyntje and Her Children.*[7]

In the late eighteenth century, a woman named Steyntje argued that she deserved freedom because she had had relationships with two of her masters. A resolution issued in 1772 by the Court of India had stipulated that upon the death of a master who fathered a child with a slave woman, the woman should be manumitted. But Cape law had ignored the statute. Three different courts took seven years to resolve Steyntje's case. Her first master, Stadler, had abused her as a teenager, and she had his child in 1799. Apparently, he had promised to manumit her in his will, but this did not come to pass. Indeed, when he died, Steyntje was sold to a man named Weeber, who apparently told her he that had bought her explicitly to make her his mistress. The couple lived together for three years and had a child. The settler community acknowledged the relationship, and Steyntje dressed in good clothes and acted as mistress of the household. However, Weeber got into financial trouble in 1803, and to pay off creditors, he sold Steyntje along with his other "assets." As a result, Steyntje found herself once again a domestic slave and much reduced in status, first in the household of a German named Dieleman, and then in the household of his widow and her second husband, Anderson, whom the widow married in 1813.

Two years later, Steyntje, with the encouragement of a group of abolitionists, decided to go to court to secure her freedom on the grounds that she had been the concubine of Stadler and Weeber and had had their children. The Court of Justice rejected her claim, but the governor, Lord Charles Somerset, as head of the Court of Appeals, granted her and her children their freedom in May 1819. Anderson appealed this decision all the way to London. After much to and fro, the King in Council finally agreed with Somerset, and Steyntje and her children became free.[8]

Another case dates from seven years later, in 1826, when Leentje, a slave woman owned by one Hendrik Greef, complained to the protector of slaves that her owner had registered their child, Sina, as his slave. Leentje argued that this contravened an agreement between her and Greef. According to the protector, two witnesses confirmed that Greef had used them to persuade Leentje to sleep with him on "a promise of freedom." A third witness verified that Leentje had often shared Greef's bedroom. The case resulted in the manumission of both Leentje and Sina.[9]

Despite slaveholder hostility to the formal marriage of slaves, some couples did marry legally. Their histories allow elusive insights into formal slave family life. Women who were defined as free black, indicating descent from slavery and freedom acquired through direct manumission or the manumission of ancestors, or women whom the law defined as the descendants of indigenous groups at the Cape, enjoyed greater opportunity to bring up their children themselves. Hence, slave men often took free local women defined as Bastard Hottentot or Hottentot as their partners, since children inherited the status of their mother and therefore in these cases would be free. Despite this official free status, these women and children often lived in conditions that rivaled slavery, because slaveholders completely dominated political and economic life in the Cape. The children were often indentured to farmers, a legal status that for all intents and purposes was the same as slavery. The only saving grace was that indentured children could not be as easily transferred from the farm of their parents as slaves could be.

An exemplary child indenture case occurred in 1830, when a slaveholder named Petrus Fredrik Rautenbach complained that he did not have control over the children of his slave Viet. Viet was married to a free woman called Flora Hartenberg, and the couple had two children, Louis, who was fourteen years old, and Valentyn, who was nine. Rautenbach complained that he had paid for the children's food and clothing when they were young, and he now wanted to indenture them to himself until they reached the age of eighteen. Slaveholders frequently argued that indenture was proper compensation for room and board as a way of gaining access to the labor of the children of slave men and free women. A procedure called the memorial system allowed individuals across the Cape, irrespective of race, gender, or creed, to petition the government if they felt that their legal rights had been infringed upon. Rautenbach wrote his memorial to the colonial office in Cape Town because he said that their mother had refused to agree to indenture her children to him, "yet can assign no justifiable reason, and, without her consent your Mem. was informed at the Office of the CC at George, it cannot be effected unless by Your Excellency's Authority."[10] Legal status as a free person thus enabled some mothers to ensure that their children remained free of the clutches of slaveholder power. But, again, this freedom was relative, since as the children grew into adulthood in the rural areas, virtually no employment was possible except for work on slaveholders' farms.

Another family's story is documented in the marriage register of the village of Paarl, wherein is recorded the marriage of Adonis Adam, age thirty-five, on April 24, 1831. He was a "baptised slave of Hermann Lambertus Bosman Snr," who lived and was registered under the name Adonis. He had married Rosia Magdalena Davidse, who had also been baptized. She was thirty-seven years old. The register noted that Rosia Davidse had seven children. It is not absolutely certain from the register whether Adonis Adam was the children's father, but such seems to be the case. The children were named Leona, Debora, Diana Christina, Johannes David, Filida Sebotier, Adam, and Rosina Dorothea.[11] Rosia Davidse appears to have been free black, as she is not identified as being of slave status. She might well have formerly been a slave who purchased her freedom. In any case, the fact that she had so many children and knew each of them certainly testifies to the strength of her family.

The example of Rosia's family may signal that slave families in the Cape in the early nineteenth century were in general quite cohesive. For example, a year or so earlier, on January 10, 1830, Johannes Cupido van Den Berg and Johanna Isabella van de Kaap, both of whose names signify slave descent at the Cape, went to church in Tygerberg, a farming region between Cape Town and Paarl. There they were married in front of the congregation and their five daughters, who ranged in age from fourteen to twenty-nine. The register does not identify the couple as being slaves, so we might well imagine that they, too, were members of the free black community who either had purchased their own freedom or were the children of former slaves.[12]

Katie Jacobs: Emancipation Day and Its Aftermath Recalled

The coming of Emancipation Day on December 1, 1838, clearly meant much to people and communities freed from slavery. It affected people who were formally enslaved, and it especially concerned those who, although technically free themselves, maintained relationships and friendships with slaves. Owners' resistance to recognizing their slaves' marriages created a complex context of monetary and emotional arrangements that inscribed personal relations within the discourse of commerce. As was the case in many slave systems in the Atlantic world, slaves in the Cape, and those in urban areas in particular, could rent out their labor. People who had been manumitted themselves sometimes bought other individuals. Sometimes they did this as a monetary investment in order to derive income from the sale of their slaves' labor. In other circumstances, freed people purchased slaves as a strategy to offer an individual de facto freedom even though she or he was still a slave de jure.

Katie Jacobs was one of the few slaves who had the chance to record her experience of Emancipation Day, and whose life is relatively well documented because of an interview published in a newspaper in 1910.[13] She was born in 1814 on a farm near Kalabaskraal in a rural area north of Cape Town and spent her youth in the waning days of slavery. She was the daughter of a man from Madagascar who had been enslaved and originally sold into the network that took slaves to East Africa. Her mother was "a Cape woman," presumably a woman born into slavery in the Cape. Many of Katie Jacobs's most painful memories relate to the way her family was decimated by casual agreements made by slave owners. For example, when her owner became too old to farm, he handed out his possessions and land to his sons. He gave Katie Jacobs and some cattle to one son, while her mother and some more cattle went to a different son, who left to live in Franschhoek. Katie vividly recalled her grief in the interview even in 1910, when she was some ninety-six years old: "From that day I never saw my mother again. I often longed to see her, but my *baas* [or master] always refused my request to visit her. I think he was afraid I would not return."

Katie Jacobs associated slavery with heartbreak and hard labor. She said that she had learned to work when she was very young. She worked both in the kitchen and in the fields herding cattle and doing agricultural labor. She labored to leave an imprint of her own values on her work. For example, she always wore men's clothes when she herded cattle, perhaps because they were more comfortable and practical for such chores. At the same time, she said in the interview that she tried to avoid strangers when she herded livestock, "for fear of being found thus oddly dressed, with a stumpy clay pipe in her mouth."

From the vantage point of her ninety-six years, Katie Jacobs recalled that her former owners had "looked after" her "well." She recalled slavery in paternalist terms, saying that she "became one of the family." It is unclear whether Katie Jacobs expressed her memories of slavery in these terms in part because of the public nature of the interview, whether nostalgia played a part, or whether she truly felt assimilated into the white family. In fact, Cape slavery could be very intimate. Owners and slaves often shared rooms and lived in very close quarters, which resulted in their knowing a great deal about one another. This intimacy also coexisted with great violence.[14]

Katie Jacobs's recollection of being a wet nurse to her owners' son illustrates how violence, degradation, and affection were all bound up together. Indeed, her memories speak to the violence and messiness of relations under slavery. She recalled that when she was a slave her "missus was not in good health, and I became a foster mother to her first-born son and heir. I was *made to* [my italics] sleep on the floor of the dining-room near the bedroom door to be on hand when the baby wanted another drink." As she grew older, Katie developed a relationship with another slave named Jacob Jacobs. This relationship was not a legal marriage because of all the barriers to slave marriage. Her husband worked on another farm, so Katie must have only seen him sporadically.

The advent of emancipation was clearly a fraught as well as a welcome experience. The final ending of slavery spoke as much to relationships lost and denied, as to ones that might be salvaged. Katie Jacobs talked about emancipation as an exhilarating moment shot through with great anxiety. According to her it came somewhat out of the blue: "One evening we slaves were ordered to appear in our best clothes the next morning. On the next day we were marched into the dining room, and without any previous warning we were told by a magistrate that in four years we would be free." Katie's father apparently did not respond with enthusiasm to this news, saying "that four years was a long time, and he did not think he would live that long. The magistrate said that he would communicate with Ounooi ['the older missus,' a term used to refer to Queen Victoria] and find out if a reduction of the term of apprenticeship could be granted." It was not. As it turned out, Katie Jacobs's father really was too old to wait four years. He died still in slavery. She said that he "did not live to enjoy the God-given freedom."

Slaves used their years of apprenticeship to start making plans. Katie reported that her husband used to visit her twice a week. They planned that he would work, and they would build their own home "where we could dwell together and be happy." Hopes that emancipation would bring a time when slaves would be able to reconstitute families and just be together were very widespread across the Cape. Indeed, for slaves, free labor involved very much a gendered reinterpretation of the meaning of labor, leading women sometimes to refuse wage labor with farmers because of new configurations in the private sphere. Apparently, Jacobs's owners were irritated "at the news of our liberation," but "were on the whole kind."

Four years later, on December 1, 1838, emancipation came on a day when heavy rains showered the Cape. That day, the former owner of Katie's husband Jacob Jacobs apparently became completely enraged and chased everybody off his farm. As a result, when Jacob arrived to collect Katie, he was already in a foul mood and wet to the bone. She recalled, "No wonder he spoke to me so harshly on that day of joy, humiliation, and prayer." Jacob was "determined to leave the district where he had suffered so much" but could not do so immediately. With few prospects and no money, Jacob and Katie stayed for some three years on the farm near Kalabaskraal. Her former owners seem to have done much to persuade the couple to stay on, offering them free room and board and some wages.

Later, though, Katie and Jacob Jacobs did move—to the village of Durbanville near Cape Town. There, like so many other former slaves, they were baptized and then married. Katie remembered, "The Reverend Back, who performed the ceremonies, was kept busy from morning to night, as there were hundreds of ex-slaves gathered together for the same purpose. I had often asked my master to allow me to be baptized, but he would never consent." For freed people in the rural areas in the immediate decade after emancipation, marriage was a significant marker of freedom. It also legitimated children, brought respectability in the eyes of the community, and, in general, denoted separation from the era of slavery. By the 1850s, however, the push to marry in churches and on mission stations waned. After working in different parts of the Cape, the Jacobs couple finally moved to District Six, the area in Cape Town where many former slaves moved and where they created a vibrant urban post-emancipation culture.

Emancipation and the Quest for Children

While Katie Jacobs did not talk of children, some records from the emancipation era allow exploration of this important dimension of Cape slavery. Many slaves knew their children, even if they had been sold and separated from them. In 1839, for example, a man named Moos returned to Stellenbosch to be reunited with his children. He had originally been a slave in Stellenbosch district, but he was later sold to an owner from Beaufort district, hundreds of miles in the interior. The fact that Moos knew where to find his children suggests that some form of communication existed across district lines. Perhaps slaves traveling with masters when taking cattle to grazing pastures served as messengers. Slaves sold into Beaufort from Stellenbosch might also have passed on news of the children. Moos saw freedom precisely as a means to bring his family together. Like many other freed parents, however, Moos discovered that former slaveholders viewed emancipation less as a break with slavery than as a time to readjust the terms of control. The widow Peppler, who seems to have owned Moos's children, had indentured the children to herself on emancipation. Moos's daughter had been passed on to Peppler's daughter, who lived in another district. His son Africa was still indentured to the widow and she refused to give him to his father.[15]

Other freed parents also were able to trace their children across time and space. In 1839, the year after emancipation, Mina July and her husband Platjes also set out to search for family. The couple lived in Worcester district, while Mina's sister was indentured to a Hans Brewer in Swellendam. They set out on a journey whose first leg by wagon or on foot was twelve miles, followed by a long journey up through the Breede River valley to Swellendam—a trek that took many days. Happily, though, the couple finally found the sister and freed her from her indenture.[16]

Similarly in 1838, a freed couple appeared at the magistrate's office in Worcester, a district in the interior beyond Stellenbosch. The man, named Saul, detailed how he had been married to a free woman with whom he had had a son called Theunis. The mother died a year after her son was born. Saul subsequently married Martha, another free woman, and they apparently lived on the farm where Saul was a slave. After the period of apprenticeship when emancipation came, the couple sought to leave the farm. It was then that they discovered that the former slaveholder, Jacobus Stephanus du Plessis, had already indentured Saul's child to himself. This would have been illegal, given the fact that the mother and stepmother were free and had not given their permission for the indenture arrangement. Martha, the stepmother, said to the magistrate that "[w]e are both very anxious to have the Boy with us, as we are able to provide for him and we should feel great gratitude if you would interfere on our behalf."[17]

One of the most detailed glimpses we have of a rural slave family comes to us as the result of a grandmother's determination that emancipation truly have meaning for her dead daughter's children. Clara was a former slave who in 1839 lived with her husband February, a name designating former slave status, in Wynberg, a suburb of Cape Town. While we know that February was a tailor, we do not know Clara's occupation. Clara's three sons lived with them. Clara seems to have wanted her grandchildren to come and live with her in part so that they could also be under the care of their uncles.[18]

Prior to emancipation, it appears that Clara, along with her daughter and three grandchildren, had been the slaves of one Franciscus Kavericus Jurgens. By 1838, Clara's daughter was dead, as was Franciscus Jurgens. Clara then moved to Cape Town, but the children stayed behind in the Jurgens household. Hence, Claartje, Louisa, and Christina now lived with Franciscus's son, Jan Jurgens, a merchant in Paardeberg. The terms of the Abolition Act allowed for the indentureship of freed children if they were shown to be orphans or in grave need of care.[19] By representing to the Stellenbosch clerk of the peace that the children were in a state of "utter destitution and orphancy," Jurgens succeeded in being granted their indenture on February 11, 1839, and he denied Clara's right to retrieve the children.

Clara decided to appeal to the colonial office, which many freed people seem to have regarded as a bulwark against the intransigence of former slaveholders who refused to acknowledge the legal realities of the new era of contract. Using the memorial system, in February 1839, some two months after the end of slavery, Clara sent a memorial to the colonial office. She asked that her grandchildren "be delivered to her." She further stated in her memorial that Jan Jurgens had misrepresented the status of the children to the clerk of the peace, given that she, Clara, had already been in touch with him about the children. Although she had managed to take Christina away, shortly thereafter Mrs. Jurgens had forcibly taken Christina back to her household. The secretary to the government was apparently persuaded by Clara's memorial, for in July 1839 he directed that the three children be delivered to her.[20]

Manisa: Emancipation Came but the Dream of Freedom Was Still Deferred

As detailed by Jackie Loos, Manisa of the Cape was a former slave interviewed by Judith Cuthbert in the *Cape Times Weekly* in 1914. At the time of the interview, Manisa was eighty-nine years old. We are not told her last name. Some sixty years after the ending of slavery, she lived in Stellenbosch in a building that had originally been urban slave quarters. Manisa was born in 1824 in Groot Drakenstein near Paarl, at the farm Baylon's Tooren. A slaveholder called Johanna Barbara van Biljon, who had married twice, owned Manisa. When Johanna's second husband died, Johanna owned sixty-one slaves. Then, in 1831, the widow died, and according to the provisions of her will, the slaves were distributed to different family members. Manisa and several other slaves were given to one W. A. Marais, who sold them at a public sale only a year later. Thus, in twelve months, Manisa's life had been completely turned upside down. At nine years old, she found herself, along with two other children and two older slaves, transferred to Johannes Jacobus Haupt, who lived in Moddergat, closer to the town of Stellenbosch.

Two years later, in 1834, the apprenticeship period commenced. In 1914, Manisa recalled, however, that apprenticeship had not meant much:

> The apprentice system came in, and you were then sent with a note to the nearest landdrost, who was supposed to hear both sides, but most of us found they thrashed us there without bothering to hear if we were in the right or the wrong, and then we had to make up our work when we got back to the farm; so we rather let the master whip us and say nothing about it.[21]

When emancipation finally came in 1838, Manisa was about twenty years old. Echoing Katie Jacobs's story, Manisa recalled that on a stormy day, owner Haupt called his domestic servants together and told them they were now free. "We did not know what that meant, and so the master let us stay and fed us until we either got new places or were taken on by him as paid servants."[22]

One of the major themes of the early years of emancipation was the great desire of missionaries in the rural Western Cape to proselytize to freed people. A key dimension of this activity was that missionaries encouraged freed people to be baptized and then formally married in the church. Indeed, across the Western Cape missionaries conducted many marriage ceremonies in the aftermath of emancipation. Couples were first baptized and then married, despite the fact that many of them had already been married in a customary way for a very long time.[23] Manisa's parents married at this time, and she remembered it as a very happy occasion attended by their growing and adult children. Her mother had kept the names of her children and their birth dates in a book and also recorded details of her husband's heritage. Unfortunately, the book was later lost in a fire, and with it, the records that this freed family had so carefully maintained.[24]

Like the lives of many other people freed from slavery, Manisa's life continued to be shaped by the political economy established by the slaveholding classes, who owned most of the good land in the rural areas and dominated economic and political life. She continued to live in Stellenbosch and worked as housekeeper for the Haupts, her former owners. She stayed on with them into her old age, in a room that had formerly been a part of the slave quarters. According to the woman who interviewed her, Manisa at age eighty-nine looked forward to "the freedom of death." Although Loos notes that Manisa spoke with affection of her former owners/employers, her hope for the freedom of death also speaks eloquently to the truncated promises of emancipation and to the deferral of justice and equality to a very much later time in the history of South Africa.

Conclusion

The stories of slavery and emancipation in the Western Cape demonstrate the centrality of ideas and practices of family to the lives of enslaved and freed people. During the era of slavery, enslaved people and unfree laborers worked and lived and loved together despite laws that divided partners and did not recognize slave parents' rights to their children. Under slavery, women navigated a particularly intimate gendered slaveholding order, often working and sleeping in the house of the slaveholder in conditions that made them particularly vulnerable to sexual violence. While slave and unfree women could not choose to reject such relationships, they were able to use existing conventions to advocate for their manumission and that of their children by slave owners. During the long era of amelioration and slave emancipation from the 1820s through 1838, enslaved people came to view liberty as a condition that would give freed people the ability to form enduring and legally protected affective relationships.

Slave emancipation brought changes in legal status. The new era brought the possibility of having one's emotional ties more readily recognized in law and in the wider colonial society. In the villages and mission stations of the Western Cape in 1834, and then with full emancipation beginning in 1838, freed people found new avenues that made emancipation matter. They learned crafts, tended gardens, and for a few years were able to avoid labor on the farms. But farmers soon campaigned against the missions as places of idleness and freed people again found themselves working as day laborers on farms. For those people living on the farms, the transition to freedom was a transition in name only. Only at the end of the nineteenth century, with the expansion of railway construction in the Western Cape and growing demands for labor in the city of Cape Town, did farm laborers, both men and women, find alternative employment that allowed some of them to escape the conditions of servitude that prevailed on the farms of the Western Cape for more than a half-century after Emancipation Day.[25]

Further Reading

A good overview of slavery is provided in *The Shaping of South African Society*, ed. Richard Elphick and Hermann Giliomee, 2nd ed. (Middletown, Conn.:

Wesleyan University Press, 1988). The pioneering work on Cape slavery is Anna Boeseken's *Slaves and Free Blacks at the Cape, 1658–1700* (Cape Town: Tafelberg, 1977). Nigel Worden's *Slavery in Dutch South Africa* is a fine history of the VOC period that situates Cape slavery within a broader comparative context. Robert Ross's *Cape of Torments: Slavery and Resistance in South Africa* (London: Routledge and Keegan Paul, 1983) illuminates the world of slaves and their struggles for freedom. In *Children of Bondage: A Social History of the Slave Society at the Cape of Good Hope, 1652–1838* (Hanover, N.H.: University Press of New England for Wesleyan University Press, 1994), Robert Shell argues that slaveholders viewed their relations with slaves through the lens of family relations. Jackie Loos's *Echoes of Slavery: Voices from the South African Past* (Cape Town: David Philip, 2004) is a good introduction to the experiences of individuals and is written for a broad audience.

Slave emancipation is covered by Pamela Scully, *Liberating the Family? Gender and British Slave Emancipation in the Rural Western Cape, South Africa, 1823–1853* (Portsmouth, N.H.: Heinemann, 1997). Scully argues that gender was a central organizing principle of British abolition and analyzes emancipation paying particular attention to domestic life and sexual relations. See also Scully, "Rape, Race, and Colonial Culture: The Sexual Politics of Identity in the Nineteenth-Century Cape," *American Historical Review* 100, 2 (1995): 335–59. *Breaking the Chains: Slavery and Its Legacy in the Nineteenth-Century Cape Colony* (Johannesburg: Witwatersrand University Press, 1994), an edited collection by Nigel Worden and Clifton Crais, includes pioneering articles on Cape slave emancipation. John Mason's *Social Death and Resurrection: Slavery and Emancipation in South Africa* (Charlottesville: University of Virginia Press, 2003) provides helpful narrative of the period of emancipation. See also his article "Hendrik Albertus and His Ex-Slave Mey: A Drama in Three Acts," *Journal of African History* 31 (1990): 423–45. For a study that includes Cape slavery in a longer analysis of South African history, see Wayne Dooling, *Slavery, Emancipation, and Colonial Rule in South Africa* (Athens: Ohio University Press, 2008). Local studies of Cape slavery include for the Eastern Cape, Clifton C. Crais, "Slavery and Freedom along a Frontier: The Eastern Cape, 1770–1838," *Slavery and Abolition* 11 (1990): 190–215.

Notes

1. Personal correspondence with Ebrahim Rhoda. Also see Ebrahim Rhoda, "Islam in the Strand 1838–1938: The Slave Kandaza and the Founding of the Muslim

Community of the Strand" (paper presented at University of the Western Cape, March 2004).

2. See Pamela Scully, *Liberating the Family? Gender and British Slave Emancipation in the Rural Western Cape, South Africa, 1823–1853* (Portsmouth, N.H.: Heinemann, 1997).

3. See Diana Paton and Pamela Scully, "Introduction: Gender and Slave Emancipation in Comparative Perspective," in *Gender and Slave Emancipation in the Atlantic World*, ed. Pamela Scully and Diana Paton (Durham, N.C.: Duke University Press, 2005).

4. See Scully, *Liberating the Family*.

5. John Edwin Mason, "Fit for Freedom: The Slaves, Slavery, and Emancipation in the Cape Colony, South Africa, 1806–1842," PhD diss., Yale University, 1992, vol. 1, 111.

6. For a comparative discussion, see Sue Peabody, "Négresse, Mulâtrese, Citoyenne: Gender and Emancipation in the French Caribbean, 1650–1848," in *Gender and Slave Emancipation in the Atlantic World*, ed. Pamela Scully and Diana Paton.

7. George Greig, *Papers Relating to the Manumission of Steyntje and Her Children* (Cape Town, 1827).

8. The information on this case is also drawn from Jackie Loos, *Echoes of Slavery: Voices from the South African Past* (Cape Town: David Philip, 2004).

9. Cape Archives (hereafter CA), 1/SO (Slave Office), 3/1, no. 29, 18 October 1826. See also no. 59, 12 March 1827, case of Clara.

10. CA, CO (Colonial Office), 3949, no. 73, Memorial of Rautenbach, 18 December 1830.

11. CA, CO 422, Letters Received from Missionaries, no. 32, 28 April 1831.

12. CA, CO 37, Letters Received from the Master of the Supreme Court, no. 8, 17 January 1831.

13. Reprinted in *Die Banier*, 2 June 1963.

14. See Scully, *Liberating the Family*, chap. 1. For a more sanguine view that also focuses on the intimacy of Cape slavery, see Robert Shell, *Children of Bondage: A Social History of the Slave Society at the Cape of Good Hope, 1652–1838* (Hanover, N.H.: University Press of New England for Wesleyan University Press, 1994).

15. CA, 1/STB 22/37/ Memorandum by H. Piers, resident magistrate of Paarl; statement by Moos, 1839.

16. CA, 1/SWM 16/33, Note in letter book of clerk of the peace, 15 January 1839.

17. CA, CO, 2779, no. 161, 18 December 1838.

18. CA, CO 4000, no. 109, 23 February 1839.

19. See Isobel Eirlys Edwards, *Towards Emancipation: A Study in South African Slavery* (Cardiff, UK: J. D. Lewis and Sons, 1942), chap. 8; Scully, *Liberating the Family*, 51–56.

20. CA, CO 4000, 26 July 1838.

21. Quoted in Loos, *Echoes of Slavery*, 140.

22. Quoted in Loos, *Echoes of Slavery*, 141.

23. On marriage in this period, see Scully, *Liberating the Family*, chap. 6.

24. On Manisa's recollections, Loos, *Echoes of Slavery*, 141.

25. See Pamela Scully, *The Bouquet of Freedom: Social and Economic Relations in the Stellenbosch District, South Africa, 1870–1900* (Cape Town: University of Cape Town, Centre for African Studies, 1989), Communication No. 17.

~

CHAPTER SEVEN

Mama Adolphina Unda
(c. 1880–1931)

The Salvation of a Dynastic Family and the Foundation of Fipa Catholicism, 1898–1914

Marcia Wright

As a young woman, Mama Adolphina Unda derived confidence from her royal birth and upbringing. Her immediate family wielded power within a small but coherent dynastic state, Nkansi, in southwestern Tanzania. In the 1890s, as the dynasty and people confronted Catholic missionaries who turned out to be harbingers of the approaching German colonial administration, they preferred diplomacy to armed resistance. Adolphina, the eldest daughter of this entrenched branch of the dynasty and the wife of the newly installed king, ultimately chose his rival, her own brother, over her husband, and facilitated the new ruler's conversion to Christianity. As an outcome of this colonial encounter, her brother until his death in 1916 and her sister until 1931 remained the recognized local rulers.

Among the challenges to a reader of this life story is how to deal with Mama Adolphina Unda as a gendered figure. How important was her childlessness during the years of her marriage? How did the example of the missionary white sisters and the sororal life in a religious order fit into her personal experience and a dynastic heritage where women held offices and harked back to a foundress? More simply, did the fact that Unda was a woman play a role in her achievements? Or did elements of the traditional male roles that she assumed contribute to her influence and success? Or might she have forged a role or roles entirely her own, distinct from those of royal men and women around her?

It is probable that Mama Adolphina thought and acted strategically in ways that preserved the influence of her family. However, her story is not a tale of cold calculation. She did not feign being attracted to the new Christian faith; her life suggests that she truly became a believing Christian. At the same time, she thought strategically enough that she managed to get the missionaries to establish an order of African sisters and became its first mother superior. Her commitment led her entire family to convert to Christianity. Yet she withdrew to the embrace of family when her brother became ill and World War I incapacitated the institutional church.

Mama Adolphina's life as a religious leader, therefore, illustrates clearly that the coming of Christianity and colonization was a far more complex event than simple conquest. The new faith and the European colonial presence presented new options to many people in African societies. Africans, then, did not perceive that they faced a stark choice between resistance or collaboration, but a wide variety of ways to deal with these new outsiders. The newcomers were quite powerful in terms of brute force, but they were at the same time entirely dependent on the Africans around them when it came to learning about and governing the societies over which they had formally declared hegemony. Was Mama Adolphina Unda successful in her efforts both to accommodate herself to the new order and profit from it? The answer is complicated, for it depends on how we interpret her objectives.

Examination of a single life cannot be fruitful without attending to the historical setting. Only rare figures by their actions compel reconsideration of culture and conjuncture. Such was Mama Adolphina Unda, who was born about 1880 and died about 1931. She held many positions: the senior among royal siblings, the childless wife of a ruler, a convert to the Catholic Church, a nun, and an apostle who succeeded in converting her family, thereby saving their dynastic fortunes during the early colonial period in the southwest corner of today's Tanzania. What valence did these roles assume, and when? In a time of structural change, what scope was there for her agency or initiative?

This biographical essay focuses on the middle years of her life, 1898–1914, which are the most completely documented. Over this decade and a half, Mama Unda moved about Nkansi and Lyangalile, the two dynastically linked principalities of Ufipa, and to the nearby ecclesiastical center of the white fathers' mission at Karema on Lake Tanganyika. The geography of her life covered a dramatic landscape, on a plateau that was sometimes mountainous and sometimes characterized by sweeping grasslands, and bordered by nearly vertical drops to Lake Tanganyika and Lake Rukwa to the west and northeast, respectively. Although she never became the ruler, or *mwene*, she was the eldest royal child of Mwene Kapufi, the great king of the decades before 1890; the wife of Mwene Kapere, who reigned in 1897–1905 and 1931–1957; the sister of Mwene Kilatu, who reigned in 1905–1916, and of Mwene Ngalu, who reigned in 1916–1931. She was also the senior cousin of the mwenes of Lyangalile, who beginning in 1905 were all women.

Mama Adolphina Unda's shifting roles are evident in the following narrative, which seeks to capture events and, in addition, to illuminate the ideology of dynastic reproduction, the substance of female power, and the compatibility of Catholic teaching and institution building as they all framed her choices.

Several important changes in her public persona may be signaled simply by the various names she took on. It should be underscored that Mama Adolphina Unda was not a name she adopted. Rather, it is a summary. Upon taking initial vows to become a nun, she renounced her "pagan" name of Unda, in favor of her baptismal name, Adolphina Marie.[1] "Mama" is an honorific, prefixed popularly after she ceased to be a nun and returned to her family to become the de facto regent in 1914, and then, after 1916, when she was associated with her sister Mwene Ngalu, as a power behind the scene, acting in effect as queen mother. Her names identify the sequence of phases in her life: Unda before she decisively threw in her lot with the Church; Adolphina Marie as the adherent and baptized Christian; and Sister Adolphina, the nun. Our Mama Adolphina Unda, then, reflects a synthesis that she both embodied and promoted.

The available historical sources reflect the high stakes for all parties around the turn of the twentieth century. As the white fathers saw it, there was a struggle under way among the ruling family of Nkansi that generated a highly desirable opportunity for them as missionaries. The white fathers themselves were in the forefront of colonization, antedating and rivaling the newly established German administration in the region. They were also well aware that Muslim traders had for decades been active and influential both at the court of Nkansi and as managers of the long-distance trade routes that traversed the central plateau and southern reaches of Lake Tanganyika to and from Shaba/Katanga in today's Congo.[2]

In part as a consequence of the events narrated here, by the time Mama Adolphina Unda faded from the Catholic records at the onset of World War I, a substantial number of subjects in Nkansi and Lyangalile had joined the Catholic Church, forming the nucleus of the major stronghold of Catholicism that the Sumbawanga Diocese is today.[3] According to her patron and godfather, Bishop Adolphe Lechaptois, Mama Adolphina Unda had set this movement in train by converting her family, which can for convenience be called the House of Kapufi.[4] While Catholic sources yield the most intimate information, official German and British records, as well as a few publications by contemporary observers, add to the available evidence. Embedded in British records is also a set of "histories" by Mwene Kapere, Unda's former husband, whose recollections erase his former wife from the political scene entirely. Kapere's accounts are nonetheless invaluable because they are direct, even if self-interested, descriptions of the injustices he endured as his rival Kilatu advanced his ambitions to unseat him.[5]

Unda

Unda was born when her father was in his middle age, with some gray hair but entirely in control of his domain. In 1880, Nkansi, the Ufipa principality that he ruled, was at peace, enjoying agricultural prosperity and providing security for long-distance trade. At Kisumba, or Mwakapufi, as the explorer Joseph Thomson called the royal capital, lived a handful of Arabs, one of whom served as the liaison between foreigners and the king. After meeting Kapufi, Thomson paid his respects "to Kapufi's principal wives, his mother, and sisters," all of whom were "delightfully plump and fat, wonderfully light of colour, well-oiled, with heads shaved and lower incisors knocked out."[6] Their activities included weaving, pounding grain, cooking, and preparing skins to be made into garments.

Thomson knew that this "picture of native domestic life" was not typical. Royal women, for example, had a good deal of milk to drink, and although he was not fully aware of it, the fine herd of cattle belonging to the mwene was a hallmark of royal distinction. Cattle belonged almost exclusively to Mwene Nkansi.[7] As she became conscious of her milieu, Unda would have learned more and more about her royal status as a Twachi, a female descended from the female founders of the dynasty. Her very name, Unda, was that of the senior of the three stranger women who, according to the dynastic charter, usurped the pre-existing chiefs. Unda's narration of this mythical charter, recorded word for word by Bishop Lechaptois, has become a cornerstone of recorded oral tradition for Ufipa.[8]

On one formal occasion in 1888, the mwene-in-council was flanked by a woman on one side and two on the other, with court functionaries and others seated according to rank.[9] Before the death of Mwene Kapufi in 1890, there were only vague references to how the royal family functioned as a ruling constellation, or regnum. With experience, closer observation, and inquiry, it became established that in addition to the mwene, the regnum included the queen mother (*mwene wa kulosi*), the heir apparent (*iWakunkwilo*), and the ritual wife (*inka mwene*). The queen mother and heir apparent enjoyed a degree of material autonomy, because particular villages were obliged to pay tribute directly to them.[10]

The incumbents of the high royal court positions in the regnum, as well as the king himself, had to be of full Twachi blood, made possible through endogamy, or marriage within the group. Such royal endogamy, well known to have weakened dynastic families in Europe and practiced in an extreme form in ancient Egypt, was highly unusual in modern Africa. It did, however, exist with disastrous effect among the Sakalava of Madagascar, where in the earlier nineteenth century a male heir ran away and converted to Islam, leaving women to rule.[11] In Nkansi there was a small hedge, in that sons never directly succeeded their fathers and the heir apparent was either the brother, nephew, or cousin of the mwene. Upon Kapufi's death, his heir apparent ruled for only a few months before he died, allegedly poisoned as a penalty for having hastened Kapufi's death.

The next in line, Mwene Msulwa, ruled for seven years until he committed suicide, in part, one rumor had it, because of impotence.[12] In any event, even though he had an inka mwene or ritual wife, he did not produce royal offspring. The shadow of infertility had already lengthened in the neighboring principality of Lyangalile. To assure that there would be royal progeny, the rulers earlier dispatched a princess to conceive a child by Kapufi.[13] Such paternity was a convenience and in no way constituted grounds for a political claim, yet the resulting bond of blood closely connected Unda with the Lyangalile female ruler and princesses she later came to proselytize. The number of Twachi princesses descended from the female founders of the dynasty well outnumbered princes, perhaps in part because some males may have abandoned their status and political ambitions by opting for exogamy.[14] In any case, when Msulwa died in 1897, there were only two remaining twa, as males of the dynasty were called: Unda's brother Kilatu and her cousin Kapere, the heir apparent with whom she had been matched as inka mwene.

Unda reached adolescence at Kantalamba/Sumbawanga, the new royal village where Msulwa succeeded as mwene. At Kantalamba, the House of Kapufi officially occupied only one of the several royal offices of the regnum, but it was the key one of queen mother. The queen mother, Unda Kankilwa, seems to have carefully aligned herself with the councilors and elders, encouraging the conservative courtiers and maneuvering for the succession of Kapufi's son, Kilatu, who had become the heir apparent following the death of Msulwa in 1897. The pairing of Unda with Kapere as inka mwene placed another member of the House of Kapufi among the principal titleholders of the regnum, so their faction was exceedingly strong. Hauptmann Ramsay, the German commandant, who arrived on the heels of the succession rituals, understood that Kapere had been "made Sultan" by the powerful queen mother. Ramsay described Kapere as a very alert young man of about twenty-two years of age who was well disposed toward Europeans and who, like his main advisers, spoke "really fluent Kiswahili."[15] Ramsay endorsed Kapere's mwene-ship and left. But Ramsay's blessing by no means guaranteed anything in terms of local politics. Unda Kankilwa remained bent upon seeing to it that Kilatu supplanted Kapere.

In 1898 and 1899, Kapere's position went from weak to unviable, as he failed to gather the support he required to become an effective mwene. He agreed to allow the white fathers to establish a mission at Zimba in the Rukwa Valley, their first station away from the shores of Lake Tanganyika in the interior of Nkansi. It was not far from the royal village of Ngongo. In the middle of 1898, Kapere had moved from Sumbawanga on the plateau to Ngongo, putting the escarpment between himself and the hostile Kapufi faction, who presided in the heartland of Nkansi on the plateau and abridged his authority over functionaries, especially district governors.[16] Kapere's courtiers were few, led by Mwanakapufi, the nyampara or headman who had been at Ngongo for many years. One of his military chiefs was an eighteen-year-old youth, just a few years his junior, who in later life became the catechist Fabiano Mgawe Tayari at Mpui, the residence of Mwene Nti of Lyangalile.[17] A royally connected group bearing the title of mwanangwa (because one parent was Twachi) constituted a group of potential officials and loyal notables. However, in these uncertain times, they did not flock to the young mwene.[18] Hence Kapere turned in 1898 for help to the missionaries at Zimba, and in early August he traveled to Karema to see the bishop himself. The visit was entirely political, for the Germans in 1897 had stipulated that the white fathers would serve as Kapere's local contact with the administration and as intermediaries in communications with colonial officers in distant Ujiji.[19]

For the missionaries, politics and religion were inseparable. The white fathers certainly encouraged Kapere to shake off the constraints of tradition. When he first set out for Karema in early July, he was "arrested" by Kanyika, the mwenekandawa, or district governor, on the grounds that mwenes were ritually prohibited from going to the Tanganyika lakeshore. The father superior of the white fathers at Zimba countered that a monarch had the power to do anything he liked. In a display of local power, the priest not only neutralized Kanyika but also proceeded to fine him four goats—two for Kapere and two for the mission that had approved the journey. Unda, although she remained behind, had earlier sent a gift of a goat to the white sisters in her own name, asking them to make a gown for her. They did so, entrusting it to Kapere, who pleased them by being dressed "a little bit in the European fashion" rather than in the customary cloak of indigenously woven cloth. The missionaries at Zimba, too, had reason to be hopeful of conversion because Kapere and Unda undertook to be instructed and allowed them to post a catechist to Ngongo.[20]

When important chiefs from a wider region were called to Sumbawanga in February 1899 to hear Otto Schloifer appeal for a huge number of porters to carry parts of a steamer from Lake Nyasa to Lake Tanganyika, Schloifer considered Sumbawanga to be the residence of the "Mwini Fipa," whom he described as the widow of Kapufi. Kapere and Kilatu had enjoyed more or less equal status as her subordinates, he reported. He also noticed Unda, remarking that Kapere's wife was "very attractive and slender."[21] The almost simultaneous arrival of a German military administrator with a company of Schutztruppe and the recruitment of porters reversed Kapere's fortunes. By the middle of the year, his position as mwene was reconfirmed, and he had received the sizable sum of seventeen hundred rupees, his reward for recruiting seventeen hundred Fipa porters.[22] Kapere had found an enduring patron in Schloifer.

Unda's place in this new situation was initially opaque. She was certainly an important element in Kapere's legitimacy. At least some rites of rulership were still performed. For example, each evening, in a ritual to close the day, the couple appeared dressed in locally woven cloth with a page carrying a basket containing royal regalia and the mwene blowing on certain pipes while drummers played. Kapere and Unda withdrew and were told which notables had paid their respects.[23] Adrien Atiman, the observer who recorded this particular performance, was a major Christian influence at Ngongo at this time. A remarkable "médecin-catechist," Atiman had been ransomed by the white fathers in Sudanic West Africa and trained in medicine at Malta before becoming a significant member of the mission establishment headquartered at Karema.

Embracing Christianity: From Unda to Adolphina Marie

Unda's position was made precarious by the queen mother's continuing animosity toward Kapere and Kilatu's demands for autonomous responsibility on the plateau. Although both Kapere and Unda had announced their intention to be instructed in the Christian faith, Unda proved to be a far more serious Christian. Kapere wanted literacy, above all. Indeed, he later became a nominal Muslim. By 1901, however, Unda was an accepted catechumen, a Christian teacher who wore the signature cross. Politics continued to be in play. The missionaries noted her absence on the plateau and greeted her return to services at the end of July. By November, she declared her wish to separate from Kapere, citing his accumulation of twenty other women, and proposed either to go live with the white sisters at Kala mission on Lake Tanganyika, or to go home to her "mother" in Sumbawanga. The missionaries asked her to delay while they sent to Karema for the advice of the bishop, Monseigneur Lechaptois. In the interim, they called upon Unda to substitute as female catechist for another who had fallen from grace, and allowed her to stay temporarily at Zimba.[24]

Kapere responded by sending a letter to the German commandant in which he complained that missionaries and Christians were interfering in the affairs of Ngongo. Forced to return to Ngongo, Unda fell ill, and she apparently endured detention in mid-February, when all she could do, as she told the missionaries, was "to pray all day to the Good Lord." The commandant took up the matter of Unda's separation when he arrived on tour at Ngongo and declared that she was free to stay or go. But the following day, to the dismay and disappointment of the Zimba missionaries, she returned her notebook and the cross, saying that she would remain with Kapere and abandon her new religion since he would not accept monogamy. At the same time, Kapere, having been severely admonished by the commandant, began to repair his relations with the missionaries, and with a large entourage attended Easter mass followed by an afternoon of feasting, drinking, and entertainment.[25]

A new episode opened in September 1902, when Unda returned to mass and her brother Kilatu requested permission to come to Zimba for several months for intensive instruction. The missionaries agreed, on condition that he not exercise his prerogative to requisition the services of the people, who by this time had become burdened with multiple extractions—labor and tax levies imposed by the German administration along with similar customary obligations owed to Kapere personally. By this time, Kapere faced widespread popular opposition, channeled in part by indigenous religious adepts, but also in more diffuse ways. Gone were the days when he could deliver seventeen hundred men as porters, who were themselves paid directly and whose recruitment also brought Kapere capitation fees. By April 5, 1903, Mwanakapufi, the nyampara, was said to have defected to Kilatu's side. Because he was late in delivering tax labor in early 1905, Kapere was replaced as mwene by Kilatu, who hastened to visit Zimba to declare his continued friendship and to say that he had taken on the name Kapufi.[26]

Unda was absent at this time. On August 23, 1903, after a public ceremony of separation orchestrated by the missionaries, she had left with

Monseigneur Lechaptois when he returned to Karema after visiting Ngongo and Zimba. At Karema, with only one girl servant, she took up residence under the wing of the white sisters. The bishop and the sisters were equally aware that she was a prize convert. For the previous several years, the mission had taken steps to break from its association with liberated slaves and to build more purposefully its constituency among ordinary people. Even so, the white sisters could not have anticipated the enthusiastic popular reception given to Unda on her arrival. Gifts, including many domestic animals, flooded in from the Fipa who lived in Karema. Before long, Unda had organized her response, a huge feast. As she settled in, her conduct was much approved by the sisters, although they were again surprised by her decision to assign the two servants who now attended her to work for the good of the religious community rather than for herself personally. Having successfully passed her examination, Unda was duly baptized Adolphina Marie—Adolphina after her patron and now godfather, Monseigneur Adolphe Lechaptois. It was probably in 1904, after her accelerated catechumenate and baptism on Christmas Day in 1903, that she began to work closely with Lechaptois as his principal informant on royal traditions and history.[27]

Assiduous in her studies and increasingly pious in her devotions, Unda quite soon asked to be accepted as a nun. Lechaptois, who had not anticipated founding an order of African sisters, had to secure approval from his ecclesiastical superiors, and before long Adolphina became a postulant. Joining her almost immediately were two other women, followed by another daughter of Kapufi, who became known as Sister Augustina. Somewhat later, two others became postulants, a daughter of Captain Joubert, the former Papal Zouave, by his African wife, and a daughter of one of the West African catechist-doctors attached to the white fathers. These young women were all of uncommon parentage; attracting ordinary girls proved to be difficult.[28]

In August 1906, three years after she left Zimba, Unda Adolphina returned, having been permitted by the bishop to go home to influence her family. Lechaptois later admitted that it had been a risk, but the speculation paid off hugely, setting in train the "sensational conversion" of the royal family. This work was continued in May 1908, when she, several other newly professed African sisters, and three white sisters embarked on a "triumphal progress" from Karema to Kala to Sumbawanga and the royal capital, and finally on to Zimba to set up the first convent of African sisters.[29] From Zimba, Sister Adolphina toured not only the Twachi strongholds in Nkansi but also those in Lyangalile.

Kilatu had proved to be more than receptive to these initiatives. In the last six months of 1908, when he traveled to the coast, Kilatu had selected one of his wives to marry in a Christian ceremony on his return. He left her with the white sisters at Karema for instruction. In severing ties with his other wives, he cushioned the loss with reparations to their families. Even though a mission station at Kate on the plateau had increased the missionary presence in Nkansi, Lechaptois gave all the credit for the conversion of the royal family to Sister Adolphina Unda. The process climaxed with the baptism and confirmation of not only the royal pair, but also of two of Adolphina Unda's sisters, Ngalu and Mwati, whose marriages to well-born catechists were blessed. The catechists and their royal wives were subsequently posted to old royal villages.[30] A kind of dynastic salvation had been achieved in this fusion with the Church.

Unda then turned to the conversion of the Lyangalile Twachi. The Mwazye mission, established in Lyangalile in 1904, had amicable relations with Mwene Kundawantu, but elements opposed to the Germans drove him to resist the administration and flee. Apprehended, he was executed in 1906. Through Adolphina Unda's influence, one of the daughters of the new mwene sought to follow her to Karema, only to be held back by councilors. Rather, she settled at Mwazye mission to receive instruction, shortly after the establishment of a convent of white sisters there in 1908. The following year, the white sisters found the princess and the girls who attended her lacking in humility and all too influential with the female youth of Mwazye. Arriving shortly after the sisters had ejected the princess from her dwelling, Monseigneur Lechaptois came down hard on the father superior, who had caved in to pressure from the white sisters, and, in so doing, threatened the prospects for conversion from above. Adolphina Unda was dispatched to repair the damage, and in due course the princess became the formidable Christian heir apparent and subchief, Mwene Maria.[31]

After the wave of preoccupation with royal conversion subsided, the African sisters assumed normalized routines. Their order was assigned responsibility for Utinta, on Lake Tanganyika between Karema and Kirando, and then for Kirando and its outstations. The tasks of the African sisters were much like those of their white counterparts. At Utinta, two taught reading and arithmetic, while one looked after the sacristy and church. They kept a small dispensary. Always in pairs, they made home visits. But far more than the white sisters, they cultivated their own food.[32] As mother superior, Sister Adolphina reigned "like a queen."[33]

In 1908, when Kilatu left for the coast for medical attention, he implored Adolphina Unda to act as regent. She declined. But when he prepared to go again to greet the German crown prince, who was due to arrive in Dar es Salaam in 1914, he repeated his request. This time, Sister Adolphina agreed.

From 1913 on, therefore, she was effectively back within the family, on a leave that became permanent once the upheavals of World War I shattered the order of African sisters. Her dimming eyesight also played a role in her retreat to her family.

By 1920, Adolphina was blind, but she remained an eminence, backing her sister Ngalu, who in 1916 had become mwene on the death of Kilatu. She lived to the end of her sister's reign in 1931. She thus lived through the end of German colonial rule into the era of British administration after World War I. However, the obscurity into which Mama Adolphina Unda had fallen was dramatized by the complete surprise of British colonial officers when Ngalu included in her pension negotiations the demand, which was conceded, that her sister be awarded a small recurrent sum as well.[34] However diminished, the regnum persisted.

Conclusion

Returning to the questions posed at the outset of this chapter, two inter-linked issues deserve discussion in order to better assess Mama Adolphina Unda's actions: the dynamics of gender relations among Twachi, notables, and commoners, and the compatibility of Catholicism and Fipa society, com-moner as well as royal.

As has been argued in this biographical essay, Adolphina Unda played a part in the survival of at least a semblance of the Twachi regnum into the high tide of colonial rule between the two world wars. This regnum was never static, exemplified by the fact that in addition to their positional functions, the powers of the kings or mwenes from the later eighteenth century onward had been wielded by women under certain circumstances, especially in the midst of crisis. One of its chief ideological features, dynastic endogamy, however, ended once and for all with the separation of Unda and Kapere in the first decade of the twentieth century. By the 1920s, the office of mwene was entirely in the hands of royal females. Moreover, they were popular, even though Kapere, in his campaign for restoration, claimed that Ngalu was only a regent and he was the true, ritually installed mwene who had been unjustly deposed in 1905. The notables and elders of Nkansi stood by Ngalu, who satisfied and played to their sense of heritage and proved to be capable of opposing fathers superior when they overreached.[35]

After 1927, the British administration and its officials increasingly viewed Ngalu as an obstacle to efficient local government. They were convinced of Kapere's superior capability. At the same time, the father superior at Zimba saw Ngalu positively as a "good Catholic." When she came to Ngongo in

1927 to conduct local court proceedings, Père Bigot reported: "Our King is an excellent mother to her family; she has six living children, is a good Christian, and is named Jeanne."[36] At play in this description is an ideal of Catholic motherhood, monogamous and prolific. The praises for Ngalu as mwene preserved the conventional "Our Father," leaving her husband to be praised as "wife of the King" (mki wa mwene).

Royal display and associated threads of cultural continuity carried through the era of change and reconstruction associated with Catholic Christianization, to which Mama Adolphina Unda had so conspicuously contributed. In the eyes and writings of Bishop Lechaptois, who died in December 1917, she was all-important. A more complete analysis of conversion in Nkansi and Lyangalile shows, however, that the tale recounted in this chapter was not simply a fulfillment of Cardinal Lavigerie's instructions to the white fathers "to convert from the head to the body of a people." In Buganda, part of today's Uganda in East Africa, the white fathers had crowed over their earlier successes. Bishop Lechaptois presented royal conversions in his diocese as equal to these missionary achievements. But the stories of Buganda and Ufipa differ markedly. In Ufipa the compatibility of Catholicism and social life had many facets. These included the attractions of mission stations to a people who in any case periodically shifted residence from place to place and the ways in which Catholic beliefs amplified the existing rituals of the life cycle, thereby providing an appealing notion of an afterlife. In addition, Christian monogamy did not challenge the basic model of family composition in a culture with strong leveling patterns among commoners suspicious of accumulation by their peers, but tolerant of wealth among a few notables who could facilitate circulation and protection. European missionaries, as well as exceptional Africans, qualified for this tolerance. Catholicism also fit in with the lives of men whose outflow as migrant workers intensified from 1903 onward. The faith facilitated their networks as sisal plantation workers and become part of a predictable rural life of inheritance and retirement. Although the missionary ethnographer Père Robert did his best to show how much of Fipa belief was still "pagan" and Christian in name only, from one to the other became a relatively seamless continuum.[37] To detail these facets would require another essay. Suffice it here to say that the conversion of royalty was paralleled by an incipient and autonomous conversion of a significant number of subjects, and thus buttressed legitimacy.

Where does the figure of Mama Adolphina Unda stand on this wider canvas? As readers and future scholars probe the times and historical forces that make up her context and come to conclusions about her importance, they must credit her agency, even while recognizing that she was not the sole agent of conversion. She dramatized a direction of religious and political change that profoundly affected the people of Ufipa, as well as the House of Kapufi. The specificity of Mama Adolphina Unda's life circumstances adds a very human dimension and texture to our depictions of the variations of family, politics, and historical change in Africa.

Further Reading

This biographical essay has relied upon unpublished and published primary sources to explore not only a particular individual and cultural heritage, but also the wider circumstances of the period 1880 to 1914. The following readings extend this frame of reference by suggesting titles that cover the same time period, dynastic maneuverings by high-status women, queen mothers as political actors, and the advance of Christianity.

The enhanced monarchies found in Africa in the later eighteenth and nineteenth centuries entailed state formation and a reordered society. The Asante kingdom in present-day Ghana and the Buganda kingdom in Uganda have rich historiographies concerning the buildup of central power and its disruption as colonial conquest and rule usurped sovereignty. On Asante, see Ivor Wilks, "The Dynastic Factor in Asante History: A Family Reconstruction," in his *Asante in the Nineteenth Century: The Structure and Evolution of Political Order* (Cambridge, UK: Cambridge University Press, 1975). The active political role of the queen mother (*asantehemaa*) Yaa Kyaa in securing the succession of her son is evident in Thomas McCaskie, "Ahyiamu—'A Place of Meeting': An Essay on Process and Event in the History of the Asante State," *Journal of African History* 25, 2 (1984). Holly Hansen, in "Queen Mothers and Good Government in Buganda: The Loss of Women's Political Power in Nineteenth-Century Africa," in *Women in African Colonial Histories*, ed. Jean Allman, Susan Geiger, and Nakanyike Musisi (Bloomington: Indiana University Press, 2002), contends that the traumatic events for Buganda monarchy between the 1880s and the turn of the century came when Buganda's rulers had effectively disabled this female office.

The most well-known queen mother to preserve a monarchy in the face of colonial alienation was Labotsibeni, queen mother of the Swazi kingdom from 1890 and queen regent from 1899 to 1921. See Thoko Ginindza, "Labotsibeni/Gwamile Mdluli: The Power behind the Swazi Throne 1875–1925," published in a valuable collection, *Queens, Queen Mothers, Priestesses, and Power: Case Studies in African Gender*, ed. Flora Kaplan (New York: New York Academy of Sciences, 1997).

If the linkage of dynasty and spiritual leadership secured continuity in Nkansi, elsewhere it figured in insurrection. See Alison Des Forges, "'The Drum Is Greater than the Shout': The 1912 Rebellion in Northern Rwanda," in *Banditry, Rebellion, and Social Protest in Africa*, ed. Donald Crummey (Portsmouth N.H.: Heinemann, 1986). On women as Christian religious agents during the early colonial period, much has yet to be written. In the African Great Lakes sphere of the white fathers, the early and discontinuous fostering of religious orders of Catholic African women is mentioned briefly by several authors, most notably by Birgitta Larsson, *Conversion to Greater Freedom? Women, Church, and Social Change in North-Western Tanzania under Colonial Rule* (Uppsala, Sweden: Uppsala University, 1993). The best general history of the Catholic Church remains Adrian Hastings, *The Church in Africa, 1450–1950* (Oxford, UK: Clarendon, 1994).

Notes

1. Adolphe Lechaptois, "Tanganyika," *Missions d'Afrique* 188 (1908): 258.

2. See Roy G. Willis, *A State in the Making: Myth, History, and Social Transformation in Pre-Colonial Ufipa* (Bloomington: Indiana University Press, 1981), and Kapepwa Anselm Tambila, "A History of the Rukwa Region (Tanzania), ca. 1870–1940: Aspects of Economic and Social Change from Pre-Colonial to Colonial Times," PhD diss., University of Hamburg, 1981.

3. By 1985, there were 402,382 Catholics, 122,721 Protestants, 16,087 Muslims, and 22,146 "pagans" in the Sumbawanga diocese. See F. Kapufi, ed., *Historia ya Jimbo la Sumbawanga, 1885–1985* (Peramiho, 1985), 101. In 1898, the population of Nkansi and Lyangalile portions of the same area probably did not exceed fifty thousand.

4. Monseigneur Adolphe Lechaptois became apostolic vicar or bishop of the Tanganyika vicariate in 1891. He wrote an ethnography that dwelled at length on Nkansi and fully credits Mama Adolphina Unda. See his *Aux Rives du Tanganika* (Algiers: Imprimerie des Missionaires d'Afrique, 1913).

5. See especially the versions of local history influenced by Kapere's renderings and inscribed in 1927 in the Sumbawanga-Ufipa District Book (DNB), volume 2, and his own signed account "Habari za Wene (Watatwala) wa Nkansi-Ufipa," 1955, also included in the Sumbawanga DNB, volume 2, Tanzania National Archives (TNA), MF Reel 12. I rely on a translation by Dr. John Kiango.

6. Joseph Thomson, *To the Central African Lakes and Back: The Narrative of the Royal Geographical Society's East Central African Expedition, 1878–80*, 2nd ed. (London: Cass, [1881] 1968), vol. 2, 220–21.

7. Rinderpest in 1892 destroyed almost all the cattle, and later mwenes were never great cattle owners. See "Cattle in Ufipa: Short Historical Review," Sumbawanga DNB.

8. Lechaptois, *Aux Rives*, 44–46, 51–54. See also Willis, *A State in the Making*, 215.

9. Report by Père Randabel on his negotiations with Kapufi in mid-1888, 25 October 1888, Archivo Padri Bianchi (APB), Rome, C17–204.

10. Willis, *A State in the Making*, 158, 160.

11. G. Feeley-Harnick, *A Green Estate: Restoring Independence in Madagascar* (Washington, D.C.: Smithsonian Institution Press, 1991); chapter 2, "Deadly Blessings," discusses the effects of "ruinous incest."

12. See J. E. S. Lamb, "History before British Occupation," 1927, Sumbawanga DNB, vol. 2.

13. Lechaptois, *Aux Rives*, 67.

14. Willis, *A State in the Making*, 174–75.

15. Hauptmann Ramsay, "Über seine Expeditionen nach Ruanda und dem Rikwa-See," *Verhandlungen Gesellschaft für Erkunde zu Berlin* 25 (1898): 320–21.

16. Kapere, "Habari za Wene" and Zimba Diary, 1898–1899, APB Rome, passim.

17. See biographical note on Tayari, in Willis, *A State in the Making*, 231–32.

18. The autobiography of Magdalena Ntaalu Ngalawa, written in September 1966, contains unique details of life and status among the mwanangwa. See Roy G. Willis, ed. and trans., *There Was a Certain Man: Spoken Art of the Fipa* (Oxford, UK: Oxford University Press, 1978), 133–35.

19. Kapere, "Habari za Wene." See also Tambila, "A History of the Rukwa Region," beginning on 125.

20. Zimba Diary, 2 July 1898, APB Rome; White Sisters, Diarie, Karema, 1, 7, and 8 August 1898; Zimba Diary, 2 July 1898, APB Rome.

21. Otto Schloifer, *Bana Uleia: ein Lebenswerk in Afrika: Aus den Tagabücher eines alten Kolonial pioneers* (Berlin: D. Reimer/Andrews and Steiner, 1943), 105.

22. Schloifer, *Bana Uleia*, 109.

23. Adrien Atiman, "Adrien Atiman: By Himself," *Tanganyika Notes and Records* 21 (1946): 68.

24. Zimba Diary, 29 July 1901, APB Rome; Zimba Diary, 3 November 1901, APB Rome; Zimba Diary, 17 December 1901, APB Rome.

25. Zimba Diary, 5 January 1902, APB Rome; Zimba Diary, 21 February 1902, APB Rome; Zimba Diary, 25 February and 30 March 1902, APB Rome.

26. Zimba Diary, 5 October 1902, APB Rome; Zimba Diary, 30 August 1905, APB Rome.

27. *Missions d'Alger* 15 (1907–1908): 259; Mathias Hallfell, "Unda, die Königen von Ufipa," *Afrika Bote, Nachrichten aus den Missionen der Weisse Väter* 16 (1909–1910): 211; *Missions d'Alger* 16 (1909–1910): 135.

28. Hallfell, "Unda, die Königen," 232, 238; Karema Diocese, "Annual Report," 1913/1914, APB Rome, 20.

29. Zimba Diary, 19 August 1906, APB Rome; *Missions d'Alger* 15 (1907–1908): 259; Hallfell, "Unda, die Königen," 235.

30. *Missions d'Afrique* 187 (1908): 230; Kate Diary, 8 February 1916, APB Rome.

31. Mwazye Diary, 10 March 1905, 10 December 1905, and 7 February 1906, APB Rome, gives a serial account; Lechaptois to Livenhac, 18 August 1908, APB Rome, vol. 1, 103; Mwazye Diary, 9 January 1910, APB Rome.

32. Karema Diocese Annual Report, 1910/1911, APB Rome.

33. Karema Diocese Annual Report, 1912/1913.

34. The only British officer to pay close attention to the Twachi and the regnum was Philip Mitchell. His 1921 report from Namanyere (Nkansi) was incorporated with further commentary in "Native Laws and Customs—Kigoma Province" (1925), TNA SMP 7794/4; P. H. Harris, D. C. Ufipa to F. D. Bagshawe, P. C. Kigoma, 29 October 1931, and F. D. Bagshawe to Chief Secretary, 26 November 1931, TNA SMP 13332.

35. Philip Mitchell, *African Afterthoughts* (London: Hutchinson, 1954).

36. Armand Bigot, "Une séance judiciaire au pays noir," *Missions Catholique* 59 (1927): 326.

37. J. M. Robert (White Father), "Croyances et coutumes magico-religieuses des Wafipa païens," Tabora, 1949. Mimeographed drafts were distributed to missionaries beginning in 1931.

PART III

THE CONTRADICTIONS OF COLONIALISM, 1910–1960: EXPLOITATION AND NEW RIGHTS

CHAPTER EIGHT

~

Colonial Administrator Adolphe A. M. Taillebourg (1874–1934)

Strict Interpreter of the Law or Humanitarian?

Issiaka Mandé

In the early decades of the nineteenth century, the campaign to end the slave trade, the rise of a clandestine trade in slaves north of the equator, the intensified commerce in people south of the equator, and the beginnings of European missionary, political, and commercial penetration into the interior of the continent marked a new era in relations between Africans and Europeans. European hegemony in Africa reached its high tide between the two world wars in the twentieth century. European colonial administrations intervened more intimately than ever before in the workings of African societies, attempting to refashion them in ways that conformed to European ideas of modernity and progress and that supplied European companies and consumers with inexpensive raw materials and agricultural products.

Mandé's chapter describes a controversial European colonial administrator in terms that are both human and complex. The historical literature on colonization in Africa usually describes such agents as venal instruments of European interests. More often than not, these men and the occasional woman are dehumanized, portrayed as one-dimensional reflections of European imperialism. This sketch of Adolphe Albert Marie Taillebourg and his career in the French colony of Upper Volta makes us scratch our heads. He does not conform to the stereotype. Taillebourg is eccentric, to say the least. A maimed war hero whose injuries transformed him into a bleating buffoon at times, he was also steadfast in his concern for the well-being of Voltaic workers recruited for the two biggest railroad construction projects in French West Africa. Taillebourg's official reports described in sensitive and exacting detail the perils and human consequences of recruiting African workers in an atmosphere of European economic self-interest, Eurocentrism, and vile racism. Moreover, Taillebourg had the capacity to step back and analyze the ultimate impact of such practices on the ethical and economic well-being of the overall colonial enterprise.

Mandé also asks us to think about another important question, the evaluation of sources for writing biography. After coming across Taillebourg's reports in the colonial archives, Mandé readily came to the conclusion that this administrator defied the stereotype. Later, Mandé read with incredulity the very derisive descriptions of Taillebourg by Amadou Hampâté Bâ, a respected African auxiliary in the colonial administration and a novelist whose memoirs have become a classic. To get a sense of the man, Mandé explores Taillebourg's own reports, reports by his superiors and peers in the colonial service and the military, official documents about his health and retirement, and Bâ's account. In a way, these documents are also characters in this chapter. As a result, they are more often quoted and cited than is the case in other chapters. Think about what each kind of source contributes to understanding Taillebourg and why Bâ may have presented him as he did.

Reading through archival documents on the social history of colonial Upper Volta (today's Burkina Faso), I was struck by the rigor and detail of reports written in the 1920s by French colonial administrator Adolphe Albert Marie Taillebourg. His sincerity and style compelled me to ferret out everything he wrote about the use of Voltaic labor in agricultural projects and railroad construction in the colonial era in French West Africa. Taillebourg's reports, unlike many others, are well organized and written in a style that is lively, direct, and straightforward. He minutely documented facts pertinent to situations at hand, placed them in the context of the relevant legislation, and then situated them in the appropriate broader contexts. Consequently, the publication of *Oui mon commandant!* in 1993, the second volume of the memoirs of Amadou Hampâté Bâ, shook me up.[1]

Taillebourg: A Character in a Musical Comedy?

Contrary to my understanding of Taillebourg, Bâ describes him as a monster and a liar—a figure whose simple physical presence in a district he likened to a swarm of locusts. As a result, I faced several challenges in writing this chapter: First, any attempt to rehabilitate Taillebourg flies in the face of con-

temporary trends in African historiography, which depict colonial administrators in a uniformly negative light. Second, as a junior African historian,
should I take a position opposed to Amadou Hampâté Bâ, an icon of African
literature? Finally, do I have the legitimacy that would allow me to recast the
image of a colonial administrator who many thought had horns? Moreover,
Taillebourg was, in fact, cantankerous and sometimes quite brutal.

In *Oui mon commandant!* Hampâté Bâ rallies readers to his point of view
from the first lines of his description of Taillebourg: "Of very nervous tem-
perament, it only took a 'yes' or a 'no' for him to throw a fit, braying like a
donkey, only stopping when he collapsed in a faint like an epileptic."[2] Bâ's
caricature is relentless. He never acknowledges, for example, that Taillebourg's wife had accompanied him to Upper Volta, information that would
have bestowed a modicum of humanity on the Frenchman and perhaps soft-
ened his crotchety image.

For Bâ, Taillebourg is a buffoon who erupts into his career and his memoir—a madman. He puts his description in the mouth of Taillebourg's cook:

> The commandant has the voice of a lion, but the tender heart of a young girl.
> One should not pay any mind to his yelling and swearing. Scatterbrained as a
> chicken, he immediately forgets what he said, as well as what you say to him.
> Everywhere he goes, he has to have three chairs—one for him, another for
> his wooden leg, and a third for his belly. He suffers enormously from his war
> wounds and especially from the amputation of his leg. Every fifteen or twenty
> minutes or so, he yells as if he were pushing the pain out of his leg, and then
> drinks a gulp or two of water to moisten his throat, which was always dry. . . .
>   When he has an attack, he sometimes yells so long and loud that he falls
> into a faint. When that happens, you don't get upset. You just wait quietly for
> two or three minutes, and he regains consciousness and comes back to him-
> self as if nothing had happened. His fainting spells might last as long as five
> minutes, but rarely much longer. When he speaks, don't interrupt him with
> questions. That's the best way to irritate him. Finally, every time he comes in
> or goes out, and every time you cross his path, even on the veranda, you have
> to salute him like soldiers do.[3]

Bâ nicknames Taillebourg "Ball of Thorns." Despite the fact that Taillebourg entered the administrative ranks as a colonial administrator first class,
Bâ ridicules his status: "He is a burlesque character worthy of an operetta,
someone we might run across in a novel. Taillebourg is not a personality of
first rank in the French colonial system, but a simple 'king of the bush.'"[4]
Hence the Frenchman appears as both handicapped and incompetent,

parachuted in to head the local administration simply because of his hero-
ics in the First World War. Bâ claims that Inspector of the Colonies Dulac,
who came to inspect the *cercle* or district of Dédougou where Taillebourg was
commandant, observed, "The presence of Monsieur Administrator first class
Taillebourg in a cercle is worse than an invasion of locusts."[5]

Hampâté Bâ acknowledges that Taillebourg was a learned man and that
he spoke Bambara and Fulfulde, two major languages of the region, quite
well. Hence it is legitimate to doubt another of Bâ's stories that a crowd
that gathered to welcome Taillebourg sang a nonsensical couplet to him in
Bambara. Taillebourg would have undoubtedly recognized the hoax. Unlike
many administrators of his rank, Taillebourg was recruited in French West
Africa following his meritorious military service. William Ponty, the governor general of French West Africa, described him as "an educated, intelligent, and devoted agent—an untiring worker [who] has offered fine service
in the districts where he has been employed in the [French] Soudan as an
officer and an administrator since 1899."[6] So what else do we know about
this man who apparently simultaneously was a loudmouth, a royal buffoon,
and bizarre, as well as cultivated, sentimental, and courageous?

Taillebourg, War Hero

Although *Oui mon commandant!* presents Taillebourg as a curiosity, he was
not at all plunked down in the colony as Bâ suggests. He arrived in Africa as
a soldier in 1891 and enjoyed a career as a low-level officer first in the second
regiment of the colonial infantry and then in a regiment of the Senegalese
sharpshooters. Engaged on the battlefield in World War I, he was promoted
to the rank of *sous-lieutenant de reserve* on March 1, 1915. Taillebourg's military record notes that he was at the front and then relieved for health reasons
with a fractured left femur and a deep incision in the joint of his left knee.
He was designated a "fine officer in wartime" with the following evaluation:
"very devoted, animated by the desire to do well, active, and courageous."[7]
An official document pronounced him 60 percent handicapped[8]—not 100
percent, as wrote Bâ.

By the time he joined the colonial administration, "Ball of Thorns" had
risen to the rank of captain in the colonial infantry. His right foot had been
amputated, and he suffered from the aftereffects of his wounds. He had been
awarded ten decorations for his wartime service, including the prestigious
Croix de Guerre 1914–1918 with Three Palms. He also received the title of
Chevalier de la Légion d'Honneur for military service. Taillebourg's personnel file also notes, and literally underlines the fact that he was categorized as

"gravely wounded."[9] Despite chronic suffering, Taillebourg the administrator pushed the envelope in a way uncommon for his epoch, arguing that all wounded in war should be proclaimed heroes of France—even if they were black or African. Taillebourg demanded that honor be bestowed on such men, even though Hampâté Bâ claimed that he was the one who initiated such efforts. Taillebourg's campaign is little remembered in France.

Taillebourg, Colonial Agent and Administrator

Taillebourg's file also documents that he had a most honorable career in the French Soudan (today's Mali) as a colonial administrator. Governor Clozel wrote that he was a "very active administrator, very energetic and very devoted, meriting the highest esteem of his heads of service."[10]

Taillebourg began his career as an *agent des services indigènes*, or an agent in the native service. In French colonial Africa, such agents were usually Europeans, whereas analogous positions in the British colonies were almost always held by local people. Whereas most French colonial administrators were civil servants recruited and sent from Paris, the agents des services indigènes were colonial functionaries entirely under the authority of colonial governors. After the creation of the federations of French West Africa (FWA) and French Equatorial Africa (FEA) in 1910, each of which brought together several separate colonies, administrators were both named and removed by the governors general of the federations.

Recruiting procedures, advancement, and the compensation and benefits extended to agents varied from one French colonial federation to another. French citizenship was the only formal prerequisite for being named an agent des services indigènes, whereas colonial administrators appointed from Paris had to have at least a secondary school diploma.[11] Hence Taillebourg, who was awarded a *baccalauréat ès-lettres* at the end of secondary school, qualified for the higher status of a regular colonial administrator. Nonetheless, he started at the bottom and tenaciously rose through the ranks.

As part of his duties as a subaltern official dealing with local people, Taillebourg was obliged to learn Bambara. Such fluency in a local language made it possible for him to ask people questions without the intermediary of an interpreter. As a result, during his later tours to evaluate colonial administrators and their operations he was not easily misled, because African agents under his control could not easily be pressured by local African auxiliaries of the colonial administration to tell him only what they wanted him to know. His language skills also were a major asset in his efforts to evaluate how well local colonial administrations served their populations.

Taillebourg, Inspector of Administrative
Affairs and Voltaic Migrant Labor

In October 1921, the lieutenant governor of Upper Volta named Taillebourg to be his inspector of administrative affairs charged with overseeing the internal affairs of local administrations throughout the colony. In keeping with the guidelines of the inspection unit, he

> dealt exclusively with the Lieutenant Governor in all matters that concerned inspections, presenting him with his observations and propositions. In keeping with colonial regulations, he issued no orders to local administrations. His sole mission was to observe the political, economic, and social situation in each district. He documented how they performed their functions and formulated whatever observations seemed appropriate. Decision-making power remained solely with the Lieutenant-Governor.[12]

In the same year, the lieutenant governor expanded Taillebourg's duties to include representing him and the colony of Upper Volta to the offices charged with supervising work on two major railroad lines in French West Africa, the Thiès-Kayes-Niger (TKN) in Senegal and French Soudan, and the Chemin de Fer de la Côte d'Ivoire (CFCI). The lieutenant governor named Taillebourg to this position for three reasons: the increasing numbers of laborers from Upper Volta working on the railroads; the large numbers of Voltaic workers returning to Upper Volta who looked like walking skeletons or "wrecks";[13] and the insistent complaints of the commandants de cercle about the negative impact of labor migration on their subjects.

As he performed his inspection duties, Taillebourg's principal interlocutors were local and regional colonial administrators in Upper Volta, to whom he communicated the lieutenant governor's thoughts and from whom he solicited concerns and protests about labor issues. Because Taillebourg was very conscientious in his adherence to the instructions, rules, and laws that were supposed to govern the administration and limit its powers, he became the target of enmity. In representing the lieutenant governor in affairs related to Voltaic migrant laborers, Taillebourg dealt with the governors of neighboring colonies that relied on workers from Upper Volta for construction and industrial or administrative projects. In these colonies, which were clamoring for Voltaic labor, Taillebourg was also regarded as a spoiler. His concern for the welfare of local people inside and outside Upper Volta led many of his fellow administrators to label him the "crackpot of the colony," an expression he came to use in his own correspondence. To place Taillebourg in this larger context requires an overview of railroad construction projects in FWA and the recruiting and treatment of the workers from Upper Volta who built them.

Railroad Construction, Migrant Labor
from Upper Volta, and Taillebourg

Railroad construction projects in FWA after World War I confronted great obstacles in finding enough labor. Apart from forbidding recruiting by the administration in Senegal, the governor general of FWA also decided that migrant workers in Senegal from French Soudan should be assigned to other projects. As a result, beginning in 1922, the entire workforce on the work sites of the TKN railroad was replaced by workers from Upper Volta.[14] In 1925, the same shift took place on the CFCI work sites in Côte d'Ivoire, despite polite protests from the lieutenant governor of Upper Volta, who suggested rather that the recruiting reservoir should be enlarged to include French Soudan. The lieutenant governor of French Soudan argued against this proposal. Table 8.1 demonstrates the crucial role that migrant laborers from Upper Volta played in the construction of the TKN and CFCI railroads between 1920 and 1931.

On the railroad in Côte d'Ivoire, part of the labor contingent was made up of laborers from Dahomey (today's Benin) called up before World War I to build the first section of the railroad from Abidjan to Bouaké. But in

Table 8.1. Workers from Upper Volta Recruited to Work on the Railroads in FWA, 1920–1931

Year	CFCI[a]	CFCI[b]	CFCI[c]	CFCI[d]	TKN[a]	TKN[b]	TKN[c]
1920	1,924	1,921	1,922		3,002	3,002	3,002
1921	3,510	3,510	3,510		7,724	7,724	7,724
1922	4,900	4,900	4,900		9,550	9,550	9,550
1923	6,800	6,800	6,800		4,500	4,500	4,500
1924	2,150	2,150	2,150		500	500	500
1925	3,700	3,700	3,700	2,342	500	500	
1926	4,885	4,885	4,885	2,876	500	500	
1927	5,060	5,060	5,060	2,400	500	500	
1928	5,967	5,967	5,957	3,000	500	500	
1929	5,095	5,095	4,515	3,000	65	65	65
1930	6,600	6,600	903	6,000			
1931	6,500						

[a]Archives Nationales du Sénégal (ANS), Dakar, 2G (1920–1931), data revised and corrected.
[b]ANS, Dakar, K121 (26).
[c]Gouvernement Général de l'AOF, *Exposition coloniale, Haute-Volta*, 1931.
[d]Centre d'Archives d'Outre-Mer (CAOM), Aix-en-Provence, France, Travaux Publics, 1e série, carton 13, dossier 10.
Note: The major differences between these four sets of data for the CFCI and three sets for the TKN are due not only to statistical distortions but also to how the authors interpreted and presented their information. The differences range from a multiple of 1 to 2, depending on whether the data represent the total numbers of workers present on the work sites at any one time, or the total numbers of workers recruited in the colony over a year's time.

general, recruiting strategies in FWA designated Upper Volta as the labor reservoir for the federation. Unequal treatment of workers from different colonies translated into disdain for workers from Upper Volta. Pay discrimination came along with social segregation. On TKN work sites, for example, Voltaic labor recruits made only 1½ francs each day, even though they were assigned the most disagreeable tasks—in contrast with workers who signed on voluntarily, who were paid 2½ francs daily.[15] In contrast, much-sought-after skilled workers came from Senegal, French Soudan, and Côte d'Ivoire.

The lieutenant governor of Upper Volta sent Taillebourg to inspect the work sites of the CFCI in June 1922. Taillebourg's task was facilitated by the confidence that the lieutenant governor placed in him. Taillebourg believed that work sites managed by the colonial administration should serve as examples for private sites. As a result, he mounted a veritable inquisition against the practices and customs of the railroad administrations. He raised questions about the organization of recruiting, living conditions of workers on the work sites, health services, and workers' pay. In short, Taillebourg confronted the problems that underlay the use of forced labor in the French colonies.

In the case of the TKN, Voltaic migrants recruited by the administration for employment as "specialists and hired laborers" enjoyed no privileges whatsoever—in contrast with workers from Senegal or French Soudan. Such discrimination served the purposes of officials in charge of the TKN, who wanted to turn Voltaic migrants into a pliable workforce that they could push to the limit. Given this situation, it is not surprising that one of Taillebourg's first acts was to call for an end to the discrimination in pay and benefits between workers from Upper Volta recruited by the colonial administration and those recruited from other colonies as free labor. At the same time, Taillebourg expressed scorn for work site supervisors who were more preoccupied with the pace of their project than the living and working conditions of the laborers.

Despite the fact that the TKN had access to automobiles, for example, Voltaic workers were obliged to work as porters, transporting food supplies to work camps. They also carried water and even dirt for embankments at railroad work sites. It is difficult to dismiss Taillebourg, who sharply criticized the differential treatment of workers on the TKN:

> Those who put the railroad in place, those who push the wagons, transport the stone, gravel, go find wood, water, straw, clear the land, and so forth, are better able to withstand the exhaustion that comes with their work. But the dirt mover lost in a group, who for hours on end repeats his machine-like movements, this man, be he the most primitive, the most besotted, the most void

of all thought, and the most dominated that one could imagine, will endeavor to work as little as possible. This man has been compared to a machine, but one takes care of a machine, and when it does not do what it should, it is not [the machine] that is subject to accusation, but rather he who does not know to use it.[16]

Apart from enduring endless forced labor, Voltaic workers also were victimized by railroad companies that seized on any pretext—illness, stealing food, empty sacks, lies, or laziness—to deduct money from their wages. Railroad authorities also multiplied verification procedures. For example, they underscored the need for a period of adaptation and delousing as an excuse for slowing down the incorporation of new laborers into the workforce, a practice which again saved them money at the expense of the workers.

Such treatment of Voltaic workers by the railroad companies also brought severe criticism from the commandants in charge of their districts of origin. Humanitarians such as Albert Londres denounced these practices. Paradoxically, worker productivity, which was undercut by poorly adapted and poorly maintained tools, seemed to be of little concern to the companies. In Taillebourg's opinion, such treatment of workers undermined France's colonial enterprise over the long term by weakening the labor force. It led him vehemently to denounce a technocratic bent so blinded by outcomes, results, and planning that human beings had no place:

> Saving several thousand francs while uselessly losing tens of lives is a mistake that is not only administrative, but political. The Thiès-Kayes [railroad] tracks how the work advances by the cost of each cubic meter of earth moved— that's all well and good. But moving earth and laying rails with a minimum of deaths—that would be better.[17]

Among those who shared Taillebourg's concerns was Sorel, the inspector general of health and medical services in French West Africa, who observed, "Once a specific number of workers had been identified, making that number became a mindless imperative. Managers calculated that a certain number of kilometers of track required a certain number of laborers, and they moved heaven and earth to find them."[18] Sorel's criticism rang particularly true in Upper Volta, whose human capital had been placed at the disposal of labor-recruiting campaigns for a long time. For many years, recruiting took place under the auspices of traditional chiefs and the whips of guards in each district. In response, local people devised a strategy of sending along the ill and those infected with sleeping sickness in order to keep able people at home to work family farms. In 1922, for example, recruits who arrived on work sites were "afflicted with illness that led to chronically swollen testicles, advanced goiter problems, chronic abscesses, or disabled arms and legs."[19]

In the same year, this situation led Lieutenant Governor Hesling to proclaim that colonial subjects recruited for the army, public works, or private works projects outside Upper Volta should be examined by the same doctors who examined men for military service. Henceforth, workers leaving the colony were taken first to Bobo-Dioulasso or Ouagadougou in Upper Volta for medical examinations. Unfortunately, in the case of workers bound for the CFCI, the physical capacities of each worker were not evaluated individually. Rather they were classified in terms of a five-level profile derived from the requirements for joining the military: Class 1, very vigorous subjects; Class 2, vigorous subjects; Class 3, normal subjects; Class 4, weak subjects; or Class 5, unfit subjects.[20] Several tragic developments arose from simply classifying potential workers rather than evaluating their individual health status. In the late 1920s, men classed as "unfit subjects" inapt for work were sent home to their cercles without any provisions for health care. They tended to be ill, underweight—defined as weighing less than fifty kilograms—or too young to work. On the other hand, workers tagged as "weak subjects" were kept on and assigned to light labor, while waiting to be assigned to more physically demanding work sites.

Opinion is divided regarding responsibility for the decline in the health of workers following recruiting. The railroad companies did not evaluate the health of workers until they arrived on work sites, thus exonerating themselves from responsibility for injuries or diseases that labor recruits contracted along the way. This policy irritated colonial administrators, who remarked that men left their districts in good health only to arrive exhausted. In addition, ambiguities in the legal texts and the refusal of the railroads to assume responsibility for taking care of workers who were not able to work when they arrived exacerbated tension between the railroads and the administration.

In the case of the TKN railroad, Taillebourg saw to it that workers from Upper Volta were assembled at the administrative post of Abidédi for delousing to kill fleas that potentially carried recurrent fever when they arrived and when they left TKN work sites. While the health service deloused their clothes, laborers bathed in a nearby stream. According to attending doctors, this was the only time that most of the workers were able to wash during the period of their six-month labor contract, due to water rationing during the dry season. On some work sites, workers could not even find water for the ablutions required of Muslims before prayer. Nor did the workers have soap or antiseptic products to combat parasites. This absence of provisions that favored personal hygiene and proper clothing, along with promiscuity and abject poverty, promoted the spread of disease. Little attention was paid to proper nutrition, despite regulations and recommendations about how to plan proper meals. Hence the colonial slogans that promised education along with work were hollow words. Workers were nothing but simple tools for production.

Upon Taillebourg's recommendation, these shortcomings led Upper Volta in 1922 to begin requiring indemnities for victims of accidents and deaths on work sites outside the colony. Local administrators, sensitive to complaints among local people about the railroads, echoed these calls for the application of labor legislation to bring down the high mortality rates. These policies had three objectives. First, they encouraged work sites for which the administration provided workers to serve as models for private work sites. Such measures also allowed the administrators to take the high moral ground when they took action against the forestry companies for exploitative practices. Finally, such measures allowed the administration to build up political capital among local populations overwhelmed by numerous deaths.

Thereby affirming its good faith and goodwill, the Voltaic administration hoped that the allocation

of a substantial indemnity to families of the deceased would oblige the management of the TKN and the Travaux Neufs to no longer limit themselves to palliative measures that consist most of the time of just more papers, but to take radical measures. Hit in the pocketbook, the administration of the TKN would be obliged to tell work site overseers that they will be evaluated not only in terms of the cubic [meters] of terrassing finished or the number of meters of rails laid, but inversely according to the number of deaths among their recruits.[21]

By committing to pay damages for workers who had died, the Upper Volta administration also pushed those responsible for the railroad work sites to face up to the issue of paying damages for "work site accidents." Despite regulations, many wounded and mutilated workers were abandoned to their fates without any protest from the administration. Indeed, the Upper Volta administration had its own strategy for not indemnifying them. Taillebourg's report highlighted the fact that the names of many workers who were ill or dead were simply added to lists of either units scheduled to be released or units already departed. Nor did the railroads assume hospital costs for injured workers, benefits that they dismissed as charity beyond their mission. Moreover, they only paid their laborers' travel costs while they were actually employed—sometimes even going so far as to cut off food rations for travel. This absurd situation obliged administrator Taillebourg, in caustic correspondence, "to beg for alms" for the people he administered.[22]

Probably the best way to improve the welfare of workers would have been to intervene earlier, when they were recruited. Surprisingly, many authors have assumed that proper formal procedures for recruiting laborers from Upper Volta were respected throughout the colonial period. This idea was also propagated by numerous official documents through the late 1920s—until the recriminations of the International Labor Organization publicized at the time of the Universal Colonial Exposition of 1931 in Paris. The reality was quite otherwise.

Taillebourg: The Fall

Taillebourg's mission ended with the end of work on the TKN railroad. Despite a decision to delegate to him administrative oversight of Voltaic workers destined for Côte d'Ivoire to the south, he was instead reintegrated into the central administration. Following a leave and an assignment in French Soudan, he was named commandant du cercle in the district of Dédougou in Upper Volta, where he encountered Hampâté Bâ, probably for the second time. Very ill when he arrived, Taillebourg stayed only a month and a half. Local French settlers and missionaries attacked him. Bâ wrote that Taillebourg's problems in Dédougou stemmed from his attacks on the Catholic Church and its priests, whom he charged with interfering in administrative affairs. Bâ reported that Taillebourg's criticisms provoked a vigorous counterattack from the vicar of Ouagadougou, the capital of the colony. Bâ added that when a colonial inspection mission arrived in Dédougou, its head, Inspector of the Colonies Dulac, judged Taillebourg harshly and ordered his repatriation due to ill health.

But the story is more complicated than the tale told by Hampâté Bâ. Bâ's version leaves out an altercation between Taillebourg and Mengant, who later was Bâ's mentor and whom Bâ described in glowing terms. Following Taillebourg's repatriation and despite his poor health, he wrote letters to his superiors between 1932 and 1934 explaining that when he arrived in Dédougou in November 1931, he was received with hostility by Mengant, who had been the commandant du cercle in Dédougou, but with Taillebourg's arrival was relegated to administrating Tougan, one of its constituent districts. Apart from arousing the ill will of Mengant, Taillebourg also questioned another administrator named Gratiant about the disappearance of five thousand francs from his coffers, which had not been reported to the higher authorities. Mengant and Gratiant were friends and, according to Taillebourg, plotted against him over the new telephone line between Dédougou and Tougan.[23]

Mengant ultimately requested an audience with the lieutenant governor to discuss the situation. The lieutenant governor then ordered Taillebourg to come meet with him in mid-January 1932. Taillebourg later wrote, "I recall the hostility that I left behind in the cercle of Dédougou [among] the White Fathers, the agricultural agency, employees of the Cercle, and others. They did not pardon me for wanting to be the sole head of the Cercle. I told the governor all of this." From the lieutenant governor, Taillebourg learned that "unbelievably slanderous charges from several quarters had spread through the country—as much about my wife as about me." These included the accusation that Taillebourg himself was implicated in the disappearance of four hundred francs from his administrative coffers. He vociferously defended himself: "I wrote to my governor: 'If you have the slightest suspicions concerning the disappearance of this sum by my hand, I would be pleased if sanctions against me were proposed to the higher authorities.'" No formal charges were ever levied against him.

To add another dimension to the story, Taillebourg acknowledged that he indeed was ill when Colonial Inspector Dulac arrived in Dédougou. His illness apparently inspired no sympathy from Dulac, who severely criticized Taillebourg's fierce adherence to regulations:

> We uncovered in these 45 or 50 days that Monsieur Taillebourg is a maniac about authority, and only knows how to exercise it with brutality. While between 1 January and 10 November [before Taillebourg's arrival], 20 punishments were inflicted, the new commandant de cercle found a way to raise this total to 135 in a month and a half. Given that the circonscription has a large population, M. Taillebourg had the chance to break his own record. In any case, he is the best illustration of what we have written about the dangers in the present system of native laws and regulation.[24]

Taillebourg wrote that he was repatriated in 1932 following a heart attack, although the medical certificate mentions instead pulmonary congestion stemming from the flu and complicated by insufficient cardio-renal function, and anemia followed by asthenia.[25] In an action unusual for the colonial administration, Inspector Dulac decided that due to Taillebourg's poor health, he would not be allowed to see his evaluation. Probably the most objective and accurate source about the last months of Taillebourg's career is the document that the lieutenant governor of Upper Volta, Fournier, sent the governor general of French West Africa. Fournier wrote, "In his last tour, M. Taillebourg, serving in Upper Volta, had to be repatriated after 16 months, [including] four consecutive months when he was incapacitated due to a very serious attack of typho-malaria." He noted further that Taillebourg's chronic heart problems along with pulmonary congestion had exacerbated his already authoritarian personality, leading to extreme antipathy toward Europeans as well as local people. The lieutenant governor concluded that the problem had become so acute that Taillebourg could not fulfill duties commensurate with his rank. And so, in a decree issued by the *président de la République* dated May 17, 1933, we read that "M. Taillebourg (Adolphe, Albert, Marie), a colonial administrator first class, is authorized to exercise his right to a retirement pension due to injury that occurred during his service."[26]

Conclusion

Given the detailed portrait of Taillebourg available in public records, one has to ask why Hampâté Bâ attacked him a half-century later. Did Bâ hope to profit from Taillebourg's unpopular reputation by taking a partisan position? Did he feel obliged to defend his friends in Dédougou who clearly had a bone to pick with Taillebourg? Or was he just looking for a burlesque character to liven up his account? At the very least, the historical record raises questions about Hampâté Bâ's sincerity. For example, why did Bâ introduce Taillebourg into his autobiography only by writing about his time in Dédougou, rather than acknowledging that they had both served together earlier in the relatively small cabinet of the colonial governor?

The omissions in Bâ's depiction suggest perhaps that Taillebourg may have been poorly understood and disliked in colonial circles because he belonged to an oppositional line of colonial administrators, all of whom compromised their careers at one time or another to defend the interests of the "natives." But when he was delegate of the lieutenant governor of Upper Volta, Taillebourg never presented himself as a reformer, even though he believed in humanitarian principles. He positioned himself rather as a legalist who required that the *Code de l'indigénat*, or the native legal code, be faithfully applied. Taillebourg's tenacity and ill-tempered insistence on respecting the letter of the law in managing African workers led to a bad reputation. Seemingly paradoxically, he also pressured the lieutenant governor to fulfill his moral obligation to improve the lot of Voltaic laborers working elsewhere in FWA. At the same time, even the lieutenant governor remarked that Taillebourg never called the colonial enterprise into question:

M. Taillebourg, a duty-bound man of great conscience, took to heart the mission confided to him. Nothing escaped either his investigations or his control. He is as committed to being a collaborator on the Thiès-Kayes [railroad], as to extracting the most from [workers from Upper Volta], as to being their protector and guaranteeing as best he can that their working conditions will reflect the regulations.[27]

Taillebourg's desire to see colonized people placed at the center of administrative concerns was more broadly reflected in the later arrival of a new species of humanitarian administrators and doctors. They were sensitive to demographic issues and particularly concerned about undermining the human capital and, with it, the fiscal capital of French West Africa. The governor general's policy "faire du nègre," loosely translated as "developing the black," grew out of ideas enunciated in 1923 by Minister of the Colonies Albert Sarraut, but it lacked theoretical underpinnings.[28] In practice, the policy took the form of reinforcing the structures of Assistance Médicale Indigène, or Indigenous Medical Assistance, which led campaigns against epidemic diseases such as sleeping sickness in Upper Volta, or the form of establishing rules for the use of local labor.

In the end, what shall we conclude about Taillebourg? Through dedication and insistence on improving the conditions of railroad workers, he allowed the colonial administration in French West Africa to avoid replicating the disastrous "drama of the railroad" on the Congo-Océan line in FEA.[29] But Taillebourg's measures did not at all please the colonial technical agencies and ironically led to his disgrace.[30] With great self-knowledge Taillebourg later wrote,

For more than 30 years, I was considered in French West Africa to be a rabble rouser, a vague term often repeated which stereotyped an employee and allowed the lazy minds who repeated it not to think any more about it. Beginning in 1921, I was the crackpot of the Thiès-Kayes from the point of view of the railroad men. M. Hesling himself counseled me to calm down when I told him about the hundreds of useless deaths [from hunger or thirst that I saw] with my own eyes. On Friday, April 3, 1925, M. Terrasson treated me like a crazy person and a hysteric in his office at 10 in the morning. It is true that at the end of our stormy interview I said to him, with my hands held open, "in any case, my hands are clean." "I know that," answered Terrasson. In 1927, when I was in Timbuktu, M. Carbou set about encouraging me to stay in France given my mental fatigue. By 1932 I was [deemed to be] a crazy person and was so recognized.[31]

Further Reading

The Government General of French West Africa came into being by decree on June 16, 1895. Jurists set about codifying disparate administrative regulations into colonial legal manuals, which offer insights into how the government was meant to function. See, for example, Paul Dislère, *Traité de législation coloniale*, 2nd ed. (Paris: P. Dupont, 1897), 3 volumes; Étienne Antonelli, *Manuel de législation coloniale* (Paris: Presses Universitaires de France, 1927); and Louis Rolland and Pierre Lampué, *Précis de droit des pays d'outre-mer: Territoires, départements, États associés* (Paris: Dalloz, 1949).

Despite such efforts at standardization, colonial administrations differed from one colonial power to another and within the French empire itself, according to the personalities of the individual governors general. Several excellent studies explore this topic: Michael Crowder, *West Africa under Colonial Rule* (Evanston, Ill.: Northwestern University Press, 1968); Patrick Manning, *Francophone Sub-Saharan Africa, 1880–1895* (Cambridge, UK: Cambridge University Press, 1988); Alice L. Conklin, *A Mission to Civilize: The Republican Idea of Empire in France and West Africa, 1985–1930* (Stanford, Calif.: Stanford University Press, 1997); Thomas Martin, *The French Empire between the Wars: Imperialism, Politics, and Society* (Manchester, UK: Manchester University Press, 2005).

Below the level of the federal government in French West Africa, each colony except Senegal was governed by a lieutenant governor, who was supported by a central colonial administration and by district administrators, or *commandants*, who headed territorial divisions called *cercles*. Early on, colonial administrators generally came from the ranks of the military units that had participated in the conquests or from Europeans who had settled in the colonies. After 1912, however, administrators had to have training at the École Coloniale. The "genealogy" of these officials is well documented in William B. Cohen, *Rulers of Empire: The French Colonial Service in Africa* (Stanford, Calif.: Hoover Institution Press, 1971). Robert Delavignette, former colonial official and former director of the École de la France d'Outre-Mer, offers insights into the experiences of an administrator in his own memoir, *Freedom and Authority in French West Africa* (London: Cass, 1968).

In the contest for hegemony on the ground, pitting French and African societies against each other, the commandants of districts were omnipotent because they concentrated both administrative and judicial powers in their hands. In theory limited by the laws and decrees of the colonial regime, they often acted as if their authority had no limits. Albert Londres describes such arbitrary exercise of authority in *A Very Naked People*, trans. Sylvia Stuart (New York: H. Liveright, 1929). The commandants are also mocked and ridiculed in novels and plays, such as Amadou Hampâté Bâ, *The Fortunes of Wangrin*, trans. Aina Pavolini Taylor (Bloomington: Indiana University Press, 1999); Yambo Ouologuem, *Bound to Violence*, trans. Ralph Manheim (New York: Harcourt, Brace, and Jovanovich, 1971), and Ahmadou Kourouma, *Monnew*, trans. Nidra Poller (San Francisco: Mercury House, 1994).

Notes

1. Amadou Hampâté Bâ, *Oui mon commandant!: Mémoires II* (Paris: Actes Sud, 1993). This volume focuses on Bâ's early adult years and his career in the French colonial administration. *Amkoullel, l'enfant Peul* (1991) deals with Bâ's childhood and adolescence in the French colony of Soudan (Soudan français).

2. Bâ, *Oui mon commandant!* 400–401.

3. Bâ, *Oui mon commandant!* 397–411. The cook's description is found in these pages.

4. An expression referring to *commandants de cercle* popularized by historian and former administrator Hubert Deschamps in his memoir *Roi de la brousse: Mémoires d'autres mondes* (Paris: Berger-Levrault, 1975).

5. In contrast to what Hampâté Bâ wrote, Inspector Dulac's comment was a question rather than a declaration. See Centre d'Archives d'Outre-Mer (CAOM), Aix-en-Provence, Inspection des colonies, carton 3069, rapport 26: Cercle de Dédougou, Mission Haute-Volta, 1931–1932.

6. Archives Nationales du Sénégal (ANS), Dakar, 1C769, "Taillebourg Adolphe: Note présentant Taillebourg pour l'ordre de la Croix de Chevalier de l'Étoile Noire du Bénin en 1904." This file includes three folders: (1) "Affaire Taillebourg," which recounts the ups and downs of Taillebourg and administrators in Upper Volta, and his early retirement; (2) a dossier including his administrative record along with assessments by governors, 1920–1932; and (3) a dossier on the reasons he retired.

7. See Service Historique de l'Armée de Terre, Château de Vincennes, Dossier Taillebourg, no. 4679, rés. Des cadres, 23è infanterie coloniale.

8. ANS, Dakar, 1C769, "Note circulaire: Taillebourg Adolphe."

9. ANS, Dakar, 1C769, "Affaire Taillebourg Adolphe."

10. ANS, Dakar, 10G11 (107), Lettre du Lieutenant-gouverneur de la Haute-Volta au Gouverneur général de l'AOF, no. 1363 A.G, 7 October 1922.

11. William B. Cohen, *Empereurs sans sceptres: Histoire des administrateurs de la France d'Outre-Mer et de l'École Coloniale*, trans. Louis de Lesseps and Camille Garnier (Paris: Berger-Levrault, 1973), 39–40. Originally published in English as *Rulers of Empire: The French Colonial Service in Africa* (Stanford, Calif.: Hoover Institution Press, 1971).

12. "Arrêté No 14, Portant création dans chacune des Colonies du Gouvernement Général, le territoire civil de Mauritanie excepté, un ou plusieurs emplois d'inspecteurs des Affaires administratives dans les cercles de la Colonie," *Journal officiel de l'Afrique occidentale française (JOAOF)*, 13 January 1906; and "Circulaire no. 57, a/s de la politique indigène et du fonctionnement de l'inspection des Affaires administratives, Dakar, le 12 August 1911," *JOAOF*, 19 August 1911.

13. Lieutenant Governor Hesling rarely used such expressions in his correspondence. See ANS, Dakar, 10G11 (107), Lettre du Lieutenant-gouverneur de la Haute-Volta au Gouverneur général de l'A.O.F, no. 1363 A.G., 7 October 1922.

14. ANS, Dakar, 10G11, Lettre du Directeur du Chemins de fer du Thiès-Kayes au Lieutenant-gouverneur de la Haute-Volta, Thiès, 6 September 1922; Lettre du Lieutenant-gouverneur de la Haute-Volta au Gouverneur général de l'A.O.F, 7 October 1922.

15. ANS, Dakar, 10G11 (107), "Compte-rendu de la visite des chantiers des Travaux Neufs du Thiès-Kayes par l'Administrateur en chef Bernard et le médecin-major de 1ère classe Heckenroth," 31 December 1922.

16. ANS, Dakar, 10G11 (107), "Rapport de Taillebourg."

17. ANS, Dakar, 10G11 (107), "Rapport de Taillebourg."

18. ANS, Dakar, 10G29, Note de l'Inspecteur Général des services sanitaires et médicaux, Sorel, Dakar, October 1931, Mission SOL, annexed to the report titled "Situation économique de la Haute-Volta"; K128 (26) and K60 (19), "Rapport sur le danger proche de dépopulation que font courir à l'Afrique occidentale française des recrutements excessifs et mal repartis"; 1H26 (26), "Rapports d'inspection des services sanitaires de l'A.O.F, 1930–1934."

19. ANS, Dakar, 10G11 (107), "Rapport de Taillebourg."

20. CAOM, Aix-en-Provence, Travaux Publics, 1ère série, carton 13, dossier 10, document: "Mission d'inspection Haranger, 1931."

21. ANS, Dakar, 10G11 (107), "Rapport de Taillebourg."

22. ANCI, Abidjan, 5KK50-XXI-1-17, Lettre de l'administrateur des colonies en mission près du CFCI au Gouverneur de la Côte d'Ivoire, a/s des recrutés de la Haute-Volta libérés sans ressources, 8 October 1922.

23. ANS, Dakar, 1C769, Affaire Taillebourg, Lettre du Lieutenant-Gouverneur de la Haute-Volta, Fournier, au Gouverneur général de l'Afrique occidentale française, 30 March 1932. The following several quotations are taken from this file.

24. ANS, Dakar, 1C769, "Affaire Taillebourg."

25. ANS, Dakar, 1C769, "Dossier Taillebourg Adolphe."

26. ANS, Dakar, 1C769, "Dossier Taillebourg Adolphe." Copy of the decree of the Président of the république, 17 May 1933.

27. ANS, Dakar, 10G11 (107), Lettre du Lieutenant-gouverneur de la Haute-Volta au Gouverneur général de l'A.O.F, no. 1363 A.G., 7 October 1922.

28. Albert Sarraut, La mise en valeur des colonies françaises (Paris: Payot, 1923), 83–127. Sarraut defends the notion of association, according to which

a distant possession would no longer be just a trading post, a storehouse of wealth, or an outlet where the "conqueror" comes to gather spices and dispense merchandise while pressuring the native race to work to the limit. Colonies are not only markets: they are living entities, human creations, loyal parts of the French state, for whom, through scientific, economic, moral, and political progress, one will provide access to the greatest of destinies, on the same level as other parts of the national territory.

29. See Gilles Sautter, "Notes sur la construction du chemin de fer Congo-Océan (1921–1934)," Cahiers d'Études Africaines 26 (1967): 219–99, and Rita Headrick, "The Congo-Ocean Railway and Its Impact on Health," in Colonialism, Health, and Illness in French Equatorial Africa, 1885–1935 (Atlanta: African Studies Association Press, 1994), 273–310.

30. ANS, Dakar, 10G11 (107), Lettre du Directeur du Chemin de Fer de Thiès-Kayes à l'Inspecteur Général des Travaux Publics, Thiès, 2 August 1922.

31. ANS, Dakar, 1C769, "Affaire Taillebourg."

~

CHAPTER NINE

Louis Brody (1892–1951) of Cameroon and Mohammed Bayume Hussein (1904–1944) of Former German East Africa

Variety Show Performers and the Black Community in Germany between the Wars

Andreas Eckert

For the last half-century, at least since the founding of the Journal of African History *in 1960, research on African history in the European colonial period has focused almost exclusively on the impact of European conquest and rule in Africa. Yet, as recent work in British and French history attests, the carving out of European empires in Africa in the late nineteenth century, their administration over the following seventy-five years or so, the attempts to reengineer African societies to extract mineral wealth and produce cash crops more efficiently, and responses to increasing African demands for autonomy also profoundly affected the histories of the European centers of empire.*

The life stories of Louis Brody and Mohammed Bayume Hussein strongly suggest that even for Germany, whose imperial history in Africa was quite short, the reverberations of the experience at home lasted as long as if not longer than the colonial era itself. First, German governments and the German people had to come to terms with Africans from the former colonies who remained in or came to Germany. Brody's and Hussein's stories illustrate the complexities and contradictions of that presence. Both spent years in legal limbo. They were not recognized as either citizens or subjects of Germany, since the empire no longer existed. At the same time, German governments, even after the rise of the race-conscious Nazis, allowed them to remain—visible vestiges of the empire that was, and harbingers of the new empire that might again be. Second, people from Germany's former colonies had to exercise extraordinary initiative to find ways to fit in and survive in the métropole, which they did in part by becoming part of Germany as best they could—whether by re-presenting to Germans images from their former empire or by becoming part of German society through relationships with German women. At the same time, they actively protested their ill treatment and lack of recognition by the government. Hussein's negotiation of this complex set of identities and contradictory relationships with power led to his execution. Brody's itinerary was "successful" in so far as he made it through the Reich to die a natural death after World War II. Yet the murder of one and the survival of the other illustrate the fragility and serendipitous quality of the position of Africans in German society.

Finally, the stories of Brody and Hussein foreshadow the later "colonization" of the métropole by people from the former colonies, raising questions about how Africans have been incorporated into German society since World War II. After World War I, the French set the stage for conflict by stationing African soldiers from French colonies in the Rhineland. Brody protested the racism and hate crimes visited upon Africans from the former German colonies by Germans protesting this French policy. Then, after World War II, American troops, including African Americans, began to be stationed in Germany, where they remain today. Much more recently the rise of the European Union and easier travel between member countries has led to increased numbers of African immigrants from the former French and British colonies in Germany. African refugees have also made their way to Germany. Hence, the stories of Brody and Hussein not only closed the book on empire; they heralded new African presences in Germany.

German Colonialism and Africans in Germany before 1945

Until very recently, Germany's colonial past was more or less ignored by both professional academics and the wider public.[1] This neglect stemmed from a widespread tendency to equate colonialism with colonial rule, and thus to locate Germany at the margins of colonial involvement. It is indeed true that the German colonial empire was not very important in economic terms and only lasted for a little more than three decades—from the 1880s to World War I. Still, it would be wrong to argue that just because German colonial rule was short-lived, it was irrelevant to German history. Colonial possessions are one thing, colonialism and colonial thinking quite another. Charles Maier argued that the creation of nation-states and colonial imperialism were two sides of the same coin, and that the colonial project was a Western project, shared by most people in Europe.[2] Even those who did not directly take part in the colonial project approved of it, because it promised markets and raw materials, knowledge, progress, and civilization. Thus, one could argue that Germany with and without colonies was a close ally of the colonial project, and that the effects of the colonial experience deeply influenced German culture and society both when Germany possessed colonies and after World War I.[3] A particularly controversial discussion has arisen around the question of what German colonialism had to do with National Socialism, and to what extent colonial racial doctrines and practices, and especially the genocide of the Herero in German South West Africa, shaped the Nazi wars of extermination and the Holocaust.[4]

Increasing interest in the history of German colonialism has also led to a fresh look at those Africans who before 1945 spent part of their lives in Germany. For the most part, the migration of Africans to Germany began during the period of formal German colonialism in the late nineteenth and early twentieth century.[5] After 1884, immigrants from Germany's African colonies were mainly men who temporarily or permanently established their home in Germany, most often in the big cities of Berlin and Hamburg.[6] Their overall number is very difficult to determine. Estimates in the secondary literature differ considerably. The totals range from five hundred colonial migrants for the entire period from 1885 to 1945, to around three thousand individuals for the 1920s and 1930s alone.[7] But whatever the precise figure, their numbers were very small. Compared to France and Britain, the impact of Africans on German society was less significant, and there was never a "Black Berlin" or "Black Hamburg" comparable to the pre–World War II "Black Paris."[8] Nevertheless, the lives and experiences of Africans in Germany constitute an important and hitherto little-known chapter at the intersection of African history, German history, and the history of the African diaspora.

Africans in Germany made up a heterogeneous group, and they came for very different reasons. During the three decades of German colonial rule in Africa, some immigrants—especially chiefs' sons—were brought or sent as children or young adults for training at Christian mission societies and trade workshops. Others taught African languages at the universities and colonial institutes of Berlin and Hamburg. Still others accompanied returning colonial officers as servants or were recruited for one of the ethnographic exhibitions (*Völkerschauen*) that were very popular in Germany at the end of the nineteenth century.[9] Some Africans tried their luck as businessmen,[10] while many, especially after 1918, worked as servants or in the field of entertainment. For the most part, African migration to Germany took place only occasionally and without coercion.

The history of African migration to Germany and the African presence between the late nineteenth century and World War II falls into three phases. The first phase lasted up to World War I. In general, colonial migrants were regarded as an unwelcome by-product of colonial politics. Such attitudes fueled efforts by the colonial administration to restrict African immigration. German authorities sought to make sure that no Africans would stay in Germany permanently. For the authorities, the ambiguous legal status of African migrants was a major problem. In the colonies, Africans were classified legally as "natives," or *Eingeborene*. When in Germany, however, they had to be treated either as "domestic citizens" (*Inländer*) or as "expatriates." Moreover, people in both of these legal categories enjoyed greater rights than the colonial administrations granted their "native subjects" in the colonies. In addition, the state kept close watch on Africans in Germany, attempting to control their movements as much as possible because of the potential political threat they posed.

Africans who asserted themselves politically, self-consciously claiming rights and status, faced massive reprisals. Between 1902 and 1911, for example, Mpundu Akwa, the son of an important Cameroonian chief from Douala, lived in Germany, where he supported Duala protests against German misrule in Cameroon, and also tried—with little success—to do business. Mpundu enjoyed considerable notoriety. The public seems to have been "highly entertained by the image, portrayed in both newspaper interviews and music hall burlesques, of a black man speaking excellent German, wearing a monocle and formal attire, who gave himself the airs of both metropolitan *Herr* and an African prince."[11] Despite Mpundu's dashing image, his demands to be treated as the equal of European authorities, and probably even worse, his appearances as the public escort and possibly private lover of bourgeois and even aristocratic European women apparently threatened the racial order. The retired naval captain Liersemann went so far as to accuse him of grand larceny and brothel keeping. Mpundu Akwa combated this charge with a lawsuit. In the course of the trial, Liersemann withdrew most of his accusations, but Mpundu's long record of financial embarrassment came to light. Mpundu won his initial lawsuit, but two subsequent appeals resulted in Liersemann's being acquitted entirely on the grounds that "the concept of sensitivity to honor is not as developed among Negroes as among *Kulturmenschen*."[12] Mpundu returned to Cameroon, where he was eventually imprisoned by the colonial authorities.[13]

The second phase in African immigration began with the end of the German empire in 1919, when migrants from the former German colonies in Germany became subjects of the new mandatory powers: Britain, France, Belgium, and South Africa. In legal terms, this change meant that Africans in Germany acquired a status closer to that of expatriates. Despite this change in status, the Weimar authorities and especially the foreign office strictly refused to naturalize Africans. Africans in Germany were either identified with the observation "stateless" stamped in their passports, or they received certificates identifying them as a person "formerly belonging to a German protectorate" or as a "former German protégé," or *Schutzbefohlener.* Thus, the legal status of Africans remained murky.

Some Africans created cultural and political networks in order to look after their rights and interests. In 1918, for instance, the Cameroonian Peter Makembe founded the African Aid Association, or Afrikanischer Hilfsverein, in Hamburg. One of the tasks of this organization was to support Africans in their search for jobs and lodging or to help them in dealing with German authorities and employers. German politicians had mixed feelings about the presence of Africans, who were more or less without rights but, nonetheless, were increasingly self-confident. While some officials preferred to "carry these people directly back to Africa,"[14] others went so far as to regard the small African diaspora in Germany as a positive development. Because these officials were convinced that one day Germany would get the colonies back, Africans living in metropolitan Germany were seen as potential multipliers who, once back in Africa, would spread a positive image of Germany. Divided opinion about Africans and their ambiguous status meant that, for the time being, forced deportation was out of the question. Rather, the foreign office employed a strategy meant to encourage Africans to leave the country "voluntarily." At the same time, the authorities took care to secure the livelihood of Africans while they remained in Germany. For this purpose, the German Society for the Study of Natives, or the Deutsche Gesellschaft für Eingeborenenkunde, was charged with supporting needy Africans.[15]

Even German officials who found it useful to treat Africans well vehemently rejected relationships between African men and German women, although African-German marriages were not illegal. In the years after World War I, there were heightened "race anxieties" due to three causes: the so-called Black Horror on the Rhine, the presence of several thousand African soldiers among the French troops that occupied the Rhineland; the prevailing sense that the "proper racial order" had been inverted by the Versailles Treaty, which treated Germany as an "object" rather than a full subject of international law; and the perceived "reverse colonization" of the Rhineland by French colonial soldiers.[16] In eyes of the German public, the African soldiers were cannibals and rapists. To quote only one of many similar statements, the medical journal *Ärztliche Rundschau* offered a harbinger of the future in 1920: "Shall we silently endure that in future days not the light songs of white, beautiful, well-built, intelligent, agile, healthy Germans will ring on the shores of the Rhine, but the croaking sounds of grayish, low-browed, broad-muzzled, plump, bestial, syphilitic mulattos?"[17]

Beginning in the mid-1920s, Germany, especially Berlin and Hamburg, became an important scene for the activities of "black revolutionaries," who were often supported by the Soviet Union and the Comintern.[18] According to the Trinidadian George Padmore, a leading figure in the pan-Africanist movement and for many years a prominent member of the Comintern, Moscow did not want to attract attention to itself and, therefore, carefully chose Germany as the center of anti-imperialist activities:

> They assigned the responsibility of organizing the new anti-imperialist movement to the German Communists. . . . Shorn of her African and other colonies' defeat in the First World War, Germany was no longer a colonial power; and it was thought that an anti-imperialist call from Berlin would arouse less suspicion among colonial and dependent peoples than one coming from Western European capitals—London or Paris—possessing overseas empires.[19]

The so-called Negro Bureau, established in Hamburg in 1930, served as a center for the exchange of information. Directives from Moscow came there, and political operations were planned and directed from there. The rise of the Nazis to power in 1933 put an end to these activities.

The third phase in African migration to Germany began after 1933, when a number of African political activists left Germany for France. For Africans remaining in Germany, the situation deteriorated. The German government declared nearly all "members of the German protectorates" as "stateless" people, and due to the increasingly open racism of the German population, it became impossible for most Africans to continue working publicly as artists and so on. Nonetheless, many Germans who had lived in the colonies expressed concern about the negative impact that Nazi race policies might have on former colonial subjects.[20] They argued that at least some Africans in Germany had earned membership in German society by virtue of their service as colonial soldiers. As former "comrades in the protectorate," they deserved jobs. Moreover, they maintained, it was more desirable to employ former colonial subjects than to let them become burdens to society. These arguments eventually convinced some higher Nazi leaders, and in 1936 a circular was sent to all district leaders, or *Gauleiter*, stating:

> About fifty Negroes from our former colonies live with their families in Germany. These natives are almost entirely without secure jobs, and when they find work, the employer is treated with such hostility that he is forced to let the Negro go. I point out that these Negroes must be offered a means of living in

Germany. It must also be taken into consideration . . . that some of the Negroes remain in contact with their homelands and will report there on their treatment in Germany. The Foreign Minister and I have therefore agreed that it must be determined which Negroes [are] to be put under special protection for their deployment for Germany. These will then be given a permit from the Foreign Office roughly stating that there are no reservations about their employment.[21]

The idea was that these Africans would serve as colonial propagandists for Germany. To this end, the German Africa Show was launched—a traveling exhibit that employed black performers, some of whom were German citizens and almost all of whom had spent many years in Germany, who played the part of Africans for the German crowds.[22] The show offered a means of survival to some blacks in Germany, who found it nearly impossible to find employment under the repressive regime legislated by the Nuremberg Laws. In exchange, however, they were forced to market the political message of colonial revisionists: that German colonizers had not been brutal to their colonial subjects, as the Versailles Treaty claimed, but had rather been especially benevolent and caring, for which reason Africans wanted nothing more than for Germany to recolonize their continent.

The show was shut down in 1940. With the outbreak of World War II and especially after the German government gave up its colonial ambitions following the defeat at Stalingrad in 1943, there were no reasons left to create space for Africans in German society or to shelter them from persecution. Overall, as von Joeden-Forgey states, "the Nazis never created a coherent race policy for Africans and other blacks in Germany."[23] The cancellation of the German Africa Show in 1940 was supposed to be part of a wider prohibition against public appearances by blacks. Although the Reich Theater Chamber officially forbade such appearances, many German Africa Show performers still found jobs in the theater. Others landed roles in the state-sponsored colonial nostalgia films that became popular during the war. Despite the availability of film and jobs in the theater, however, many African Germans, especially those categorized as Mischlinge, or mongrels, were forced into concentration camps. The total number of blacks murdered in the camps is disputed, but some estimates put the number at around two thousand.[24] In any case, documents do exist showing that individual Africans received death sentences or were murdered in concentration camps for alleged attempted rape or for Rassenschande, or racial pollution.[25] All in all, despite the space created for Africans due to an incoherent race policy, "the Nazi state still reserved to murder them on an individual basis as unwanted race aliens."[26]

Life Stories: Louis Brody and Mohammed Bayume Hussein

The scattered information about the fate of many members of the German Africa Show is symptomatic of the limited source material we have on the life histories of Africans in Germany between the two world wars. But despite their limited number, biographies and autobiographies offer one important, if not the most important, access to the study of the African community in Germany. They show that people of African background have been part of German history for more than a century. An important impetus to this biographical literature came in the mid-1980s through the work of a group of feminist African-German women who operated largely outside established academic historiography. In 1986, they published a book titled *Showing Our Colors*, which attempted to connect the formation of an African-German identity with the struggle against racism and discrimination in contemporary Germany.[27] Their main concern was to challenge the widespread idea that "black" and "German" were irreconcilable opposites. The life stories of Afro-Germans established a counter-discourse to the dominant nationalist paradigm, which excluded the experiences of Africans in German society.

Since that time, historical research has unearthed much more information about individual members of the African community in Germany. The following pages analyze how two men struggled for survival in an often hostile environment. Instead of presenting them as objects of German rule, as mere victims of racism and paternalism, these two narratives stress their agency, their self-representations, and their complex experiences.

Louis Brody

Louis Brody, whose first name was also spelled Lewis or Lovis, was by turns an actor, musician, dancer, wrestler, and singer who achieved prominent status in Germany during the Weimar Republic in the 1920s.[28] His fame was reflected in his depiction on artists' postcards and by mentions of him in film reviews, film credits, and press releases. In his films Brody, like other black actors, was forced to represent a long-standing stereotypical image. His film parts were the products "of white fantasies and projections: page boys, bartenders, butlers, musicians, sailors, dancers, bell boys, porters, chauffeurs, and 'wild' native people." Nonetheless, Brody acted in some of the most important and popular movies of the early 1920s, such as Joe May's monumental eight-part series *Die Herrin der Welt* and Fritz Lang's *Der müde Tod*. His roles were restricted to "exotic" characters, and so he also appeared on-screen as a Malaysian and a Chinese. At the time there was a tendency in film "to layer different forms of ethnic and racial difference into one singular image of the exoticized 'Other.'"

Brody was born on July 15, 1892, as (Ludwig) B'bebe Mpessa in Douala, Cameroon. He arrived in Germany under unknown circumstances. His first documented appearance on the silver screen came in 1915. There is little information on Brody's life during World War I and the early years of the Weimar Republic. At the end of the war, he lived in Berlin at Kurfürstenstrasse No. 40 and was a member of the African Aid Association (discussed below). As representative of this organization, Brody wrote in 1921 to the B. Z. am Mittag, a widely read Berlin newspaper, to protest diplomatically against the so-called campaign of Black Shame, the movement protesting the presence of black soldiers during the occupation of the Rhineland. Under the title "The German Negro and the Black Shame" he set out his argument that "Blacks who came from the former German colonies and now live in Germany suffer greatly because of the accounts regarding the 'Black Shame' that are being published in certain papers." Germans, he complained, would not acknowledge that they once had colonies and that the German state had failed to reach a decision about the fate of its former African subjects living in Germany: "Will they become members of the entente or will they remain Germans?" Brody argued that Africans from the former German colonies were Germans, at least politically speaking. For this reason their return to their home countries from Germany was very difficult. "We kindly ask Germans to consider that we have to suffer just like they do and please not to treat us with disrespect. We want to point out especially that we are not a wild race without morals, as is currently maintained everywhere in Germany." He also reminded the readers of the newspaper that Lettow-Vorbeck did not fight the war in Africa alone, but that many Africans fought alongside the Germans and risked their lives for the German flag. "Blacks who live in Berlin and in the unoccupied territories of Germany are not the same blacks and yellows of the occupied territory. We ask Germans therefore to be considerate of these blacks and not to persecute them because of news about the 'Black Shame.'" Brody added that his appeal was occasioned by the following incident: "14 days ago one African was attacked by pedestrians and seriously beaten because he was taken for a black person from the occupied territory."

Official or other responses to this article are not recorded. In later years, Brody's name occasionally appeared in the context of political and social activities of the African community. For instance, at the end of 1926, he was one of seventeen Africans to sign a power of attorney allowing Dr. Arthur Mansfeld of the German Society for the Study of Natives to "represent us in all legal matters of social and economic interest before the German government." It appears, however, that Brody never required any such help.

During the late 1920s and early 1930s, he apparently landed enough engagements as an actor and musician to survive. For a short time, he and many other Africans were targeted by surveillance, as German authorities became increasingly nervous about the possible communist influence on them. After a conversation with a journalist, an employee of the Foreign Ministry noted in January 1930 with surprise "that the natives are now preparing a revue in which only colored performers and one or two whites will appear." Furthermore he reported that "a certain Brodi [sic], apparently a West African native, whom Geyer [the journalist] describes as very intelligent, wrote the texts and poetry for this revue." He ended by writing that he could not imagine "how the natives are planning to produce this revue."

Brody's career did not suffer a significant interruption with the Nazi takeover. Between 1933 and 1945 he starred in twenty-three films. During the 1930s, he also appeared as a wrestler and a singer. In 1938 he was recommended as an "artist and wrestler" for the German Africa Show, but whether he appeared in it remains unknown. He did have roles in many popular films, especially colonial films shot during the war such as *Carl Peters* (1941), *Ohm Krüger*, (1941) and *Germanin* (1942/1943). They all showed Brody "stereotypically as a 'chief' in native attire." Brody seems to have occupied a quite unique position among black actors in Nazi Germany. His pay was three or four times as high as that of other black Germans. He survived the war and lived through the collapse of the Nazi regime in Berlin. After the war he continued his career as an actor, artist, and musician in Berlin and Leipzig. Forever without a German passport, he died a natural death in Berlin on February 11, 1951.

Mohammed Bayume Hussein

During the shooting of *Carl Peters*, Brody met Mohammed Bayume Hussein from the former colony of German East Africa, which became Tanganyika after World War I.[29] Hussein served as a "Negro Chief and coach for Swahili" and was the only black whose salary came close to that of Brody. Unlike Brody, Hussein unfortunately did not survive Nazi rule.

Hussein was born in 1904 in Dar es Salaam under the name of Bajume bin Mohammed. A ten-year-old boy when World War I broke out, he followed his father into the German colonial armed forces. He was wounded in combat. Some time after the war Hussein made his way to Germany. During the 1920s, the young veteran earned his livelihood as a "boy" or servant on British and German ships. He also worked in Berlin as a circus performer or artist in variety theater. In April 1930, he worked as a waiter at the nightclub Wildwest, part of the famous Haus Vaterland in Berlin. Two years later he married Maria, a Sudeten-German woman, with whom he had two children. During the Nazi period, he played bit parts in colonial films. For a short period, he also appeared with the German Africa Show. In addition, he taught Swahili at Friedrich Wilhelm University in Berlin, as a part-time lecturer in 1931–1932 and full-time after 1936.[30]

Hussein regularly appeared in the public record because he "never held his tongue when it came to sueing them [the German authorities] for his rights and was always short of money."[31] In 1930, for instance, Hussein claimed, without success, belated pay for the time that he and his father had served as *askaris*, or African troops, in the German colonial army in East Africa. After the Nazis took over, Hussein protested in vain against the decision of the new regime to issue papers labeling as "stateless" Africans living in Germany along with German wives. Beginning in 1934, Hussein filed the first of several applications to receive a badge of honor for his military service in World War I, but in the end, the Ministry of the Interior decided that such a badge should be restricted to white people. In a letter to the Ministry of Foreign Affairs, Hussein complained bitterly about this decision:

I was there from the beginning to the end of the war. . . . I don't want much, I only want my medal. I am entitled to it. It is not a lie, neither am I trying to obtain something for myself illegally. It is my right. I implore the respected gentlemen of the Foreign Ministry to help me. . . . I did not receive my or my father's payment in the war, and now you even want to deprive me of my reward? . . . We never thought the Germans were like that.[32]

At the time Hussein wrote this letter, he was in dire economic straits. He had been fired from his job as a waiter at the Haus Vaterland following charges by a German colleague that he had stolen money. Hussein consulted a lawyer but lost his case in labor court. In the years that followed, he regularly asked different authorities and agencies for money. In 1940, a conflict put Hussein at odds with his superior at Frederich Wilhelm University, Diedrich Westermann. The reasons for the disagreement are not documented, but it is obvious that Hussein's days at the university were numbered.

Hussein's final chapter came when he had an affair with a German woman. He was accused of *Rassenschande*, or racial pollution, put in prison, and then taken without trial or judgment to Sachsenhausen concentration camp. When informed of his confinement, the university authorities reacted deplorably by simply sending him a notice of termination. After three years' imprisonment, Hussein was murdered at Sachsenhausen in November 1944.

Conclusion

The story of Africans in Germany in the 1920s and 1930s belongs to both German and African history. It is also part of the wider history of the African diaspora in the twentieth century. Africans came to Germany for a variety of reasons. During Germany's colonial period, their presence was desirable only as long as it could be controlled and used for colonial purposes. After World War I, Africans living in Germany technically became stateless foreigners. Even so, they were considered to be a bridge to the "lost colonies," and they were expected to serve as future ambassadors of Germany after the eventual restoration of the German colonial empire in Africa.

In the interwar period, the German state thus consigned Africans to uncertainty and ambiguity. They were under constant threat. They reacted to their difficult situation with different strategies and different outcomes. The life stories that have survived are testaments to surprising agency as Africans turned to concrete action to claim and preserve their status in the face of a racist state. Although Africans in Germany between the two world wars indeed suffered discrimination, humiliation, and terror, their stories are not mainly the tales of victims, but rather the histories of individuals who maneuvered with sometimes surprising success to situate themselves between different worlds and in difficult times.

Further Reading

Only in recent years have historians turned their attention to the fate of Africans or individuals of African origin in Germany. As a result, much of the relevant literature is in German and has not yet been translated into English, which is why we cite it here. Given that many scholars of German studies in the United States have shifted their focus to colonial topics, several important studies in English have appeared in the last few years. Two essay collections provide solid introductions to the topic, along with interesting case studies. See Eric Ames, Maria Klotz, and Lore Wildenthal, eds., *Germany's Colonial Past* (Lincoln: University of Nebraska Press, 2005), and Patricia Mazón and Reinhild Steingröver, eds., *Not So Plain as Black and White: Afro-German Culture and History, 1890–2000* (Rochester, N.Y.: University of Rochester Press, 2005).

On the history of Africans in Germany before World War I, the key monograph is still Peter Martin, *Schwarze Teufel, Edle Mohren: Afrikaner in Geschichte und Bewusstsein der Deutschen* (Hamburg: Junius, 1993). Interesting biographical information is found in Hans W. Debrunner, *Presence and*

Prestige: Africans in Europe; A History of Africans in Europe before 1918 (Basel: Basel Afrika Bibliographien, 1979). On people from Cameroon, and especially the Duala people in Wilhelminian Germany, see Ralph Austen with Jonathan Derrick, *Middlemen of the Cameroon Rivers: The Duala and Their Hinterland, c. 1600–c. 1960* (New York: Cambridge University Press, 1999). Illuminating source material on Mpundu Akwa is made accessible in English by Elisa von Joeden-Forgey, ed., *Mpundu Akwa: The Case of the Prince from Cameroon; The Newly Discovered Speech for the Defense* (Münster: LIT, 2002).

The turbulent years of the Weimar Republic are brilliantly analyzed by Eric D. Weitz, *Weimar Germany: Promise and Tragedy* (Princeton, N.J.: Princeton University Press, 2007), although he does not mention Africans. For other references on the Weimar era, see the notes to this chapter. The literature on the Nazi period is more comprehensive. See Tina M. Campt, *Other Germans: Black Germans and the Politics of Race, Gender, and Memory in the Third Reich* (Ann Arbor: University of Michigan Press, 2004), and Clarence Lusane, *Hitler's Black Victims: The Historical Experience of Afro-Germans, European Blacks, Africans, and African-Americans in the Nazi Era* (London: Routledge, 2003).

For interesting biographical and autobiographical information on Afro-German women covering much of the twentieth century, see May Opitz, Katharina Oguntoye, and Dagmar Schultz, eds., *Showing Our Colors: Afro-German Women Speak Out* (Amherst: University of Massachusetts, 1992).

Notes

1. Examples of this failure to acknowledge the German colonial past are apparent in recent syntheses of German history, such as Hagen Schulze, *Germany: A New History* (Cambridge, Mass.: Harvard University Press, 1998).

2. Charles S. Maier, "Consigning the Twentieth Century to History: Alternative Narratives for the Modern Era," *American Historical Review* 105, 3 (2000): 807–31.

3. Sebastian Conrad, "Doppelte Marginalisierung: Plädoyer für eine transnationale Perspektive auf die deutsche Geschichte," *Geschichte und Gesellschaft* 28, 1 (2002): 145–69; Andreas Eckert and Albert Wirz, "Wir nicht, die Anderen auch: Deutschland und der Kolonialismus," in *Jenseits des Eurozentrismus: Postkoloniale Perspektiven in den Geschichts- und Kulturwissenschaften*, ed. Sebastian Conrad and Shalini Randeria (Frankfurt: Campus, 2002), 372–92; Birthe Kundrus, *Moderne Imperialisten: Das Kaiserreich im Spiegel seiner Kolonien* (Cologne: Boehlau, 2003); Sara Friedrichsmeyer, Sara Lennox, and Suzanne Zantop, eds., *The Imperialist Imagination: German Colonialism and Its Legacy* (Ann Arbor: University of Michigan Press, 1998); Eric Ames, Maria Klotz, and Lore Wildenthal, eds., *Germany's Colonial Past*

(Lincoln: University of Nebraska Press, 2005); and Lore Wildenthal, *German Women for Empire, 1884–1945* (Durham, N.C.: Duke University Press, 2001).

4. See Pascal Grosse, "What Does German Colonialism Have to Do with National Socialism? A Conceptual Framework," in *Germany's Colonial Past*, 115–34. On the Herero, see the numerous publications by Jürgen Zimmerer, including "The Birth of the 'Ostland' out of the Spirit of Colonialism: A Postcolonial Perspective on Nazi Policy of Conquest and Extermination," *Patterns of Prejudice* 39, 2 (2005): 197–219.

5. On Africans in Germany before the 1880s, see Peter Martin, *Schwarze Teufel, Edle Mohren: Afrikaner in Geschichte und Bewusstsein der Deutschen* (Hamburg: Junius, 1993); Hans W. Debrunner, *Presence and Prestige: Africans in Europe; A History of Africans in Europe before 1918* (Basel: Basel Afrika Bibliographien, 1979). For later periods, see Katharina Oguntoye, *Eine Afro-Deutsche Geschichte: Zur Lebenssituation von Afrikanern und Afro-Deutschen in Deutschland von 1884 bis 1950* (Berlin: Hoho, 1997); Tina M. Campt, *Other Germans: Black Germans and the Politics of Race, Gender, and Memory in the Third Reich* (Ann Arbor: University of Michigan Press, 2004).

6. See Ulrich van der Heyden and Joachim Zeller, eds., *Kolonialmetropole Berlin: Eine Spurensuche* (Berlin: Berlin Edition, 2002), and Heiko Möhle, ed., *Branntwein, Bibeln, und Bananen: Der Deutsche Kolonialismus in Afrika; Eine Spurensuche in Hamburg* (Hamburg: Libertäre Assoziation, 1999).

7. For the first estimate, see Pascal Grosse, "Zwischen Privatheit und Öffentlichkeit: Kolonialmigration in Deutschland, 1900–1940," in *Phantasiereiche: Der deutsche Kolonialismus in kulturgeschichtlicher Perspektive*, ed. Birthe Kundrus (Frankfurt: Campus, 2003), 107n1; the second is taken from Peter Martin and Christine Alonzo, eds., *Zwischen Charleston und Stechschritt: Schwarze im Nationalsozialismus* (Hamburg: Dölling and Gallitz, 2004), 9.

8. Tyler Stovall, *Paris Noir: African Americans in the City of Lights* (New York: Houghton Mifflin, 1996).

9. The literature on these exhibitions is quite vast. The most recent study is Anne Dreesbach, *Gezähmte Wilde: Die Zurschaustellung "exotischer" Menschen in Deutschland 1870–1940* (Frankfurt: Campus, 2005).

10. Leroy Hopkins, "Einbürgerungsakte 1154: Heinrich Ernst Wilhelm Anumu, African Businessman im Imperial Hamburg," in *Die (koloniale) Begegnung: AfrikanerInnen in Deutschland 1880–1945, Deutsche in Afrika 1880–1918*, ed. Marianne Bechhaus-Gerst and Reinhard Klein-Arendt (Frankfurt: Peter Lang, 2003), 161–70.

11. Ralph A. Austen, "Cameroon and Cameroonians in Wilhelminian Innenpolitik: Grande Histoire and Petite Histoire," in *L'Afrique et l'Allemagne de la colonisation à la coopération, 1884–1986: Le cas du Cameroun*, ed. Kum'a Ndumbe III (Yaoundé: Editions Africavenir, 1986), 204–26, especially 219.

12. Quoted in Austen, "Cameroon and Cameroonians."

13. Andreas Eckert, *Die Duala und die Kolonialmächte* (Münster: LIT, 1991).

14. The former German governor in Cameroon and German Southwest Africa, Theodor Seitz, quoted in Fatima El-Tayeb, *Schwarze Deutsche: Der Diskurs um Rasse und nationale Identität 1890–1933* (Frankfurt: Campus, 2001), 108.

15. Heiko Möhle, "Betreuung, Erfassung, Kontrolle: Afrikaner aus den deutschen Kolonien und die 'Deutsche Gesellschaft für Eingeborenkunde' in der Weimarer Republik," in *Die (koloniale) Begegnung*, 225–36.

16. The literature on this topic is large. See, for instance, Iris Wigger, *Die "Schwarze Schmach am Rhein": Rassistische Diskriminierung swischen Geschlecht, Klasse, Nation, und Rasse* (Münster: Westfäalisches Dampfboot, 2007).

17. Quoted in Fatima El-Tayeb, "Dangerous Liaisons: Race, Nation, and German Identity," in *Not So Plain as Black and White: Afro-German Culture and History, 1890–2000*, ed. Patricia Mazón and Reinhild Steingröver (Rochester, N.Y.: University of Rochester Press, 2005), 27–60; here: 49.

18. For brief summaries of their activities, see Peter Martin, "Schwarze Sowjets an Elbe und Spree?" in *Zwischen Charleston und Stechschritt*, 178–93; Immanuel Geiss, *The Pan-African Movement* (London: Methuen, 1974), chap. 16; Jonathan Derrick, *Africa's "Agitators": Militant Anti-Colonialism in Africa and the West, 1918–1939* (London: Hurst, 2008). An interesting biographical sketch is Robbie Aitken, "From Cameroon to Germany and Back via Moscow and Paris: The Political Career of Joseph Bilé (1892–1959); Performer, 'Negerarbeiter,' and Comintern Activist," *Journal of Contemporary History* 43 (2008): 597–616.

19. George Padmore, *Pan-Africanism or Communism: The Coming Struggle for Africa* (London: D. Dobson: 1956), 323.

20. For the following paragraph, see Elisa von Joeden-Forgey, "Race Power in Postcolonial Germany: The German Africa Show and the National Socialist State, 1935–40," in *Germany's Colonial Past*, 167–188, especially beginning on 172.

21. von Joeden-Forgey, "Race Power in Postcolonial Germany," 173.

22. See Susann Lewerenz, *Die Deutsche Afrika-Schau (1935–1940): Rassismus, Kolonialrevisionismzus und postkoloniale Auseinandersetzungen im nationalsozialistischen Deutschland* (Frankfurt: Peter Lang, 2006); Elisa Forgey, "'Die große Negertrommel der kolonialen Werbung': Die Deutsche Afrika-Schau 1935–1943," *Werkstatt Geschichte* 3, 9 (1994): 25–33.

23. von Joeden-Forgey, "Race Power in Postcolonial Germany," 180.

24. von Joeden-Forgey, "Race Power in Postcolonial Germany," 181.

25. See Marianne Bechhaus-Gerst, "Alexander N'doki: Ein Opfer nationalsozialistischer Justiz," in *Zwischen Charleston und Stechschritt*, 557–65.

26. von Joeden-Forgey, "Race Power in Postcolonial Germany," 181.

27. May Opitz, Katharina Oguntoye, and Dagmar Schultz, eds., *Showing Our Colors: Afro-German Women Speak Out* (Amherst: University of Massachusetts Press, 1992).

28. The following biographical sketch is mainly based on Tobias Nagl, "Louis Brody and the Black Presence in German Film before 1945," in *Not So Plain as Black and White*, ed. Patricia Mazón and Reinhild Steingröver (Rochester, N.Y.: University of Rochester Press, 2005), 109–35. All of the quotations that follow about Brody are from this essay.

29. Especially thanks to Marianne Bechhaus-Gerst, we have some biographical information about Mohammed Bayume Hussein. See her *Treu bis in den Tod: Von*

Deutsch-Ostafrika nach Sachsenhausen—Eine Lebensgeschichte (Berlin: Links, 2007), and "Kiswahili-Speaking Africans in Germany before 1945," in *Afrikanistische Arbeitspapiere* 55 (1998): 155–72. My sketch relies heavily on these publications.

30. On his work as a Swahili teacher, see Holger Stoecker, *Afrikawissenschaften in Berlin von 1919 bis 1945: Zur Geschichte und Topographie eines wissenschaftlichen Netzwerkes* (Stuttgart: Steiner, 2008), 62 and following pages.

31. Bechhaus-Gerst, "Kiswahili-Speaking Africans," 164.

32. A copy of this letter in Swahili is reprinted in Bechhaus-Gerst, "Kiswahili-Speaking Africans," 172.

CHAPTER TEN

Siti binti Saad (c. 1885–1950)

"Giving Voice to the Voiceless," Swahili Music, and the Global Recording Industry in the 1920s and 1930s

Laura Fair

The story of Siti binti Saad, famed singer of Zanzibar in the 1920s and 1930s, raises questions about continuity and change in popular culture in Islamic and colonial East Africa at the high tide of colonial rule. Descended from slaves, Siti mastered the musical forms of the Arab ruling class, transforming taarab music, usually sung in Arabic, into popular music sung in Swahili for everyone—ironically including the elite. Siti and her band built their careers by singing for gatherings of the wealthy and powerful in Zanzibar in the customary setting of their great houses, and by performances open to all in Siti's home and in the streets of Zanzibar Town. She performed live, as had generations of earlier musicians, but she and her band also traveled to make recordings that carried their music to thousands of people in East Africa and elsewhere.

Siti's singing and her songs also helped crystallize a new civil society in British East Africa. Especially her lyrics, but also her success and the widespread popularity of her music, explicitly and implicitly called into question the hegemony and the discourse of the descendants of Arab settlers who dominated politics, society, and economy along this stretch of the East African coast. Although British colonial power by and large supported the continuation of their control, Siti binti Saad's biting social commentary raised both consciousness and questions about the legitimacy of their prominence and authority. Moreover, she and her band performed their message in the language and idioms of local Islamic society. They grounded their critical commentary in Muslim concepts of justice and proper behavior, not in the language of nationalism and democratic rights that had by this time begun to influence the Western-educated ranks of teachers and government employees elsewhere in British East Africa and South Africa.

The story of Siti's life, even the partial chronology that we know, illustrates other important points. First, her career underscores the ways that individual agency allowed a person—indeed, a woman—of very modest birth to navigate the shoals of prejudice and restriction to become prominent and influential in a society that in many ways continued to look down on her and her peers. Second, Siti's story demonstrates that during the late nineteenth and early twentieth centuries, Islam in East Africa was undergoing changes. This chapter gives rise to many questions about how Siti managed to become such an accomplished musician and why she appealed to such a large and diverse following. What is certain is that for Siti binti Saad—a woman of slave ancestry whose skin was probably darker than that of her patrons of the Zanzibari ruling class, who was a colonial subject at the bottom of the hierarchy—Islam and Islamic intellectual and cultural traditions opened the door to influence in East Africa. Indeed, Laura Fair suggests that Siti was every bit as popular in her world as were her African American female contemporaries such as Ma Rainey, Bessie Smith, and Billie Holiday.

The East African World of Siti binti Saad

In March of 1928, a Zanzibari woman by the name of Siti binti Saad traveled with her band to Bombay, India, where they became the first East Africans to have their voices and music recorded on gramophone disc. Over the course of three sessions, Siti and the four male members of her band recorded and released some 130 titles with the Bombay branch of His Master's Voice (HMV). These records became major hits back home, selling nearly seventy-two thousand copies by 1931, making her songs among the most widely circulated recorded music in East African history.[1]

Siti's recordings marked a breakthrough not only for industry executives anxiously searching for new markets, but also for coastal East Africans looking for cultural affirmation in an era of colonial hegemony. Prior to the release of Siti's 1928 recordings, the only gramophone discs available in East Africa were in the languages of the colonies' economic and political overlords. According to both Zanzibar Island residents and company executives, Siti's records served to elevate the social and cultural position of Kiswahili speakers and affirm their status among the "civilized" and "modern" peoples of the world. Siti's success as a recording artist, combined with the deep and

profound mark she left on East African music culture, has led her to be me-
morialized by generations of East Africans as "giving voice to the voiceless."[2]
Eighty years after her recordings were first released, it is still difficult to find
anyone in coastal East Africa who does not recognize her name.

Sold from the coast to up-country Tanganyika and Kenya, in the Belgian
Congo and throughout the Indian Ocean, Siti's records also helped temporarily to renew Zanzibar's waning position as the cultural capital of East
Africa. According to one of her contemporaries, these recorded songs gave a
new and decidedly modern meaning to the old saying, "When the pipes play
in Zanzibar, they dance on the lakes." First coined in reference to Zanzibar's
position as the finance and market center of the East African slave trade, the
use of this phrase to refer to Siti's success is highly ironic, given that Siti's
ancestors were themselves forcibly brought to the isles as slaves in the 1800s.
Unlike the majority of famed Swahili-language poets, who were descended
from learned Islamic scholars or urban families that ranked among the most
economic and socially prestigious on the coast,[3] the woman who created
this treasure of songs was born into a family of poor, servile farmers from the
Zanzibar countryside. In 1897, after the abolition of slavery, Siti binti Saad
joined Zanzibar's version of the "Great Migration" from the countryside to
the city—searching for economic opportunity as well as new possibilities for
social and personal autonomy. Former slaves of Siti's generation used a range
of tools to effect their liberation, including cultural tools that allowed them
to assert their status as free and independent individuals. While few urban
migrants achieved Siti's economic and social success, her life story served as a
poignantly powerful example of the transformative potential of the era. Here
was a poor woman who had risen above her servile beginnings to become the
most acclaimed musician in Swahili history. Here was the daughter of rural
slaves being received, both locally and internationally, as the cultural icon
of Swahili civilization.

Siti's life history and her musical career highlight several themes that are
central to an understanding of this period in East African history. This was
an era of major economic, social, and political changes, and former slaves,
who accounted for some three-fourths of Zanzibar's total population, initiated many of them. The turn of the century also witnessed the imposition of
colonialism in Africa. Between the 1870s and 1920s, European powers gradually managed to wrestle economic and political power from those who had
previously ruled East Africa, including powerful Swahili dynasties, and in the
case of Zanzibar, the sultan of Oman, who moved his capital to Zanzibar in
the early 1800s in an attempt to increase the profits he earned from lucrative
trade networks in the region. The British forced the sultans of Zanzibar to

abolish the trade in slaves coming out of East Africa, but they were reluctant to abolish slavery itself, due to their reliance on alliances with slave owners for their very power and to their own stereotypes about the alleged laziness of slaves.[4]

Abolition was decreed by Europeans, but emancipation was achieved only as a result of the persistent efforts of slaves themselves. While former slaves may have considered abolition to be a blessing, not all of the changes wrought by colonialism were appreciated. The political and economic policies introduced by the British meant that many people—particularly those who were poor and female—were increasingly marginalized and excluded from the political arena. Analyzing Siti's songs and the context in which they were performed and created provides a unique view into the myriad changes taking place during this period, as well as the critiques and alternative visions circulating among Siti's contemporaries.

Siti binti Saad: A Life

Binti Saad, or "the daughter of Saad," was born in the countryside a few miles outside of Zanzibar Town in the mid-1880s. Her given name, Mtumwa, translates literally as "slave" or "servant" and reflects the subordinate status into which she was born. As a child, Mtumwa binti Saad shared the life of many village youth, playing in the fields and streams of the countryside, helping with domestic and agricultural chores from an early age, and gradually learning from her mother and other village women the skills of a potter that would allow her to earn cash income as an adult. Like many women of her day, Mtumwa married while still in her early teens. This first marriage did not last long and shortly after the birth of her only child, Mariam, more commonly known as Kijakazi—a diminutive of "female slave"—Mtumwa and her daughter returned to her parents' home, where they lived for the next ten years.

But binti Saad's mind was elsewhere. According to biographers, "she hungered for change and new experiences."[5] So Mtumwa began collecting pottery from women in the village and carrying it to town, some six miles away, where she sold her wares while wandering neighborhood streets. Through her regular trips to town she became acquainted with the people and possibilities of urban life, and in 1911, as one biographer phrased it, she decided to leave "her dusty life in the countryside and to enter into the city."[6] Like tens of thousands of others during the first decades of the twentieth century, binti Saad left the countryside and moved to the city in search of better economic opportunities, as well as new possibilities for social and personal autonomy in the post-abolition era.

In order to draw attention to her pottery and to make her work more enjoyable, binti Saad sang while she wandered the streets carrying her pots. Marketing her pottery throughout town, she earned a reputation as an engaging and entertaining singer of folk songs and riddles. Word of her wit and the power of her voice earned her quite a reputation. Once she moved to town permanently, she was recruited by several performers of Islamic ritual music who convinced her to begin training to become a performer herself. In her late twenties or early thirties, binti Saad began to learn the Qur'an and the rules of recitation, known as *tajwid*, which emphasized correct pronunciation, breathing techniques that allowed phrases to remain intact, and the importance of tone and timbre to convey textual meaning. The vocal training, introduction to Arabic, and knowledge of the Qur'an that binti Saad received from her tutors were instrumental in her transformation from a quaint singer of colloquial tunes into a highly sought-after performer of Islamic ritual music.

Transformations in Islamic ritual and cultural practices were part and parcel of the larger social transformations taking place in East Africa around 1900. For more than a thousand years, most Swahili townspeople had been Muslims, but many of the people brought from the interior of Africa to the East African coast as slaves practiced indigenous religions. Slaves and other immigrants were encouraged to convert to Islam, but poverty prevented most from devoting extensive periods of time to deep study of the religion. Many poor Muslims, like Mtumwa, knew the basic tenets of the religion and how to pray, but they had not had the benefit of attending Qur'anic school as children, where students memorized the chapters of the Holy Book in Arabic and then graduated to advanced studies.[7] Islam professes the spiritual equality of all believers, yet along the Swahili coast there were marked differences between the status and rank of free and slave practitioners. Wealthy, freeborn members of society had the time and money to indulge in extensive study of texts and exegesis, and they tended to dominate the leadership of Islamic schools and mosques. As in most cultures across the globe, the wealthy also wrote and administered the laws, which privileged their needs. Socially, the elite also established customs that differentiated themselves from the poor and served to symbolically identify them as more devout. Among these token signs that served to enhance the status and mark the alleged piety of wealthy Muslims were local prohibitions that prevented poor Muslims of both genders from covering their heads or wearing shoes in the presence of the freeborn.

However, with the abolition of slavery, many former slaves began to take a greater interest in learning about Islam and participating in various ritual forms of practice. As increasing numbers of former slaves began to swell the ranks of practitioners, they also fought to transform ritual practice to make it more inclusive. In the 1890s, Sheikh Habib Salih (d. 1935), a reformer widely credited for his efforts to introduce African musical and ritual practices into Islamic worship along the coast, was literally drummed out of the neighboring island town of Lamu by the religious establishment for his efforts. He was accused of heresy for his attempts to be more inclusive in regard to the island's African community through the incorporation of drumming, Kiswahili, and women into ritual performance.[8] Although he was scorned by the orthodox religious establishment, Habib's innovations became very popular among the poor in Lamu, and they spread quickly up and down the East African coast, including Zanzibar.

Building on the innovations introduced by Habib, others began to spread the performance of *maulid*, ritual expressions of individual or communal gratitude in appreciation of God's mercy. In the nineteenth century, maulid were rarely performed in Zanzibar, and when they were, they were austere, private recitations of the Qur'an to commemorate the birth of the Prophet Mohammed. In the 1910s, however, the public performance of maulid poems, performed either in Arabic or in Kiswahili and accompanied by tambourines and drums, became widely popular. People began performing maulid to celebrate not only the birth of the Prophet Mohammed, but the births and weddings of their own children and grandchildren. By the time binti Saad and her band took off to record their first records in Bombay, an average of eight hundred private maulid were performed in Zanzibar Town every year.

Binti Saad's natural talents as a singer and her training in the Qur'an allowed her to ride this wave of new devotional practice to become one of the most sought-after performers of the day. The growing popularity of more performative and musical maulid coincided with a general shift away from a literate and orthodox Islamic tradition to one that more openly embraced devout, yet poor and nonliterate, men and women. Innovations in religious practice introduced at the turn of the century thus opened up new possibilities for individuals, including women like Mtumwa, who were from poor, servile, and Kiswahili-speaking backgrounds to earn respect for their knowledge and performance of religious ritual. No less significant, such opportunities also provided new opportunities for earning a living.

By the mid-1910s, Mtumwa's skills were in high demand. The quality of her voice, her range of tones, resonance, nasality. and intonation are said to have moved her listeners to another plane of existence. In fact, according to the legends that surround her life, it was in the course of one particularly dynamic performance that the title of "Siti," the Arabic term for "Lady," was bestowed upon Mtumwa by a member of the island's gentry out of reverence for her allegedly impeccable pronunciation of Arabic and performance of Islamic ritual text. As a result of her training in the Qur'an, Mtumwa, the slave, had transformed herself into Siti, the lady. As one of binti Saad's approbators suggested, "From being a nonety [sic] with a slave name, Siti captivated wealthy Zanzibaris such that they became her slaves. No occasion was deemed successful, be it a wedding or the celebration of a birth, among Zanzibar's elite, without Siti's performance."[9]

Siti was also among the first generation of Zanzibari women to begin to wear the *buibui*, a form of black veil commonly worn by women along the Swahili coast in the twentieth century. In the nineteenth century, while slaves were encouraged by their masters to convert to Islam, they were prohibited from dressing in the fashions of the elite. The necessities of work, combined with a lack of money for clothes, also meant that most walked the streets wrapped in only one piece of cloth, which men tied around their waists and women under the armpits. After the abolition of slavery, slaves of both genders began to dress more modestly in public, covering their heads, shoulders, and legs when possible and wearing shoes when practical. When they had the money, they also began to invest in the cloth and styles of dress that slaves had previously been prohibited from wearing. Women also began to veil with the buibui, as yet another assertion of their spiritual and social equality with former owners.[10]

Siti, the Legend

The urban legends that surround Siti's life and career suggest that transforming her identity from slave to lady was not at all easy. The rich may have adored Siti's voice, but they were not necessarily all willing to accept her as a social equal. One example of Siti's struggles for social recognition can be found in the work of Ali Ahmed Jahadhmy, a child of the Arab elite in Zanzibar, who studied in the United Kingdom during the colonial era and went on to become a scholar of Kiswahili language and poetry. In one of his books, *Waimbaji wa Juzi*, or *Singers of Yesteryear*, Jahadhmy goes to great lengths to praise Siti's voice and power as a poet, while simultaneously denigrating her for her heritage, arguing that the reason she veiled her face while singing was to draw her audience nearer, rather than making them run away.[11] According to Jahadhmy, Siti's voice may have shone, but she lacked the light skin, the long thin nose, and the soft hair that he and other members of the Arab elite associated with beauty. What Jahadhmy fails to mention is that tens of thousands of women in Zanzibar began to veil their faces in public during this era. Siti did not veil because she was ashamed of her looks—she veiled as a public display of her status as a free, devout, respectable woman.

Others also attempted to denigrate Siti and qualify her hard-won status among the "civilized." The Swahili have a long tradition of utilizing the performance of poetry competitions and verse exchanges to debate ideas in public,[12] and these "poetry slams" were also used to question her stature. One widely remembered song that circulated about her went like this: "Siti binti Saadi / When did you become 'someone' / You came from the countryside wearing only the cloth of slaves / If it wasn't for your voice / What would you be eating?" Siti responded to her detractors with the following lines: "It isn't enough / To appear gracious / To be a member of the elite / With a noted genealogy / The true deprivation of a person / Is to be without intelligence." Siti's response earned her wide praise as someone who could compete quite effectively in these poetry exchanges, and many more people were allegedly drawn to her future shows in anticipation of what she would say to her detractors. The importance of earning the respect of the community, through wit and good deeds, became a hallmark refrain of many of Siti's songs. On numerous occasions, she used her position onstage to critique the practice of giving reverence to those with "old money" or "blue blood," while ignoring and demeaning the ideas of the poor. As a few lines from another song lamented: "There is nothing you can do to make a poor person look good / If you compare them with someone who is rich / Poverty is powerlessness, its example like a reed. Even if you commit great acts and shine like a jewel / You will be treated like you are insipid / You will never be consulted. Your intelligence can never compare to someone with money / People will treat you like a baboon, or worse, like a female slave / A rich person is always among those who is counted without even having to speak."

Siti binti Saad and her band are also widely remembered for their innovative transformation of *taarab* music into a popular genre that became widely enjoyed among all classes of people along the Swahili coast. Taarab is a unique form of musical expression that originated along the East African Coast.[13] Like other elements of Swahili culture, taarab reflects the cosmopolitan blending of African, Arab, South Asian, and Indian Ocean elements into something distinctive and uniquely Swahili. It is based upon an ancient Swahili tradition of poetry, with precise rules regarding meter, rhyme, and verse. This poetry is then set to music played on instruments from Africa, Arabia, India, and, after the 1950s, Europe as well. The rhythms and melodies are also drawn from a wide range of peoples with whom the Swahili traded and interacted.

While taarab is known today for its wide-ranging blend of musical influences, at the turn of the century it was regarded by many as the cultural preserve of the coastal ruling class. Most of the songs were composed in

Arabic, and many of the well-regarded performers were children of the elite. Siti and her band were probably not the first taarab performers to compose in Kiswahili, the dominant language of the coast, but they were among the first to be widely recognized by the elite as legitimate taarab performers. Like those who initiated transformations in Islamic rituals, musical performers also had to toe a careful line between adherence to accepted practice, and innovations that would mark them as creative, yet reputable, entertainers. Like previous taarab musicians, Siti's band incorporated musical instruments from Arabia, such as the *ud* (lute), *nai* (end-blown flute), *tari* (tambourine), and violin, but they also incorporated many rhythm patterns and melodies brought to the Swahili coast by slave and free immigrants from throughout East Africa and across the Indian Ocean. The music of Siti's band was thus more cosmopolitan and culturally inclusive than early genres of taarab.

Yet another innovation in the performance culture of taarab popularized by Siti and her band was to move taarab performances out of the walls of the palace and the compounds of the coastal elite and into the streets, neighborhoods, public gardens, and cinema halls of Zanzibar, where a greater cross section of the community could enjoy them. Again, there were many other Swahili bands that performed in these public spaces. What made Siti's band unique was its ability to cross over from the public spaces of the masses to the inner rooms of the sultan's palace, where the band performed every Friday. In fact, it was in the course of one such performance at the palace that the band was introduced to the HMV agent who arranged for the recording sessions in Bombay.

While Siti was lauded and employed by the elite throughout the Swahili coast, she was absolutely revered by the poor among whom she lived. Long before Siti rose to fame as an international recording star, she earned the respect and adoration of her neighbors for her ability to transform the latest news and local gossip, as well as individual and collective struggles, into song. Much of this material went unpublished, yet a great deal of it remains etched in the memories of elderly men and women, who frequently credit themselves as coauthors of Siti's work. The band's nightly practices were held at Siti's home in the poor section of Zanzibar Town, and island residents were encouraged to attend. Siti and the other members of her band composed the poetry that became the lyrics to the songs. However, they did so along with feedback from the audience, which openly praised the power of some phrases or suggested reworking others. Siti's home thus became one of the central gathering places in town for members of her generation. And when guests came from the countryside or elsewhere in East Africa, hosts might take them out for a nightly practice session at Siti's home, a treat they would never forget.

Siti prided herself on her ability to compose extemporaneously, and her contemporaries were regularly amazed by her ability to transform their talk into a poetic song. Private and public scandals—from abusive husbands to corrupt public officials—generated endless urban gossip as well as the material for many of the band's songs. Siti used her performances not only to entertain her audiences but also as a means of circulating and editorializing upon the news of the day or the week. The band's songs became akin to a newspaper, circulating information on the latest scandals, as well as ideas for improvements in society. Siti's songs were not background music one could listen to without bothering to hear, but poetic expressions that demanded, indeed forced, engagement. Through the process of meeting, talking, and debating, the women and men who gathered at Siti's home for practices, discussed her music after performances, or sang the band's songs while doing their daily chores actively helped constitute bonds of community, evaluate reputations, and formulate discourses of social and political values. Many of Siti's contemporaries contend that her willingness to spark debate around issues of class, gender, and political inequality accounts, at least in part, for the unforgettable place Siti and her songs occupy in the collective memory of the era.

Musical Culture and Civil Society

The vast majority of those who lived in colonial Africa were utterly excluded from formal participation in the political institutions of governance, yet they remained actively involved in formulating the debates that constituted civil society. Taking part in the vibrant music culture of the day was just one of the many ways they did so. Drawing on nineteenth-century patterns of political critique, Zanzibaris in the twentieth century continued to use gossip and song to undermine the status and reputation of the wayward. Songs that chastised and made fun of wrongdoers embarrassed the person who was the subject of scandal and publicly articulated the community's lack of respect for those engaged in such behavior. By listening to the lyrics to these songs and the stories that surround them, we can hear snippets of the daily conversations and heated debates of Siti's contemporaries. The British certainly did not solicit the opinions of the poor regarding questions of governance, but these songs tell us that the men and women of Zanzibar struggled nonetheless to make their thoughts and opinions heard through less formal, but no less effective, means.

In colonial Africa, political authority was vested in Europeans, who appointed and oversaw local administrative officials. In Zanzibar, these local officials owed their positions of power and authority to the British, and they were not much accountable to the people over whom they governed. Siti's band used their positions onstage to raise awareness of corruption by appointed officials, as well as to chastise those who used their public position for personal gain. One song that is widely remembered, even though it was not among the songs recorded by HMV, celebrates the fall from grace of a corrupt government official, Bwana Msellem. Msellem was widely despised by the poor of Zanzibar for his habit of demanding bribes, which few could afford. He was also said to use his office to cheat people out of their property, by having those who could not read and write affix their thumbprints to legal documents that ultimately transferred their property or homes into Msellem's greedy hands. While citizen complaints about his behavior fell on deaf British ears, Msellem eventually lost his job after being caught embezzling money from office accounts to finance an elaborate seven-day celebration in honor of his daughter's wedding. As punishment for his crimes, Msellem was sentenced to hard labor in the town's rock quarry. The citizens of Zanzibar were ecstatic, and Siti's band wrote the following song in celebration: "There is no pedigree, I am the child of so-and-so / A word like a sudden blow which burns in the chest / The name is yours, my man, and the rock is on your head, the rock is on your head / You men should stop oppressing and stealing from the poor / Especially those who are said to be the stupidest of the stupid / Forever their pen is ink upon the thumb, is ink upon the thumb / You men should not be deceived, this is mine I should take it / A memento should be created so it does not leave their hearts / You clerks should be satisfied with what you are entitled to, with what you are entitled to."

Despite the fact that the poor of Zanzibar were unable to effectively use the tools of colonial power to challenge the dominance of appointed officials like Msellem, they certainly celebrated those rare instances when courts convicted the wealthy who had committed crimes. The poor also used the tools at their disposal, including rumor and song, regardless of prosecution, to popularize perceptions that what these men did was wrong. Each time such a song was repeated—whether by Siti, a woman washing clothes, or a fisherman hauling in a catch—alternatives to the dominant colonial discourse of the just and selfless service of bureaucrats were advanced. Common people were fully aware of the ways in which political power was being abused. With lines such as "You men should stop oppressing and stealing from the poor," they voiced the demand that the situation be changed. Msellem was only convicted after he was caught stealing from the state, but in the song the band makes clear that stealing is wrong and that embezzlement should be punished, regardless of whether it is property taken from the government or from the "stupidest of the stupid."

Critiques of judicial authority make up another substantial part of the band's corpus of songs. Colonial courts were known for siding with the wealthy and sending the poor to jail while the rich were let off. Colonial courts were also widely perceived as misogynist. They tried to enhance the social and economic power of men over women; typically refused to punish perpetrators of domestic violence; and rarely granted women divorces, even in cases of abuse and neglect. The band used their power as performers to voice popular resistance to such decisions. In one song called "Judge Grant Me Justice," the band criticizes the courts for refusing to grant a divorce to a neighbor of one of the male band members, even though her husband repeatedly abused her and neglected his obligation to support her—either of which should have been conditions for divorce according to both Islamic law and local practice.

In another widely remembered song, "Kijiti," the band chastises the courts for their decision to punish the victim and her witnesses, rather than the perpetrator of the crime. Kijiti is the name of the assailant, who raped and murdered a woman with whom he went on a date after a party. Rather than sending the police to search for the assailant, the courts sentenced the victim's friends to jail for organizing the party and serving the alcohol on which Kijiti and the victim got drunk. People were appalled, both by Kijiti's actions and by the decision of the judge. How could the witnesses be held accountable for their friend's death while the murderer was left to run? The following song tells the story, while simultaneously voicing the community's outrage over this gross miscarriage of justice: "Look you all, look at what Kijiti has done / He took a guest and played the game of tag with her / He went with her to the bush and brought her back as a corpse. We left home, we did not ask for permission from our elders / Our alcohol in the bag, we brought it with us / The party is near the beach in Chukwani / death in the neighborhood of Sharifmsa. / Kijiti said to me, 'Come on girl, let's go!' / Oh, if only I had known I would have refused / Kijiti you got drunk and murdered me. / The judge was mad in his chair where he sat / And said, 'You bloody fools!' to the witnesses / He put you in jail Sumaili and Kay, the daughter of Subeiti. / These things are amazing every time we look at them / Kijiti killed someone and in her stomach was a baby / Kijiti escaped, but the witnesses have drowned. / Kijiti I warn you, do not go to the town of Dar es Salaam / You will meet an old man with a razor waiting just for you / People are swearing about you, may God give you elephantiasis."

These songs provide evidence of local awareness of and resistance to colonial attempts to further the institutional marginalization of women in island society. Be they calls for the imprisonment of men who assaulted women, or pleas for the recognition of women's right to sue for divorce, the songs suggest that community standards of justice were evaluated against a different moral standard than those used by British magistrates. Moreover, the fact that many of the songs that spoke out against violence against women, be it physical or institutional, were written by the male members of the band indicates that these concerns were not perceived as being solely "women's issues." In an era in which the struggles by the poor to overcome economic and social equality were paramount, there appears to have been a general recognition among both men and women of the importance of advancing gender equity as well. In many of the band's songs, there is also an explicit critique of British efforts to secularize Zanzibar society, and a call to retain a religiously infused equation of justice and morality. Though poor victims and women had difficulty achieving justice from British courts, the band's songs often included a prayer for God to make amends.

The music of Siti binti Saad lives on in the memories of Zanzibaris today. Although Siti herself died in 1950, her songs are still performed. Like the music of her contemporaries Ma Rainey, Bessie Smith, and Billie Holiday, Siti's music continues to enrapture listeners and evoke both the dreams and struggles of people of African descent in the first half of the twentieth century. Siti's music was so immensely popular not only because it voiced the critical consciousness of her contemporaries, but also because it comforted them as well. By listening to these songs, audience members gained assurance that at least the problems they were facing were not theirs alone. Their poverty was not a result of personal failure but of systemic economic injustice. In addition, songs like "Kijiti," which had the power to bring tears to people's eyes, helped initiate catharsis and begin the often painful process of personal and communal healing. The laughter and friends that were part and parcel of an evening's performance allowed audience members to temporarily forget their cares and to restore the courage they needed to carry on. While there were certainly aspects of Zanzibar society that could be improved, the band and the audience also consistently reminded each other of the need to rejoice and enjoy the many good things that life had to offer—not the least of which were the nightly practices in Siti's home and the free Thursday and Friday night performances in the neighborhood squares.

Further Reading

No individual is as widely written about in Kiswahili as Siti binti Saad. Unfortunately, there is much less available in English. Those who are able to read Kiswahili are encouraged to explore Shaaban Robert, *Wasifu wa*

Siti binti Saad (Dar es Salaam: Mkuki na Nyota, [1958] 1991); Ali Ahmed Jahadhmy, *Waimbaji wa Juzi* (Dar es Salaam: Chuo cha Uchunguzi wa Lugha ya Kiswahili, 1966); Issa Mgana, *Jukwaa la Taarab Zanzibar* (Helsinki: Mradi wa Medafrica, 1991); and Mohammed Seif Khatib, *Taarab Zanzibar* (Dar es Salaam: Tanzania Publishing House, 1992).

English-language sources on the historical development of taarab in East Africa include Laura Fair, *Pastimes and Politics: Culture, Community and Identity in Post-Abolition Urban Zanzibar, 1890–1945* (Athens: Ohio University Press, 2001); Werner Graebner, "Taarab: the Swahili Coastal Sound," in *The Rough Guide to World Music,* ed. Simon Broughton et al. (London: Rough Guides, 1999), 1: 690–97; Werner Graebner, "The Interaction of Swahili Taarab Music and the Record Industry: A Historical Perspective (Tanzania)," in *African Media Cultures: Transdisciplinary Perspectives,* ed. Rose Marie Beck and Frank Wittmann (Cologne: Rudiger Koppe Verlag, 2004), 171–92; Jan Knappert, "Swahili Taarabu Songs," *Afrika und Ubersee* 60, 1 and 2 (1977): 116–55; Jan Knappert, "Swahili Songs with Double Entendre," *Afrika und Ubersee* 66, 1 (1983): 67–76; Janet Topp-Fargion, "The Role of Women in Taarab in Zanzibar: An Historical Examination of a Process of 'Africanization,'" *The World of Music* 35, 2 (1993): 109–25; and Kelly Askew, *Performing the Nation: Swahili Music and Cultural Politics in Tanzania* (Chicago: University of Chicago Press, 2002).

There are many CDs of taarab music available, including one recently released with some of the only examples of Siti's music commercially available in the United States and Europe, titled *Poetry and Languid Charm: Swahili Music from Tanzania and Kenya, 1920s–1950s* (World and Traditional Music Section of the British Library Sound Archive). This CD also features extensive liner notes by Janet Topp-Fargion, an ethnomusicologist specializing in taarab who is responsible for the collection at the British Library Sound Archive. Werner Graebner has recorded and produced an extensive library of taarab music from Zanzibar, Kenya, and Tanzania. To get a sense of how taarab has changed over time, consult Graebner's multivolume CD set, *Zanzibara* (Buda Musique) or his *Mila na Utamaduni: Spices of Zanzibar* (Network). Other multivolume CD sets include *Music of Zanzibar* (Globe Style) and *Zanzibar: Soul and Rhythm* (Jahazi). The styles of taarab vary, not only over time, but also from place to place. Kelly Askew's book *Performing the Nation: Swahili Music and Cultural Politics in Tanzania* includes a CD featuring taarab groups from Dar es Salaam and Tanga, recorded between the 1960s and 1990s.

Notes

1. H. Evans, "Report by Mr. H. Evans on His Tour of Kenya, Uganda, Tanganyika, Zanzibar, and Portuguese East Africa, May–July, 1931," unpublished manuscript, Hayes, Middlesex: EMI Archives, generously provided to me by Werner Graebner. See also Werner Graebner, "The Interaction of Swahili Taarab Music and the Record Industry: A Historical Perspective (Tanzania)," in *African Media Cultures: Transdisciplinary Perspectives*, ed. Rose Marie Beck and Frank Wittmann (Cologne: Rudiger Koppe Verlag, 2004).

2. Shaaban Robert, *Wasifu wa Siti binti Saad* (Dar es Salaam: Mkuki na Nyota, [1958] 1991), 62; Leila Sheikh-Hashim, "Siti's Magnetic Voice," *Sauti ya Siti* 1 (1 March 1988): 3–4.

3. Mohamed H. Abdulaziz, *Muyaka: Nineteenth-Century Swahili Popular Poetry* (Nairobi: Kenya Literature Bureau, 1979); Ibrahim Noor Sharif, "Islam and Secularity in Swahili Literature: An Overview," in *Faces of Islam in African Literature*, ed. Kenneth Harrow (Portsmouth, N.H.: Heinemann, 1991), 37–58.

4. Frederick Cooper, *From Slaves to Squatters: Plantation Labor and Agriculture in Zanzibar and Coastal Kenya, 1890–1925* (New Haven, Conn.: Yale University Press, 1980).

5. Robert, *Wasifu wa Siti binti Saad*, 7; Issa Mgana, *Jukwaa la Taarab Zanzibar* (Helsinki: Mradi wa Medafrica, 1991), 34–60.

6. Mohammed Seif Khatib, *Taarab Zanzibar* (Dar es Salaam: Tanzania Publishing House, 1992), 15.

7. As late as 1948, only 19 percent of Zanzibar's population had attended Qur'anic school, and fewer than half of those people had completed the basic course of study, which included memorizing the entire Qur'an. Students often learned to read and write in Arabic script, which was the script used to write the language of Kiswahili until 1905, when the British changed the common script to the Roman script. See Edward Batson, *Social Survey of Zanzibar Protectorate* (Cape Town: School of Social Sciences and Social Administration, University of Cape Town, 1910), vols. 10 and 11.

8. Peter Leinhardt, "The Mosque College of Lamu and Its Social Background," *Tanganyika Notes and Records* 52 (1959): 228–42.

9. Sheikh-Hashim, "Siti's Magnetic Voice," 3.

10. Laura Fair, "'Dressing Up': Clothing, Class, and Gender in Post-Abolition Zanzibar," *Journal of African History* 39 (1998): 63–94.

11. A. A. Jahadhmy, *Waimbaji wa Juzi* (Dar es Salaam: Chuo cha Uchunguzi wa Lugha ya Kiswahili, 1966), 97.

12. Ann Biersteker, *Kujibizana: Questions of Language and Power in Nineteenth- and Twentieth-Century Poetry in Kiswahili* (East Lansing: Michigan State University Press, 1996).

13. Werner Graebner, "Taarab: The Swahili Coastal Sound," in *The Rough Guide to World Music*, ed. Simon Broughton et al. (London: Rough Guides, 1999), 1: 690–97; Kelly Askew, *Performing the Nation: Swahili Music and Cultural Politics in Tanzania* (Chicago: University of Chicago Press, 2002).

~

CHAPTER ELEVEN

Maryan Muuse Boqor (b. 1938) and the Women Who Inspired Her

Memories of a Mogadishu Childhood

Lidwien Kapteijns and Maryan Muuse Boqor

In light of Somalia's recent history, Maryan Muuse Boqor's recollections of her coming of age, as recorded by Lidwien Kapteijns, seem to describe a paradise lost.[1] This is not at all to say that Maryan's early years were without challenge and loss. Rather, it is to say that, as the country struggled toward independence, Maryan's family and people around them believed in a brighter and more hopeful future. The descriptions of these times inevitably lead us to ask if we can see the elements of future developments in Somalia through the details of everyday life in the middle twentieth century recounted in the pages that follow. Is it possible to connect the local lives of Maryan and her family and friends with larger issues that may help Somalis recover from the civil war that began in 1991 and rebuild their state?

Maryan also tells a wonderful story of intergenerational solidarity among women. Her mother, her aunts, and older women friends of the family provided encouragement to her and served as crucial role models in her youth. She indeed emphasizes that she would not have become the woman she is today without their example. It is also true that she had close ties with some men in her family, notably her father, and that some of them also encouraged her to think beyond the boundaries often assigned to women in Somalia. These dimensions of the chapter lead us to ask how similarities and differences in age and gender roles between women and men influenced Maryan's early years and transition to young adulthood.

Finally, Maryan's tale, with its wealth of detail recorded by Lidwien Kapteijns, shows how the roles and possibilities open to women in Somalia were perhaps more various and more public than might be expected in a Muslim society. What paths were open to Maryan for personal and professional development? At what point did she strike out in new directions on her own? What were the benefits and burdens of being part of a generation that spearheaded such changes for women? Were the very high expectations of women only positive or perhaps at times also constraining? What specific aspects of Maryan's story change our impressions of Somalia and growing up there in the years between World War II and Somali independence?

To be a Somali in this era of civil war and communal violence is hard and heartrending. In the diaspora of Somalis living abroad, many people, especially women, fight the bitterness in their hearts with the memories of earlier solidarity and try to repair the social fabric through innumerable and never-ending small acts of kindness and mutual support. Nevertheless, since the civil war, even presenting a narrative about an individual or family exposes one to the mistrust that remains among people representing the many sides of the civil war. The complex civil conflict has also left distorted hate narratives in its wake, constructed especially by people with bad consciences or unsavory ambitions. Although women, generally speaking, played a different and less destructive role in the civil war than men, no man or woman, insider or outsider, has remained untouched by what we know, or think we know, about the war. In addition, although Somalis generally acknowledge the value of oral history, many still frown upon anyone who makes the personal public and the ordinary special, and even more so if that person is a woman: "*Maxay dadka dheertahay?*" ("What makes her better than other people?"); "*Yay is moodday?*" ("Who does she think she is?"). Despite these obstacles, we must tell the life stories of real women. Unless we do, the collective historical experiences of Somali women and their efforts and contributions to Somali history will remain unknown and unacknowledged.

Maryan Muuse Boqor presented her life story, part of which is represented here, as an "exemplary narrative."[2] To categorize it this way does not imply that it is sugarcoated, but rather that it brings to the fore the ideals that the people whose experiences are recounted here tried to live up to, in the hope that these values will inspire the current generation of Somali youth. As a result, this narrative is a rescue action that attempts to save a usable past from the ravages of civil war. It is a set of reminiscences and reflections on the values that Maryan's family members and many of their Somali contemporaries held and passed on to their children.

Maryan's reasons for telling her story are threefold. First, she has always believed in women's solidarity, whose power she witnessed in her own life and in the history of Somalia. Although her narrative is about her own life, it is also a record of the efforts and contributions of all of the women of her generation, a history that Somali men must learn to acknowledge more fully. Second, Maryan has always been committed to education and scholarship. She belonged to the first group of Somali girls to be sent to Egypt for primary and secondary education. She later studied law in Morocco. As a former teacher of Arabic and religion, she believes in the value of history—including the history of Somali women. Third, when Maryan became a refugee and was resettled in the United States, she joined the working poor of Boston's less affluent neighborhoods. She noticed that in the diaspora her grandchildren rapidly integrated into mainstream society but knew very little and felt very ambivalent about their Somalia homeland, where people had driven each other out at gunpoint. Through her story, she wanted to give these youth, who have inherited so little in terms of material wealth, a sense of the Somalia she loved in spite of its imperfections, and the families she takes pride in regardless of all their shortcomings.

For the historian and the general reader, the value of creating public space for a personal story lies in how it elucidates wider social realities. In this case, the story of how a young Somali girl in the city of Mogadishu was raised and experienced her youth in the heady days of the 1950s and 1960s may throw light on the history of the single generation that witnessed both the creation and the collapse of the Somali state. Maryan hopes that her narrative, which is just one thread in the complex fabric of Somali social history, will inspire other men and women to tell their own stories about their youth.

The narrative presented here has two themes. The first focuses on Maryan's youth, which involves socialization into two very different cultural settings, one in Mogadishu and the other in Hilwan, Egypt, where she attended boarding school for six years. The second theme explores women's leadership and solidarity, exemplified in Maryan's early youth by her female relatives, a maternal grandmother and two aunts. For Maryan, these women were inspiring female role models for two reasons. First, they contributed actively to the upkeep of their families, both before and after the deaths of their husbands. Second, they actively served their wider communities in a variety of ways, including active participation in the nationalist movement. Maryan believes that these women prepared her for her later active participation in activities directed at the political and social well-being of the Somali community. They also prepared her for a life, including motherhood, lived largely without the presence and support of her husband, who was a political prisoner for about twenty years.

Historical Background

Precolonial Somali society consisted of small states as well as non-state communities. From Zeila to Harar, Mogadishu, Afgoye, and Brava, trade, especially when combined with agricultural production, formed the material basis of these city-states, ruled either by a sultan or *amir* (emir) or by a group of elders. The non-state communities also often had titled leaders—*boqor, ugaas, garaad, islaw, islaan, malaak, suldaan,* and so forth—who may have been associated with special ritual and religious functions before the coming of Islam.

Two small, late precolonial principalities in northeast Somalia were ruled by Maryan's ancestors. Although their power over the nomads of the interior was limited, their favorable geographical location on the Gulf of Aden and the Indian Ocean gave them access to and some control over the seaborne trade with South Arabia, the Benadir Coast, Zanzibar, and the wider Indian Ocean. The older northern sultanate was called "Migiurtinia" (as transliterated into Italian) and centered on Baargaal and environs. Its southern offshoot, based on Hoobyo, was founded in the 1870s. Maryan descended from the leaders of these two sultanates, as well as from the titled leaders, or *islaans,* of a nomadic non-state community. Through her father, she descended from the *boqors* of Baargaal and the *garaads* of the Warsangeli; through her mother's father, she descended from the *suldaans* of Hoobyo, and through her mother's mother, she descended from Islaan Aadan Faarah of the Mudug and Haud regions. In some cases, such precolonial leadership positions translated into political positions after independence. For this and other reasons, Maryan's father became a government minister.

It is no wonder that Maryan takes pride in her family and its historical accomplishments. Although social inequities have limited the potential achievements of many, other Somali families also possess an equally rich family history and a highly developed sense of identity and pride. Somali families often see themselves as a sort of *grande famille* or even dynasty, like the Kennedy or Bush families in the United States. In Maryan's case, such a view has some historical merit.

Maryan's Youth

Maryan was born in one of the large stone houses in Hamarweyne, the historical heart of Mogadishu, then the capital of Italian Somaliland. The neighborhood was inhabited by the original city population, the Reer Hamar, with their own language and cultural habits, as well as a sprinkling of other Somalis, Indians, Arabs, and Italians. Initially, the house had been an upscale prison for Maryan's paternal grandfather, the boqor of Baargaal, who, after his defeat by the Italians in about 1927, was exiled to Mogadishu. Maryan's father was a small boy at the time. One day when he was near the coast having a horseback-riding lesson, an Italian ship showed up to take his father away. Although the ship's captain had orders not to let anyone accompany the boqor, the little boy refused to let go of his father's hand and was allowed on board. With only a warm shawl handed to him at the last minute by one of his uncles, the boy went into exile with his father. During the twilight years of Italian rule in Somalia in the 1950s, Maryan recalls, her father, encouraged by a local lawyer, petitioned for ownership of the house.

Maryan's early memories of life in this big house are very happy, at least up to the premature death of her mother, Faduumo-Jawaahir, or Jawaahir for short, in 1952 when she was thirteen or fourteen years old. While her father was very private, her mother, whose grandfather had been sultan of Hoobyo, was very outgoing and social. Maryan's mother not only tried hard to fit into the culture of Hamarweyne but also hosted friends and relatives from other neighborhoods and was friendly with Italian women, from whom she learned some Italian, needlework, and even some fashions new to Somalia, such as the brassiere. Jawaahir initially had trouble bringing her pregnancies to term. Since the Italian hospitals were closed to Somalis, an Italian nun and friend of her father found an Italian midwife, fondly called Haaja Faay by Somalis. The midwife's guidance proved successful. Thus Maryan's own safe birth came to pass, a product of cross-cultural collaboration between women.

The house consisted of two large apartments, each of five and seven rooms with an upstairs and downstairs. Apart from Maryan and her three siblings, it housed thirteen young boys, first cousins from northeast Somalia, who lived with them so that they could go to school. Female relatives also visited for extended periods, especially young wives who came to the city to check on long-absent husbands and often found in the tall house in Hamarweyne an opportunity to reconcile. Jawaahir loved to help other women. She also had many friends and relatives in the nearby neighborhood of Iskuraran. Since women were allowed out only under the veil of darkness, they would come on foot at night to visit in groups of as many as ten or fifteen. They ate fritters at Maryan's house, filling the women's quarters with lively talk and laughter.

But the most dramatic visits were those from her father's seafaring brothers and cousins from Bari, that is to say, the northeast, who would stop off at Mogadishu on their way to and from Aden, Zanzibar, and other places.

They turned the house on its head with their informality and loud joviality and teasing, their gifts to the children and their mother, and their can-do attitude. They made themselves at home anywhere in the house and mixed easily with its permanent residents. Maryan remembers how they rose before most other people in the house and the neighborhood, and how, after praying at the local mosque, they used to read the Qur'an out loud. If their cargo were of use to the household, they would bring some of it home. These uncles from Bari knew how to tease their little city niece, whose looks and manners were so different from the girls of the countryside. There a girl initially had her head shaved except for a little tuft (*food*). Once she became eight years old or so, she would let her hair grow out and plait it into small braids, whose length would be an easily recognizable indication of her age. However, Maryan had a full head of long hair, as was the custom among the Reer Hamar, earning her the nickname of *tuurkuhalesh*, "the long-haired girl." Another aspect of her city ways was that she wore long dresses with petticoats of a different length.

If anyone failed to meet their expectations, the visiting uncles would compose mocking verses, so that Maryan would do her small errands for them as carefully as she could, just to avoid being immortalized in verse! However, at times she disappointed them: "Maryan, how many uncles do you have?" Maryan could think of only two relatives of her father living in their neighborhood. In reality, she had eight. "And how many aunts?" Maryan could think of only one, even though she had four. Indignation! "These Benadir[3] folk are really not with it! Let's take her to Bari!" About this time her parents began to teach her the names of other uncles and aunts who did not live in Mogadishu. Of course, little Maryan learned her parents' northeastern dialect of Somali well. However, even today, she still has a special love for and is most fluent in the old city language (or so her children claim).

In the evening sometimes Maryan's father quizzed his children, and especially Maryan and her brother, with general questions about general knowledge: "Abdullahi, how many teats are there on a camel?" The boy had once seen a male burden camel, and so he answered full of confidence, "One." "Wrong!" Maryan, miffed that her father had asked her younger brother a question first, opted for deductive reasoning: "If the goat has two and the cow has four, then the camel must have six!" Laughter!

As she grew up, Maryan noticed quite a few differences between the culture of her Hamarweyne neighborhood and the cultures of other Somalis. She remembered, for example, that the Reer Hamar people were very private and did not enter each other's houses unannounced or without clear invitation. However, if there were a death, neighbors were expected to drop whatever they were doing and come running to a place where they could hear the customary wailing. If a woman stopped so long as to put on her shoes, she risked criticism. Maryan's mother hated to walk outside barefoot and Maryan remembers occasions when she, as a little girl, accompanied her mother and waited outside holding her mother's sandals—not always acquitting herself successfully of her job. She played hide-and-seek among and inside the tall houses of her neighborhood and is still surprised at how tolerant people were of the children's noise and running around. But when they were about ten years old, Reer Hamar girls went into *purdah*, or seclusion. All girls married young, but in contrast to other Somalis, Reer Hamar girls often married close relatives. "Other Somalis wanted their children to have significant *abtis* or maternal uncles," Maryan noted, and thus looked for spouses beyond the circle of close relatives.

When she was six years old, Maryan went to school, joining her younger brother and the other boys of the household. She remembers how hard it was to keep up with the bigger boys, and how she was fearful of the boys' loud pushing and shoving during breaks and on the way to and from school. Because parents and other adults of the community attached great value to education, however, they encouraged the children. An uncle who had a store on their way to school gave them bread and dates to make their school day more pleasant, and he always lectured them on the importance of education.

Although Maryan remembers being a bit annoyed by the importance given to her younger brother and, more vaguely, saddened by the loss of a sister to complications resulting from female circumcision, the early years of her youth were happy ones. Tragedy struck when she was barely a teenager: Her beautiful, young, joyful mother suddenly died, possibly of a disease of the liver. Jawaahir died in her own mother's home in Galka'yo, where Maryan's father had taken her in the hope that a change of air might do Jawaahir good. It was not until several years later that Maryan returned to her father's house in Hamarweyne, for she could not bear seeing it or the neighborhood. In spite of her sadness about her mother's death, she found joy in the attentions of her aunts and great-aunts in Galka'yo and learned to milk a little goat she named Qaato. After this extended visit to her grandmother in Galka'yo, Maryan moved back to Mogadishu. This time she moved to Iskuraran, another downtown neighborhood but one that was very different from her old, historical, coral-built neighborhood in Hamarweyne. Indeed, the name "Iskuraran," which means "piled on top of each other," reflected the informal character of the settlement, many of whose inhabitants had arrived not long before.

Women's Leadership and Solidarity

When Maryan moved to Iskuraran, the neighborhood was very cohesive and highly politicized. Most residents, although from a variety of family backgrounds, shared a nomadic rural background and originally hailed from the three regions of Bari, Mudug, and Haud. Most of them also belonged to the Somali Youth League, the leading nationalist party in the country, which was committed to create an independent, unified nation-state. Even though this densely built neighborhood of wooden houses and closely connected residents was known to her from earlier visits, living there was a new experience for Maryan. Here people were loud and outgoing, visiting each other unannounced, sharing meals on the spur of the moment, and actively and unabashedly involving themselves in each other's daily lives. In the morning, the older married men, on their way to work, would gently bang their canes on every door and ask whether all was well that morning: *"Ma barideen?"* ("Have you all woken up well?" "Are the children fine?") If someone ran out of something, a neighbor would provide it. If someone's cooking fire was not lit, others would notice and offer help, or the woman herself would ask for assistance: "Are you a bit better off than me today?" People also disciplined each other's children; Maryan still remembers her shock at being slapped once by a neighbor! For a girl who had grown up in Hamarweyne, where families valued privacy highly and minded their property and social relations carefully, this new environment was impressive and surprising mayhem. Maryan saw that for the people of Iskuraran, money and food existed only to be invested in people, not to be valued or saved for their own sake. Maryan particularly remembers the support women gave to men whose political activism for the nationalist movement led the Italians to fire them from their jobs. Women either provided free room and board for them, or they raised needed money by selling needlework. Maryan still remembers the first piece of embroidery she sold for this cause.

Maryan and her siblings moved in with three female relatives: her mother's mother (the same formidable Hirsiyo Aadan whom she had visited in Galka'yo); Hirsiyo Aadan's daughter (Maryan's aunt) Maryan Haaji `Ismaan; and `Ambaro Husein, Hirsiyo's cousin, who was also the widow of her son Yaasiin.[4] Thus, Maryan and her younger brother and sister, three children who had lost their mother, joined two children who had lost their father. During these formative years, Maryan recounts, the women of this household, her grandmother and aunts, taught her the values that she has tried to live by ever since.

Hirsiyo Aadan, her grandmother, was a tough character who built quite a reputation for herself in the wider family. She was the sister of Islaan Faarah and daughter of Islaan Aadan Mahmuud, whose sister Dahabo was married to the sultan of Hoobyo. Another sister, Faduumo, had been sought in marriage by the famous leader of the Somali anticolonial resistance Sayyid Mohamed `Abdille Hassan (d. 1921).[5] To formalize the political alliance that marrying Faduumo represented, and with great regret, Sayyid Mohamed then gave up his favorite war pony Hiin Finiin. The praise poem the Sayyid composed for his horse on this occasion is unequalled in Somali oral literature and includes a tribute to the Islaan Aadan: "Since the Sultan to whom I owe respect insists on having it," the Sayyid ended his poem, "take its bridle; I would not have honored any other human being with it!" (*"Mar hadduu suldaan igu xil lihi igaga xaydaantay, xariggiisa qabo aadni kale kuma xurmeeyeene."*)[6] Hirsiyo herself was valued at least as much as her sister, Maryan recounted, for when the Sayyid's marriage proposal arrived, family elders refused to let Hirsiyo go, sending her sister Faduumo instead. Hence Hirsiyo was given in marriage to Haaji `Ismaan Sharmarke, a widower with children and a great poet, who had also composed a religious treatise with different chapters for each letter of the Arabic alphabet. When she was older, Hirsiyo was that rare woman who was invited to the formal gatherings of her clan and attended the settlement of customary law cases.

Hirsiyo was very religious and had earned the honorific of *haaja* by making the pilgrimage to Mecca. However, her religiosity was also pragmatic. At one point, Maryan remembers, she asked her daughter, who was using prayer beads, "If you had to choose between those prayer beads and the Jubba and Shabeelle hotels, what would you choose?" Her daughter answered, "The prayer beads." At this, Hirsiyo scoffed: "I can pray to God using my fingers, without prayer beads, but with the wealth represented by those two hotels I would be able to provide work and food for many people. Religion is `amal, that is to say acts or work, not just `ibaado, or devotion." It was Hirsiyo's son Yaasiin who had been a cofounder of the Somali Youth League. When his colleagues came to console her over his premature death, she had little patience: "He made it clear who was to succeed him," she said. "What are you waiting for? The work is waiting to be done."

She was pragmatic in other ways as well. When Maryan got married in 1964, her grandmother explained why she had not put together a beautiful trousseau for her: "You like things that are in fashion," she said. "I was afraid that, had I prepared bed sheets in fashion several years ago, with snakes embroidered on them, you would wonder today why I wanted to put snakes in your bed." Until she died in the early 1970s, Hirsiyo's mission in life and her definition of honorable behavior and noblesse oblige was to provide for others. She never encouraged her grandchildren to save money but always directed them to support this or that family, because so-and-so had fallen sick or died, or so-and-so was out of work or had had bad luck. Looking back on her life in her old age, Hirsiyo told Maryan, "The principles that guided my action always were that when people need you, you make yourself useful, but when you are in need yourself, you bear it and protect your good name." Throughout her life, Hirsiyo prayed to God for "an honorable life and an honorable place in the hereafter." Only after she witnessed a deadly cholera epidemic in Mogadishu, did she change her prayer, adding "an honorable death" to her earlier prayer: *"nolol sharafleh, geeri sharafleh, aakhirana maqaar sharafleh."*

Maryan's aunt `Ambaro Husein, widow of Hirsiyo's son Yaasiin, also lived with them in Iskuraran. `Ambaro came from a very religious nomadic family in the countryside, the kind of family that believed that girls' voices or footsteps should not be heard, but taught both boys and girls the Qur'an and the `Ismaaniya script.[7] `Ambaro was very young when she was brought to the coast to be married. When she first saw the tall, light-skinned man who was waiting for her, she thought he was a foreigner because she had never seen a Somali wearing European-style pants. Only after he had taken her home, on horseback under a canopy of cloth, did she realize that he was her husband. Whatever the beginnings, theirs was a happy marriage, although short-lived. `Ambaro's husband was so fond of her, the story goes, that when he learned in the mosque about the houris of paradise, he raised his hand and asked the sheikh "whether God would allow you to just stick to your own wife?" This quiet, deeply religious woman became a second mother to Maryan and her siblings. She clearly spoiled the young girl who had just lost her mother, giving her few chores and cheering her up when she could. `Ambaro was also quite a poet, composing topical rhymes about both the small incidents of daily life and the hot political issues of the day. One time, Maryan noted that her aunt's *fisileeta,* a small headscarf of fine, transparent cloth, was sagging, Aunt `Ambaro improvised her response: "Dear God, my scarf is sagging! Please send me heaps of splendid clothes!" (*"Allow fisileetigayga faruuranyeey, waxaad i siisaa dhar faro ka badan!"*)

`Ambaro also commented in verse on the political events of the day. Although Maryan's memories of politics in this pre-independence era are limited, she remembers her family's support for the Somali Youth League as expressed in a popular poem, set to the music of a march, which became the league's theme song: "We are the men who wear the logo of our party on our hearts and are not afraid of clan. Let all good people who want to join come to the Somali League." (*"Karaawilkan ragga koorahay ku sitaan oon kalaan* ka *cabsanin baannu nahay. Kal wanaagsan iyo ninkii doonaayo, kaalaya Somaaliya Leeg.*")[8]

Maryan still vividly remembers how closely the women of the family followed political events. In the house in Hamarweyne, the men gathered downstairs in the courtyard to listen to the news on the radio, while upstairs the women clustered at windows overlooking this space to hear. One evening, between 1948 and 1949, when the United Nations was deciding what would happen to the colonies of the powers defeated in World War II, they all stayed up late, listening to the radio for news from North America. Would the UN agree to Somali independence?[9] At one point the women heard the men clapping, but they didn't know why. "Let's send Maryan down to ask." "Wait, wait, let's give the girl a message!" And so Maryan went down with a message crafted by `Ambaro: "Is the signing [of the UN decision] near? People are worried, and men are not able to sleep normally. This clapping of yours we hear, is it what we have been hoping for?" ("*Saxiix baa dhow [in la kala baxo], oo saxwi baa dadka ku jiraa. Rag baa ka suxuumay hurdada la seexan jiray oo idinku sacabtaad tumaysaan saraad miyaa?*")

The little girl was even more impressed by her aunt's anger upon hearing that the Italians would return to Somalia to head a UN trusteeship administration in 1950, a decision opposed by the Somali Youth League.[10] `Ambaro lamented with irony: "If we were Muslims, we would set out in submarines and torpedo their ships in their harbor. We would kill those who are jeering at us and happily praise God." ("*Muslim haddaan nahay, mariina ku kicin lahayn. Nuulka maanyada maraakiibtaan gelin lahayn. Kuwii na maagahayaa maytkoodaan dhigi lahayn. Mahad Ilaahay aan makhsuud ku noqon lahayn.*") The political activism of `Ambaro and many women like her, moreover, went beyond words and moral support. They helped recruit members for the Somali Youth League, collected funds, and made great personal sacrifices—financial and otherwise. While in school in Egypt and also following her return to Somalia in 1961, Maryan too stayed politically engaged, with considerably more freedom to move in the public sphere than her aunts had enjoyed.

The third aunt who had a great impact on Maryan was Maryan, Hirsiyo's daughter. Aunt Maryan was also serious and religious. After the death of her first husband and a short, unhappy marriage to another man, she married `Ismaan Yuusuf Keenadiid, brother of the sultan of Hoobyo, author of the `Ismaaniya script, and a brilliant poet. Aunt Maryan, however, also had a community project. Given the name "Maryan dejjiya," or "the one who settles people," by her mother, Maryan built a mosque, a school that she ran, and three houses. She gave one house to the son of her deceased first husband, she lived in the second, and she gave the third to a new wife she found for her husband when her responsibilities at the school began to take up most of her time. Aunt Maryan had studied religion. If she heard something at the mosque she did not understand or with which she did not agree, she would ask the imam to stop by her house on his way home. Then she would either straighten him out or be educated by him. In her great knowledge of tafsir—made up of interpretation of hadith, the corpus of sayings of the Prophet Muhammad, and the Qur'an—Aunt Maryan appears to have been unique among women in her community. Yet her case was not unique in Somalia. In the southern coastal town of Brava, for example, women were the Qur'anic schoolteachers par excellence.

Even as a young girl, Maryan was struck by the differences in behavior between her mother's mother's people, from the interior, and her father's father's and mother's father's people, from the sultanates on the coast. The serious, quiet, and religious ways of the people from the interior contrasted with the informal, spontaneous, and boisterous teasing of those on the coast. Nonetheless, all the grown-ups in her life had a highly developed sense of communal responsibility—a belief that one's good name, as an individual and a family, brought with it responsibilities for others, irrespective of whether one's material circumstances allowed for it. Thus, her grandmother's motto was "Gob awood baa looga roon" ("Being honorable means that you go beyond your means [to provide for others]"), while her father taught her that "one pays dues on one's name," or "magaca canshuur buu leeyahay."

For Maryan, this philosophy encapsulated the kind of leadership that existed in Somali society in the past, among both women and men. She illustrated this belief with a story about her ancestors during the time of Sayyid Mohamed. Some of her great-uncles from the Islaan family had traveled to Baargaal to ask for assistance from Boqor `Ismaan. They were received in a beautiful room, high up, with windows in all directions. As they were sitting there, they heard a woman's voice: "Help, `Ismaan! This filthy son of a filthy father's sheep has chased my donkey! What will you do about it?" The boqor got up and called out to the woman by calling her "Auntie," and he ordered his men to give her a bale of cotton cloth and a case of dates. The men of the Islaan family were flabbergasted. Eventually, one asked the boqor why he allowed the woman to address him so impolitely and insult him and his son on top of it. The boqor smiled and said, "Listen, we have the sultanate. The least we can do is to give the people things and let them speak freely!" Maryan feels that this kind of democratic spirit, as well as leadership that provided for people rather than exploiting them, represented the ideals (if not always the practices) of Somali leadership in the past. She asked herself whether this kind of leadership could inspire Somalia's new transitional government.

Maryan stayed in Iskuraran only a year or two. Once her father had remarried—he married her mother's sister—he redecorated her room and persuaded her after a time to come back to the tall house in Hamarweyne. By then he had resolved to send Maryan to school in Egypt, began teaching her Arabic, and brought her Egyptian women's magazines to prepare her. The Rabitah al-Islamiya, to which Muuse Boqor belonged, was a group of men who, in modern parlance, would be called Islamic modernists or liberal Muslims. They chose to educate their children in Egypt, fearing that study in Europe might distance them from their religion and culture. At the same time they also strove to be modern. Thus, in 1955, two years after they sent their sons to school in Egypt, they sent fifteen girls. Throughout her years in Egypt, until she returned in 1961, Maryan's father helped her balance her objectives of becoming a modern, educated woman, who would be able to act in the public sphere with confidence and competence, as well as elegance and joy, with her desire to remain grounded in the core values of Islam. However modern her father's support for girls' education and his confidence in her capabilities may have been, Maryan suggests, his attitude toward women had also been shaped by the female role models of his youth. When his mother, one of the wives of the sultan of Hoobyo, had lost favor, the sultan's young nieces made sure that when the ships with provisions came in, all wives, including his mother, received a fair share.

When they were leaving for Cairo, the women of Iskuraran impressed on the girls that they were not only responsible for their own success but that they were also blazing a trail for other Somali girls: "The struggle for independence is coming to an end," they said, "but [the struggle] for the progress of Somali women is only beginning, and much will depend on you." They also showered the girls with blessings. Maryan remembers those of Aunt `Ambaro: "You are leaving at 2:00 a.m. May God make things easy on you! May not even the smallest harm befall you, and may you reach the country safely. May everything there that breathes welcome you with respect." (*"Sideed saacaad baxaysaan, Allah ha sahlee! Saxar aan idiin gaarin, carliga salaama taga oo intii san ku neefleh joogta idiin sajuuda."*)

Given the women who had raised her, Maryan was well prepared to take on her new responsibilities in Egypt. She held office in the Somali students association, and at a formal celebration of Somalia's independence in 1960, Maryan was the only girl who addressed with confidence a hall full of Egyptian dignitaries. "The girl who spoke before me was so nervous she could hardly hold her piece of paper," Maryan remembered, "so I made sure I put my sheet on the lectern in front of me." Her brother was so worried that she would embarrass herself that he left the hall, returning only to witness the spontaneous ovation she received at the end of her speech. Maryan spoke about the important roles Somali women were expecting to play in independent Somalia, and indeed she focused her political and social activism on women's issues after her return to Somalia in 1961 in the hopeful aftermath of independence.

Like her brother, and in spite of the fact that her father was minister for the Somali Youth League, she joined the opposition, a new left-leaning party called the Great Somali League. Her father did not challenge her political opinions and activities, while she did her best not to embarrass or worry him. When, a decade or more later, the military dictator Mohamed Siyad Barre complained to her father about Maryan's opposition to his "scientific socialist revolution," her father retorted, "She was in the opposition when I was in the government. Why would it be different under you?" During these years, Maryan combined a job as a teacher with enthusiastic political and social activism for the Great Somali League, contributing to the party's newspaper and serving as secretary to the women's, youths', and students' sections. She took part in delegations, fact-finding missions, and conferences throughout the country, reporting on unequal access to educational or health services, and raising awareness about the lack of Islamic sanction for female circumcision.

In 1964, in defiance of the wishes of her father, who had betrothed her to someone else, Maryan married a young and dashing member of parliament, who also belonged to the Great Somali League. Her wedding was a great social event and consisted of three celebrations: one in the style of the Hamarweyne neighborhood where she had been raised, one according to the Somali customs of Iskuraran, and one in European fashion. She bore her husband two sons. The future appeared to smile on the young couple. That independence would not bear all the fruits their youthful generation expected was a disappointment that still lay in the future.

Further Reading

Poetry is a wonderful window on Somali history and culture. For an excellent introduction, see B. W. Andrzejewski and I. M. Lewis, *Somali Poetry: An Introduction* (Oxford, UK: Clarendon Press, 1964). Other, more specialized studies are Said S. Samatar, *Oral Poetry and Somali Nationalism: The Case of Sayyid Mahammad ʿAbdille Hasan* (Cambridge, UK: Cambridge University Press, 1982); John W. Johnson, *"Heelloy": Modern Poetry and Songs of the Somali* (London: Haan, [1974] 1996); and Lidwien Kapteijns, with Maryan

O. Ali, *Women's Voices in a Man's World: Women and the Somali Pastoral Tradition in Northern Somali Orature, 1899–1980* (Portsmouth, N.H.: Heinemann, 1999). For examples, see www.doollo.com, www.aftahan.com, or www.golkatumo.com.

For books on the Somali past (colonial and post-independence), see Robert L. Hess, *Italian Colonialism in Somalia* (Chicago: University of Chicago Press, 1966); Lee V. Cassanelli, *Shaping Somali Society: Reconstructing the History of a Pastoral People, 1600–1900* (Philadelphia: University of Pennsylvania Press, 1982); Abdi Ismail Samatar, *The State and Rural Transformation in Northern Somalia, 1884–1986* (Madison: University of Wisconsin Press, 1989); David D. Laitin and Said S. Samatar, *Somalia: Nation in Search of a State* (Boulder, Colo.: Westview, 1987); Ahmed I. Samatar, *Socialist Somalia: Rhetoric and Reality* (London: Zed Books, 1988); and I. M. Lewis, *A Modern History of the Somali*, 4th ed. (Athens: Ohio University Press, 2002).

For the history of Islam in the Horn of Africa, see Lidwien Kapteijns, "Ethiopia and the Horn of Africa," in *The History of Islam in Africa*, ed. Nehemia Levtzion and Randall L. Pouwels (Athens: Ohio University Press, 2000), 227–50.

For women and gender, see Kapteijns with Ali, *Women's Voices in a Man's World* and Lidwien Kapteijns, "Women and the Crisis of Communal Identity: The Cultural Construction of Gender in Somali History," in *The Somali Challenge: From Catastrophe to Renewal?* ed. Ahmed I. Samatar (Boulder, Colo.: Lynne Rienner, 1994), 211–32; and Cawo Mohamed Abdi, "Convergence of Civil War and the Religious Right: Reimagining Somali Women," *Signs: Journal of Women and Society* 33, 1 (2007): 184–207.

For the ongoing Somali civil war, see Said S. Samatar, *Somalia: A Nation in Turmoil. A Minority Rights Group Report* (London: Minority Rights Group, 1991); Terence Lyons and Ahmed I. Samatar, *Somalia: State Collapse, Multilateral Intervention, and Strategies for Political Reconstruction* (Washington, D.C.: Brookings, 1995); Ahmed I. Samatar, ed., *The Somali Challenge: From Catastrophe to Renewal* (Boulder, Colo.: Lynne Rienner, 1994); and Catherine Besteman and Lee V. Cassanelli, eds., *The Struggle for Land in Southern Somalia: The War behind the War* (Boulder, Colo.: Westview Press, 1996).

For the study of Somalis in the diaspora, see *Yesterday, Tomorrow: Voices from the Somali Diaspora* (New York: Cassell, 2000) by Nuruddin Farah, the famous Somali novelist; and Abdi M. Kusow and Stephanie R. Björk, eds., *From Mogadishu to Dixon: The Somali Diaspora in Global Context* (Trenton, N.J.: Red Sea Press, 2007).

Notes

1. This is a substantially revised version of an article published in *The International Journal of African Historical Studies* 42, 1 (2009): 105–16. We gratefully acknowledge the trustees of Boston University for permission to include this version of Kapteijns and Boqor's essay.

2. Maryan Muuse Boqor now resides in Boston. We recorded the interviews during the month of Ramadan (January/February) 2001.

3. "Benadir" literally means "ports" in Persian. Here it refers to the people of the cities on the southern Somali coast, such as Mogadishu.

4. Yaasiin Haaji `Ismaan Sharmarke was one of the original thirteen founders of the Somali Youth League, initially called the Somali Youth Club.

5. Sayyid Mohamed `Abdille Hasan led a religious war of anticolonial resistance from 1898 until his death in 1921. Sayyid is in this context a religious title. See Said S. Samatar, *Oral Poetry and Somali Nationalism: The Case of Sayyid Mahammad `Abdille Hasan* (Cambridge, UK: Cambridge University Press, 1982).

6. For the poem, see B. W. Andrzejewski and I. M. Lewis, *Somali Poetry: An Introduction* (Oxford, UK: Clarendon Press, 1964), 66–71. *Hiin finiin* is onomatopoeia, indicating the whizzing sound of a fast object, in this case the flying horse.

7. Devising their own way of writing Somali was part of the program of Somali nationalists of this period.

8. *Koorahay* is from the Italian *cuore* ("heart"). The reference to "clan" reflects the nationalist party's principled resistance against the Somali people's tendency to want to promote the political interests of their clans rather than to see themselves as members of a unified Somali nation.

9. After the Four Powers Commission visited Somalia to ascertain the wishes of the population, the UN decided that Somalia would get its independence following a period of trusteeship. The decision to consign the trusteeship to Italy was very unpopular with many Somalis, including the Somali Youth League.

10. The trusteeship period (1950–1960), when Italy governed Somalia as a United Nations Trust territory, was meant to prepare Italian Somaliland for independence.

PART IV

GLOBALIZATION, FAMILY STRATEGIES, AND NEW THREATS IN THE ERA OF INDEPENDENCE, 1960–2012

CHAPTER TWELVE

~

Wambui Waiyaki Otieno Mbugua (b. 1928)

Gender Politics in Kenya from the Mau Mau Rebellion to the Pro-Democracy Movement

Cora Ann Presley

This chapter examines the life of Wambui Waiyaki Otieno Mbugua, a noted Kenyan activist and advocate for women's rights. Wambui's life experiences reflect the evolution of women's involvement in the political struggle in Kenya and their agenda for social change. She became involved in the anticolonial struggle during the 1950s and emerged as a leader of women in the Mau Mau rebellion. After independence, she served in the national assembly and directed government initiatives for improving the economic status of women. In the 1980s, Wambui gained international notoriety when her legal challenge to inheritance laws and widows' rights reached the highest courts in Kenya. The court case came to symbolize African women's struggles for equality and became a cause célèbre in the international feminist movement. When the pro-democracy movement emerged in Kenya in the 1990s, Wambui Otieno also played a prominent role in this challenge to the legitimacy of the Moi regime in Kenya, which had been in place for many years.

Wambui Otieno's story echoes many themes in the history of modern Africa. Three topics in particular prompt us to think beyond the Kenyan historical experience to include other African colonies, which later became independent countries. First, Wambui comes from a family with a long history of defending African rights in the face of European transgression. Four generations before Wambui herself set out to be a freedom fighter, her great-grandfather resisted British laws aimed at tak-ing over his people's land. Although the British prevailed, Wambui's grandparents and her parents continued to champion African rights. The contours of British domination changed dramatically over this time, as did the strategies for contesting it. Wambui's family engaged the new colonial order, taking advantage of mission education to become, in some ways, part of the colonial project. Yet, members of her family ultimately used their changed situation and the advantages acquired dur-ing British rule to resist more effectively.

Second, Wambui's own activism spilled over from one arena to another—from resisting the rule of the British and their local collaborators during the Mau Mau era to championing women's rights in the face of oppression by patriarchal clan authority. She then joined the struggle for democracy in Kenya, condemning the one-party government of President Moi. More recently, in the face of widespread condemnation of her marriage to a much younger man, she proclaimed a woman's right to marry whomever she wishes.

Third, Wambui lodged a lawsuit that demanded recognition of her rights as a wife to make decisions about the burial of her husband, S.M. Otieno, after his death in 1986 and to inherit his property. Since she was Kikuyu and her late hus-band was Luo, Wambui's initiative and the response to it underscores the intensity of ethnic identities and how political leaders manipulate them to set groups against each other. The violence that followed the presidential election of 2008 between Kikuyu and Luo candidates is a sober example of the destructive force of ethnic-ity. In the same year, the Kenyan response to the dramatic contest in the United States between Hillary Clinton and Barack Obama for the Democratic nomination illustrated the same issue. Even though Obama spent very little time in Kenya and only barely knew his father's Luo relatives, the Kikuyu in Kenya were vocal sup-porters of Clinton. They figured that because his father was Luo, Obama would "naturally" oppose Kikuyu interests if he became president of the United States. Ethnicity in Africa, like ethnicity in the big cities of immigrant America in the nineteenth century, serves to monopolize power and wealth.

In the following pages, Cora Ann Presley focuses on how Wambui carried forward her family's tradition of resistance. This history of political activism raises questions about whether and how it is possible to transmit a will to resist from one generation to another. Wambui's experience also leads us to explore how it is that a struggle for rights in one sphere may lead to demands for freedom in others.

In 1986, Silvano Melea Otieno, one of the most prominent lawyers in Ke-nya, died of a heart attack. His wife, Wambui Waiyaki Otieno, rushed to the hospital. By the time she arrived, her husband, known as "S.M.," was already dead. This new widow with fifteen children notified his brothers of the death. Suddenly, Wambui Otieno found herself in a struggle with her brothers-in-law over the right to marital property and the right to make decisions about burying S.M. The struggle over burial rights lasted for over a year, while S.M.'s body lay in the morgue. During that year, the trial was watched closely by the Kenyan press and by the Luo and Kikuyu peoples. S.M.'s death inflamed the conflict between these two major ethnic groups, which had for decades competed for political power. At stake were issues of women's rights. Could women inherit marital property? Were they entitled to flout tradition and bury a man apart from his blood relatives and place of birth? Could widows ignore traditions that prescribed that a widow be passed on to a male relative of her late husband? Was it time for modern notions of women's independence, thought to be Western, to replace African traditions of male dominance? These questions were debated with passion in the press, homes, and streets of Nairobi, while Wambui Otieno struggled to keep her family together and to secure her rights.

Wambui Waiyaki's life and experiences capture the tension between changing African traditions and the challenges of modernity epitomized by a progressive agenda that would open to women all dimensions of political and economic life. Along with other female activists engaged first in the nationalist struggle and then in the pro-democracy movement, Wambui Otieno found herself marginalized and under attack when she took part in activities that called into question the hegemonic, patriarchal institutions in colonial and contemporary African societies.

Decades before the S.M. burial saga, Wambui was involved in the struggle for African rights in Kenya. During the 1940s, her father, Tiras Waiyaki, joined with other Kenyans who committed themselves to bringing an end to the British colonial occupation of their country. Wambui became politically aware as a result of being exposed to nationalist talk in her parents' home.

British Colonial Rule and Kenyan Resistance

The British declared Kenya to be a British protectorate in the late nineteenth century. Along with other European powers, Great Britain aimed to claim and control great stretches of Africa. At stake was European access to African natural resources such as gold, ivory, rubber, copper, and diamonds, and control of potential new markets for European products. In some parts of the continent, European interests also hoped to found new white settler colonies whose inhabitants would play key roles in developing agribusiness and increase the African production of cash crops for export.[1]

Kenya quickly became one of Britain's most important African colonies. Once the invasion and conquest were complete, the colonial government set about imposing British law and customs and encouraging British settlement. To ensure the prosperity of the settlers and build the necessary infrastructure, the British colonial government enacted laws requiring that African people pay taxes, surrender thousands of acres of land to the British, and offer their labor. As a result, hundreds of thousands of African families found their lives fundamentally changed as white settlers took over their ancestral lands and transformed them into European settler estates. Africans were required to work on these estates as low-paid laborers, or live as squatters who could cultivate the land but also had to provide agricultural labor for the settlers. Africans also constructed roads and government buildings, and they staffed the lower ranks of the army and civil service.

From the beginning, Wambui Waiyaki's family was deeply implicated in the new European regime in Kenya. Indeed, even before official British rule, her great-grandfather, Waiyaki wa Hinga, worked with representatives of the Imperial British East Africa Company (IBEAC) to establish an economic enterprise sphere in his lands. The IBEAC was a privately owned, government-chartered company whose goal was to open up Kenya and Uganda for economic exploitation. Its charter granted it broad powers, some of which closely resembled later colonial government control. In the case of Waiyaki wa Hinga, the company's British agents and African employees violated the treaty, which stipulated that no land would be taken by force and that Kikuyu women would not be molested, leading to war between his Kikuyu people and the IBEAC. Another conflict broke out in 1892. The Kikuyu won the first battle, but after a fight with an agent in the IBEAC company office, Waiyaki was arrested. He was severely beaten and died as he was being hauled off for deportation.

In her autobiography, Wambui presents Waiyaki wa Hinga as the first Kenyan nationalist. She claims that Waiyaki's children and grandchildren played substantial roles in winning Kenyan independence, and she argues further that his descendants are the natural leaders of Kenya because of this heritage. She also believes that her extended family was targeted for government repression during the regime of President Moi because "Kenya's current leaders live in fear that the children of Waiyaki, whom they believe have the potential to unite the nation, will take leadership again."[2]

The Role of the Waiyaki Family in Early Kenyan Nationalism

Well before the independence movement, the descendants of Waiyaki wa Hinga positioned themselves to become members of the African elite. Munyua Waiyaki, who was Waiyaki's son and Wambui's grandfather, donated land to the Church of Scotland Mission. Munyua's son Waiyaki Wathoni, Wambui's father, popularly known as Tiras, was among the first young Kikuyu to be educated by the missionaries. This background positioned him for a high-ranking position in the colonial administration. Despite this success, Tiras and his children harbored bitterness over the inequities of colonialism: land alienation, high taxation, the dismantling of African social customs, and the race-based social segregation that characterized colonial Kenya. As a result, Tiras gravitated toward nationalist ideas.

Tiras Waiyaki's involvement with the nationalist movement grew out of contradictions inherent in the colonial enterprise. After he completed his education, he joined the colonial administration. By the 1940s, he held the rank of an African chief inspector of police, placing him among the African elite of the colony. But his mission education had an unintended outcome. Mission education provided him practical skills in industrial education and literacy in English; it also brought close contact with Europeans. As was often the case with other members of the Western-educated elite, the study of history, literature, and the other humanities broadened Tiras's worldview, providing him with the critical tools for understanding and critiquing the colonial experience. Tiras also saw to it that his children and grandchildren received a mission education—the only option since the missions monopolized the schools until the 1930s, when Africans rebelled. Fueled by an upsurge in cultural nationalism associated with what came to be called the female circumcision controversy,[3] the Kikuyu established their own rival, independent schools.

The contradictions of mission study are apparent in Wambui Waiyaki's education. At the mission she became aware of the negative attitude her teachers held about Kikuyu culture. Students were punished if they spoke their own languages at school. Other practices also raised her ire. She was especially offended that each female student was subjected to an annual physical exam to determine if she were still a virgin. When she learned how the British characterized her great-grandfather's war with them, she became radicalized. Taken together, the curriculum and practices of the school aimed at erasing or modifying students' African identities. In Wambui's case, she was pushed to answer to a European name but often refused to do so, which led to her detention at school on weekends when her classmates went home.[4]

Wambui's experience reflected issues that concerned all Africans in Kenya. The confiscation of land, harsh labor laws, rising taxation, and extreme racial segregation had led by World War I to a second phase in African challenges to the British authorities. Africans living in towns and cities, many of whom were mission educated, began to form political associations to pressure the government for change. The key associations among the Kikuyu were the East African Association and the Young Kikuyu Association. Led by Harry Thuku, a mission-educated clerk in the government, urbanized young African men sent letters and telegrams to the colonial office in London and the governor's office in Kenya about their concerns. They requested that the high taxes be reduced and that Africans receive services—such as roads, schools, and hospitals—commensurate with the level of taxation they paid.

Their demands for reform were rejected, and between 1914 and 1920 their growing urban-based movement became more insistent. They organized rallies in Nairobi and neighboring districts. The spread of these mass movements alarmed the government and its African allies. In 1922, after a mass rally in Nairobi, Harry Thuku was arrested and imprisoned. The urban crowd responded with a mass rally outside the jail. The police fired on the crowd, killing dozens of Africans. Harry Thuku was deported to the coast, where he spent more than ten years in exile, and political associations were banned. These measures did not suppress nationalist feelings for long. Rather they spurred the founding of more radical groups, and successor organizations such as the Kikuyu Central Association (KCA) broadened their goals in pursuit of African liberation. Between the 1920s and the 1940s, these activists came to be closely associated with the African independent schools movement and the independent church movement.

In the 1940s, the most prominent leaders of the nationalist struggle, figures such as Mbiyu Koinange and Jomo Kenyatta, were frequent guests at Wambui's home. Kenyatta had been raised by Wambui's grandmother, who was also his aunt. He forged still stronger ties to the Waiyaki clan when he married Ngina, daughter of Senior Chief Muhoho wa Gatheca, a descendant of Waiyaki wa Hinga.[5] During his visits to Wambui's home, they would "lie on the grass outside our house and have discussions with my father for hours on end."

Kenyatta's role in the nationalist movement was well established by the time the young Wambui met him. In the 1930s, as a member of the KCA, Kenyatta was sent to Great Britain to represent African interests. For the next twenty years he lived in London, where he participated in nationalist meetings and represented his people. He also studied at the School of Oriental and African Studies at the University of London, where he wrote a thesis later published with the title *Facing Mount Kenya*. The book has become a classic and is the standard insider view of the Kikuyu people and their early history. Ironically, Kenyatta fit in with British society and developed a real understanding of the British people. For decades Kenyatta was the most well-known Kenyan nationalist. Kenyatta absorbed nationalist sentiments from both maternal and paternal relatives. Such was also the case with Wambui. She thought through her anticolonial positions early in life as a result of family connections with the nationalist movement.

Wambui Joins the Mau Mau Resistance

As a result of growing up in her immediate family and through ties with nationalist leaders, Wambui's political awareness and commitment matured after 1950. By then, a new nationalist organization, called Mau Mau by the Europeans, attracted the impressionable sixteen-year-old girl with its radical call to expel the Europeans via armed insurgency. During school holidays in 1952, when oaths of loyalty to Mau Mau were secretly administered in her neighborhood, Wambui took the step that secured her place in Kenya's history as one of its most prominent women leaders. She took her first oath of loyalty to the movement before the British declared an official state of emergency. Because she had openly expressed her resentment of colonialism and had vowed to do anything to avenge her great-grandfather, her cousin Timothy Chege took Wambui and a woman related to her mother to a secret location.[6] Like countless others who were taken by friends or relatives to an oathing ceremony, Wambui was not aware that she was going to be inducted into the Mau Mau movement until she arrived at the gathering. She thought that she was going to a meeting of the Girl Guides.[7]

In taking the oath, Wambui meant to strike a blow to avenge her family. She also believed that membership was an important weapon against collaborators who were in the pay of the colonial government. From 1952 to 1954, she hid her connection to the movement from her family. Using the code name of Wagio, later changed to Msaja, she attended meetings in secret and was privy to local level Mau Mau plans for attacks on government installations and African loyalists.

In 1954, her secret association with the rebels was revealed. On April 24, 1954, her father was arrested in Operation Anvil, a massive police sweep intended to arrest prominent nationalist members and root out Mau Mau. While her father was held for questioning, their home was raided repeatedly. During one of the raids, her mother was beaten by a European officer, and Wambui went to the district office to complain. She forced her way to the head of the line of people awaiting an audience with the district officer. She and the assistant district officer, "Mr. Martin," shouted at each other. Wambui later wrote that in the heat of the moment she was so angry that she did not care if the authorities killed her. Indeed, she dared them to do so, facing down armed soldiers who leveled their guns at her.[8]

Throughout 1954, Wambui and her mother struggled to support the family while her father was in government custody. Her brothers were forced to interrupt their schooling in England. She and her mother went into the forests to gather wood from wattle trees and sold the bark to the local gin factory to earn money. Her mother retreated into her faith, oblivious to the upheavals that the state of emergency produced. Wambui, on the other hand, became more involved with Mau Mau. Toward the end of the year, she ran away to Nairobi to become a full-time participant in the rebellion. For months her family did not know where she was. Her frantic mother reported her absence to the police and secured a detective to help look for her.

Nairobi, the capital of Kenya, was as young as the colony; it had been founded by the British on land taken from the Masaai in 1902, part of an agreement that forced them to surrender thousands of acres. Nairobi was a way station on the railroad to Uganda, and the life of the town focused on the railway and government. It quickly became a bustling settlement with a growing population of British, Indian, and African agents and settlers. By the time Wambui arrived in 1954, Nairobi was officially segregated by race, with Asians, Africans, and Europeans living in separate neighborhoods.

Gender discrimination was also policy in the capital. Early in the colonial period, the government and African male traditionalists had conspired to pass ordinances that kept women, especially single women, out of town. African elders feared that if young women moved to the city, they would slip out of their cultural control. In addition, in the early 1950s women were not able to obtain employment in the city as readily as males. Most careers were closed to them; even secretaries were male. Female education was controlled by the missionaries and did not prepare women for jobs in the new colonial regime. They were taught "domestic science," not the industrial arts that would qualify them for any occupation other than wife and farmer. As a result, the few single women in Nairobi worked as maids, street hawkers, or prostitutes. Wambui's family searched for their runaway daughter in their ranks.

In Nairobi Wambui embarked on daring missions for the Mau Mau organization. Her first assignment was to obtain secrets from the offices of high-ranking officials in Government House. She approached the governor's secretary, "telling a lot of lies and making false promises. I had to keep the man's advances at bay yet remain friendly enough for him not to suspect my real interest in Government House."[9] These tactics were so successful that Wambui was told to organize a spy ring in Nairobi. She enlisted household servants to spy on their masters and spirit away sensitive government documents when their masters were asleep or intoxicated. Even the governor's driver, Mzee Shiyuka, became a secret supporter of the Mau Mau and helped secure sensitive government memoranda for the movement.

Over time, Wambui was given responsibility for scouting and smuggling firearms. She daringly created a ring of women agents in Nairobi. Using a well-coordinated fleet of taxis, these women frequented bars and even barracks, dressed to attract British soldiers, whose weapons they intended to steal. As they encouraged the soldiers to get drunk, the women agents would use various tricks, such as vomiting in the toilets, to avoid getting drunk. When it was time to leave for the girls' lodging, Mau Mau operatives driving taxis by prearrangement would assist the girls in stealing the soldiers' weapons.[10]

The successes of these strategies led to Wambui's steady rise in the movement. The war council gave her responsibility for important surveillance missions in rural areas. Using disguises, she made frequent trips to government facilities, such as the Kendra Home Guard post. Intelligence she gathered there was later used in the assault on the post. She was nearly caught and arrested, as she could not produce a movement pass.[11] When questioned, she pretended that she was an innocent young girl who had been abducted by a local man who wanted to marry her. Claiming that he had abandoned her, she was such a sympathetic figure that the guards gave her food and escorted her to Kihumbu-ini, another town.[12]

By the time the war drew to a close with the defeat of the Mau Mau, Wambui Waiyaki had been entrusted with numerous missions and was a member of the inner circle of the movement. She was engaged to Tom Mboya, one of the most prominent nationalist leaders, who also led the trade union movement. By 1960, she had had three children with him, and the young mother was one of the top women organizers in Nairobi. After the war, the British recognized that it was inevitable that Kenya would, like the other African colonies, become independent. Between 1959 and independence in 1963, the British allowed Africans to form political parties. Wambui became a leader in the new Nairobi People's Convention Party (NPCP).

Wambui, Nationalist Leader

In the NPCP, Wambui mainly organized anticolonial demonstrations and disseminated propaganda leaflets. Even though the British administration allowed political parties to organize, most politically aware Africans believed that real progress toward independence would only come when Jomo Kenyatta was released from detention. (Kenyatta had been arrested in 1952 and charged with being the leader of the Mau Mau organization.) Over the following eight years, people came to recognize him as the leader of the independence movement, and nationalists insisted that he be freed. Wambui organized and participated in boycotts and demonstrations demanding his release; she also coedited the NPCP newspaper. Beyond that, Wambui served as secretary of the women's wing of the party, whose members helped organize campaigns against racial segregation in schools, hotels, hospitals, and residential areas. But the campaign to release Jomo Kenyatta was their most pressing issue.[13]

Wambui's notoriety and visibility led to her arrest on several occasions. In 1959, she was sentenced to restriction, forced to leave Nairobi, and had to remain in rural areas outside the city. She had to report daily to the district officer and submit to interrogation. One day she had had enough of the daily interrogations. She walked out and refused to return despite orders to do so. When the district officer tried to force her to return, she slapped him so hard that he fell to the floor. The African Home Guards who served the British ran in, ready to shoot.[14] Wambui's truculence nearly got her killed, but she was willing to risk her life for her principles.

Ultimately Wambui came to be so difficult to deal with that the authorities ordered her to report to an African chief at Dagoretti Location at Waithaka, where she locked horns with a different interrogator for the remainder of her sentence. In Dagoretti Location she had to travel on foot fourteen miles every day. Several times she broke restriction and slipped away to Nairobi to attend political meetings. Finally, eighteen months after her restriction began, the news broke that the state of emergency was over. Hearing the news on the radio, Wambui decided to never go back for interrogation by the chief. Chief Kinyanjui told her that he was different from the European officer she had defied, stressing that he was an *African* man. If she defied him, he said, she would be taught a lesson. Moreover, after the Europeans had left, he would still rule the area.[15] These remarks implied that after independence, African men would enforce the cultural values that assigned women a lesser status. Although Wambui found his remarks to be contemptible and ignored them, his words foretold what would happen to her years later during the infamous controversy surrounding her husband's burial.

Although the state of emergency was over, Africans still faced political repression. Even as the British were meeting with representatives of Kenyan political parties at Lancaster House in London to negotiate independence, a new series of roundups began. Claiming evidence of new subversions, Governor Swan proscribed the Kiama Kia Muingi (KKM) or Kenya Land Freedom Army, a newly formed organization of younger nationalists, and other parties associated with it. Under Public Security Restriction Regulation 1960 L.N. 313, issued on July 8, 1960, large numbers of Africans were arrested and sent into detention. Wambui Waiyaki and her young children were among them, even though she was not a member of the Kenya Land Freedom Army.[16]

This time, Wambui found herself in a detention center on Lamu Island off the Kenyan coast, hundreds of miles away from Nairobi and her home in Kiambu district. For a few days, Wambui was separated from her children and other detainees. She was questioned, and during the last night she was raped repeatedly by her interrogator, Rudolph Speed. The next day, she was sent to the barracks to join other women detainees.[17] Because she had contracted malaria, she was released from detention on January 23, 1961, pregnant with a child conceived as a result of the rape.

Once in Nairobi, Wambui determined to hunt down her rapist and have him charged with the assault. She enlisted the aid of her brother, who was a lawyer. But before they could bring a case against Speed, he was given a pension and fled to England. Around this time Wambui met S.M. Otieno, an attorney who knew her brother. She told him about her experiences with Speed and how her former fiancé Mboya had informed her after her return that they could never marry because he was seeking a more advantageous union. Nonetheless, he wanted to purchase a house for her and his children and visit them regularly. Wambui felt deeply betrayed and ended the ten-year relationship that had lasted through the Mau Mau uprising and the early days of party politics in Nairobi.

Wambui, a Kikuyu Woman, Marries S.M. Otieno, a Luo Man

These experiences of rape and betrayal led Wambui to be leery of close relationships. S.M. Otieno pressed the unconventional Wambui to marry from the outset. She refused because she was a Kikuyu and he was a Luo, and there was historic tension between the two ethnic groups. S.M.'s sister Helen opposed the relationship, though his brother Isaiah defended Wambui when Helen asked why S.M. had bought a car and allowed it to be driven by a "Kikuyu prostitute."[18] Eventually Wambui and Otieno became intimate, and she gave birth to their son in 1963. When they married shortly thereafter, most of S.M.'s relatives boycotted the ceremony.

Wambui had worried that marriage would change her lifestyle, that she would have to assume the role of a traditional African woman. S.M., however, supported her work as a politician, and the two became partners in their law firm. Through the 1960s and 1970s, Wambui was an active politician. She was a member of the ruling party and ran for office unsuccessfully. She rose to prominence in the main women's organization, called Maendeleo ya Wanawake (Women's Progress). She led the women's cooperative movement and frequently represented the government at national and international conferences on gender issues. Several times she was sent to the United States, and once to Mexico as a member of the Kenya delegation to the international conference on women in 1975.

In 1983, Wambui represented Kenya at meetings in the United States. One of these visits included a tour of the American South, where she visited the Federation of Southern Cooperatives in Epes, Alabama. The federation was chartered in 1967 by poor black Southern farmers. During her travels, she visited sites where Martin Luther King Jr. had delivered speeches during the local struggle against racial discrimination. She also visited sites of slave auctions and wrote that she was moved to tears as she "felt the lingering spirits' pain."[19] Wambui also noted that racial segregation was still visibly evident. Her visit to Alabama and Mississippi showed her the other side of the United States, where race relations were so unlike those in New York or Washington, D.C. She was able to ask questions of slaves' descendants and to finally understand how the colonial education system in Kenya had used pictures and stories of slavery in America to prove that British colonialism was more considerate toward Africans.[20]

During her travels, Wambui developed an acute appreciation of the global aspects of racial oppression and gender discrimination. During these years, Wambui and S.M. lived a sophisticated urban life in Nairobi and raised their children in relative affluence. When their children were old enough to go to college, they were sent to the Europe and the United States. And yet, the sophisticated Wambui and S.M. remained deeply connected to their traditions and cultures. The traditional rivalries between the Kikuyu and Luo had their corresponding contemporary dynamics. They were also played out within their marriage. For example, when S.M.'s father, Jairo Ougo Oyugi, died in 1978, Wambui took charge of the domestic details of the funeral, preparing the body for burial, cooking and arranging for the funeral. At African social gatherings, the women typically spend most of their time in the kitchen preparing food and talking. But during this funeral, Wambui reported that the Luo women refused to help and subjected her to rude comments: "The women snidely told me that Mzee had said that I should do the cooking, bury him, and so on. I ignored their comments. Only my husband's stepsister and Simon Odhiambo's daughter assisted me."[21] These minor jealousies were apparent in the first years of her marriage to S.M.

S.M.'s Death and Wambui's Struggle against the Constraints of Ethnicity and Gender

S.M. died in 1986, leading to a struggle between Wambui and her in-laws and his Kager clan that lasted more than a year. During the conflict, S.M.'s body lay in the Nairobi morgue. At issue was whether or not Wambui, as his widow, had the authority to bury S.M. and whether she owned their marital property. According to traditional Luo law, the eldest male relatives of the deceased husband had undivided authority over not only surviving children, but over the widow and property as well. Wambui Otieno argued in court that traditional Luo law should not apply because S.M. was an urbanized man who rejected the customs of the past. The trials were closely followed in Kenya and in the international press. Many people saw them as a case that illustrated the tension between traditional law and women's rights.

By this time, Kenyan women had fought for a decade to reform the traditional laws that discriminated against them. According to these laws, for example, widows of state employees lost their deceased spouse's pensions if they remarried, whereas widowers of state employees continued to receive the pensions of their deceased spouse if they did the same. Indeed, several ethnic groups, such as the Luo, did not allow a widow to remarry at all. Luo traditions provided for the transfer of the property of the deceased husband to his father and brothers. The widow had no rights of ownership.

The contest between S.M.'s widow and his kin played out publicly in the press. Wambui was roundly vilified. She was accused of being a loose woman, since she had given birth to children during the Mau Mau struggle when she was Tom Mboya's lover.[22] She was also condemned for being a disobedient wife, since she refused to comply with Luo burial and inheritance traditions. Finally, she was charged with being a "tribalist" who favored Kikuyu domination over the Luo. Wambui fought these accusations with the courage she had found within herself as a Mau Mau fighter. She believed herself to be the victim of a conspiracy extending from the Kager clan all the way to the office of President Arap Moi, a Luo. Indeed, on one occasion, while speaking at a women's fund-raiser in Wambui's home district, the president said that if a woman married a Luo, then she should follow Luo customs.[23] On another occasion, emissaries from the president urged Wambui to abandon her battle and, after leading the group in prayer, told her that the president wanted her to attend the funeral arranged by S.M.'s people. If she stayed away, they threatened, he would not go. Wambui still refused because she knew that if she went the issue would disappear from the news, along with discussion of how the entire incident was a violation of human rights and a flagrant example of discrimination against women. When Winifred Mwendwa and Julia Ojiambo tried to persuade her to fall in line, citing the system's injustices to them, Wambui replied that she was not like them. She could not condone injustice.[24]

Wambui lost the final appeal on February 12, 1987, and was ordered to bury her husband jointly in his family's village. The court upheld the version of a woman's place that Richard Otieno Kwach, the lawyer for the Otieno clan, underscored in an interview with Blaine Harden of the *Washington Post*:

> Wambui was nothing but a woman of the streets, a bossy whore. . . . A woman cannot be the head of a family. There are things she cannot do; she cannot preside over the negotiations for the marriage of her daughter. There is traditional regalia for attending burials, which she cannot wear. She cannot sit on her husband's traditional stool. She cannot organize a beer party. Women accept this. Not a single Luo woman, I repeat not a single Luo woman has ever gone to Court over these matters ever since the world began.[25]

Wambui's persistence showed that she was determined to defy so-called custom. She believed that Kenyans constantly adjusted tradition. Indeed, she had testified during the trial that Joash Ochieng and others of the Kager clan had lied about Luo traditions. Further, she asserted that these laws were outdated and needed to be modernized so that Kenyan women could have full rights.[26] She refused to attend the funeral, but she did send a team to record the event. In her autobiography, she ridiculed the ceremony as a "mixture of Christian and traditional burial practices . . . by people who have no traditional beliefs [to] impress a community that does not give a damn or even understand."[27] Following the bitter battle, Wambui built a private family shrine to S.M., and, together with her children, family, and friends, observed the anniversary of S.M.'s death each year.

Wambui's New Struggle: Democracy in Kenya

Wambui Otieno's public defiance of the state's executive and judiciary in the late 1980s mirrored brewing dissatisfaction and dissent in Kenya. By the early 1990s, the Moi regime was viewed by many as being corrupt and repressive. Numerous cases of human rights violations were attributed to the government, including provoking violent interethnic fighting and fiscal malfeasance. Kenyans, like Africans in many other countries, demanded democratic governments and an end to dictatorships. The Kenyan government suppressed dissent, jailing dissenters. When the government jailed several young men who pushed for democratic reforms and held them without trial, women in Kenya staged a yearlong protest. They built a shantytown in the middle of Nairobi, held daily demonstrations, and went on a hunger strike, demanding that the government release the young men. The protest garnered international attention for the pro-democracy movement.

International pressure on the Kenya government finally led to an agreement that one-party rule would end and Kenyans would be allowed openly to form political parties whose candidates could run for office. By 1991, several alliances had formed. The most active was the Forum for the Restoration of Democracy (FORD). Wambui was one its first members.

> I was very excited because now I was able to share my views with other people. No longer would I be in the ignominious position of being a political pariah. . . . People had avoided me solely because I opposed the president. However, the truth was that I was not against the president as such, but I was opposed to his undemocratic rule.[28]

Even though FORD and other political parties were able to register, their opposition to undemocratic rule was stymied. Hired thugs, known as KANU youth wingers, played dirty tricks on them, attacking them at rallies and waylaying them while they campaigned in the countryside. On one occasion, when Wambui Otieno was campaigning with Wangari Maathai, they were so badly beaten that they had to be taken to the hospital for treatment.[29] After years of struggle for the restoration of democracy, including accusations of electoral fraud by the ruling party in the 1992 and 1997 elections, the 2000 election resulted in the selection of a new president, who was democratically elected under a multiparty system. Wambui had been asked to run for president by many of her supporters. However, she did not do so because, she said,

> Now that our men have been stripped of their political power, politically minded women must resolve to join hands with them and fight to restore it. This coalition will give us a better argument for equal rights with men. No man can tell seasoned women leaders like Professor Wangari Maathai, Honorable Phoebe Asiyo, Professor Micere Mugo, Tabitha Sei, Rose Waruhiu, Hon. Martha Karua, Grace Githu, Jael Mbogo, and a newcomer, Honorable Charity K. Ngilu, that they are not involved in fighting to liberate our country. I, an old timer, have worked with these ladies and have come to admire their courage and dedication.[30]

Wambui Waiyaki Otieno expressed these sentiments in her memoirs in 1998, forty years after she first became involved in political movements in Kenya. By then, she was recognized by women in Kenya and elsewhere as a national and global leader for women's rights. She had participated in two

major political events: the Mau Mau rebellion and the pro-democracy movement. She had traveled internationally and overcome efforts to besmirch her
reputation and hold her up to national public ridicule because of her defense
of her rights as a Kenyan woman and a widow in the S.M. burial case. One
might have expected that Wambui would have eased into a graceful retirement. This was not to be.

Wambui Remarries,
Once Again Challenging Gender Conventions

In 2003, Wambui appeared once again in the national and international media when she unexpectedly remarried. This time, she chose a husband who
was much younger than she. Wambui and her groom hoped to observe the
ceremony privately. Unfortunately, an enterprising photographer snapped a
picture of the sixty-three-year-old Wambui and her twenty-eight-year-old
groom, a stonemason, as they emerged from the civil ceremony. Throngs of
people stood outside the building where the union had been legalized. The
wedding was reported widely, drawing both praise and censure. Wambui's
children boycotted the ceremony, saying that their mother would come to
regret the shameful marriage to a man so much younger. The groom's mother
also opposed the marriage. Some members of the clergy in Kenya also issued
statements condemning it.[31]

As in the S.M. Otieno case, shocked and outraged traditionalists condemned the marriage, while feminists and advocates for women's rights
praised Wambui's courage in challenging convention. At the time, Kenya's
politicians were contemplating a constitutional amendment to give women
equal rights in Kenya. When Wambui appeared at the conference where the
constitutional amendment was being discussed, there was a general outcry
to eject her.[32] Led by Bonny Khalwele, a member of parliament, the male
members of the conference tried to eject Wambui. Hubbie Hussein defended
Wambui's admission as a delegate. Wambui remarked that delegates to the
conference included land grabbers, murderers, and looters and that their
presence at the conference was not questioned.[33]

According to Wanjiru Kariuki, Wambui's defiance stemmed from her
life experiences as "a freedom fighter and feminist par excellence." Wambui
said that her remarriage was a love match—a direct challenge to African
patriarchy in Kenya in general, and among the Luo in particular. When male
delegates to the constitutional convention first attempted to eject Wambui
and then walked out to protest her lawful inclusion in the assembly, Wambui
refused to be silenced. She declared, "I will continue attending the constitu-

tional conference in my capacity as an observer, a former freedom fighter and a politician."[34] The Federation of Women Lawyers–Kenya (FIDA) publicly supported Wambui Waiyaki Otieno Mbugua. FIDA's head, Mrs. Majiwa, pointed out that that the society was patriarchal, and that "no Kenyan, man or woman has a right to cast aspersions against another for being married to whomever they choose, so long as the concerned parties are not married to other individuals."[35] FIDA took the position that family laws in the country did not deter anyone from marrying whomever he or she wished. Clear feminist lines were drawn when Majiwa declared, "To humiliate Wambui just because of stereotypes in the name of social decorum is tantamount to infringing on her rights as an individual. . . . And the Kenya Human Rights Commission (KHRC) has termed the treatment accorded Mrs. Wambui Otieno-Mbugua at Bomas of Kenya as shocking and scandalous."[36]

Conclusion: Gender, Patriarchy, and Women's Rights in Kenya

This final shock to Kenya's patriarchal culture was delivered by Wambui as she neared her seventh decade. Several questions emerge from this reading of Wambui's life: What lessons do we learn? How do Wambui's life and experiences show transformation in women's attitudes about modernity? Why did this one story become so famous, when countless widows in Kenya and elsewhere in Africa are routinely dispossessed by their in-laws as poverty deepens in Africa, and as tradition is fractured by urbanization and the pressures of modernity? As a Mau Mau fighter, Wambui was an accepted and respected public heroine. As the wife of one of Kenya's most prominent lawyers and a women's leader in the 1970s and 1980s, Wambui exemplified elite Kenyan women for whom service to the nation and their roles as wives and mothers are paramount. Her actions did not challenge national and cultural norms. But the S.M. burial saga and Wambui's persistent public and vocal defiance in the face of attempts to silence her somewhat tarnished the image of this heroine of the independence struggle. In some senses, her status was redeemed by her later participation in the pro-democracy movement that led to the reestablishment of multiparty democracy in Kenya. The final challenge of her remarriage to a much younger man again thrust her into a divisive public and personal controversy. This controversy reflects the ongoing gender war in Kenya—dismaying traditionalists and encouraging those who seek to elevate the status of Kenyan women.

More particularly, Wambui's life experiences capture a set of challenges, first to colonial oppression through her engagement in the Mau Mau struggle, and then to the antidemocratic government via participation in the pro-democracy movement. Her personal struggle to challenge Luo traditions and the state's support for them in her husband's burial case perhaps did set the terms of debates over "tradition versus modernity," or tradition versus more liberal laws about the status of women. Nonetheless, it is certainly true that through her actions, Wambui Waiyaki Otieno Mbugua exposed the depths of gender conflict in Kenya and emboldened other women to take action and demand that the issue of equal rights for women be a part of the national discourse.

Further Reading

In addition to works cited in the notes, further discussion of political and social issues in Kenya exemplified by Wambui Waiyaki Otieno Mbugua's life can be found in the literature on the anticolonial movement in Kenya, the pro-democracy movement, and African women's issues. For general histories of Kenya that discuss colonialism and the Mau Mau rebellion, see William Ochieng', *Modern History of Kenya, 1895–1980* (Nairobi: Evans Brothers, 1989); Caroline Elkins, *Imperial Reckoning: The Untold Story of Britain's Gulag in Kenya* (New York: Henry Holt, 2005); Wunyabari Maloba, *Mau Mau and Kenya: An Analysis of a Peasant Revolt* (Bloomington: Indiana University Press, 1998); David Anderson, *Histories of the Hanged: The Dirty War in Kenya and the End of Empire* (New York: Norton, 2005); and Alam S. M. Shamsul, *Rethinking the Mau Mau in Colonial Kenya* (New York: Palgrave Macmillan, 2007).

On the pro-democracy movement and ethnic politics, see Bruce Berman, Dickson Eyoh, and Will Kymlicka, *Ethnicity and Democracy in Africa* (Athens: Ohio University Press, 2004); David Throup and Charles Hornsby, *Multiparty Politics in Kenya* (Athens: Ohio University Press, 1998); and Bruce Berman and John Lonsdale, *Unhappy Valley, Book 2: Violence and Ethnicity* (London: James Currey, 1992).

Mau Mau freedom fighters' personal narratives began to appear the 1960s and are still being written. These include Don Barnett, ed., *The Urban Guerrilla: The Story of Mohamed Mathu* (Oakland, Calif.: LSM Information Center, 1974); Josiah Mwangi Kariuki, *Mau Mau Detainee: The Account by a Kenya African of His Experiences in Detention Camps, 1953–1960* (London: Oxford University Press, 1963); Waruhiu Itote, *"Mau Mau" General* (Nairobi: East African Publishing House, 1967); Henry Muoria I, *The Gikuyu and the White Fury* (Nairobi: East African Publishing House, 1994); and Kinuthia Macharia and Muigai Kanyua, *The Social Context of the Mau Mau Movement in Kenya* (Lanham, Md.: University Press of America, 2006). Despite nearly forty years of Mau Mau narratives, Wambui Otieno's account, *Mau Mau's Daughter* (Boulder, Colo.: Lynne Reinner, 1998), remains the only one written by a woman.

For discussions of women's roles and gender issues, see Claire Robertson, *Trouble Showed the Way: Men, Women, and Trade in the Nairobi Area* (Bloomington: Indiana University Press, 1997); Tabitha Kanogo, *African Womanhood in Colonial Kenya, 1900–50* (Athens: Ohio University Press, 2005): Jean Davison, *Voices from Mutira: Change in the Lives of Rural Gikuyo Women, 1910–1995* (Boulder, Colo.: Lynne Reinner, 1996); and Cora Presley, *Kikuyu Women, the Mau Mau Rebellion, and Social Change in Kenya* (Boulder, Colo.: Westview Press, 1992).

Finally, the S.M. burial saga exposed gender discrimination in Kenya and conflicts between traditional customs and westernization. For analysis of the controversy, see Atieno Odhiambo and David William Cohen, *Burying S.M.: The Politics of Knowledge and the Sociology of Power in Africa* (Portsmouth, N.H.: Heinemann; London: James Currey, 1992); Patricia Stamp, "Burying Otieno: The Politics of Gender and Ethnicity in Kenya," *Signs* 16, 4 (Summer 1991), 808–45; and April Gordon, "Gender, Ethnicity, and Class in Kenya: 'Burying Otieno' Revisited," *Signs* 20, 4 (Summer 1995), 883–912.

Notes

1. From the late 1400s through the early 1900s, Europe's primary interest in Africa was extracting slaves for the trans-Atlantic slave trade. Over more than four centuries it is estimated that more than eleven million Africans were taken from Africa and transported to South America, the Caribbean, and Central and North America to work on plantations producing sugar, cotton, tobacco, indigo, and other agricultural goods. After abolition of the slave trade in the North Atlantic in 1807, the traffic declined; by 1878 it had more or less ended. Between 1807 and the later 1800s, British philanthropists promoted substituting "legitimate trade" for the slave trade. Only in the 1880s did European powers shift focus and begin dividing up the continent of Africa into colonies.

2. Wambui Waiyaki Otieno, *Mau Mau's Daughter: A Life History*, ed. Cora Ann Presley (Boulder, Colo.: Lynne Reinner, 1998), 17–18.

3. The female circumcision controversy grew out of a conflict between Kenya's indigenous people and missionaries. The practice of genital cutting was a cultural tradition among the Kikuyu. Medical missionaries condemned it because it caused death and complications during childbirth. As early as 1912, authorities attempted to force the Kikuyu to abandon the custom without success. In 1928, the Church of Scotland Mission, led by Dr. John Arthur, issued an ultimatum to the Kikuyu to end the practice within their families or be expelled from the church and its schools.

Most Kikuyu refused to comply and started their own independent churches and schools. Ironically, then, a custom that oppressed women became a symbol of the Kikuyu desire for liberation.

4. Otieno, *Mau Mau's Daughter*, 29.

5. Mbiyu Koinange's leadership in the nationalist movement rivaled Kenyatta's position in the 1940s. Like Kenyatta, he was one of the few Africans to receive post-secondary education overseas. When the controversy over female genital mutilation gave rise to the independent schools movement, Koinange became the founder and head of Kikuyu independent schools.

6. Otieno, *Mau Mau's Daughter*, 33.

7. The Girl Guides are the British equivalent of the American Girl Scouts.

8. Otieno, *Mau Mau's Daughter*, 36.

9. Otieno, *Mau Mau's Daughter*, 37.

10. Otieno, *Mau Mau's Daughter*, 39.

11. The *kipande*, or pass, was a document that Africans were required to carry whenever they traveled out of their designated reservations. The authorities introduced the kipande as an instrument for controlling population movement and access to employment. During the state of emergency, pass checks were regularly done, making it difficult for Mau Mau operatives to move freely. Africans who did not possess passes were sent to jail and eventually deported back to the reservations.

12. Otieno, *Mau Mau's Daughter*, 40.

13. Otieno, *Mau Mau's Daughter*, 51–56.

14. Otieno, *Mau Mau's Daughter*, 67.

15. Otieno, *Mau Mau's Daughter*, 68.

16. Otieno, *Mau Mau's Daughter*, 72–73, 77–79.

17. Otieno, *Mau Mau's Daughter*, 79–84.

18. Otieno, *Mau Mau's Daughter*, 89–98.

19. Otieno, *Mau Mau's Daughter*, 123–24.

20. Otieno, *Mau Mau's Daughter*, 124–25.

21. Otieno, *Mau Mau's Daughter*, 111–12.

22. Tom Mboya led the African labor movement in Kenya.

23. Otieno, *Mau Mau's Daughter*, 164.

24. Otieno, *Mau Mau's Daughter*, 180–181.

25. Blaine Harden, "The Battle for the Body," in his *Africa: Dispatches from a Fragile Continent* (Boston: Houghton Mifflin, 1991), 95–129.

26. Otieno, *Mau Mau's Daughter*, 158–62, 188–91.

27. Otieno, *Mau Mau's Daughter*, 190.

28. Otieno, *Mau Mau's Daughter*, 211–12.

29. Otieno, *Mau Mau's Daughter*, 211–23.

30. Otieno, *Mau Mau's Daughter*, 36.

31. Kariuki wa Mureithi, "Kenya Split by Wedding Row," BBC News Online http://news.bbc.co.uk/2/hi/africa/3083877.stm (accessed 1 February 2005).

32. Francis Openda, "Jeers and Cheers for Wambui at Bomas," http://www.kenya constitution.org/docs/news55.htm (accessed 10 February 2006).

33. Wanjiru Kariuki, "Keeping the Feminist War Real in Contemporary Kenya: The Case of Wambui Otieno," *JENdA: A Journal of Culture and African Women Studies* 7 (2005) http://www.africaknowledgeproject.org/index.php/jenda/article/view/113 (accessed 1 February 2006).

34. Waithera Karuri and Lucy Ndichu, "Wambui Vows to Stay at Bomas," http://www.kenyaconstitution.org/docs/n (accessed 23 February 2006).

35. Karuri and Ndichu, "Wambui Vows to Stay at Bomas"; Brian Carnell, "Wambui Otieno Mbugua Sets Kenya Abuzz," http://www.equityfeminism.com/archives/years/2003/000087.html (accessed 1 February 2006).

36. Karuri and Ndichu, "Wambui Vows to Stay at Bomas"; Carnell, "Wambui Otieno Mbugua Sets Kenya Abuzz."

CHAPTER THIRTEEN

~

Tina (b. 1942) of Côte d'Ivoire

Success in the Masculine
World of Plantation Managers

Agnès Adjamagbo

This biographical sketch of Tina grows out of a larger study about the processes of population or demographic change in a region of Côte d'Ivoire with high rates of fertility and population growth. The study also aimed to learn more about the factors and logic underlying fertility behavior. To achieve these goals, Agnès Adjamagbo and her colleagues supplemented quantitative data collected during their research with information derived from qualitative research using what is called the life-story method. The life-story approach is designed to uncover elements of social life as they are perceived by the population being studied. Life stories situate individual actors in their larger historical contexts. In this case, the collection of life stories helped social scientists understand the nature of social relationships in a rural area of Côte d'Ivoire totally devoted to cash crop production in the early 1990s.

A qualitative approach to analyzing social relationships does not require that the case under review be statistically representative of a larger group. Consequently, individuals like Tina are worthy of consideration. In quantitative or statistical research, such individual cases are set aside because they do not represent the dominant norm or "average" behavior. The story that follows shows that Tina's life is clearly not typical. She defied the norms of the farming world of southwest Côte d'Ivoire by setting herself up as head of a farm of ten hectares that produced a cash crop. In this part of Côte d'Ivoire, this economic sector is entirely controlled by men. Although she is exceptional, Tina's experience nonetheless highlights important social dimensions of local society. Indeed, precisely because her life course contrasts with the norm, it reveals structural elements and themes that underlie social relations in this plantation society. As you read about Tina, identify and think about what these elements and themes may be. How do they help us understand the recent history of the larger society in this part of Africa?

Over the last half of the colonial period, from the 1920s to 1960, Côte d'Ivoire came to be the most prosperous colony in French West Africa. Because it lies on the coast, French authorities targeted it for economic development, focusing on the forestry industry and commercial agriculture. However, the coastal zone of this part of West Africa was lightly populated when compared to lands to the east, such as the British colony of Nigeria, or other French colonies to the north, such as Upper Volta (today's Burkina Faso) and French Soudan (today's Mali). Indeed, the northern part of Côte d'Ivoire was more densely populated than the south.

As a result, French rulers deployed a variety of mechanisms—including head taxes payable only in French colonial currency, coerced labor contracts, and forced labor at derisory rates of pay—to force Africans to leave colonies in the interior and migrate to work in southern Côte d'Ivoire. The colony's economy grew markedly. Based largely on the production of cash crops and propelled by inexpensive labor, the Côte d'Ivoire economy boomed in the decades immediately after independence in 1960. Tina tells us her story about the last years of this era of extraordinary expansion and the ensuing economic crisis that came with the fall in prices for Ivoirian cash crops and the rise in xenophobia directed toward settlers from elsewhere and their descendants. Early in the new century, civil war tragically closed the chapter on what economists shortly after independence had labeled the miracle Ivoirien, or Ivoirian miracle.

The woman I call Tina was about fifty years old in the early 1990s. She lived in Beyo, a small village in the Sassandra region of southwest Côte d'Ivoire. At that time, this part of Côte d'Ivoire was a center for export crop production. Coffee and cocoa were the main crops, but there were also lemon orchards and oil palm trees.

This chapter is divided into two parts. The first part retraces the history of the plantation economy in this humid tropical zone in West Africa, focusing on the organization of production and social relationships. Hence I provide the major historical and sociological landmarks necessary to understand the larger contexts in which the different episodes of Tina's life unfold. The second part is Tina's own story, a life history illustrated by quotations from her own account of her life.

Cash Crop Production in Sassandra

Tina lived in the *sous-préfecture* or district of Sassandra, which had a population of about 100,000 people in the early 1990s. Crossed from north to south by the Sassandra River, the district is made up of three regions: the Neyo area on the Atlantic coast around the mouth of the river; Bakwé to the west of the river; and Godié to the east, where Tina's village of Beyo is located.

With the arrival of the earliest European ships in the fifteenth century, this part of today's Côte d'Ivoire (literally, the Ivory Coast) opened up to maritime commercial exchange, which later became its main economic activity. By 1900, the port town of Sassandra had developed at the mouth of the river and came to be an important assembly point for natural resources collected in the interior for export to Europe.[1] By the late 1960s, after the construction of a new deepwater port in San Pedro in the west of the country,[2] Sassandra had lost its position as the major regional port. But broader development in the larger region helped open up the rural areas. Agro-industry based on plantations of rubber, oil palm, and scented citrus flourished; the development of timber resources accelerated; and coffee and cocoa plantations spread. Thus commercial agriculture took off following the earlier decline in exports. By the 1970s, the Sassandra region was a strategic pole for the production of Ivorian agricultural exports.[3] A demographic boom in the rural areas paralleled this economic expansion.[4]

Social Relations in a Plantation Economy

As elsewhere in the region, the rise of the plantation economy in southwest Côte d'Ivoire was accompanied by several social changes.[5] Among these, the autonomous unit of production came to be a domestic group limited to the nuclear family. The rapid spread of tree crop farming in cacao and coffee and the widespread drive to acquire land generated a great demand for labor. In the absence of more sophisticated farming techniques and advanced technology, increasing the size of the labor force—whether through salaried workers or family labor—constituted the major strategy for expanding the plantation economy.[6]

Gender Inequalities

With the onset of cash crop farming came changes in the gender division of labor.[7] As usual, women continued to engage in subsistence production, growing rice, bananas, cassava, yams, herbs, and so on, but they now also assisted their husbands in maintaining the farm and harvesting cash crops such as coffee and cacao. But this new proximity of men and women in the production process did not imply that they enjoyed equal power. Men exercised exclusive control over land management as well as the production and commercialization of the harvest. The transformation and commercialization of food products, which fell into the women's sphere of domestic activities, only generated a small income supplement that helped purchase goods for household consumption.

The subjection of women's productive labor to their husband's authority is tied to a patrilineal system and virilocal marital residence. In this part of Côte d'Ivoire, even within the domestic units where women live and work, wives are regarded as temporary sojourners who will return to their family when their husband dies. This status brings women few rights in their husband's village. Land cultivated by women belongs to their husband or their in-laws, who must give them permission to use it.

Why Tina?

The organization of production in southwest Côte d'Ivoire offered little support for women's ventures beyond their role as caregivers. Few women became plantation managers.[8] For this reason, we have chosen to present here the life history of an exceptional woman who managed to succeed in cash crop production, when others were unable to do so or did not even dare to try. But Tina's story is not only about success. She also confronted failure and disappointment. Her tale also offers a woman's perceptions about the situation of women. The particular nature of Tina's case underlines the difficulties encountered by women in their daily life. Being a female plantation owner in Sassandra in the 1990s truly challenged societal norms. Yet the few women who, like Tina, have succeeded in such endeavors have also earned social recognition among both men and women in their communities.

Tina's History

Tina was fifty-two years old when we interviewed her. She was born of a Bété mother and a Ghanaian father who owned a plantation in the region. She grew up with her parents in a village near Soubré with five brothers and sisters. Her childhood was tranquil, spent going to school and working on the farm. She left school at the end of the first level to live with a maternal aunt who traded in clothes in Soubré.

Tina enjoyed working with her aunt and liked trading. After some years, in the 1960s, she met a young man, a distant relative of her father who had come to spend the holidays with him. He courted her, and Tina found him alluring. In the few weeks he stayed in the village, they saw each other often. The man returned home but came back some months later to ask for Tina's hand in marriage. A year later they got married in Sassandra and moved to Abidjan, where he worked as a civil servant with the Régie de chemin de fer Abidjan-Niger (RAN) railroad company.[9] In Abidjan, Tina engaged in small-scale trading in cakes and clothes. Very quickly, the couple had a son. But after a few months, her husband started drinking and became violent. Life quickly became impossible for Tina and her son. One day, during a quarrel, Tina's husband threatened her with a knife. Terrified, Tina took their child and sought refuge with her parents at Soubré.

Her brothers-in-law and father-in-law knew about her husband's abuse and disapproved of his attitude. After the incident, they came to Tina's parents to offer a formal apology, hoping to pave the way for her return to her husband. But the idea so frightened Tina that her family rejected the apology. She and the child stayed with her parents in Soubré, where she again took up petty trade. When her son was older, he returned to his father in Abidjan to go to school. Tina learned that her husband had married a Baoulé woman. She asked him for a divorce but he refused. Tina then told the sous-préfet, a local official, about her plans to ask for a divorce, but he advised her to abandon them, given the difficulty in convincing a husband whose drinking made him unreasonable. Ultimately, Tina gave up the idea.

Tina's business in Soubré was not very successful, so in the early 1970s she decided to return to Abidjan to take up her trade in clothes. There she met a trader with whom she lived for a number of years. He wanted to marry her, but after her last experience of marriage, she hesitated and then refused. The prospect of a difficult divorce from her first husband reinforced this decision. Nonetheless, they had two children, a boy and a girl. The girl died when she was little.

A short time after the birth of Tina's last child, her partner took ill and died. She was then thirty years old. Unable to cope alone with her two children, Tina decided to leave Abidjan. She left her son in the care of one of her late partner's brothers and joined her own brothers in Beyo in 1974: "When I became a widow, I stayed there alone with the children for a year. But I could not survive. Where I was living in Abidjan, I must confess, life was hard. So, I returned to my parents here." At first, she stayed with her brothers, and in short order opened a bar-restaurant at the intersection of two dirt roads leading to Sassandra and the large industrial complex called Palmindustrie.

When I came from Abidjan, I first stayed with my parents. They live close by. The little houses you passed on your way to that crossroads—that's my father's camp. So that's where I stayed with my parents, and then very quickly, in a month, I built my own house and settled here [she shows the little house next to the bar-restaurant where our interview was taking place], and thank God, business started to take off. That is why I stayed here.

Tina left her father's house to become independent. She became the head of a household of eleven members, because even though her brothers allowed her to live alone, they sent their children to live with her. Tina thus took on her nephews and nieces. Fairly quickly, three of the nieces got married and left. Tina remained single, which, she explained, was a personal choice:

After the death of my husband [or partner], I did not want to remarry, because in my life, I had wanted only three children, and I had my three children: two boys and a girl. I lost my daughter but did not wish to have other children anymore. That is why I came to sit here without thinking of marriage anymore.

Tina worked hard. She woke up very early every morning to take the seven o'clock bush taxi to Sassandra to get provisions at the market. It took several hours to cover the fifty kilometers between Beyo and Sassandra. But business was good and the local economy was promising. Palmindustrie, just down the road, played a major economic role in the area. Created in the 1970s as part of a government project to promote industrial development, it specialized in the production of palm nuts and their transformation into oil. Palmindustrie provided a regular income to local farmers who supplied it with their palm nuts. In addition, its factories attracted many foreign workers, mostly from Burkina Faso but also from Mali and Guinea. For many who worked at this industrial complex lost in the bush fifty kilometers from Sassandra, Tina's bar-restaurant offered a much-appreciated place to relax. From workmen up to management staff, all were good clients. Some became Tina's friends.

One day, one of her clients suggested that she start an palm oil plantation. Tina, who had never imagined such a possibility, hesitated for a long time. The project seemed audacious. First of all, she needed sufficient land, which was not easy for a woman to acquire. Her family had land but her brothers had divided it up among themselves, and she did not dare attempt to renegotiate for her own share. She explained her hesitation in the following way: "My father is an outsider here. He himself had to ask for land here. My brothers who are here did the same. I could hardly go and ask to be given as well. You know, Africans will say: 'You are a woman; you are coming to fight with us.'" But her friend marshaled many arguments to convince her, including the fact that he could use his position at Palmindustrie to get her the best oil palm seedlings to start. In the face of his insistence, she decided to give it a try. She gave up asking for help from her brothers and decided to negotiate directly with the village authorities for land. It turned out to be easier than she had thought, and very quickly the village chief agreed to give her ten hectares of land in exchange for drinks. She explained her success by the fact that her business gave her a certain importance in the village. Many villagers also benefited from the presence of salaried workers.

Tina started her plantation in 1977. Using the profits from her bar-restaurant, she hired contract workers. She then decided to bring her first son back to help her. Since his school results were disappointing, she thought that agriculture might offer him a profitable alternative occupation:

> My son came to join me when I started my plantation in 1977. School was not working out for him. Paper did not suit him, so I brought him close to me. I wanted him to see what I was doing here in Beyo. Perhaps that would interest him more than schooling. So he came and with my advice, he understood and started work. Now, I'm still with him and he is in charge of the workmen and all that.

Afterward, "to help the family," according to the saying, she decided to put her nephews to work. But the nephews neglected their work and played on family ties to demand high salaries when the oil palm plantation had barely begun to produce. Although disappointed, Tina preferred to do without their help. But in order to avoid family quarrels, she gave them some land to farm on their own. They failed. Her nephews could not do the heavy labor required on a plantation. So Tina ended up taking over everything again with the help of contract workers. This is how she recounted the story:

> At first I employed contract workers whom I paid as I went. Thereafter, when the plantation entered into production, I wanted my nephews to work with me. I told my nephews, who are also my children, to join me. That is how it is with us Africans, the children of your brother, you must help them. But that did not work, because as soon as it started to produce, they wanted me to pay them each month. They did not understand that my resources were not very stable. In addition, they did nothing, so I said to them, "OK, I'll share the plantation; take this part and take care of yourselves." But even then, they did not succeed. They went away, leaving the plantation in bad shape. Me, I could not stand seeing the plantation in that state. I had even put some money into it! So, I uprooted everything and got contract workers to maintain it.

By dint of hard work, Tina's plantations became profitable. She went through a very exciting phase of her life when her bar-restaurant was always full and the oil palm plantations produced a good yield. Tina felt she had made the best choice by opting for an oil palm plantation. In her own words, the oil palm

is "the most in vogue" in the region, compared to coffee and cacao. The problem with coffee is that during the year, you have only one yield. So, you must wait to earn money only once a year and often it is not much, whereas with the oil palm, you are assured of being paid every month. It is like being a salaried worker. Each month the truck comes to collect your harvest and they pay you by its weight. For a hectare, if it rains well, you can easily make twelve to fifteen tons in a year. Fifteen tons at twenty [West African] francs a kilo, that comes to three hundred thousand francs. They provide you income because they are the ones who gave you the initial seedlings, the fencing, and the fertilizer. So, when your plantation enters into production, they start to deduct little by little what they spent on your start-up. Even in lean periods, you are sure to gain at least ten thousand francs at the end of the month.

But the prosperity did not last long. By the early 1980s, the first signs of the decline of the plantation economy were felt across the region. Cacao lost its value in international markets, with negative repercussions on the income of local producers, who experienced a drastic fall in their purchasing power:

Here, previously, the price of cacao was good because we sold a kilo of cacao for 400 francs, so parents lived well and did not allow their children to suffer at home. But now, the price has dropped: A kilo of cacao sells at 75 francs; sometimes it climbs a little to 100 francs, maximum 125 francs. At the same time the price of everything has increased in the market. How shall we live?

Palmindustrie, affected by the recession that struck most public-sector industries in Côte d'Ivoire, could no longer provide the same levels of remuneration to plantation owners. Even though oil palm was still the most lucrative crop, its price was falling and payments came late:

In 1984, the palm nut rose to 20 francs a kilo, then [fell] from sixteen to fourteen, and from fourteen to twelve. Today, it is at twelve; it has dropped a lot. In addition, now you have to wait long before being paid. Sometimes you are sick, and you are there waiting to be paid before you can seek treatment.

Hence Tina's business slowly dropped off. The golden age of the plantation and of the bar-restaurant came to an end. The crisis hit everyone, including the salaried workers of Palmindustrie, who did not come to eat and drink as often at Tina's place. For some months, her trading volume amounted to about half what it had been before. Then health problems forced Tina to go to Abidjan for treatment. She left her business in the care of a nephew, who "ate everything." On her return, she was forced to close down when she saw the disastrous state of the accounts. When Tina was interviewed, she planned to reopen in the near future but had the feeling that business would not be as good as before.

Tina's social and economic success brought many requests for help that she felt obliged to respond to, even though her own income was declining. She had an obligation to the villagers who gave her land to start her plantation. Sometimes she helped out when someone fell ill. She maintained a close relationship with her maternal family in Beyo, near Soubré. Her mother's brother was still alive, and she sent money regularly to him. Tina was head of her household. Her youngest son lived under her roof along with his partner and their two children. They were not married, but Tina strongly wanted them to regularize their status and intended to start the marriage preparations soon. She would have to make the bridewealth payment to the bride's family, and she was waiting for things to improve before making the marriage request to the girl's parents. She was also responsible for four nieces who lived with her. One of them was single but was expecting a third child by a man who, yet again, had no intention of marrying her. These young women did not work, and Tina deplored their failure to help her either at home or on the plantation. She complained of being obliged to hire contract workers despite a crowd of relatives in her home who could have helped her. She judged the girls severely, considering them to be unsteady and even venal:

> When a man approaches them, instead of first looking at him alone, they will look elsewhere. As soon as one of their friends calls them to say, "Come, there's another man waiting for you here," they rush there. Then how do you expect this man to be serious with them afterwards? In any case, according to what I see here in this village right now, it is the fault of our daughters if they cannot get married. For me, friendship comes before marriage. When a young girl and a young man like each other, they first become friends. They go out, they study one another, and if the girl behaves well with him, he, too, will behave well with her, and then they can think about marriage. But these daughters of ours, from the beginning, they spend the night together, and after the second night if the man does not give them this or that, if he does not give them gifts, then they do not want to marry. . . . They are only faithful to money. If money does not come, then they are unhappy. In my opinion, if you

love the person and you know that he loves you also, even if he doesn't have the means, at least you make an effort to prove to him that you love him, too. And then together, you try to do something.

Tina was sad about the passive attitude of these young girls and their lack of imagination:

Today, whatever the situation, you must work. In town it is easier. Even if you are not a salaried worker in an office, if you have a little money, at least you can succeed. By trading, the people in the city can get along quite well. You open a shop, or if you are a woman, a little restaurant or a hairdressing salon. Or you can sew. You can get by. Here, it is true that things are different, but you can also make a go of it. Even if you do not have money, you can always start by petty trading. Every morning, you can prepare cakes that you can sell. Some do that, but here in this village of ours, that's not what I see, especially among the youth who have been to town. One wonders what they are waiting for.

Tina was also indignant about the lack of a sense of responsibility among girls who lived off their parents and had babies indiscriminately. She remembered her childhood with her aunt and her early interest in trading. She did not understand young girls who do not seize opportunities for work and sit by idle while their parents are forced to sell off their lands:

Take my example. I had it in my head to trade from the time my aunt raised me. For me, trading is necessary for a better life. Even if I live with a man, I have to trade. I try to help him by doing my petty trade. Since my parents were plantation owners, I started working in the farm early with them also. I went away with my aunt at twelve. So, I know both sides. The girls of today, who have just left school, I call to them and say: "If you are in the village, do not remain there with your arms folded," but they do not listen. If they only had the courage to do the same thing as me, their parents would not be forced to sell plots of their land everywhere. Now, everything is being sold!

Armed with her own experience, Tina believed that a young divorced girl who returns to the village with her children is not a failure. Her integration depends, according to Tina, on her courage alone. She was convinced that men do not give sufficiently to women because women themselves do not know how to show their abilities. She would have liked to bring her experience to the service of these women who were not doing anything:

You know, these young girls who see me working, if they were interested, they could come towards me and ask, "Auntie, how did you build up this trade?" I could advise and help them. For example, I could explain how, when you do not have money, you have to start little by little. They could, if they were not jealous, instead of hanging around like that, doing nothing. That is what is killing the village, little jealousies. That is what is killing the village.

At the same time, Tina knew that her case was exceptional and recognized that things are not easy for a woman who decides to work in agriculture.

You know, here, a woman is a woman. Men respect me but they did not know that a woman could run a plantation, especially ten hectares like this. So, they cannot advise their daughters to go into plantation work. Whoever says her relative advised her in that direction is a liar.

Tina's view of the future was relatively morose. It was becoming more and more difficult to make ends meet, and she hardly saw any solution to the current situation:

What I observe sincerely is that everything has become too expensive in the market right now. In our area, especially, women grow everything on their farms: okra, pepper, cassava, bananas. Everything is available at home. Yet, what I see is that everything is more expensive than in Abidjan. In the market in Abidjan, you buy pepper and you are given a little extra. The little quantity of pepper that you buy here for 25 francs, in Abidjan you can get two, three times the quantity for that amount. For tomatoes, it's the same story: What you buy for 25 francs in Abidjan, will cost you 100 francs here. No, the problem is here. The women are selling too dear to us! All this is because of women who come from all over, from Sassandra, from Lakota; some even come all the way from Abidjan now. Every Thursday, the day before our village market, they arrive and they take away everything: pepper, palm nuts, everything, . . . everything. Those of us who are here cannot eat. We live in the midst of problems. You see, they come to buy wholesale. The women here, rather than hanging around sitting all day to sell a small quantity of pepper here and another quantity there, would rather sell the whole basket for one thousand francs. They sell wholesale and we who are living here can no longer buy pepper.

She was also worried about her son, whom she finally judged "not very skilled for farmwork," and she wondered especially about the future of her grandchildren:

My grandchildren, right now, I worry about them. I ask myself how they will cope later on because times are getting harder and harder every day. This is what I was saying to my son: "You must not give up and just let your children become unhappy someday." I pray a lot that my grandchildren will grow up to be happy. When a child hasn't had the luck to go to school but comes back home with courage, he can take up trading. He can do a little of everything to succeed.

Since there was no hope for a prosperous future in oil palm plantations, Tina had to look at other options. She had projects. She wondered about changing to coffee and cacao, whose official prices seemed recently to be going up. But she needed new land. It also would take a long time for the trees to begin producing, whereas her financial needs were immediate. She was also thinking of raising food crops for sale—especially cassava, which she would have ground into flour to sell in town. She was planning to reopen her bar-restaurant soon. She knew that all this would be difficult, but she thought that she had the fortitude to succeed.

By this time, Tina no longer believed in collective solutions for fighting the economic crisis. In an era of hard times, she sensed that there was a climate of individualism that did not favor collective well-being:

> Here in our village, I must say that people do not love each other. Even if you are brothers from the same mother, that doesn't count for much these days. Some say you should help each other farm, but those same people come to your farm to cast their gris-gris [or spells] in order to destroy your harvest. Some women tried to set up a cooperative in the village. One day they met to work on one woman's rice farm, and the next day everyone went to work in the farm of another one and so on. You know, if you are ten women working a hectare of land, you can do most of the work in a day. Unfortunately, it did not succeed because there are women who join to these cooperatives only to destroy other people's farms. After you plant your rice, you are happy, but then in the end the rice doesn't come up. When you work like crazy and at the end of the year you have nothing to eat, you know that your efforts have been in vain. One thing is sure: The next year, you won't ask the same women to put a foot on your farm. If you find that by working alone you earn more than by working with ten people, you work alone. In any case, we women here, when we try to organize, it's always the same thing. Some always want to keep their little change. The treasurers are often dishonest. The day comes when they take the cooperative's money and spend it on their own needs, and this leads to quarreling. This is why we can no longer work together.

Tina also thought that social relations were falling apart due to the loss of arable land. She worried that this difficult period would lead to increased ethnic prejudice, which would threaten peace in the village. "Before, families loved and respected one another, but now, it is no longer the case. Our children are very jealous of foreigners." Although she had lived with her family in the village for a long time, Tina sensed that she was now considered to be a foreigner. Her success, which previously earned her respect, now aroused jealousy and meanness. She sensed that she was being progressively isolated from public life, and no longer enjoyed the same authority in the eyes of her neighbors. At the end of the interview, she expressed a weariness that contrasted sharply with the dynamism of her life history. Now that she felt herself aging, she regretted not being married. She would have liked to have at her side a companion with whom she could share her daily troubles. She did confess to having a secret love life. Tina would have liked to live this relationship fully and openly but could not get herself to take the step. For a woman of such a ripe age, unveiling a secret love relationship might have further undermined her already fragile social position.

Tina Looks Back on Her Life

Tina's is the story of a fighter, a woman who courageously challenged the social norms of her agricultural world to rise to be a prosperous plantation owner and manager. Apart from being a relatively wealthy farmer, she also owned and managed a prosperous bar. To those from Europe or North America, Tina's story may seem ordinary, but few women in southwest Côte d'Ivoire have ventured into the cash crop economy, a sphere exclusively controlled by men. Tina was conscious of how difficult it is for a woman to take up such a challenge. Everything around her conspired against it. But even after her prosperity came to an end, she could not fathom why young girls were so reluctant to try to change their situation.

Tina, who forwent marriage and had only two living children, did not realize how difficult it was to upset social models. Many women still saw marriage as the only lever for social and economic progress. In the minds of young village girls, life in the village was a stopgap. They dreamed of city life, far from the physically demanding work in the fields.[10] At Beyo, many of them threw themselves at the senior staff of the agro-industrial complexes, hoping for a lifestyle compatible with their dreams. But the hard reality was that this strategy led them into successive love relationships that never culminated in marriage. Moreover, these unsuccessful and unhappy experiences led to the exacerbated monetarization of relationships between men and women that are unbearable to a woman like Tina, who all her life has rolled up her sleeves to work hard and manage her destiny.

Although everyone acknowledged Tina's success—she was called "Tantie," or "Auntie," throughout the village—her courage and her tenacity attracted as much jealousy as respect. She believed that the rising tension she felt around her was closely related to the economic downturn and declining access to land, which have hit the region hard. In the end, then, the euphoria that accompanied the boom in export agriculture in the Sassandra region did not last long. In less than twenty years, the conditions that allowed this system to flourish have disintegrated, destroying all hope of maintaining a comfortable standard of living.

Even for Tina, who launched her plantation in the late 1970s, the rewards for her efforts lasted only a short while. In the twilight of her life, she faced painful economic difficulties alone, including heavy family obligations. These responsibilities, which she had always borne, weighed on her mind. However, she was even more vexed by the xenophobia that she had endured for some time. Unfortunately, Tina's fears have been confirmed by the tumultuous political history of Côte d'Ivoire since the interviews with her. Southwest Côte d'Ivoire has been a theater for major confrontation between local people and those who have moved there from other parts of Côte d'Ivoire or neighboring countries. The melee has prompted thousands of people to flee. We do not know if Tantie Tina, the daughter of a father from Ghana, was among them.

Conclusion

Tina's story highlights the social relationships between men and women in striking ways. Her life underlines how the unequal distribution of power and responsibility between men and women in both family and production limits the economic power of women. Married women who wish to farm independently are almost always restricted to subsistence crops. Tina was able to circumvent this restriction and get into oil palm production because she lived alone and created her own domestic and economic unit. Her estranged husband lived in Abidjan. Free from his control, she had access to opportunities closed to married women living with their husbands. Had Tina's husband been with her, local authorities would probably not have allowed her access to land for cash crop production on a large or even medium scale.

Family ties and obligations are another theme in Tina's story. In assuming the right to farm cash crops, Tina took on associated obligations. She obtained the right to farm ten hectares of land as she wished, but family obligations dictated the terms of her access to labor, another key factor of production. Her enterprise brought appreciable manna to the extended family at a time when land disputes and a decline in agricultural income had begun to undercut the living standard of such larger domestic units. When Tina launched her plantation and her bar, family obligations compelled her to offer work to her idle nephews even though their poor performance jeopardized her success. To be sure, the obligation to distribute the benefits of success to members of the extended family is not limited to women but is also imposed on men. Similar customs of solidarity characterize many African societies.

Tina discovered that the sons of her brothers were interested in getting money, not in working. Even though she realized that her nephews would not farm, she had to exercise great care in pushing them aside. She only managed to do so by demonstrating goodwill in another way—by giving up some land so that the family could launch a plantation. Her family did not take advantage of this opportunity either, and the land was neglected, which afforded Tina the excuse to take it back and farm it on her own.

Agriculture was the only profitable activity in the region, and the lack of interest in agriculture among young people frustrated Tina. She thought they took advantage of her generosity and could not understand their inertia. Her resentment underscores a broader characteristic of this region, whose economy is based on cash crops: the precarious condition of female heads of household. At the time of our study, women headed 8 percent of the households.[11] Female-headed households most often arise out of the breakup of marriages or the death of a spouse. Households headed by women usually find it much more difficult to attract productive members than households headed by men. Moreover, because female heads of household do not have access to means of production, they are more often solicited to take in members who are not productive, such as young children or idle youngsters. This situation leads to a social paradox. Despite limited productive capacities, female household heads are supposed to support young dependents who do no work in return. Although Tina was a household head at the time of the study, she was different because she had access to means of production similar to male heads. Nonetheless, she failed to attract dependents who worked in exchange for living with her. Tina's disappointment was all the more acute because she, unlike other female heads, did have the means to support younger people in a profitable line of work.

Without knowing it, Tina paid for the failure of earlier strategic choices when cacao production brought prosperity to southwest Côte d'Ivoire in the middle decades of the twentieth century. At that time, local farmers turned to education as a way of integrating their offspring in the modern sector of the urban economy. This choice made sense because the loss of labor occasioned by the exodus of young people could be compensated by hiring local workers. Unfortunately, the later deterioration of the country's economy made it difficult to find employment in urban areas, and many trained young people resigned themselves to returning to their villages to live with their parents. They viewed this "return to the land" as anything but exciting, and many of them dreamed of finding other careers. This lack of enthusiasm for farming, harshly pointed out by Tina, led to conflict between generations that faced different realities. The older generation was motivated by the hope for another agricultural boom, while younger folks yearned for an easier life in the city.

Tina's nieces were not any more motivated than their brothers to work in the fields. Like most village women, they showed little enthusiasm for living in the village and devoted enormous energy to finding a husband who would take them to live in town, far from the exhausting work in the fields. They found relationships, but they did not last. At best, these young women were left with a few gifts, such as jewelry, local cloth, or money; at worst, they found themselves with a child whom they faced raising alone. These unhappy experiences led women to focus on ways to extract money from their relationships with men, a development absolutely unbearable for a woman like Tina. Tina was annoyed that young women lacked professional ambition and condemned their obsession with an ideal marriage that was not meant to be.

Tina knew that these women would find it difficult to deal with the challenges that she had faced. She knew, too, that everyone and everything conspired against women embarking on such a venture. Yet, given the collapse of prosperity, and with it, all hope of an easy urban life, Tina did not understand why these young girls did not try something—why they made no plans for the future. Having failed in her efforts to set up an economic springboard for her nephews, then, Tina suffered a second setback. She was unable to serve as an example for her nieces.

Further Reading

Since the end of the 1980s, numerous studies have brought to light the various forms of inequality between the sexes in developing countries, and in sub-Saharan Africa in particular. An encyclopedic synthesis of these questions is available in *Women in the Third World: An Encyclopedia of Contemporary Issues*, ed. Nelly Stromquist (New York: Garland Publishing, 1998). Another synthesis published by the United Nations surveyed francophone Africa; see United Nations, *Condition de la femme et population: le cas de l'Afrique francophone* (Paris: ONU/CEPED/FNUAP/URD, 1992). In *The Status of Women: Indicators for Twenty-Five Countries* (Calverton, Md.: Macro International, 1996), Sunita Khisor and Katherine Neitzel offer an enlightening comparative analysis of data from demographic and health surveys conducted in 1990–1994, including twelve in sub-Saharan Africa.

Since the early 1990s, the amelioration of the condition of women has been generally acknowledged to be a precondition for development; see the

Déclaration of Dakar/NGor on population, the family, and durable development, formulated in 1994 by representatives of African countries in Addis Ababa. Nonetheless, the condition of women has improved only slowly. Women continue to endure distinct disadvantages compared to men in terms of excess female mortality linked to childbirth, low levels of literacy and education, and so on. For an overview of the contemporary situation, see the essay collection titled *L'Afrique face à ses défis démographiques: un avenir incertain*, ed. Benoît Ferry (Paris: Karthala/CEPED/AFD, 2007).

In the urban economy, the underrepresentation of women in the modern sector, their underremuneration, and their tendency to be recruited for the most precarious forms of employment must be pointed out. In rural areas, discrimination takes the form of very limited rights of access to land. In both cases, it is a question of differential access to resources to the detriment of women whose emancipation through economic activity faces numerous obstacles, especially in agriculture. For a subtle analysis of women's strategies for circumventing such barriers and related issues, see Christina Gladwin, Anne Thompson, Jennifer Peterson, and Andrea Anderson, "Addressing Food Security in Africa via Multiple Livelihood Strategies of Women Farmers," *Food Policy* 26 (2001).

Recognition of the right of women to work has been a challenge for a long time, an obstacle that stems in part from the social representations of female identities in most societies in sub-Saharan Africa. Catherine Coquery-Vidrovitch explores the place of women in the economies of precolonial African societies; see *African Women: A Modern History*, trans. Beth Gillian Raps (Boulder, Colo.: Westview Press, 1997). Coquery-Vidrovitch argues that the tendency to deny women a place and a role in the economy—which extends well beyond the colonial period—stems from overemphasis on reproduction. The employment of female labor for food production and the production of agricultural goods for exchange is certainly considered to be crucial for survival in many societies. But the use of their bodies for reproduction is usually deemed to be even more important. The productive strength of a group dependent on a large labor force rests largely on the ability of women to produce offspring.

Since the 1990s, one might ask if the proliferation of official proclamations favoring women is, more than anything else, a sad reflection of the inability of African states to put in place concrete measures able to guarantee progress. See the Declaration of Luxembourg, signed in 2000 at the conference "Femme, pouvoir et développement," sponsored by the Organisation Internationale de la Francophonie; or the solemn declaration of the equality of men and women in Africa formulated at the Conference of the African Union in Addis Ababa in July 2004. These lofty declarations stand in marked contrast with the singularly timid advances of women in the legislative domain.

Notes

1. Anne-Marie Pillet-Schwartz, "Chronique d'une région en mal de décolonisation: La basse-vallée du Sassandra," in *Tropiques, lieux et liens*, ed. Florence Pinton (Paris: ORSTOM, 1990), 565–77.

2. These measures were included in a development project for southwest Côte d'Ivoire launched in 1969 by the South West Region Development Authority (ARSO).

3. François Ruf, "Les crises cacaoyères, la malédiction des âges d'or," *Cahiers d'Études Africaines* 31, 1–2, nos. 121–122 (1991), 83–134.

4. Between the censuses in 1975 and 1988, the *département* of Sassandra experienced a growth rate of 8 percent, leading to a quadrupling of its population. Population density grew from nine inhabitants per square kilometer in 1975 to twenty-one inhabitants per square kilometer in 1988, and even up to forty-five inhabitants per square kilometer in some areas. See Olivia Bocquet, "Situation du système agraire de l'arrière pays de Sassandra: histoire et situation économique actuelle" (Mémoire de DÉA, INA-PG, IEDES, Paris/CNEARC, Montpellier, 1994).

5. André Quesnel and Patrice Vimard, "Famille plurielle en milieu rural africain, un exemple en économie de plantation, le plateau de Dayes (Sud-Ouest Togo)," *Cahiers des Sciences Humaines* 25, 3 (1989): 339–55; Jean-Pierre Dozon, "Économie marchande et structures sociales: Le cas des Bété de Côte-d'Ivoire," *Cahiers d'études Africaines* 17, 4, no. 68 (1985): 463–83.

6. Claude Meillassoux, *Femmes, greniers et capitaux* (Paris: François Maspero, 1975); Jean-Pierre Chauveau, "Organisation socio-économique Gban et économie de plantation," *Cahiers des Sciences Humaines* 8, 2 (1975); Philippe Léna, "Transformation de l'espace rural dans le front pionnier du sud-ouest ivoirien," PhD diss., Université de Paris X, 1979.

7. Alfred Schwartz, *Sous-peuplement et développement dans le sud-ouest de la Côte d'Ivoire: Cinq siècles d'histoire économique et sociale* (Paris: ORSTOM, 1993).

8. In the course of our research in the study region, we met only three women who were independent plantation owners, defined as heads of a plantation of more than ten hectares.

9. Or the Abidjan-Niger Railway Authority.

10. Agnès Adjamagbo, *Crise en économie de plantation ivoirienne et transformation des rapports sociaux: Le dilemme féminin à Sassandra (Côte d'Ivoire)* (Paris: Centre Français sur la Population et le Développement, 1999).

11. Agnès Adjamagbo, "Changements socio-économiques et logiques de fécondité en milieu rural ouest africain: Le cas de la région de Sassandra en Côte-d'Ivoire," PhD diss., Université de Paris X, 1998.

CHAPTER FOURTEEN

~

Samba Sylla (b. 1948), Doulo Fofanna (b. 1948 or 1949), and Djénébou Traore (b. 1972)

The Colonies Come to France

Dennis D. Cordell and Carolyn F. Sargent

This chapter is about three immigrants from the West African countries of Mali and Mauritania who went to France in the second half of the twentieth century.[1] These countries, along with Senegal, Burkina Faso, Niger, and Chad, are located along the southern edge of the Sahara desert, a part of West Africa called the Sahel. All are former colonies of France and all gained independence in 1960. The lives of these migrants illustrate the historical shifts in Sahelian migration to France. Samba Sylla arrived in Paris in 1965 at age seventeen, having left his village in western Mali near the border with Senegal. Doulo Fofanna was born in a small town in eastern Mauritania on the border with Mali. He deplaned in Paris in 1971, when he was in his early twenties. In 1982 Djénébou Traore, a ten-year-old girl, went to Paris to live with her parents. They all came from a small village in southwestern Mali.

The French began trading on the coast of today's Senegal in the seventeenth century (see chapter 4). In 1659, they founded a settlement at the mouth of the Senegal River, which they baptized Saint-Louis. French traders made their way east up the river, which later would become the border between the French colonies of Senegal and Mauritania. Local African traders also plied the Senegal River, exchanging goods and slaves for European wares. Regions along the river began producing foodstuffs for Saint-Louis, smaller French trading posts, and even the oceangoing ships that linked these settlements with metropolitan France. Eventually, this commercial network extended east to the region around the river's headwaters in today's Mali.

These commercial connections laid the foundation for the French empire in West Africa, which embraced ever-larger regions and numbers of people over time. The empire also produced a system of circular migration that sent French men and a few women to the colonies for stints as officials, soldiers, traders, missionaries, explorers, and adventurers (see chapter 8). The African men and the few women who had been pulled into the French orbit as traders were joined by other Africans who became migrant workers, soldiers, students, and lower-level bureaucrats in the colonial regime. For example, seasonal migrants made their way from the western part of today's Mali to work on farms in Senegal that produced crops such as peanuts for export. Other migrants worked in the French ship repair yard near Saint-Louis. Still others actually joined the crews of French ships. In both World War I and World War II, soldiers from this part of West Africa served in the French armies in France. After the end of hostilities, most of those who survived returned to Africa.

From the early twentieth century through the mid-1970s, migrants to France from the Senegal River valley thought of themselves as temporary sojourners. The French agreed. Despite the history of African empire, France and Africa were perceived on all sides as two separate worlds. With time and greater numbers, however, the Africans in France brought Africa to France. In ways that offer rich topics for discussion, the experiences of the three migrants recounted in the following pages represent an unforeseen culmination in French efforts to shape colonial migration over a much longer period. This intersection and interpenetration of the former colonies and the former métropole, or metropolis, has produced a new postcolonial world.

Leaving Mali and Mauritania and Arriving in France

Samba Sylla was born in 1948 in Diataya, a small town in western Mali, whose population today is about three thousand people.[2] Diataya was built alongside a small stream that feeds into Lake Magui, and easy access to water in this otherwise semi-arid region allowed the cultivation of two crops a year, as well as fishing. Samba was the second son in a family of farmers—although he had a grandfather who migrated to Abidjan, a coastal city in the French colony of Côte d'Ivoire to the south, where he became a trader. Samba remembers that he had to "accept a lot of responsibility." In 1963, when he was only fifteen, Samba made his way to the colonial cities of Dakar in Senegal, Bamako in French Soudan (today's Mali), and Bobo-Dioulasso in Upper

Volta (today's Burkina Faso), hoping to set himself up as a vendor with a table of goods or work for a merchant. But fortune did not smile on him, and he went back home to Diataya.

Around 1965, he left again, this time for France with tickets provided by family members and friends and accompanied by elders who already lived there. The first leg of his journey took him again to Dakar, where he sought passage on a ship. In Dakar, he found out that the ship was completely booked. He stayed on in the Senegalese capital, doing odd jobs around the port—accompanying people to the market and helping others with their baggage. Friends and fishermen often invited him to join them for a meal. Frequenting the colonial cinemas in Dakar, Samba recalls that he became enamored of films of all kinds—westerns, gangsters, gladiators, karate, "even Eddie Constantine." Five months later he heard that he could probably get a ship for France from Abidjan, now the capital of the newly independent country of Côte d'Ivoire. He hopped the train from Dakar east to Bamako, the capital of Mali. From there, he set out again for Bobo-Dioulasso, the second-largest city in colonial Burkina Faso, and journeyed on south to Abidjan.

Like Dakar, Abidjan is a major port. Samba stayed for a month with his grandfather, who was by that time an important merchant, in a house filled with other relatives. Samba finally arrived in Paris in 1965, having traveled by ship from Abidjan to the port of Marseille and by train north to the French capital. France was both familiar and foreign. To be sure, Samba had seen French people in West Africa, but never French people who actually did manual labor like the farmers in the fields that he saw from the train. Samba was one of many young men who came to France around this time from Mali, Senegal, and Mauritania, following their independence from France in 1960.

Another young man was Doulo Fofanna, who came from Bouli, a small town on Lake Karakoro in the Guidimaka region of eastern Mauritania near the border with Mali.[3] During the rainy season every year, the lake overflowed its banks and his village became an island. Not surprisingly, then, people lived by fishing and farming rice. They also raised cattle and grew sorghum, peanuts, and rice. When Doulo left home in 1968, about twenty-five hundred people lived in Bouli. By 2000, the population had grown to five thousand.

Born in 1948 or 1949, Doulo was the third son in a family of ten children. He had two older brothers, five older sisters, and two younger brothers. All of his sisters died. Unlike Samba, Doulo went to the colonial primary school, finishing his seventh year—called *sixième*, the first postprimary year. He wanted to continue his studies, but because he did not do well on his exams his father pulled him out of school and sent him to work with his uncle in a neighboring village. Doulo's two older brothers had already gone to school, so his father did not think Doulo needed to continue.

Doulo's family also had a history of migration. His father moved to Senegal in the 1930s, where he worked in the peanut fields. In 1960, Doulo's two older brothers also left, one going to Paris and the other to Nouakchott, the capital of Mauritania. Doulo and all four of his brothers eventually made their way to France at one time or another. His eldest brother died in Paris in 1965, and two other brothers went back to West Africa. In 2002, Doulo and another brother still lived in France. But migration was not simply a family tradition; it was a village tradition in Bouli. Doulo remembered that when he left Bouli in 1968, only four or five of his friends were still there. All the others had left.

Like Samba, Doulo first set out for Dakar. He also planned to take a ship to France. A brother in France who was supposed to send a ticket dragged his feet. Doulo thinks that his brother probably hoped he would return to Bouli to take care of the family, but Doulo waited him out in Dakar, living for a year with an aunt. His brother finally sent money for passage, and Doulo set out for Marseille in November 1969. When he arrived, French authorities refused him entry, saying his papers were not in order. Frustrated, he swore off France, and went to Nouakchott, where he worked with another brother for a French company. Six months later the brother in France sent him an airplane ticket. Doulo let it gather dust for a year, but he finally left for Paris in 1971. Doulo, then, like Samba, set out for France twice. Given their youth and limited means, their perseverance was quite extraordinary.

More than a decade later, ten-year-old Djénébou Traore, born in Djiu-idada in southwestern Mali, left her paternal grandmother in the Malian capital of Bamako for France.[4] Her father had migrated to France in 1972, the year Djénébou was born. Her mother followed in 1974. Djénébou hence spent the first ten years of her life with her grandmother and aunt, her father's sister. Her childhood was much like those of other girls in Bamako. When she was five or six, she remembers going with her grandmother to the market to sell peanuts and sometimes mangoes and oranges or watching over a stand in front of their house. She did not go to "French school" but rather to Qur'anic school, not an odd thing for a girl at the time. Indeed, her female cousin learned to read Arabic and the Qur'an quite well. Djénébou, on the other hand, did not do so well because she often went off with her grandmother rather than going to school. In the meantime, her aunt gave birth to a daughter, so Djénébou was no longer alone. She thought of her cousin as her sister. Her uncle married a second wife. But catastrophe struck in 1979, when her first aunt died in childbirth. Djénébou stayed on in her uncle's house, with his second wife, her grandmother, and a female cousin. Not long afterward, her uncle married a third wife because his second wife had not had children.

When he arrived in France, Djénébou's father took the well-beaten path of earlier West African migrants to factories that made automobiles. Djénébou offered few details of his work history, but when interviewed in 2002, she said that he would probably retire in a couple of years from Renault, where he worked in the parts department. In any case, following his initial departure from Mali in 1972, Djénébou's father returned for a visit ten years later. He brought dresses, a doll that talked, and other presents for his daughter, but she did not regard him as her father. When first introduced to him, for example, Djénébou remembered saying, "Bonjour, Monsieur," shaking his hand, and then running away. To her, her real father was her uncle.

Djénébou's father came in part to take his daughter back to France, but he knew that the move to Paris would be traumatic for his daughter, so he waited before raising the issue. Not only was he concerned about Djénébou; he also worried about how his mother, Djénébou's grandmother, would deal with her departure. When he finally broached the topic, his younger sister, Djénébou's aunt, insisted that he take Djénébou with him: "She's too spoiled. We can't do anything with her. She won't grow up right." Both Djénébou and her grandmother were very upset about her leaving. Nonetheless, her father proceeded to get the required documents, and Djénébou left Bamako by plane early one morning for Dakar and on to France. Djénébou was forced to leave her beloved grandmother as well as her cousin. She found herself living with parents she did not really know, in a country that she did not know, and where she could not speak the language. She was afraid, she was sad, and she recalls "crying for days."

Just as Samba's and Doulo's families had a history of migration, so it was with Djénébou's forebears. They did not go to France, but her great-uncles were merchants who traveled between Mali, Senegal, and Côte d'Ivoire. Her father had also been a trader and had followed similar itineraries. But he took the larger leap to France. Djénébou's early years are the story of a child left behind. Even in 1982 this tale was not unusual, since women and children had only just begun to join husbands and fathers in France.

History of West African Migration to France

Samba and Doulo were part of the first stream of migrants from the former colonies to arrive in France after independence in 1960. They were part of a phase in West African migration to France that began in 1946 and contin-ued to 1974.[5] Before 1960, the homelands of these migrants were still part of the French empire. Thus they arrived as colonial subjects and not as citizens of independent countries. For the most part men, they helped rebuild France after the war and supported the rapid economic expansion that followed. In France the three decades after World War II are called the *trente glorieuses*, referring to the "thirty glorious" years of economic boom that abruptly ended with the dramatic rises in oil prices in the middle 1970s. France also turned to West Africa because the Algerian war for independence between 1954 and 1962 had disrupted the flow of migrants from this part of North Africa.

During this era bridging the colonial and independence eras, the French government encouraged men from its West African colonies—Senegal, colonial Sudan, and Mauritania in particular—to migrate to the métropole. There were few legal barriers. In 2002, Karamoko Cissé, who arrived in 1946 from colonial Mali, recalled with pleasure that the French welcomed him as a brother come to rebuild the homeland.[6] Nor did independence initially present obstacles. According to agreements negotiated between the French government and the government of newly independent Mali, for example, Malian migrants, in effect, enjoyed a kind of double citizenship.[7] Instead of the passports and visas usually required by one country of citizens of another, Malians needed only their national identification cards to get into France.

During the trente glorieuses from 1946 to 1974, a consistent pattern and calendar of migration developed—albeit influenced by earlier migration practices in West Africa. Most of the migrants from West Africa were men who were either single or had left their wives and families behind. They found work, saved money, and sent remittances home. After a few years, most returned home to marry and settle down, and younger, unmarried male relatives then replaced them. This pattern of circular migration assured the supply of African workers to France and the return flow of money. A much smaller proportion of married migrants returned to visit their families every few years—sometimes spending as long as six months or a year in their vil-lages before returning to France.

The energy crises of the mid-1970s and the ensuing economic slowdown led the French government to declare the end of labor migration in 1974 and impose restrictions on immigration.[8] Beginning in 1975, the new regulations required that all migrants obtain a *carte de séjour*, or temporary residence permit. Additional conditions made it increasingly difficult to get the permit, so that it became much less likely that new migrants could legally take the place of those who had returned home. Because many West African families were dependent on the remittances of family members in France, this new policy interrupted the earlier system of circular migration. Following the promulgation of the new rules, migrants could, of course, return to Mali, but it became much more difficult for other family members to replace them. As a result, many migrants who already had temporary residence permits were trapped in France. Not surprisingly, the new regulations also led to a rise in illegal immigration.

Perhaps to counter these measures, the French government launched a new policy of family reunification in 1975, which marked the beginning of another phase in West African immigration to France that lasted until 1986. New legislation allowed some migrants to bring wives and children to France, prompting animated debate among Malian men about what to do—whether they should or should not bring their families to France. In their discussions, they frequently raised questions about whether the influence of French society would undermine male authority in the household; weaken adherence to Islam, the predominant religion of the community; and alienate children from their African roots. In the end, many migrants brought their wives and children to France. Others, like Samba Sylla and Doulo Fofanna, did not, preferring to continue to live in migrant hostels with other men and only occasionally visit their families in Africa.[9] For many French people and even for the government that had permitted it, the arrival of families implied that Malians and other migrants from West Africa had come to stay. Their presence also raised concerns in French circles—about women's status, reproduction and family size, polygyny, schooling, and whether and how the new immigrants would become part of French society. Still other questions stemmed from the arrival of an estimated 130,000 illegal West African immigrants in the decade after 1975.

Djénébou's mother and Djénébou arrived in 1974 and 1982, respectively, in the wake of the new policy of family reunification. They represented the first and second generations of women immigrants from the Sahel. These measures may well have figured into the decision on the part of Djénébou's father to migrate to France in 1972, to bring his wife, and then go get his daughter. To be sure, young Djénébou was not party to his thinking. In 2002, she acknowledged that her father's departure more or less coincided with the new requirement; but when asked why he left, she responded with a stylized Sahelian explanation for migration: "for adventure and to find money."[10]

The first of the so-called Pasqua Laws, passed in 1986 and named for the interior minister at the time, marked a third phase in post–World War II immigration policy in France. In the 1970s and the first half of the 1980s, French authorities either allowed or turned a blind eye to the fact that some immigrant men had brought more than one wife to France. The first of the

Pasqua Laws further restricted immigration, tightening identity and document requirements and checks. In 1993, a second round of Pasqua measures
limited the rights of citizenship for children born in France of noncitizen
parents, outlawed polygamy (with disrupting consequences for many Sahelian families), and imposed housing requirements on immigrants who wanted
to bring their families to join them. More specifically, the new measures
required men to identify one partner as the legal spouse and disown any
others, forcing them to move out and removing them from the rolls of social
programs.

These changes were accompanied by an increasingly virulent anti-immigrant discourse on the part of political parties such as the National Front, as
well as growing militancy on the part of immigrant organizations and their
supporters. Despite the more nuanced application of some of these measures
in the late 1990s and the years after 2000, immigrants no longer felt welcome
in France.

Given the impact of these shifts in French policy on the lives of immigrants and their families, it is not surprising to learn that they have tended
to date their personal histories by reference to laws and decrees governing
immigration and immigration status. They have also keenly followed the
anti-immigrant discourse of right-wing groups such as the National Front.
As a result, Sahelian immigrants in France are quite politically aware and
active. In the late 1990s and early 2000s, many actively supported the cause
célèbre of the undocumented Senegalese, Malian, and Mauritanian immigrants known as the *sans-papiers*, immigrants without papers or documents
authorizing their presence in France.[11] Having lived as adults through all
three phases in French immigration policy described above, Samba Sylla and
Doulo Fofanna have a tendency to think of France and Africa as two distinct worlds. Since arriving in France, they have fought for greater inclusion.
Djénébou Traore has lived through the second and third phases of French
immigration policy after World War II. Perhaps because she arrived as a child
to join Malian parents already living in France, she does not perceive as great
a divide between Mali, where she was born, and France, where she grew up.
In some ways, the lives of Samba, Doulo, and Djénébou in Paris illustrate
this distinction.

Immigrant Lives in Paris: Samba Sylla and Doulo Fofanna

In somewhat different ways, the professional lives of Samba and Doulo illustrate the close association between early Malian and Mauritanian labor
migrants and labor activists in France in the 1960s and 1970s. After arriving

in France, both men became politically active in astoundingly short order, given that France was very different from their homelands. Samba did not even speak any French when he disembarked in 1965. Fellow workers at the first place he worked—an African and a Frenchman—helped him learn the language. He took evening French classes offered by French labor unions until 1973. Samba also learned about French legal and political institutions, French politics, and labor militancy both in class and on the job. By 1966, a year after arriving, he had become politically engaged. He actively participated in demonstrations and other events during the tumultuous year of 1968, when protesting students, workers, and even government bureaucrats shook the foundations of French society.

Doulo, on the other hand, learned French in primary school and was better situated to make his way in France. His turn to political militancy stemmed rather from the arbitrary way he was treated by the medical authorities attached to the Office de la Migration Internationale (OMI), the French immigration office. After being admitted to France in 1971, he later learned that he had tuberculosis. Initially, the authorities told him that he had to leave the country. He appealed the order and was rewarded by being bundled off to a sanatorium in the Pyrenees. Near the end of his treatment eight months later, he had to prove he had a job to stay in France. His previous employer wrote a letter testifying that Doulo could come back to work, but the OMI rejected him anyway. He then sent a letter directly to the Ministry of Health. Two weeks later, his authorization card from the OMI appeared. He returned to work in 1972, where, moved by his tenacity, his fellow workers asked if he would be their spokesman. With that, Doulo, like Samba, became involved in French unions and union causes. Doulo said that the union, La Confédération Générale du Travail (CGT), taught him and other migrants "their rights—the Rights of Man." Or, as he put it in 2000, "I started to fight. I had to!"

Samba and Doulo signed onto the unions and their causes, whether local, national, or global. Doulo participated in strikes in the 1970s at Renault and Citroën plants protesting the exposure of workers to toxic substances and dangerous machines. Samba and other African migrants joined French activists of the left: "French and African, workers and intellos [slang for intellectuals], men and women." In the late 1960s and 1970s, unions in France often supported causes beyond their narrow economic interests. They campaigned for the independence of other African territories, in particular the Portuguese colonies; they demonstrated against the Vietnam War waged by the United States; they recruited new activists "through literacy classes, open houses in the [migrant] hostels, and cinema clubs." Doulo followed a similar path. Through his union work, he made close French friends. These activities taught both Samba and Doulo the political and organizational skills appropriate to the French context. They went on to found some of the earliest Malian immigrant associations.

Their first efforts in the immigrant arena included campaigns for improved housing. When Samba first arrived in Paris, he stayed in a poorly ventilated, dirty, and crowded basement dormitory. Landlords commonly referred to as "sleep sellers" rented beds to immigrants for shifts of several hours. French and immigrant activists eventually forced reform of housing laws to outlaw such abuse. Samba, Doulo, other immigrants, and their French allies then turned attention to what Doulo called "the great struggle of the foyers," or migrant hostels. They protested the hideous living conditions in these concrete dormitory towers that had sprung up in Paris with the explosion of immigration in the late 1950s and 1960s. In 1970, Samba remembered, a fire caused by a resident cooking on charcoal broke out in a building housing Senegalese and Mauritanian immigrants. Five people died. Fifty thousand people demonstrated at their funerals to protest poor living conditions and lack of cooking facilities.

Activists also fought for the right to govern the hostels—making their own rules and organizing their own activities. In his very carefully formulated oral history, Samba labeled this time his era of "foyer to village," referring to campaigns to make the hostels more friendly to African residents. Two of the largest enterprises in the hostel business, SONACOTRA (the Société Nationale de Construction pour les Travailleurs) and AFTAM (the Association pour la formation technique de base des Africains et Malgaches), resisted African efforts to introduce African cuisine and African female cooks; set aside places for Muslim prayer; and allow peddlers, barbers, and tailors into the residences to sell their goods and services. In response, the immigrants, influenced by their union experience and with the help of the Socialist and Communist parties, founded resident organizations in each of the several dozen buildings owned by these companies. Doulo was elected president of the organization in his building, partly due to his ability to speak French, and partly because some of his fellow residents knew that he descended from ancestors famed in the Sahel as mediators.

SONACOTRA and AFTAM eventually relented, allowing committees of immigrants to govern residence life and replacing French administrators, who were often military veterans or former colonial officers, with African personnel. Still, living conditions were far from ideal between 2000 and 2003 when Samba and Doulo were interviewed. In the Foyer Soundiata, where Samba lived, three or four men still shared very small rooms, and residents of several rooms had to share a kitchen. Despite these major shortcomings, the hostels had become African spaces by this time. Residents referred explicitly to the buildings as transnational places. In many rooms, the men watched Senegalese or Malian television programs transmitted by satellite from home. By the early 2000s, Africa had come to France.

Doulo and Samba also directed their attention to the improvement of life in Mauritania and Mali. In the 1980s, Doulo worked for the Association for the Promotion of Soninke Language and Culture (APS). Founded in 1979, the association aims at preserving the heritage of Soninke immigrants from Mauritania, Mali, and Senegal. Doulo's activities led indirectly to the foundation, in 1986, in Aubervilliers, a working-class and immigrant suburb of Paris, of an association of Soninke immigrants from Bouli, his village in Mauritania. He played a key role in the venture by calling together ten French friends and colleagues who were interested in development. They drew up a project proposal for the association and contacted municipal authorities, who eventually entered into a partnership with the APS. The organization was headed by a leader of the Diawara chiefly family in Bouli, and Doulo became the president. The APS not only tackled the problems of Bouli immigrants in France but also initiated development projects around Bouli. About the same time, another association developed among immigrants in the Paris suburb of Montreuil.

In conversation about his life, Doulo recalled that as a boy he was quiet, with little interest in politics. But when he went to France, he ran into problems and others helped him. He said that it was then his turn to help others. Doulo says that he is still quiet but can get fired up over injustices. In 1993, for example, during a conference on immigration and development held in Paris, Doulo minced no words in telling high-ranking French officials that they needed to listen to immigrants themselves:

> If we really want to deal with the problems of immigration, another approach is required. You cannot talk badly about someone behind his back. Today, at the highest levels of state institutions, there is talk about the problems of people who are not present—the immigrants! How do you think we can make progress that way? It's not possible and I will say that whenever I have a chance.

In 2000, Doulo was still president of the Bouli development association, which helped social service offices in the suburb of Aubervilliers find mediators to deal with African family and institutional problems related to school, housing, health, and domestic conflict. Of his life as an immigrant, Doulo says, "I started with the workers' struggle, but I'm now in the development struggle."

Samba, too, described a shift in the weight of his commitments over time—from union struggles in France to development in Mali. As early as 1967 and 1968, shortly after he came to Paris, he and other men from his village collected money to build a mosque at home in Diataya—a common first undertaking among Malian immigrants. They also founded an immigrant association, the Union of People from Diataya and Salamou Residing in France.[12] They created four mutual assistance funds—for Diataya immigrants, for projects in Diataya, for neighborhood projects in Paris, and for the larger Malian immigrant community in Paris or their villages at home.

Immigrant development projects in Diataya included digging a dozen deep wells in the wake of the drought of the 1970s and early 1980s. This initiative prompted a lot more discussion in both France and Mali about other initiatives. The most popular propositions dealt with education, health, and agriculture. The association began by building a school. The first phase of the building began in 1988, with six classrooms and lodging for teachers. In 1989, the school's first class included eighty-nine students. Three more classrooms were added in 1998 in order to open the school to girls. By 2000, enrollment had grown to six hundred students. In 2001, future plans included a library for children and adults, along with a VCR/DVD-equipped multipurpose room for vocational education.

For Samba, like Doulo, the later 1980s and 1990s brought increased engagement with Africa. Samba calls this phase in his life "the struggle for two spaces"—the fight for the more effective integration of African immigrants in French society and the fight for the development of rural society at home. Samba described these efforts as two sides of the same coin: "You cannot be an African in Europe and stay isolated in your little corner." At the same time, he said, "It is important to take development to the homeland. A man without history does not exist. He has his history, his culture. He cannot be cut off from Africa." Ironically, Samba and his fellow immigrants' preoccupation with African matters may also stem from two other realities: the permanent character of their residence in France, and the growing intolerance toward immigrants in France, which perhaps makes political engagement across a broad front less likely than in the 1960s and 1970s.

Samba's roster of activities in the early 2000s, like that of Doulo, is testament to both extraordinary commitment and impressive achievement. At that time he still served on the residents' council in Foyer Soundiata. He was also an officer of the Association pour la Solidarité Franco-Malienne, which operates a community radio station in Kayes in western Mali. In addition, he presided as president of the Association Jigiya and was a member of another organization that promoted housing construction in Mali. By that time, the group had built twenty-two houses and trained young people in construction techniques. Beginning in 1990, Samba worked for GRDE, the Groupe de Recherches en Développement Rural, a nonprofit research organization dedicated to research in rural development founded and run by social scientists from the Sahel. His duties included working with immigrants who want to found associations and working with associations that hoped to launch development projects. His work took him to Mali, Senegal, and Mauritania quite often, and then back to France. His personal spaces became more connected. France is in Africa, and Africa does indeed exist in France.

Immigrant Lives in Paris: Djénébou Traore

By the time Djénébou arrived in Paris, the Malian, Mauritanian, and Senegalese immigrant communities were sizable and included families. She clearly recalled the presence of Malian women and children. Given the policy of family reunification, getting to France was much easier for Djénébou than it had been for Samba and Doulo. But other challenges awaited her. Whereas Samba and Doulo came to France as young adults who had made the decision to migrate, Djénébou arrived as a young girl—a young child born in one country and culture who faced growing up in another: learning a new language, going to French schools, and figuring out how to function in France. She was a remarkable girl whose trajectory is quite extraordinary. Like other children of immigrants, Djénébou had to navigate a double socialization, first in her parents' household, a product of their Malian origins but influenced by residence in France, and second in the larger French society around her. Moreover, when she arrived, Djénébou had to learn how to fit into a family that included a younger brother and sister born in France, whom she had not met.

In the larger society, Djénébou went to school, where she faced challenges that earlier adult male immigrants from Mali had not. She had to negotiate the differences in gender roles and expectations between Malian and French societies. She began primary school in Garenne-Colombes and then moved her second year to Bois-Colombes, both immigrant suburbs of Paris. She spent the mornings at school learning French with other immigrant students "from everywhere—Hindus and so on." In the afternoon she went to regular classes—odd for her because she was older and taller than her classmates. Despite these obstacles, she learned French quickly. Djénébou continued her studies at a *lycée professionnel*, a secondary school specializing in vocational education, earning her Certificate in Professional Studies in Bioservice in 1994. Two years later, while working full-time at a military hospital, she passed the Baccalaureate in Health and Environment, a national examination allowing her to compete for management jobs in the health and environment sector. Talking about her studies, Djénébou noted that there were "no other Malians in any of my graduating classes. [They were primarily] Senegalese, and students from North Africa, the French Caribbean, and France." Shortly after finishing her baccalaureate, Djénébou moved to another large public hospital in Paris, where she was working when interviewed in the early 2000s. By this time she was a supervisor in charge of cleaning and sanitizing laboratories and operating rooms in a large section of the hospital. Her mother worked there as well, although Djénébou emphasized that she had landed her job by herself.

Following her arrival in France in 1982, Djénébou visited Mali only twice in the next twenty years. She said that she did not think about Mali very much—although she thought about her grandmother for a long time. She recalled that her parents periodically telephoned their families in Bamako. Her parents did return to Mali while she was growing up—her father once and her mother twice. In 1997, Mali became more immediate because Djénébou went to visit after getting married in Paris. She married a Malian man of her own choosing, although she and her husband-to-be sought her parents' approval. This was a little unusual because many Malian parents still arrange marriages for their children. They married in a ceremony that was as much like a wedding in Mali as her parents could arrange—complete with rituals to prepare the bride for her new role. When she went to Mali with her new husband, Djénébou got to see her dear grandmother once again and for the last time. In 2003, she and her husband went to Mali again, this time with their own young children born in France.

While the obstacles that Djénébou faced in France were perhaps not as dramatic as those that confronted her parents or men such as Samba and Doulo who arrived in the 1960s and 1970s, her early years in Europe were far from easy. Her experiences illustrate the challenges of being a child of both Africa and Europe, learning French, and making her way through a maze of education and career options. She also had to negotiate rather huge differences in gender roles and expectations. Although a transnational child, she still appreciated how the sacrifices and contributions of her parents and other earlier immigrants had paved the way for her.

African Migrants and the Creation of Transnational Identities

It is important to remember that Samba Sylla, Doulo Fofanna, and Djénébou Traore are unique individuals. Moreover, their biographies are different from

those of the tens of thousands of other people from the former French colonies who migrated to France in the last half of the twentieth century. At the
same time, their experiences are exemplary, representing core features of the
trajectories of many other migrants to France, other parts of Western Europe,
and later North America. Samba and Doulo arrived in the era of circular
migration, when migrants were mostly male. They left their parents, brothers and sisters, and other relatives behind. Family life was identified with
Africa; they were but temporary sojourners in a very foreign land. In their
struggles in France, whether for the rights of fellow migrants from the Sahel
or for workers of whatever color, they constructed new kinds of communities.
In migrant hostels they created trans-African communities. These young
men tended eventually to return home, marry, and found families. But the
continued comings and goings of migrants from Senegal, Mali, Mauritania,
and other parts of sub-Saharan Africa did lead to the institutionalization of
migrant life in France. As Samba, Doulo, and other migrants of their generation negotiated everyday spaces in Paris, they creatively participated in the
construction of transnational identities and spaces. Migrant associations,
hostels administered by migrants, and other organizations laid the foundation for African society in France. Yet for a long time the men still thought
of France and Africa as very separate worlds. To paraphrase Samba, they
continued to "struggle for two spaces"—for the more effective integration
of African immigrants into French society, and for the development of rural
society at home in Mali.

Ironically, global economic forces and the political reaction of the French
state to African immigrants brought the separate worlds of Samba, Doulo,
and other African migrants together. The French government put an end
to the practice of circular migration, tempering this abrupt policy shift by
allowing the wives and children of migrants to come to France. In so doing,
it inadvertently added the family, the building block of all societies, to the
institutions of "Africa-in-France." Djénébou's mother joined her husband
in France. For young children of the next generation like Djénébou, whose
father and mother left for France when she was a baby, France had been a
part of her world for as long as she could remember. In France, she lived with
her Malian family while going to French schools and speaking French. The
chasm between France and Africa perceived by Samba and Doulo did not
exist for her. She grew up in a transnational family.

The life stories of Samba, Doula, and Djénébou allow us to see, from their
points of view, how the shaping of the personal and political—marriage,
family, and politics—were informed by state and global structures. The two
men were of the first postcolonial generation of West African immigrants

to France, while Djénébou was a child of that generation whose life inaugurated a new era of transnational marriage and family. Samba, Doula, and Djénébou faced issues of legal documentation, housing, employment, education, changing or multiple gender roles, and anti-immigrant sentiment. In addition, they all felt the negative impact of shifting French attitudes and government policies concerning immigrants. Their experiences resonate with those of many other Africans, hundreds of thousands of whom have left their homes to seek work and a better life in other parts of Africa, Europe, the Middle East, the United States, and even South and East Asia. Collectively, they are the "new African diaspora."[13]

Further Reading

To place the life stories of Samba Sylla, Doulo Fofanna, and Djénébou Traore in the larger context of French immigration from Africa and elsewhere, see Sylviane A. Diouf, "Invisible Muslims: The Sahelians in France," in *Muslim Minorities in the West: Visible and Invisible*, ed. Yvonne Yazbeck and Jane I. Smith (Walnut Creek, Calif.: Altamira Press, 2002). See, in addition, Mahamet Timera, "Righteous or Rebellious: Social Trajectories of Sahelian Youth in France," in *The Transnational Family: New European Frontiers and Global Networks*, ed. Deborah Fahy Bryceson and Ulla Vuorela (Oxford, UK: Berg, 2002), 147–55. The evolution of viewpoints and policy on citizenship and immigration in France is traced in Alec G. Hargreaves, *Multi-Ethnic France: Immigration, Politics, Culture, and Society*, 2nd ed. (New York: Routledge, 2007), and in Jane Freedman, *Immigration and Insecurity in France* (Hants, UK, and Burlington, Vt.: Ashgate, 2004). The presence of Malians and other Africans in France raises broader issues of French identity and culture, which are incisively analyzed in Dominic Thomas, *Black France: Colonialism, Immigration, and Transnationalism* (Bloomington: Indiana University Press, 2007) and in Charles Tshimanga, Didier Gondola, and Peter J. Bloom, eds., *Frenchness and the African Diaspora: Identity and Uprising in Contemporary France* (Bloomington: Indiana University Press, 2010).

As for the history of African migration to France, *Willing Migrants: Soninke Labor Diasporas, 1848–1960* (Athens: Ohio University Press, 1997) by the late François Manchuelle illustrates how the expansion of the French empire in the Senegal River region in the nineteenth century drew increasing numbers of men into its economic orbit, paving the way for later mobility. Other roots of contemporary migration to France included the conscription of men to serve in French colonial forces in Africa, France, Europe, and other parts of the empire beginning in the nineteenth century. This history is explored by Myron Echenberg in *Colonial Conscripts: The Tirailleurs Sénégalais in French West Africa, 1857–1960* (Portsmouth, N.H.: Heinemann, 1991) and by Gregory Mann in *Native Sons: West African Veterans and France in the Twentieth Century* (Durham, N.C.: Duke University Press, 2006). For analyses of the history and lives of Malians in France, see our two articles: Carolyn Sargent and Dennis Cordell, "Polygamy, Disrupted Reproduction, and the State: Malian Migrants in Paris, France," *Social Science and Medicine* 56 (2003), 1961–72; and Dennis D. Cordell and Carolyn F. Sargent, "Islam, Identity, and Gender in Daily Life among Malians in Paris: The Burdens Are Easier to Bear," in Muriel Gomez-Perez, ed., *L'Islam politique au sud du Sahara: Identités, discours et enjeux* (Paris: Karthala, 2005), 177–206. Also see Carolyn Sargent and Stephanie Larchanche-Kim, "Liminal Lives: Immigration Status, Gender, and the Construction of Identities among Malian Migrants in Paris," *American Behavioral Scientist* 50, 1 (2006): 9–27. The best study of Malian migrant associations remains Christophe Daum, *Les associations de Maliens en France: Migration, développement et citoyenneté* (Paris: Karthala, 1998).

Malian and other African migrants to France have also played key roles in the rise of world music, contributions explored in James A. Winders, *Paris Africain: Rhythms of the African Diaspora* (New York: Palgrave Macmillan, 2006). Contemporary African migration is the topic of Isidore Okpewho and Nkiru Nzegwu, eds., *The New African Diaspora* (Bloomington: Indiana University Press, 2009).

Notes

1. This chapter grows out of a research project entitled "Reproduction and Representations of Family among Malian Migrants in Paris, France," financed by the Wenner Gren Foundation (GR6325), the National Science Foundation (BCS-0105192), and the University Research Council and the Clements Department of History at Southern Methodist University. We wish to thank all of these institutions for their support while, of course, acknowledging our responsibility for the views and analysis presented here.

2. Interviews with Samba Sylla in Montreuil, a suburb of Paris, 16 and 29 June, and 3 July 2000; 3 June 2003.

3. Interviews with Doulo Fofanna in Paris, 4, 6, 27 July and August 2000, and 17 July 2002.

4. Interviews with Djénébou Traore in Paris, July 2001 and 28 June 2002; telephone conversation, December 2004.

5. On immigration in French history, a chronology of policy changes and events since 1968, Islam and Muslims in France, and immigration from West Africa, see

Alec G. Hargreaves, *Multi-Ethnic France: Immigration, Politics, Culture and Society*, 2nd ed. (New York: Routledge, 2007), 13–31, 70–72, 99–102, 211–20, 140–64.

6. Interviews with Karamoko Cissé in Colombes, a suburb of Paris, 1, 3, and 5 July 2002.

7. See Frederick Cooper, "From Imperial Inclusion to Republican Exclusion? France's Ambiguous Postwar Trajectory," in *Frenchness and the African Diaspora: Identity and Uprising in Contemporary France*, ed. Charles Tshimanga, Didier Gondola, and Peter J. Bloom (Bloomington: Indiana University Press, 2010), 111, 114.

8. Hargreaves, *Multi-Ethnic France*, 24–32.

9. Following his retirement and our initial interviews, Doulo Fofanna married a much younger Mauritanian wife in France, whom he described as "a little wife" for his "old age." He also has at least two wives who live in Mauritania (electronic message from Carolyn Sargent to Dennis Cordell, 29 January 2010).

10. In the Sahel region of West Africa, such an explanation is a common response to questions about why people migrate. For a similar dialogue about how young men from Burkina Faso migrated to Côte d'Ivoire for adventure and money, see Jean Rouch's film, *Jaguar* (Paris: Films de la Pléïde, 1954–1967).

11. See Jane Freeman's chapter "The Sans-Papiers Movement: Mobilisation through Illegality," in her book *Immigration and Insecurity in France* (Burlington, Vt.: Ashgate, 2004), 71–88.

12. The original name of the organization in French is "L'Union des ressortissants de Diataya et Salamou résidants en France."

13. Contemporary historiography identifies the first African diaspora with the slave trade, which took millions of men and women from Africa to the Atlantic world between the fifteenth and nineteenth centuries.

~

CHAPTER FIFTEEN

Foday (b. ca. 1974) Meets the Rebels in 1991

Diamonds Are Not a Boy's Best Friend

Doug Henry

The Princess Cut—perfectly square, with more sparkle than a square cut diamond. There is no other shape like it, and this Princess Cut will be noticed by everyone. It's truly a diamond fit for a Princess.

—Advertisement

In the 1990s, horror stories of "blood diamonds" in Africa, people whose limbs had been chopped off by crazed militiamen, and kidnapped youngsters forced to become murderous child soldiers exploded on the developed world out of nowhere—still another stereotype of African barbarity that contrasted dramatically with the "civilized" North. Foday's story, as he told it to Doug Henry, is the stuff of nightmares not limited to children. The young man tells a tale of random killing and systematic murder among peasants in Sierra Leone during the months he served the Revolutionary United Front (RUF). In describing his own experiences, as well as what other boys lived through, Foday helps us see that these youth did not just endure the individual trauma of their own kidnapping—as terrible as that might have been. Capture was not a discrete act of terror. It heralded their entry into a life of terror, a day-to-day, hour-to-hour, and even minute-to-minute existence plagued by fear and insecurity.

In this altered dimension, bloodcurdling acts of violence might and did occur anytime. Comrades by your side one minute were gone the next. Not only did thousands of Sierra Leonean farmers die in this reign of terror, but the lives of thousands of child soldiers were also snuffed out. We will never know either their numbers or most of their names. Foday's account takes us beyond dramatic armed violence to show how it was linked to, and indeed grew out of, arbitrary power, poverty, and failed development. He describes the larger context that pushed him and other adolescent boys to leave villages where they saw no future for themselves to pursue dreams of wealth in the diamond fields. Foday tells his tale in a tone that suggests that he is still in shock in the wake of the dissolution of social bonds and obligations between people in the same family and same community. His story shows how life in the diamond regions and the organization of the diamond trade set the stage for the kidnapping of children and the widespread violence that engulfed Sierra Leone in the 1990s.

Doug Henry weaves a narrative about the history of Sierra Leone through Foday's immediate story in order to set the tale in a much broader context. From the initial conquest of the lands that would become Sierra Leone in the nineteenth century to the colony's independence in 1962, the British colonial administration demonstrated little regard for local people. At the same time, colonial authorities deferred to British economic interests because they were eager to reap revenue both for the colony and for the British metropolitan government. What does this chapter reveal about the colonial economy in general, and the rise of diamond mining in particular, that helps us understand what happened to Foday and his friends so many decades later? How do Foday's experiences as an individual illustrate some of the larger and seemingly removed themes in the modern history of Africa?

For years, rebel or dissident groups in African countries like Angola, Sierra Leone, and the Democratic Republic of Congo have fought for control of diamond mines within their borders. Diamonds are mined, sometimes at the end of a gun barrel, then sold illegally and smuggled out of the country for cutting and polishing elsewhere. They are then mixed with "legitimately" mined diamonds so that they can get into jewelry stores in First World countries like the United States.[1] In recent years, human rights groups and the news media have brought attention to how proceeds from these diamond sales are sometimes used to purchase weapons that lead to destabilization or campaigns of terror. These diamonds have come to be called "blood" or "conflict" diamonds, because in the process of taking over territory, mining operations, and smuggling networks, rebels more often than not commit gross human rights violations against ordinary people. In Sierra Leone, for instance, rebels were infamous for attacks during which they hacked off the limbs of innocent civilians, some of whom were children, in order to spread fear and panic. The diamond industry claims that conflict diamonds represent only 4 percent of the world's total annual diamond production, worth $6.8 billion in 2002.[2] Some observers judge this estimate to be low. Nonetheless, 4 percent of $6.8 billion still amounts to $272 million—a sum greater than the annual budget of many African countries, more than enough to equip rebel fighters with automatic weapons and rocket-propelled grenade launchers, and more than enough to wreak havoc on the lives of ordinary people struggling to make a living.

Sierra Leone is both blessed and cursed with gemstone-quality diamonds of very high value, often used to fashion the intricate box-like princess cut diamonds now popular in the United States. In Sierra Leone in 1997, I met Foday, a young man in his early twenties who already had intimate experience with diamonds, rebels, and bloodshed.[3] At least at the time that I knew him, Foday was not famous or even well known beyond his immediate circle of friends. He was just an average boy wanting a better life. His story, however, came to be much more than that, as he found himself inadvertently entangled in the relentless struggle for power, profit, hard currency, and control of natural resources that has spanned generations in the colonial and postcolonial eras. In this struggle, global greed intercepts individuals living in the smallest villages, leading to protracted turmoil and extended states of terror for everyday people.

I first met Foday in the Kamboi Hotel, a combination refugee camp and internment center in Sierra Leone for former rebels who had either managed to escape conscription on their own or who had been captured by government forces and were judged not to constitute a threat—even though they remained under the careful watch of soldiers to make sure they did not "lapse" and rejoin the other side. The Kamboi was not really a hotel at all, but more an unfinished frame of a two-story building. It had no walls and no roof, but it was surrounded by a very solid nine-foot-high cement wall with shards of sharp broken glass embedded on the top for security. Considering the residents' pedigree and poverty, the question always remained as to whom the walls were supposed to protect—the former-rebel residents, or the more than slightly nervous people who lived in the surrounding neighborhood. To be sure, they eyed the Kamboi Hotel with suspicion and fear. Theoretically, the hotel's "guests" could come and go as they pleased. In reality, there was nowhere for them to go. Most of the Kamboi's residents were penniless, and they waited around for Africare, an international agency, to hand out food or dispense medical attention each day. When residents did leave the Kamboi to walk around town, they were subjected to the accusatory whispers, finger-pointing, and name-calling of apprehensive locals, who hated and feared that dreaded rebels were living in their neighborhood.

In fact, the residents of the Kamboi were both men and women—elders, children, and youth of all ages, most of whom had been innocent civilians captured by rebels, conscripted into their cause, and forced to serve them either by preparing food, carrying heavy loads, spying, or fighting. Few had homes left or relatives who would take them back, since rebel atrocities had either killed or torn apart families that might have offered refuge. Few were inclined to leave anyway, at least immediately, because they were still quite dazed by their sudden freedom following years of captivity and forced labor. They thought it best to stay in one place and see what Africare might provide.

Foday was born forty-five miles away in Bo, the second-largest city in Sierra Leone, but he moved with his family to Liberia, where his father got a job in the timber-cutting industry. After several years his father was laid off, and the family moved to Pujehun, where they had relatives and thought they could get land to farm. Foday never went to formal primary or secondary school, though his parents did enroll him in the local Arabic school, where he learned to read Muslim prayers from the Qur'an and do basic math. In 1991, when Foday was sixteen, the rebels attacked Pujehun: "We heard they were in the forest nearby, but didn't think they would enter the town. Then we heard the firing over by the hospital, that KPOW! KPOW! of the 'AK' [AK-47 automatic rifle], and then people started hollering."

In the confusion, Foday ran first toward his house, but he was met by several friends running in the opposite direction, who convinced him to follow them into the forest. He soon learned from them that both of his parents had been killed—his mother executed while rebels looted the home, and his father killed on one of the garden paths entering town, where he had had the misfortune to run into the rebels. Foday fled with his friends, eventually walking more than thirty miles to seek refuge with his father's family in Bama Kohnta, a small village in the neighboring district. His uncle took him in and treated him as one of the family. Though he worked hard for his uncle and was treated well, the uncle had sons of his own and Foday said he always felt somewhat like an outsider. He was certain that the uncle would one day feel obligated to give his "birth" sons better or larger parcels of land to farm. Foday began to see a future of dwindling opportunities. When he was twenty years old, he began looking for economic alternatives. For many boys in Sierra Leone, this usually means mining for diamonds. When he reached twenty-two, on New Year's Day, Foday decided to try his luck. A Mandingo man, a traveling trader associated with diamond trading,[4] usually came through the village every week to recruit young men to work for his operation. One week, Foday and two of his friends joined up, with dreams of striking it rich.

Diamonds in Sierra Leone

Colonial authorities stumbled upon diamonds in Sierra Leone in 1927, when a small geological team surveying for minerals found instead two diamonds in a streambed. The British colonial government, pressured by the crown to make the colony profitable, negotiated with the giant South African firm De Beers to create a local subsidiary called the Sierra Leone Selection Trust (SLST), which was granted exclusive rights to prospect and mine in the entire territory for ninety-nine years. Within a decade, Sierra Leone was producing a million carats of diamonds each year, with profits going directly to De Beers, the colonial authority, and Britain.[5] Both the British government and De Beers were eager to keep local people from setting up and profiting from their own competing mining operations. Laws were passed that actually prohibited Sierra Leoneans from even possessing the diamonds mined on their own land. Within a few decades, however, local people became aware of the value of these "rocks" buried in their soil. Hundreds of small, illicit mining operations sprang up to challenge the government's monopoly. These illegal miners sold their yield to Mandingo and Lebanese traders, who, in turn, gave local chiefs a share of the profits in exchange for their support and smuggled the small gems out of the forest to markets overseas. Unable to police every mining zone, the colonial government granted SLST the right to field its own police force. Newspaper reports soon followed of heavy-handed violence, nighttime executions, and roadside ambushes meted out by these private security firms. In response, the Sierra Leonean miners illegally mining their own land took up arms to defend themselves. Soon privately armed groups began to compete and clash across the mining areas.

By the 1950s, the colonial government realized it was not faring well in its dealings with De Beers, and it moved to renegotiate the contract with the mining giant. At the same time and despite continued SLST patrols, increasing numbers of diamonds were making their way out of the country illegally, many of them to Monrovia, the capital of the neighboring country of Liberia. Facing increasing restrictions in Sierra Leone, De Beers itself found it increasingly profitable to simply bypass official channels and allow diamonds to be smuggled out of Sierra Leone to Monrovia, so they could buy them up across the border in a different country. De Beers opened its first office in Monrovia in 1954, paying high prices in stable foreign currency in order to gain control over as much of the trade as possible. By 1956, the colonial government in Sierra Leone had renegotiated its agreement with SLST, restricting the company's prospecting monopoly to only one zone, its richest lease in Eastern Province, which covered 230 square miles. In exchange, the colonial government made a onetime payment to De Beers of 1.6 million pounds sterling, or 2.3 million American dollars. Hoping to bring local miners and indigenous landowners under their control, the government offered them licenses. Some local chiefs accepted numerous licenses but then turned around and leased the land to wealthy Lebanese traders. Ironically, many of these traders were the smugglers of earlier years.

By the time British colonial rule ended in 1961, more than thirty thousand boys and men in eastern Sierra Leone were engaged in mining, most between the ages of fifteen and twenty-nine. Independence-era politicians, beginning with President Siaka Stevens in 1968, learned to exploit this growing population of laborers. Stevens rose to power in part through promises to miners that he would grant them more access and personal control over the diamond areas. Any real empowerment of the young men did not happen—in reality, politicians expanded their own clandestine involvement in mining and neglected to enforce formalized, state-level, structural efforts to regulate or reform the industry. Corrupt politicians soon learned that they could elicit payoffs and political contributions from illegal dealers. Young miners learned they could band together to vote in blocks for politicians who would overlook their activities in exchange for money or support. Privately armed groups directed by local strongmen learned that they could influence the supporters of competing political parties, and they could intimidate rival miners or dealers. As a result, official, legitimate diamond exports declined while illegal exports grew. From a high of over two million carats in 1970, formally reported production fell to only forty-eight thousand carats in 1988. By 1999, Sierra Leone's official exports in diamonds were valued at just under $1.5 million, compared with industry estimates that placed total exports at $70 million. In other words, $68.5 million in diamonds had been lost to smuggling in that one year alone!

Foday Tries Mining

The Mandingo recruiter took Foday and his friends to a mining camp outside Tongo, not far from Kenema, the largest city in eastern Sierra Leone. The recruiter was also a "supporter"—someone who works for a dealer, providing food and equipment to the much poorer miners and employing them to work a plot of land.[6] In this case, the Mandingo recruiter/supporter had given money to a local chief in exchange for a "lease" on several acres of land to mine. A crew of six boys worked hard for many hours every day in the sur-rounding forest, often sleeping in a makeshift shelter near one of the piles of gravel to ward off would-be thieves. Recalling the backbreaking labor, Foday simply shook his head. Mining is miserable, exhausting work. The supporter "lends" shovels and picks to the crew of boy miners, or *san-san boys*. By hand, they dug wide holes as deep as twenty-five feet through dirt, clay, and sand, looking for gravel, which is associated with diamonds. Once they hit gravel, the boys shoveled it out into piles, which they slowly sifted through with wa-ter, looking for small gems. When the rains came and the holes turned into giant soggy mud pits, the supporter might bring a generator-powered pump to pull out the water so that work could continue. Most diggers were extremely poor, but they worked feverishly in the hope of finding a large stone that would bring fabulous wealth. Foday spent more than a week at a stretch at the digging site, isolated with his fellow san-san boys.

Foday noted that women were not allowed in the mining area because the crew thought that their presence might spoil their luck. Because the chances of finding the tiny valuable stones were so slim, superstitions like this were common. Their supporter had gotten a Muslim holy man, called a *kamoh*, to give them advice as to where to dig. The man even prayed to bless the site and the work. But despite the kamoh's efforts to entice divine intervention, the crew found little of value on a typical day. On a lucky day, they might find several carats of tiny stones, which they were obliged to sell to their supporter. He paid between $30 and $100, depending on the value he estimated by examining their size, color, and clarity. He then took the stones to a local Mandingo buying agent, who Foday heard worked for Israelis. Buying agents might pay a supporter several hundred dollars, even-tually amassing a large bag of stones that they sold abroad for thousands of dollars. Buying agents are easy to spot in towns in Sierra Leone—they are the ones who sport a satellite television dish on their rooftop and drive a Mercedes Benz in a country where most people cannot afford a bicycle. Back at the beginning of the chain of production, Foday and his friends managed to save enough money every two or three weeks to travel to Ken-ema for a day or two, see a martial arts movie at a video parlor, maybe buy a new pair of jeans or a radio, and visit one of the three brothels in town. I asked Foday if boys ever pocketed the diamonds to sell to a dealer them-selves, thus avoiding the loss of money to their "middleman" supporter. Foday's face darkened at first, but then he shrugged his shoulders and said matter-of-factly:

> If somebody does that, his heart will show it and the supporter will find out. It
> would be hard to keep that from the rest of the team and someone will always

talk. And what would the rest of the boys think, anyway, when one or two start walking around with new clothes?

Besides the fear of getting caught and punished, diggers are undoubtedly kept honest by the realization that they would not know how much money to ask for a rough diamond anyway. One of the tragedies of this situation is that the san-san boys are largely kept ignorant of the fluctuations in the market price for the gems they find and would probably get cheated.

Despite the dirty, backbreaking nature of the work, this life seems, at least initially, an attractive option to many youth in Sierra Leone. For those who come from small villages, it lets them leave their homes and see something of the world beyond their immediate chiefdom. Mining also looks particularly glamorous to most boys because other economic opportunities are so few. They see no better options to improve their lot. Moreover, stories abound of people striking it rich. Though almost no one personally knows anyone who has had such good fortune, everyone has heard of a "friend of a friend" who has. Even though most boys quickly recognize the tremendous disparity in wealth between dealers and diggers, they feel stuck in their situation. There are no better alternatives. Many diggers nonetheless become disenchanted with the tough work after two or three years, realizing that they are not much better off than they were before. Some of them then shift to seasonal mining, organized around the farming calendar. Others, if they have homes to return to, quit outright. But those who abandon the mine do not pose a problem for the supporters and dealers. Legions of boys and young men arrive to replace those who leave.

In the villages and forests of the diamond areas, the impact of so many young men flowing in and out is tremendous. Most of these young men are strangers, with few or no family or regional ties to the small towns or villages where they find themselves. As a result, their presence exerts enormous pressure on the local social fabric in several ways. First, men vastly outnumber women, sometimes ten to one. I remember the first predominantly mining village I visited, a small village called Pohtéhun, about fifteen miles east of Kenema. An informal survey at dusk revealed that about 80 percent of the roughly four hundred inhabitants were young men. Most were in their twenties; 90 percent were engaged in mining. Local healers I spoke with told me that sexually transmitted diseases, particularly gonorrhea and chlamydia, were rampant in the village and represented major health problems.[7] Looking around, I saw that the village was in disrepair. For nearly a year, the roof of the central market had sported a huge hole. The pump for the village well had been broken for even longer, leaving people to draw water by hand from a dirty well by the river. Despite the presence of a few young children, the village did not have a primary school, nor were there any teachers. I asked the village chief about these problems. Somewhat embarrassed, he claimed the repairs had in fact been a high priority for several months, but he had not been able to marshal enough local support to pay for them. He actually asked me if I had access to any community development grant funds that the village could get. This was one of the few times I actually lost my temper during field research! I was sickened and disgusted to think of all the money that was leaving the village in the form of stones taken out of the ground. *None* of it ever got invested back in the community. Even when local miners got cash, they did not spend it here. Everything they wanted was in Kenema.

One week in April 1996, Foday and his friends got about $120 from selling several diamonds to their supporter. They split the money six ways. Four of them went to Kenema, while two stayed behind to guard the site. The four diggers who went to town split the cost of a bag of rice for the group. Foday also bought a new pair of sandals and a cassette of reggae music. Thursday night they all went to the Moonlight Hotel to meet prostitutes. After two days' vacation, they left for Tongo on a Friday. On Saturday morning, rebels came back into Foday's life for the second time.

The Civil War in Sierra Leone

In March 1991, a group of armed Sierra Leoneans, Liberians, and Burkinabè who called themselves the Revolutionary United Front (RUF) attacked a small village in southern Sierra Leone, launching a civil war that lasted eleven years. Though apparently supported by the National Patriotic Front of Liberia (NPFL), perhaps in retribution for the Sierra Leone government's support of the multilateral military force of ECOMOG (the Economic Community of West African States), the RUF quickly developed its own populist political agenda. But the RUF's tactics, which privileged atrocities inflicted on innocent civilians, and the absence of sincere political reforms aimed at producing a lasting cease-fire, soon raised questions about the RUF's true intentions. Despite many attempts at cease-fires, brokered amnesties, negotiated settlements, boycotts, and political power-sharing, the RUF continued to engage in hit-and-run guerrilla attacks, highway ambushes, looting and burning houses, and destruction and confiscation of crops, as well as rape, maiming, and mass human rights violations.

Most analysts attributed this violence to a combination of personal political grievances harbored by former president Charles Taylor of neighboring Liberia, who is widely acknowledged to have supported the rebels through international arms shipments; exiles fighting social exclusion and failed patrimonialism; and criminal elements battling for control over the highly profitable but illicit trade in diamonds out of Sierra Leone to neighboring countries like Liberia. It has often been pointed out that ongoing low-level violence in Sierra Leone was "functional," in the sense that it created a destabilized environment ideal for criminal activity such as smuggling. Hence, to no one's surprise, the rebels in Sierra Leone initially stubbornly resisted efforts of UN peacekeeping troops to enter the diamond regions. Indeed, it was in these areas that infrastructure damage was especially extensive. Schools, banks, health clinics, bridges, churches, and hospitals were damaged or destroyed. Across Sierra Leone, more than half the population of 4.5 million people were displaced at least once during the eleven-year conflict—either dispersed within the country or across the border into Guinea or Liberia. Estimates of casualties range from twenty thousand to seventy-five thousand. Many thousands more people lost one or more limbs in violent amputations.

Much of the money that financed these operations and the weapons used to carry them out came from illegal mining. Diamonds were exchanged for food, cheap automatic rifles or grenade launchers from Eastern Europe or China, or consumer goods. Throughout the conflict, light weapons such as Kalashnikov rifles and grenade launchers were paid for in part by the backbreaking labor of miners like Foday. Later, guns were traced to private weapons dealers, often of Ukrainian or Israeli origin.[8] Weapons were flown to Burkina Faso and then shipped through Liberia to the rebels, probably with the complicity and active support of officials at the highest levels of both governments. Both were driven by the desire for the hard currency generated by the diamond trade.

The workers in the diamond mines were young men like Foday. Aware of these sources of support, the RUF forcibly conscripted youth at the warfront to put them to work as miners, or to train them as guides, carriers, bodyguards, or fighters. Thousands of young people were forcibly recruited. Some were forced to commit horrible atrocities such as murdering family members or village elders, acts that severed their ties with their home settlements. Some boys even willingly joined rebel forces—especially those who had become disenchanted by the lack of educational or employment opportunities. As some analysts have noted, such recruits may have regarded training in the use of weapons, forest survival, and guerrilla warfare as preferable to no education or training at all.[9] War orphans like Foday were particularly susceptible to such entreaties.

Foday Meets the Rebels

In terse, dispassionate terms, Foday described what happened on the fateful day that rebels attacked their mining site. He had returned on Friday and the rebels attacked the next day. They surrounded the site, blocking off all the forest roads to prevent escape. Foday and his friends first jumped into the river to try to flee, but the current was too strong to make it to the other side. The rebels forced the mining crew to march to their forest headquarters, a base called Bandao. Almost immediately, they began forcibly training the boys to join their ranks. As with a cult, loyalty was created through "bonding" experiences born of fear, tough beatings, and hard physical training:[10]

> Sometimes they'd make us walk with loads, sometimes over thirty miles a day.
> . . . If we complained, they made us dig a hole, and then stay in it all day and night. They said if we came out they'd shoot us. . . . The killing was awful. Lots of recruits were killed. Sometimes they would just pile about twenty bodies in a hole. And if you tried to run into the bush to escape, they'd take a machete and cut you all over your body, sometimes scarring "RUF" across your forehead. That way they could say, "This one, he won't run again." Because any man you came across would know that you were a rebel!

Foday's main job was to work as a "standby" for the combatants on the front line, carrying their weaponry and equipment, though he was also forced to fight on occasion. If the commandos wanted water, the standbys would have to find a well and bail it. If the commandos wanted a shelter built, they'd have to build it. Wherever the commandos went, Foday and his team would be right behind them with their load.

For the rebels, the violence presented both political and economic opportunities. With guns, they could begin to make a living. Rebel commanders claimed the right to appropriate the produce of any farm around them. Just before harvest time, they would spread the word that foreign troops or civilian militia were about to attack, so the farmers would go into hiding. When the farmers came back, they would find that their harvest had disappeared. The stolen food was destined only for combatants, however. Standbys like Foday had to gather wild yams and bananas for themselves. Captured women were forced to harvest palm nuts to make oil, which was bartered for salt or other trade items at the Guinean border. Many women were forced to serve as "bush wives" for the rebels; rape was widespread. During fortunate weeks off from fighting, recruits were allowed to mine, though under constant surveillance. A group was allowed to keep some of the smaller diamonds to take to the border to trade. This was called by rebels the "two-pile" system: Miners would wash a gravel pile for diamonds for the rebels, and then they were allowed to wash a pile for themselves.

Under these living conditions, illnesses were rampant, especially from malnutrition, parasitic diseases, cholera, malaria, and sexually transmitted diseases. James, whom I met at the Kamboi with Foday and who had also been conscripted by the rebels, described it this way:

> We were so poor, and the place was so forested—you weren't supposed to cut any trees at all, but just build your house under them. We were afraid of helicopters and jet bombers seeing us. There were lots of people, and lots of sicknesses, because there were no medicines. Some people's bodies would swell up—especially a foot or a leg. . . . Sometimes people would die of this.

Foday's Escape

After a time, Foday managed to escape the rebels during the confusion created when a militia attacked Bandao. Though the militiamen who captured him at first threatened him with execution, they ultimately believed Foday's story of forced conscription and turned him over to soldiers who brought him to the Kamboi Hotel. Many youths just like Foday remained behind and were forced to serve the rebels until the end of the conflict in 2002. No one who has seen the destruction in the wake of the rebel war doubts that it represented a particularly horrible, bloody chapter in Sierra Leone's history. Yet, when examined against the historical backdrop of chronic violence that has surrounded the production of diamonds in Sierra Leone since the early days of the mining industry, it is apparent that the situation for youth has changed little since the 1930s.

Viewed from the perspective of boys like Foday, the exploitation of miners differs little, whether they worked for De Beers, for greedy merchants in the service of corrupt politicians, or for the rebels. Whether explicitly entrapped by force or forced to participate because of extreme poverty and lack of economic opportunity, the outcome was more or less the same: The labor of the young remained a commodity to be exploited, tapped into, manipulated, and used for profit. To be sure, this is in itself a form of violence. It began long before the actual armed violence of the civil war and continues today, even after the end of the fighting. As long as crippling poverty and lack of genuine economic alternatives grips Sierra Leone, people will continue to be caught in a spiral of violence. Formal peace or not, this situation promises to remain a persistent problem for the foreseeable future.

The End of Civil War and a "New" Diamond Regime?

In January 2002, an international coalition of UN, British, Sierra Leonean, and West African forces brought the civil war to an end. Countrywide democratic elections followed several months later. Since that time, human rights tribunals have put many of the leaders of the violence on trial for war crimes. Since human rights groups and the media have brought the diamonds–weapons–bloodshed connection to light, the diamond industry, most notably De Beers, has taken significant steps to erase its bloodstained history and begin reform. Faced with the prospect of a consumer boycott of its highly profitable product, De Beers has disavowed all trade in "blood" or "conflict" diamonds. By the end of 2000, Belgium's High Diamond Council and industry representatives had developed the Kimberley Process Certification Scheme, the current system for managing and certifying the trade in rough diamonds. According to its protocol, all uncut diamonds must be shipped in sealed packages accompanied by certificates certifying their place of origin. Any dealers or distributors who cannot identify the origins of the diamonds they trade risk fines, penalties, embargo, or even expulsion from the international Diamond Council. By 2009 the Kimberley Process included forty-nine members representing seventy-five individual countries, all pledging to reform diamond regulation.

The certification scheme also calls for a peer review system in which the mining, trading, and manufacturing sectors in political and civil society police themselves. Unfortunately, the peer review system is voluntary, and a relatively small number of countries participate in it. Nonetheless, the process has been credited with a large increase in official exports from Sierra Leone, and the end of trade in diamonds with countries like Liberia that are involved in conflict diamonds. Officials note, however, that illicit diamond mining and smuggling continue to thrive, and the structural problems of artisanal mining amid extreme poverty remain.[11] Rights groups complain that the administrative systems of reporting and analysis upon which the credibility of the Kimberly Process Certification hinge are inconsistent, and that diamonds continue to fuel violence and finance terror.

A more recent measure, the Diamond Development Initiative, may offer promise. Partnered by De Beers, the World Bank, and several nongovernmental organizations, the initiative began in February 2005. Its aim is to assess the viability of shifting alluvial mining operations more into the formal economy, with the idea that proceeds might bring substantial benefits to miners, local governments, and local communities. How well these initiatives will work, and whether they are capable of resisting corruption, smuggling, and certificate laundering, remain to be seen. However, one thing is certain. The future of Sierra Leone and legions of boys like Foday depends on it.

Further Reading

Several overviews offer historical background and more contemporary analyses of the diamond industry in Sierra Leone. Investigative reports by nongovernmental organizations have been very influential in calling international attention to the connections between diamond trading and conflict. See, for example, Ian Smillie, *Blood on the Stone: Greed, Corruption, and War in the Global Diamond Trade* (London: Anthem Press, 2010) and Ian Smillie, Lansana Gberie, and Ralph Hazleton, *The Heart of the Matter: Sierra Leone, Diamonds, and Human Security* (Ottawa: Partnership Canada, 2000). Reports by the UN have also been important. See the *Report of the Panel of Experts Appointed Pursuant to UN Security Council Resolution 1306 (2000), Paragraph 19 in Relation to Sierra Leone* (2000). On African conflict diamonds and the diamond trade more generally, see Greg Campbell, *Blood Diamonds: Tracing the Deadly Path of the World's Most Precious Stones* (Boulder, Colo.: Westview Press, 2002), and Stefan Kanfer, *The Last Empire: De Beers, Diamonds, and the World* (New York: Farrar, Straus & Giroux, 1995).

There are now many accounts of the civil war in Sierra Leone. Particularly good is Paul Richards, *Fighting for the Rain Forest: War, Youth, and Resources in Sierra Leone* (Oxford, UK: James Currey, 1996); David Keen, *The Economic Functions of Violence in Civil Wars*, Adelphi Papers No. 320 (Oxford, UK: International Institute for Strategic Studies, 1998); Ibrahim Abdullah, "Bush Path to Destruction: The Origin and Character of the Revolutionary United Front/Sierra Leone," *Journal of Modern African Studies* 36, 2 (1998): 203–35; Patrick Muana, "The Kamajoi Militia: Violence, Internal Displacement, and the Politics of Counter Insurgency," *Africa Development* 22, 3/4 (1997); Alfred Zack-Williams, "Sierra Leone: The Political Economy of Civil War, 1991–98," *Third World Quarterly* 20, 1 (1999); and William P. Murphy, "Military Patrimonialism and Child Soldier Clientelism in the Liberian and Sierra Leonean Civil Wars," *African Studies Review* 46, 2 (December 2003): 61–87.

For writings about the experiences of children in war, consult Ilene Cohn and Guy Goodwin-Gill, *Child Soldiers: The Role of Children in Armed Conflict* (Oxford, UK: Clarendon Press 1994); Nancy Scheper-Hughes and Carolyn Sargent, eds., *Small Wars: The Cultural Politics of Childhood* (Berkeley: University of California Press, 1998); and Jo Boyden and Joanna de Berry, eds.,

Children and Youth on the Frontline: Ethnography, Armed Conflict, and Displacement (New York: Bergahan Books, 2004). On Sierra Leone, see Myriam Denov, *Child Soldiers: Sierra Leone's Revolutionary United Front* (Cambridge, UK: Cambridge University Press, 2010) or Chris Coulter's *Bush Wives and Girl Soldiers: Women's Lives through War and Peace in Sierra Leone* (Ithaca, N.Y.: Cornell University Press, 2009). For a broader African view, see Elliot Skinner, "Child Soldiers in Africa: A Disaster for Future Families," *International Journal on World Peace* 16, 2 (1999): 7–22; Harry West, "Girls with Guns: Narrating the Experience of War of FRELIMO's Female Detachment," *Anthropological Quarterly* 73, 4 (2000): 180–94; and Corinne Dufka, *Youth, Poverty, and Blood: The Lethal Legacy of West Africa's Regional Warriors* (Washington, D.C.: Human Rights Watch, 2005).

For an excellent novel about a child soldier conscripted to fight in Liberia and Sierra Leone, read Ahmadou Kourouma, *Allah Is Not Obliged*, trans. Frank Wynne (New York: Anchor Books, 2006). Child soldiers have also published accounts of their ordeals. See Ishmael Beah, *A Long Way Gone: Memoirs of a Child Soldier* (New York: Sarah Crichton Books/Farrar, Straus & Giroux, 2007), and Grace Akallo and Faith McDonnell, *Girl Soldier: A Story of Hope for Northern Uganda's Children* (Grand Rapids, Mich.: Chosen Books, 2007). Finally, Emmanuel Jal, a former child soldier from Sudan, has released *Warchild*, a hip-hop recording about his experiences (London: Sonic 360, 2008).

Notes

1. American consumers, usually men, buy 80 percent of the world's diamonds.

2. So-Young Chang, Amanda Heron, John Kwon, Geoff Maxwell, Lodovico Rocca, and Orestes Tarajano, "The Global Diamond Industry," http://www4 .gsb.columbia.edu/chazen/journal/article/14252/The+Global+Diamond+Industry. Estimates of the volume of diamonds mined by Sierra Leonean rebels of the RUF vary widely. A UN panel estimated their value to be between US$25 and US$125 million per year. De Beers itself estimated that in 1999, US$70 million worth of rough diamonds came onto the world market through the RUF. See United Nations, *Report of the Panel of Experts*, http://www.un.org/sc/committees/1132/ selecdocs.shtml. Blaine Harden writes that the RUF sold at least US$630 million in diamonds to Liberia in exchange for support and weapons. See Blaine Harden, "Diamond Wars: A Special Report; Africa's Gems; Warfare's Best Friends," *New York Times*, 6 April 2000.

3. I gathered much of the data reported here as a result of participant observation, in the course of a larger anthropological research project investigating the connections between conflict, health, and the provision of relief aid during wartime. For

thirteen months in 1997 and 1998, I lived in two "refugee" and "displaced persons" camps, one on either side of the Sierra Leone/Guinea border. I visited several diamond mines, mining villages, and other self-settled and camp-settled refuges, including the Kamboi Hotel camp for displaced ex-combatants, where I met Foday. I am grateful to him for his tremendous courage in sharing his story.

4. "Mandingo" is an ethnic group usually associated with the Mandinka, originally from Mali. In Sierra Leone, traveling traders associated with diamond mining may be casually referred to as Mandingo.

5. Much of the historical data for this section comes from David Koskoff, *The Diamond World* (New York: Harper Collins, 1981); William Reno, *Corruption and State Politics in Sierra Leone* (Cambridge, UK: Cambridge University Press, 1995); H. Laurens Van der Laan, *The Sierra Leone Diamonds: An Economic Study Covering the Years 1952–1961* (London: Oxford University Press, 1965); Edward Epstein, *The Rise and Fall of Diamonds: The Shattering of a Brilliant Illusion* (New York: Simon & Schuster, 1982); and Michael Harbottle, *The Knaves of Diamonds* (London: Seeley Services, 1976.)

6. The terminology varies, but in general "dealers," "traders," "buying agents," and "merchants" are of foreign (often Lebanese) origin; they inspect the rough-cut diamonds, amass several bagsful, and then sell them up a chain of middlemen to large syndicates, usually located in Europe. The syndicates cut, polish, set, and ship the stones to jewelry stores, mainly in the United States. See Alfred Zack-Williams, *Tributors, Supporters, and Merchant Capital Mining and Underdevelopment in Sierra Leone* (Aldershot, UK: Avesbury Press, 1995).

7. In its wake, the war has left an unfortunate legacy of rising HIV rates. Thousands of foreign peacekeeping troops were sent to Sierra Leone under the auspices of the UN in the closing days of the war, some of them from areas of the world with high HIV rates. Not all of these soldiers were aware of their HIV status or had up-to-date knowledge about the prevention and transmission of the disease. On weekends, they often frequented the same group of sex workers as the miners. See Doug Henry, "The Legacy of the Tank: The Violence of Peace," *Anthropological Quarterly* 78, 2 (2005): 443–56.

8. *United Nations Report of the Panel of Experts Appointed Pursuant to UN Security Council Resolution 1306 (2000), Paragraph 19 in Relation to Sierra Leone.* This report traces some of the shadowy networks of international arms and diamond smugglers, and the hired mercenaries that often accompany shipments. http://www.un.org/sc/committees/1132/selecdocs.shtml.

9. Krijn Peters and Paul Richards, "Why We Fight: Voices of Youth Combatants in Sierra Leone," *Africa* 68, 2 (1998): 183–210.

10. Child and youth soldiers were boys most often, but their ranks also included girls. They were sought after because they were thought to be fearless and obedient. They were also polyvalent, engaging in cooking, carrying heavy ammunition and equipment, providing sexual services, spying, stealing, supporting fighters, or fighting. Some local and Western organizations in Sierra Leone are working to create new

economic and educational opportunities for child combatants who have disarmed, allowing the children to re-create new identities for themselves in turn. These transitions are not simple, because such children have particular difficulty reintegrating into their families and society following conflict. Adama, a market woman I knew in an internally displaced persons camp in Sierra Leone, put it this way:

Look at the wickedness that this thing [the fighting] has brought! You know, kids don't even want to work now! They don't want to have farms! This power that's here now—they just want guns! If you have a gun you can just "hands-up" someone or loot their property! . . . And who is a mortal man to decide when a mortal man should die?

There is an important and growing literature about child and youth soldiers in Sierra Leone. Mariane Ferme suggests that children are inherently dangerous because they exist in a liminal space where they are not yet initiated into society as responsible, knowledgeable, fully functioning adults. See Mariane Ferme, *The Underneath of Things: Violence, History, and the Everyday in Sierra Leone* (Berkeley: University of California Press, 2001). Danny Hoffman notes that there are many synonyms denoting youth combatants in Sierra Leone, all of which imply "unfinished," "chaotic," and "incoherent." See Danny Hoffman, "Like Beasts in the Bush: Synonyms of Childhood and Youth in Sierra Leone," *Postcolonial Studies* 6, 3 (2003): 295–308. Susan Shepler observes that child soldiers are the subject of multiple public discourses that portray them as either victims or perpetrators. See Susan Shepler, "Conflicted Childhoods: Fighting over Child Soldiers in Sierra Leone," PhD diss, University of California, Berkeley, 2005. These are important distinctions. Victim implies a passive casualty of an oppressive social system and, therefore, a need for social reform. Perpetrator suggests greater agency and, consequently, culpability, even approximating that of an adult. Shepler explains that children may exist on both levels; they have themselves been victimized, and yet they are also savvy users and manipulators of public and global discourses about their rights as children. Multiple means and labels lead the public simultaneously to fear these children and judge them to be in need of education and protection. In their report "Children's Experiences of Forced Migration: A Child-Centered Approach to Research on the Human Rights of Separated Children," presented to the International Rescue Committee in 2004, Brooke Schoepf and Ousmane Kabia move beyond this dichotomy, adopting a human rights approach to point out that child agency and abilities may be limited by the prolonged social marginality of poverty, bondage, hunger, and precarious health.

11. Lansana Gberie, ed., *Sierra Leone Diamond Industry Annual Review* (Ottawa: Partnership Africa Canada and the Network Movement for Justice and Development, Diamond and Human Securities Project, 2005).

Index

~

About the Contributors

Agnès Adjamagbo coedited *Santé de la reproduction et fécondité dans les pays du sud* (2007) and *Santé de la mère et de l'enfant: exemples africains* (1999). She is currently preparing a coedited volume with Anne Calves of the Université de Montréal entitled *Women's Emancipation in the Global South: New Figures, New Issues*. Adjamagbo received her doctorate in demography from the Université de Paris X. She is presently a researcher at the Institut de Recherche pour le Développement (IRD) in France in the Laboratoire Environnement, Population, et Développement.

Maryan Muuse Boqor is a Somali elder and community leader in Boston, Massachusetts. After studying in Somalia and attending law school in Morocco, she taught Arabic and Islam in secondary schools in Somalia. Maryan's husband was a political prisoner for almost twenty years during the regime of Mohamed Siyad Barre (1969–1991), and she and her children suffered much political harassment. Boqor fled to Kenya and eventually resettled as a refugee in Boston, where she now delights in her grandchildren and continues to take pride in her autonomy and her ability to help others.

Dennis D. Cordell is the author of *Dar al-Kuti: The Last Years of the Trans-saharan Slave Trade* (1984), coauthor of *Hoe and Wage: A Social History of a Circular Migration System in West Africa* (1996) with Victor Piché and the late Joel W. Gregory, and more recently coeditor of *The Demographics of Empire: The Colonial Order and the Creation of Knowledge* (2010), with Karl Ittmann and Gregory Maddox. Earlier, he coedited *African Population and Capitalism: Historical Perspectives* (1987/1994) with Joel W. Gregory. He is professor of history and associate dean at Southern Methodist University in Dallas.

José C. Curto is the author of *Enslaving Spirits: The Portuguese Brazilian Alcohol Trade at Luanda and Its Hinterland, c. 1550–1830* (2004). He also coedited *Africa and the Americas: Interconnections during the Slave Trade* with Renée Soulodre-La France (2005); and *Enslaving Connections: Changing Cultures of Africa and Brazil during the Era of Slavery* with Paul E. Lovejoy (2004). Curto received his PhD in African history from the University of California, Los Angeles. He is presently associate professor of history at York University and fellow of the Harriet Tubman Institute.

Mamadou Diouf is the author of *Histoire du Sénégal: Le modèle islamo-wolof et ses peripheries* (2001), *Le Kajoor au XIXè siècle: Pouvoir Ceddo et conquête coloniale* (1990), and with M. C. Diop and Donald Cruise O'Brien, *La construction de l'État au Sénégal* (2002). He coedited *New Perspectives on Islam: Conversion, Migration, Wealth, Power, and Femininity* (2009) with M. A. Leichtman, and *Rhythms of the Afro-Atlantic World* (2010) with I. K. Nwankwo. He is Leitner Family Professor of African Studies in the Department of Middle East, South Asian, and African Studies and the Department of History at Columbia University, and the director of the Institute for African Affairs.

Andreas Eckert is professor of African history at Humboldt Universität zu Berlin and director of the International Research Center for "Work and Human Life Cycle in Global History." He is the author of four books, most recently *Herrschen und Verwalten: Afrikanische Bürokraten, Staatliche Ordnung und Politik in Tansania, 1920–1970* (2007). More than one hundred of his scholarly articles on African history and the history of colonialism have appeared in German, English, and French in numerous journals and essay collections.

Laura Fair is the author of *Pastimes and Politics: Culture, Community, and Identity in Post-Abolition Urban Zanzibar, 1890–1943* (2001). She has published articles in the *Journal of African History*, *Frontiers: A Journal of Women's Studies*, *Swahili Forum*, *International Journal of African Historical Studies*, and *Africa*. Her essays have also appeared in collections such as *Fashioning Africa*, edited by Jean Allman (2004), and *Love in Africa*, edited by Jennifer Cole and Lynn Thomas (2008), among others. She is currently associate professor of history at Michigan State University.

Toyin Falola has written or edited many books, including *Violence in Nigeria: The Crisis of Religious Politics and Secular Ideologies* (1998), *Nationalism and African Intellectuals* (2001), *Economic and Political Reforms in Nigeria, 1945–1965* (2004), and *A History of Nigeria* (2008). His autobiography, *A Mouth Sweeter than Salt* (2004), was a finalist for the Melville Herskovits Award of the African Studies Association (USA). Falola has received major teaching awards at the University of Texas, where he is Distinguished Teaching Professor and Frances Higginbothom Nalle Centennial Professor in History.

Doug Henry is an associate professor of anthropology at the University of North Texas (UNT). He has authored or coauthored numerous articles, book chapters, and reports on Africa and violence, and more particularly on refugee health (*Medical Anthropology Quarterly*, 2006), conflict diamonds and the political economy of instability (*African Geographical Review*, 2006), extensions of violence into "postconflict" periods of peace (*Anthropological Quarterly*, 2005), and refugee interactions with the system of humanitarian aid (*Politique Africaine*, 2002).

Lidwien Kapteijns is Kendall/Hodder Professor of History at Wellesley College. She has published widely on Sudanese and Somali history. A recent monograph, Women's Voices in a Man's World: *Women and the Pastoral Tradition in Northern Somali Orature, c. 1899–1980* (1999), co-authored with Maryan Omar Ali, deals with folklore texts by and about women and with notions of proper womanhood in popular songs. An example of her current research about Somali popular culture and the violence of state collapse has appeared in *Mediations of Violence in Africa: Fashioning New Futures from Contested Pasts* (2010), coedited with Annemiek Richters.

Issiaka Mandé edited a collection of essays titled *Le Burkina Faso contemporain: Racines du présent et enjeux nouveaux* (2011) and coedited *Entreprises en movement* (2009) with Corinne Maitte and Manuela Martini. He also has published numerous articles, including "How to Count the Subjects of Empire? Steps towards an Imperial Demography in French West Africa before 1946," in *The Demographics of Empire* (2010). Mandé is a member of the faculty of the Department of History and the Laboratoire Sociétés en Développement: Études transdisciplinaires (SEDET), Université de Paris 7—Denis Diderot.

Cora Ann Presley has published two important books on the history of Kenyan women: *Kikuyu Women, the Mau Mau Rebellion, and Social Change in Kenya* (1992) and *Mau Mau's Daughter: The Life History of Wambui Otieno* (1998), which she edited and to which she wrote the introduction. Both volumes have appeared in Japanese. She has also contributed articles to journals, including the *Canadian Journal of African Studies/Revue Canadienne des Etudes Africaines*, and chapters to essay collections. She is associate professor in the Department of African-American Studies at Georgia State University in Atlanta.

Carolyn F. Sargent has published two monographs, including *Maternity, Medicine, and Power: Reproductive Decisions in Urban Benin* (1989), and coedited *Reproduction, Globalization, and the State* with Carole Browner (2011). She coedited *Gender in Cross-Cultural Perspective* with Caroline Brettell (latest edition, 2009), as well as issues of the *American Behavioral Scientist* (2006) and *Medical Anthropology Quarterly* (2006). Sargent has also published articles on Malian immigrants in France. She is professor of anthropology at Washington University in Saint Louis.

Pamela Scully is the author of books and articles on slave emancipation, including *Gender and Slave Emancipation in the Atlantic World*, coedited with Diana Paton (2005). Her latest book, coauthored with Clifton Crais, is *Sara Baartman and the Hottentot Venus: A Ghost Story and a Biography* (2009). She is chair of the Department of Women's Gender and Sexuality Studies and professor of women's studies and African studies at Emory University. She is writing a book on sexual violence and gender justice in postconflict societies.

Ibrahim Sundiata is the author of two volumes, *From Slaving to Neoslavery: The Bight of Biafra and Fernando Po in the Era of Abolition, 1827–1930* (1996) and *Equatorial Guinea: Colonialism, State Terror, and the Search for Stability* (1990). More recently, in *Brothers and Strangers: Black Zion, Black Slavery, 1914–1940* (2004), he examines the role of African Americans in labor recruitment scandals related to the Firestone Corporation's rubber plantations in Liberia. Presently he is Samuel J. and Augusta Spector Professor of History and African and Afro-American Studies at Brandeis.

Marcia Wright has published extensively on the history of East and Southern Africa, women and the law in Africa, and more recently on public health in South Africa. She broke new ground with her book *Strategies of Slaves and Women: Life-Stories from East/Central Africa* (1993), which explored the vulnerabilities and scope for agency among women caught up in this brutal slave trade. Marcia Wright received her PhD from the University of London. She is professor of history emerita at Columbia University.